A Culture of Freedom

A Culture of Freedom

ANCIENT GREECE AND THE ORIGINS OF EUROPE

CHRISTIAN MEIER

Foreword by Kurt Raaflaub
Translated by Jefferson Chase

OXFORD
UNIVERSITY PRESS

OXFORD
UNIVERSITY PRESS

Oxford University Press, Inc., publishes works that further
Oxford University's objective of excellence
in research, scholarship, and education.

Oxford New York

Auckland Cape Town Dar es Salaam Hong Kong Karachi
Kuala Lumpur Madrid Melbourne Mexico City Nairobi
New Delhi Shanghai Taipei Toronto

With offices in

Argentina Austria Brazil Chile Czech Republic France Greece
Guatemala Hungary Italy Japan Poland Portugal Singapore
South Korea Switzerland Thailand Turkey Ukraine Vietnam

Published by Oxford University Press, Inc.
198 Madison Avenue, New York, New York 10016

www.oup.com

Oxford is a registered trademark of Oxford University Press

Originally published as Kultur, um der Freiheit willen. Griechische Anfänge – Anfang Europas?
By Christian Meier © 2009 by Siedler Verlag, a division of Verlagsgruppe Random House
GmbH, München, Germany. *Geisteswissenschaften International*— Translation Funding for
Humanities and Social Sciences from Germany. A joint initiative of the Fritz thyssem Foundation,
the German Federal Foreign Office, and the German Publishers & Booksellers Association.

Library of Congress Cataloging-in-Publication Data

Meier, Christian, 1929–
[Kultur, um der Freiheit willen. English]
A culture of freedom : ancient Greece and the origins of Europe / Christian Meier.
p. cm.
Translation of: Kultur, um der Freiheit willen.
Includes bibliographical references and index.

ISBN 978-0-19-974740-5

1. Greece—Civilization—To 146 B.C.   2. Greece—Politics and government—To 146 B.C.
3. Greece—History—To 146 B.C.   4. Greece—History—Persian Wars, 500-449 B.C.
5. Europe—Civilization—Greek influences.   6. Political science—Greece—History.   I. Title.
DF77.M47513   2011
938—dc22
2011007134

Printing number: 1 3 5 7 9 8 6 4 2

Foreword

I met Christian Meier for the first time in the mid-1960s in Basel, Switzerland. I was a graduate student at the time, had completed my teacher's training, and was ready to write a dissertation. I had been fascinated by history and classical culture all along; hence ancient history, combining the two, was a logical choice, but the chair of ancient history had been vacant for several years. I was greatly excited, therefore, when a new chair, a young scholar from Germany, was appointed who was going to assume his first professorship in Basel and would help me move ahead. And I was in awe: he was a student of Hans Schaefer and Hermann Strasburger, two of the greatest names in Greek and Roman history, and he had edited the papers of Matthias Gelzer, an eminent authority on the Roman Republic. So I looked forward with great anticipation to Meier's arrival in Basel. As was his habit, he took me on long walks in the hills around the city, and we discussed possible topics. Eventually, we agreed on Caesar, and I was hooked. I wrote my dissertation and served as Meier's assistant in Basel and, for one year, in Cologne, but then went on to teach classics and history in secondary school. Still, I continued to visit Meier and had long conversations with him on walks in the countryside and over glasses of wine. In this way, too, at a crucial turning point in my life, the decision was made that eventually started my academic career in ancient history.

After Basel, Meier taught in Cologne and Bochum, before settling in Munich. Over the years, he rose to the top of his field and to great prominence far beyond it. As the first ancient historian, he served as President of the German Historical Association. Among other academic leadership positions, he was also President of the German Academy for Language and Poetry. He has received numerous fellowships and grants as well as a number of prestigious distinctions and prizes, in recognition of his work and lifetime achievement (including the Jacob-Grimm-Prize for the German Language, the Austrian Medal for the Sciences and Arts, and the Lichtenberg-Medal of the Academy of Sciences in Göttingen). He is a member of the Academy of Sciences of Berlin-Brandenburg and of the Norwegian Academy of Sciences, as well as a corresponding member of the Academy of Sciences of Athens.

His books, not to speak of edited volumes and scores of articles and chapters in books, are too numerous to list in full. They focus on three main areas: Graeco-Roman history, modern German history and politics, as well as the meaning and function of History as a discipline and the responsibility of the historian. (I give some representative titles here in English translation.) In the first area, classical antiquity, his first book was *Res publica amissa: A Study of the Constitution and History of the Late Roman Republic* (1966, many reprints). *The Greek Discovery of Politics* appeared in 1980 (in English in 1990), followed by *The Impotence of the Omnipotent Dictator, Caesar: Three Biographical Sketches* (1980), *Caesar* (1982, English edn, 1995), *Politics and Grace* (1985), *The Political Art of Greek Tragedy* (1988, English edn, 1993), *Athens* (1993, English edn, 1999), and now *A Culture of Freedom* (2009).

In the other two areas I mention *Forty Years after Auschwitz* (1987, revised and enlarged edn, 1990), *The World of History and the Province of the Historian* (1989), *German Unity as a Challenge: What Foundations for What Kind of Republic?* (1990), *The Nation that Does not Want to be One* (1991), *The Parliamentary Democracy* (1999), *The Disappearance of the Present: On History and Politics* (2001), *From Athens to Auschwitz: Reflections on the Situation of History* (2002), *and The Command to Forget and the Indispensability of Remembering* (2010).

These are some of the facts and statistics illustrating Meier's life and achievement. They tell many parts of the story. To begin with, it is the story of an immensely productive historian whose impact has been and continues to be massive: in the field of history at large and of ancient history in particular, but also in public discourse concerning urgent questions of recent history and the present. It is the story of a scholar who deals with the ancient past but never sees it as gone and alien but rather, to vary the title of one of his articles, as 'the closest alien thing'. In other words, antiquity is, at least to some extent, close enough to be accessible without constant interpretation, and distant enough not to raise emotions and affect identities; it stimulates thinking about the present and in turn becomes interesting and accessible by questions agitating the present. The record listed above also highlights a citizen who precisely as a historian, armed with insights gained through history, feels a deep obligation to assist his country and his fellow citizens in coming to terms with their terrible past and meeting the challenges of their present, and to show his fellow historians that they can ignore this responsibility only at their own peril and that of their discipline. Furthermore, the record reveals a servant to his academic profession, whose long-standing efforts on behalf of his students, academic institutions, and an interested lay public have received abundant recognition.

Less visible in that record is another dimension: a person, a true *Mensch*, who, despite all his accomplishments and honours, remains modest enough to focus (as he did at the celebration of his sixtieth birthday among friends and pupils) not on the triumphs but on the shortcomings of his academic endeavours and to derive an obligation from what he had *not* done although he should or might have. He is a person who cares, as a husband, father, teacher, friend, colleague, and a citizen of this world; a person who needs to understand what works in human society and what does not, who seeks answers to these questions in studying the ancient world and shares his insights with all who also care and want to listen. Unlike the proverbial prophet who is not heard in his own country, his works are read widely and eagerly: people listen.

The story has other parts. One is best told by students (and wider audiences) who have experienced Meier as a great and tireless presence who delights in lively narrative but especially in stimulating others to think, in raising questions, pushing the boundaries, seeking ever deeper answers, penetrating far beneath the surface and beyond the levels where others have stopped, probing, testing, refuting, and starting anew. Meier's aim is to let his audiences share in his quest for understanding the essential factors that explain the course of history—a quest that rarely pursues a straight line but proceeds along twisted paths, wherever the restless search leads. Readers of the present volume will be treated to a generous dose of this but will also be able to enjoy the delights of discovery and illumination.

Another part of the story concerns the scholar's path of search and discovery. Meier started out as a Roman historian, trying to understand in *Res publica amissa* (still a standard work) the reasons for the crisis and fall of the Roman Republic. The question soon changed: why did a socio-political structure that had initially been tremendously successful but that was mired in a deep crisis and clearly seemed doomed last so long, through a death struggle of decades if not a full century? An important part of Meier's answer is a formula that is forever tied to his name: it was 'a crisis without alternative'. It was, in other words, a crisis of which people were all too well aware but for which they were able to find a solution neither within their moribund system nor by transcending it, since all conceivable alternatives were ideologically unacceptable. Similar 'winged formulations' emerge from Meier's other works.

On the Greek side, Meier has for almost forty years been pursuing a single but encompassing question: why and how did some immensely important phenomena, profoundly different from anything that had preceded them, and profoundly influential on all subsequent history, emerge precisely in a rugged country among small communities which were long so insignificant that the great powers of the time largely ignored them? Some of the phenomena in question concern political values and terminology, politics or 'the political', democracy, political thought, the political function of drama, historiography, and now Greek culture at large. 'The Greeks, the Political Revolution of World History', is one of the most expressive and memorable of his titles. So is *A Culture of Freedom*, the present book that focuses squarely on the search for the origins of Greek culture, its connection to liberty, and its role in the beginnings of Europe.

Ancient Greece's connection to modern Europe is not obvious. Indeed, why should a book on the origins and specific nature of Greek culture begin, as this one does, with a series of chapters on the question of the beginnings of Europe and whether or why the ancient world and particularly ancient Greece can be considered part of it? This question is of obvious significance at a time when Europe is striving to achieve unity and to redefine its scope, history and tradition, and role in the world. But its importance goes far beyond Europe. Two contradictory claims often confront each other. One, often refuted and abused, emphasizes the descent of modern culture and especially democracy from ancient Greece. The other points out that the ancient world, including the Roman, though eventually encompassing substantial parts of western and central Europe, always remained focused on the Mediterranean and areas further east. History became 'European' (politically and culturally) only in the Middle Ages, and the case has often been made that 'European history' in a more precise sense thus began then and not in antiquity. Meier traces these discussions and acknowledges their importance but then changes the focus: what is true for political history may not be true in the same way for cultural history, for mainly two reasons. One is that Europe as a continent and a distinct cultural-political sphere had already been discovered and conceptualized by the ancient Greeks by the late sixth and early fifth centuries BC. The other, more important, is that, although no direct political continuity extends from the Greek through the medieval to the modern European world, culturally such continuity, even if mostly indirect and transmitted through Roman and Byzantine intermediaries, was broad and substantial. Moreover, this factor was decisive. The development of medieval and early modern culture in Europe, although directed by monarchical powers (whether religious or secular), was triggered and crucially influenced by the appropriation of ancient culture. European culture was made possible by, and grew out of, ancient and, very essentially, Greek culture. At least from a cultural perspective, therefore—and strong cases can be made for other perspectives too—there are very good reasons to study the history of the ancient world, including especially its beginnings in Greece, as the prehistory and early history of Europe—with consequences, of course, that eventually reached far beyond Europe.

The second (and main) part of this book deals with early Greece essentially in the 'Archaic Period' (*c.*750–500 BC). Meier focuses on the formation of the Greek world of *poleis* (usually small, face-to-face citizen communities) that emerged out of the 'Dark Ages' (*c.*1200–750). After the collapse of the powerful and magnificent Greek ('Mycenaean') Bronze Age civilization and a substantial contraction of populations, horizons, and cultural skills (despite manifold continuities), Greek communal life and culture essentially started anew. For several centuries these communities evolved in clusters and constant competition among each other, expanded their world through the foundation of a great number of new *poleis* along the coasts of the Mediterranean and Black Sea areas, interacted intensively with the more highly developed cultures to the east and south (from Anatolia and the Levant to Mesopotamia and Egypt) but lived outside the sphere of direct control by the great powers of the time. As a people, they were thus free, not ruled over by others. Moreover, the competitive but essentially egalitarian and balanced system of multiple *poleis* permitted the formation of a few exceptionally large and potentially powerful communities (such as Sparta and Athens), but for a variety of reasons these did not (yet) aim at dominating or even ruling over the others. The same was true for the internal sphere of the *poleis*: with very few and usually short-lived exceptions (the 'tyrants') and despite increasing social and economic differentiation and the conflicts caused by it, centralized, monarchical power was conspicuously absent in this world: the *poleis* were free internally as well, founded on a strong egalitarian base, and as much as possible self-sufficient.

All this, Meier argues, was not only a fact, resulting from highly exceptional conditions and circumstances, it was also what the Greeks wanted and embraced, what they lived and fought for, and what they were able to preserve until and beyond their eventual confrontation with the giant Persian Empire in the late sixth and early fifth centuries BC. Uniquely in world history, here a culture was born not from above, by the will and resources of monarchs, but from among citizen communities, driven by the citizens' collective will. This offered great opportunities but also posed enormous challenges and difficulties, which these citizens had to resolve with their own means and skills, finding ways to live together productively, and developing institutions and methods to govern themselves. To master these challenges, Meier contends, they needed their own particular culture. They developed it—in its entire range from poetry, political thought, and law to painting, sculpture, and architecture, and, eventually, to philosophy, geography, and the beginnings of science—because it helped them to cope with the complexities of their lives and tasks, to express themselves, and to think and work through all that they were confronted with. They had to do all this for the first time too, since they did not have the privilege shared by all later cultures: they had no Greeks to emulate and to guide them in their thinking. Although Meier is careful to take fully into account the many ways Greek culture was influenced and enriched by intense contacts with the civilizations of the ancient Near East, he also emphasizes that these societies were very different socially and politically. In shaping their communal sphere and life, the Greeks found such influences much less helpful; they had to find their own ways.

This book is special, therefore, not because it traces the development of early Greek society and culture from its beginnings to the threshold of its 'classical' greatness; others have done that. Rather, it is unique and fascinating because it does so through a constructive synthesis that is based on what we might call 'empathetic reconstruction': it leads us into the middle of the struggles, anxieties, suffering, and exhilaration the Greeks experienced in their efforts to meet the huge challenges they were confronted with and had chosen to confront. Meier thinks not only about what the Greeks achieved and why they were able to achieve it but also what problems it caused them. Most especially, he tries to understand why they needed to develop their own ways of life, their own forms of community, and their own culture, distinct and right for themselves, in which they would not follow the commands of others but live freely, by their own rules, and govern themselves, both in their own *poleis* and in the entire world of *poleis*. This book allows us not just to read about this process but to relive it and thus to understand in a fundamentally new way what it meant, and why it was necessary to develop a culture through the collective effort of citizen communities and for the sake of freedom.

Finally, the present volume is the third part of a significant trilogy. Meier once said he wanted to write three types of biography: of an important personality, of a city, and of a culture. This wish was prompted initially by dissatisfaction with the kinds of biographies that are usually written. How this should be done properly and in meaningful as well as interesting ways remained to be figured out. Meier did this in writing his *Caesar*. The principle was not to try to present Caesar as if he were one of us but to make him understandable in all his cultural difference. This in turn required a comprehensive effort to include in the biography of a historical actor not just the necessary minimum of social and factual background but all the particularities, in their rich and puzzling complexity, of the culture that conditioned his actions. Structural history, even analysis, became an indispensable foundation and part of biography. In the case of *Caesar*, the result was anathema to some traditional historians but a feast for a broad readership, encompassing everybody from scholars and students to the proverbial interested lay person. *Mutatis mutandis*, but ever more comprehensively, all this applies to Meier's 'biographies' of a city (*Athens*) and a culture as well.

A Culture of Freedom is thus the third and by far the most ambitious 'biography', encompassing an entire culture—at least in its birth and youth. (A brief outlook at the end suggests where a continuation might lead.) It represents an effort by one of the leading interpreters of archaic and classical Greek history to fit the results of his previous scholarship into a holistic picture, sketching, exploring, and explaining the remarkable phenomenon of the origins and development of Greek culture, from smallest beginnings to the threshold of its climax, by itself and in its relation to the ancient cultures of the Near East and to other parts of the Mediterranean, and under conditions that differed so totally from those which produced other leading cultures in world history.

The book also attests to Meier's qualities as a writer. A unique and difficult style had initially limited the impact of *Res publica amissa* largely to German-speaking readers; it has resisted translation to this day. This is fortunately not true of later books, most of which have seen translation into several languages. In fact, Meier is capable of writing in a beautiful, creative, imaginative, and engaging style: it is no accident that he was elected a member and then the President of the German Academy for Language and Poetry. Early on, for example, his long introduction to Helmut Simon's translation of Caesar's *Civil War* (1964) highlighted this talent: it leads the reader from the core of the immediate crisis further and further back and ever deeper into the structural problems and paradoxical conditions that made it possible to fight a civil war with the justification of defending one's honour. Another beautiful example of Meier's literary style is *Politics and Grace*. The cover of this little book shows Athena, as played by Jutta Lampe in the memorable performance of the *Oresteia* by Peter Stein's Schaubühne am Halleschen Ufer in Berlin in the 1970s and 1980s—one of my own deepest experiences of ancient drama. Shared interest in the meaning and performance of ancient tragedy brought Meier in touch with the ensemble, and he ended up working with them on other projects. He was fascinated by the challenge. What he wrote in that book, and how he wrote it, was stimulated in part by this experience—which in turn illustrates his personal engagement with the culture about which he writes.

Even though translation necessarily flattens out Meier's style, I trust that readers of *A Culture of Freedom* will still be able to notice (and enjoy) its unique character and quality—and to see that it serves multiple purposes: not only to narrate and explain a fascinating story but also to probe, search, and question, and to help the readers share the author's efforts to find the deep and hidden answers to the complex questions he is asking.

Kurt A. Raaflaub
Providence, RI

Acknowledgements

In readying the original German version of this book, I received much assistance from Katharina Weikl and Heidrun Thiel. In one of those frequent moments, when my courage threatened to fail me, Katja Wildermuth offered to read the manuscript in whatever state it was in and encouraged me to continue. I would like to express my deep gratitude to all three of them, as well as to Ditta Ahmadi.

For their help in preparing the English version, I would like to thank my former student, Kurt Raaflaub, and the staff of Oxford University Press.

If this book had a dedication, it would be to my wife, my children, and my grandchildren. Along with many other things, I owe them the relatively high proportion of independence that I have enjoyed since the beginning of my career.

Publisher's Acknowledgements

The publishers would like to extend their especial thanks to Professor Kurt Raaflaub for his editorial contribution to the preparation of the English edition of this book.

Contents

List of Maps

List of Figures

Map 1. The Greek World.

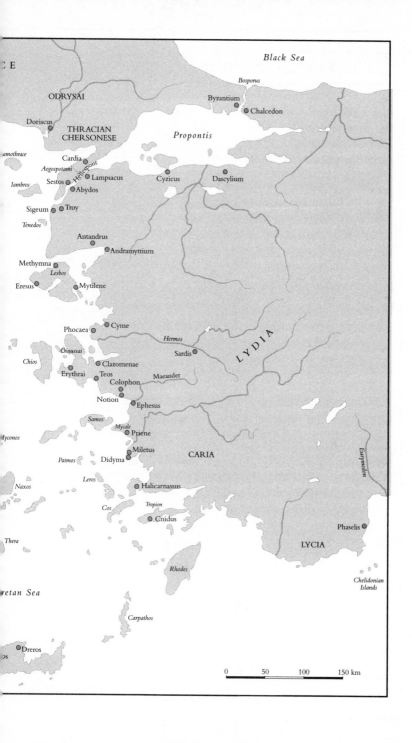

Black Sea

Bosporus

ODRYSAI

Byzantium
Chalcedon

Doriscus
THRACIAN
CHERSONESE
Propontis

amothrace

Cardia
Aegospotami
Sestos ⊙ Lampsacus   Cyzicus   Dascylium
Iambros   Abydos

Sigeum ⊙ Troy
Tenedos

Antandrus
Andramyttium

Methymna
Lesbos
Eresus   Mytilene

Phocaea ⊙ Cyme
Hermos   L Y D I A
Oinussai   Sardis
Chios
Erythrai   Clazomenae
Teos
Colophon   *Maeander*
Notion
Ephesus
Samos
Mycale
Priene
Myconos   Miletus   CARIA
Patmos   Didyma
Leros
Naxos   Halicarnassus

Cos
Tropion
Thera   Cnidus   Phaselis

LYCIA
Rhodes
*Chelidonian
Islands*

retan Sea   *Carpathos*   *Eurymedon*

Dreros
os

0   50   100   150 km

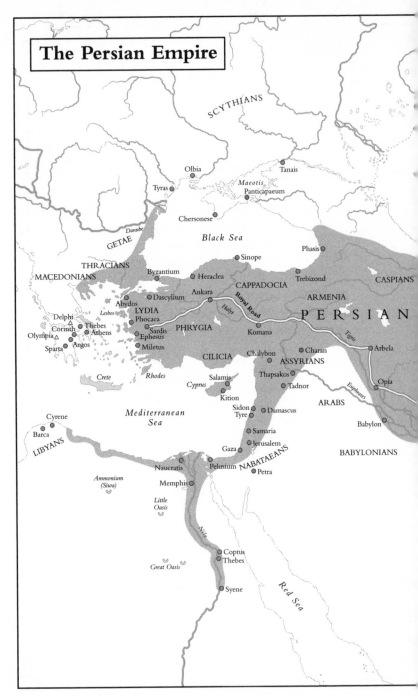

Map 2. The Persian empire.

Aral
Sea

DAHAR

SOGDIANA

⊙ Kyreschata

⊙ Maracanda

CHORASMIA

*Caspian
Sea*

Oxus

⊙ Bactra

⊙ Margiana

BACTRIANS

⊙ Taxila

Margos

GANDHARA

HYRCANIA

E M P I R E

Arios

MEDES ⊙ R.hagai

PARTHIANS

ARIA

ARACHOSIA

⊙ Ecbatana

:histun

INDIANS

⊙
Susa

SAGARTIA

Pasargadai ⊙

Persepolis ⊙

GEDROSIA

PERSIANS

MAKA

Persian Gulf

GERRHAEANS

MYKIANS

*Indian
Ocean*

PART I

The Question of Beginnings

Introduction

Where does Europe begin? Where, indeed, does anything ever begin? Nothing exists without preliminaries, predecessors, and preconditions; there is no such thing as a true 'zero hour'. Everywhere you look, when you scratch beneath the surface of ostensible beginnings, you discover still deeper origins, which seem to recede further and further before the researcher's gaze into a bottomless abyss.

Undeniably, some phenomena do have definite start dates. These include constitutions, alliances, entities such as the European Community, or institutions that are founded at a specific point in time. While such phenomena have their own prehistory, the moment at which they came into being clearly demarcates the prelude from the story proper.

It is entirely different, however, with gradually evolving phenomena, things which, when first noticed, already seem to have been in existence for quite some time. How can one determine the absolute beginning of an opinion, a custom, a situation, or a movement—to say nothing of a highly complex phenomenon like Europe, where there is considerable hesitation about whether it should be considered a spatial and temporal unit at all. If Europe is to be thought of as a discrete entity, it must have coalesced from an endless number of disparate elements, which continued to diverge and coalesce in different ways. Moreover, the longer one considers Europe to have existed, the more its continued development must have been determined by either constant or sudden additions, from within or without, of much that was novel and often very diverse. Most often, highly heterogeneous impulses would likely have given rise to and intensified one another, while other no less European and perhaps even more significant elements would repeatedly have disappeared. In any case, under these conditions, this Europe would have been in an extremely pronounced state of constant transformation, both within its separate parts and as a whole.

Or did some form of European particularity preserve itself at a basic level and even through such changes? Or is it precisely the tendency towards very rapid, often radical transformation that ultimately characterizes Europe?

An inestimable and barely comprehensible multitude of phenomena make their way forward in history, intertwining and converging with one another; they carry with them things universally forgotten about but which can suddenly re-emerge and, indeed, under certain circumstances, assert themselves powerfully. Processes entail and presuppose one another, drive this or that development, cross paths, coalesce, and then drift apart at a wide variety of different speeds. What appears as a path in history all too often turns out to be merely the lanes that later observers have hacked out of the thicket of effects and counter-effects.

And then, to this web of factors and causes—entangled so much that it can hardly be unravelled—we try to apply a measuring stick marked with years and centuries, to determine things such as *the* beginning of Europe? As if it were possible to scratch markings into an entangled bale of yarn. As if, as we so often would like to believe, incisions were simply a given?

Nonetheless, one is tempted to do precisely that. How else can we gain an overview and attempt to comprehend history? That is why we dare eventually to let historical phenomena begin at certain points and relocate everything that might have determined them—in one way or another, more or less—to a prior period in time. This is somewhat arbitrary, to be sure, but as close as we can come to a sensible historical interpretation. But when an entity as complex as Europe is in question, one first needs to be clear about what it is or should be.

Should we locate the beginning of Europe and its history at the point when the peoples, especially in the west and centre of the continent, become conscious of a commonality that they share, despite all the differences that separate them? Conscious, as was occasionally the case already in the early Middle Ages, of belonging together and being distinct from Avars, Huns, Arabs, and Turks; from the Orient, Africa, and the New World; as the centre of the entire earth being seen in new ways? Or should we go further back in time to the point at which the peoples that were later to constitute Europe began to emerge? But what would these peoples have had in common? The geographical nature of the area where they lived? The nascent, but soon to be familiar situations, together with customs and typical modes of thought and action, which they needed and developed in order to succeed in such situations? Or was the common factor certain initial conditions from the still deeper past that exerted their influence upon such peoples?

Should we then perhaps, as has been so often suggested, look for the origin of Europe in antiquity, at least in the roots of Christianity, whose Western, Latin form was to shape the European continent so strongly? After all, during the Middle Ages, people saw themselves more as members of Christianity than of Europe. But perhaps one has also to include Roman and even Greek history in the history of Europe?

At any rate, there are many reasons not to define Europe ethnically, in terms of peoples per se, but rather in terms of what uniquely permeated and challenged them, what opened up such a massive realm of possibilities for them, and what enabled them (or at least several among them), beginning, for example, in the sixteenth century, either to take possession of or exert decisive influence over the entire world. In view of this, Eric Lionel Jones speaks of the 'European miracle'. What he means by that is, ultimately, to put it simply, a discrete—European—culture.

Even if we do not want to underestimate the formative power and competency of each and every specific period in history, European culture was forcefully and lastingly influenced by Graeco-Roman antiquity. Indeed, it perhaps could never have emerged without ancient Greece and Rome. On the other hand, the creative forces that had exerted their influence in antiquity over generation after generation had more or less exhausted themselves in the western part of the Roman Empire by the third, fourth, or fifth century AD. To be sure, the Church, along with knowledge, customs, and not least many texts from earlier periods, survived. Certain dispositions persisted that were passed on with the faith that antiquity had needed and to which it had given itself in the end. Nonetheless, in the Middle Ages, it was essentially necessary to start from scratch. No matter how intensively people may have oriented themselves time and time again towards antiquity since the Carolingian Renaissance, this hardly sufficed to bridge the divide between antiquity and the Middle Ages. It was a unique process of cultural formation in Europe that went on at the time and has continued ever since.

1

A Most Unusual Case I:
The Appropriation of Antiquity by
Medieval and Modern Europe

After the first high cultures had arisen in various parts of the world, cultural development usually proceeded by means of connections to previous cultures. But there were significant differences, among other things, in the depth and duration of such connections. One can expose oneself for a time to foreign influences and then use what has been learned, without spending much time worrying about its origins. Alternatively, one can feel inferior and obligated to a previous culture for centuries, so that one is prompted constantly to study that culture and its legacy. This point distinguishes medieval and modern Europe markedly, for instance, from Greece and the Arab world. The Greeks certainly utilized the knowledge and technologies of the Orient in many ways, including its forms of expression, motifs, myths, cults, and insights. But they concerned themselves afterwards with the source of what they had appropriated only in isolated instances. The extent to which the Greeks learned Oriental languages rather than merely communicating via intermediaries and translators is unclear, as is the issue of whether they translated literary texts for anything but private usage.

The Arabs, especially under the early ninth-century Abbasids, did in fact translate large parts of Greek literature, and they used them in a most remarkable fashion, as the works of their own great philosophers show. Those books were probably also available early on in the major libraries that existed in Baghdad. But the Arabs themselves hardly learned Greek; they never developed the discipline of philology, and they picked and chose. They were interested in the sciences, such as medicine, mathematics, astronomy, and philosophy, as well as, incidentally, the rules of perspective, which Greeks scholars had developed particularly to resolve problems of the design of theatrical stage sets. But the Arabs had no use for Greek tragedy, history, rhetoric, or the plastic arts—or for Greek lyric poetry, since they already had a rich poetic tradition of their own.

The situation was completely different in medieval and modern Europe, which developed a symbiotic relationship with antiquity: Europeans not only used Latin as the language of the Bible and religious liturgy, of law, administration, diplomacy, and scholarship, and thus as a universal, indeed superior medium of communication, but Latin and, later on, Greek texts too were collected, studied, and copied wherever they were available. Initially, Greek texts existed primarily in Arabic translations, from which they had to be further translated into Latin. But, eventually, the originals became accessible. The new cultural and scientific languages schooled themselves on the classical ones. Latin and Greek texts were treated as paradigms. And the same was true of the artistic and architectural legacies of antiquity.

In the course of time, Europeans developed an intense interest in the ancient Greeks and Romans themselves. Metaphorically speaking, they were not merely content to pluck the fruits of a culture, but devoted attention to the branches and trees upon which those fruits had grown. Part of the reason was that in the long process of transmission of Greek and Roman works, with few exceptions, only the most outstanding ones had the chance of being passed down. As a result, the Greeks and Romans were not just the models and mentors, but also the objects of increasingly intense study. Europeans were constantly drawing new connections with antiquity, and, in doing so, they were following the example of the Romans themselves, who had been equally as strongly attached to the Greek sources they considered classical.

The original works produced in various European languages up to the nineteenth and even twentieth centuries were less replacements than supplements to the Greek and Roman sources. The nineteenth-century Swiss historian Jacob Burckhardt was thus correct to conclude: 'We will never rid ourselves of Antiquity unless we become barbarians again.'

Over and over again, ancient texts and works of art proved to be fresher, longer lasting, and even more modern than what modern adapters had made of them. Often that is still the case even today. Almost invariably, the rapid change that makes new adaptations necessary also quickly renders them obsolete, whereas the originals seem, in a way that is never entirely comprehensible, to have been created for the ages. That is why they seem classic.

The continuation of the Imperium Romanum was the Holy Roman Empire. In large parts of the continent Roman Law continued to be valid into the twentieth century and is still present in the civil law of various European national states. Where else has it been the case that the upper and middle classes of an entire continent have had their children learn at least one, if not two languages that no people in the world still speak? As long as it was still customary to memorize poems on a large scale, educated people included Latin and Greek ones. Even today, there is no such thing as philosophy without Plato and no political science worth the name without Aristotle. Wherever we care to look, our language, images, and ideas are still populated by ancient concepts, figures, and stories.

Moreover, in almost paradoxical fashion, Graeco-Roman antiquity helped to open medieval and modern Europe to renewal and even revolution. 'Whenever people undertook to bid farewell to their own world and find a new one beyond their previous horizons', writes Werner Dahlheim, 'they turned their gaze backward towards the faraway land of Antiquity... hoping to find a truth there over which no tradition could hold any power'. In unparalleled fashion, antiquity was thus a powerfully influential part of the history of medieval and modern Europe. Can the impression be entirely wrong, then, that Europeans did not just appropriate antiquity, but allowed themselves to be appropriated by classical Rome and Greece?

What does this mean for European history? How can it be explained? Was it just that for a long time the Graeco-Roman legacy was simply so superior? Was it impossible to catch up with it or to exhaust it—not least because of its capacity to encourage ever new interpretations? Did people in the age of Christianity need the decisive authority of the Ancients to help them to resist the demands imposed by their own faith and its zealous representatives? Had people spent so long adopting the legacy of antiquity that they no longer had the desire or the means to live without it—although, or rather, because they knew that they were inferior to it?

Perhaps, though, the legacy of antiquity contained something especially fascinating, at least for those who, thanks to the Christian transmission of that legacy, were open to perceive and receive it. In any case, at the very core of this legacy, and still resonant within it, was something unique in world history: freedom.

2

The Challenge of Freedom

Cultures can be viewed as sophisticated ways in which members of societies, however they might have come about, establish themselves together and in the world. People have to develop, maintain, and consolidate civilized forms of living with one another and to deal productively with their human and non-human environments. Society needs to structure itself. Political entities, which allow for common action, have to be created. Methods must be developed for establishing law and order, fighting wars, and organizing and increasing knowledge, perhaps even monopolizing it. Things have to be given significance. Religion, an understanding of the world, education, and role models are needed. But people also have to find ways of expressing themselves and understanding various experiences, perspectives, triumphs, fears, insights, and feelings—according to what is appropriate in each situation, not forgetting specific forms of relief, relaxation, and enjoyment, as well as the magnificent and often exaggerated self-presentation that is virtually the life-breath of every proud culture.

The process of cultural formation thus usually consists of agreeing upon and determining a great number of rules, without which it is impossible for people to find the room necessary to act and develop. Whether such rules arise from coercion or adaptation, from the self-discipline or the ability to exploit opportunities, they tend to merge and, under certain conditions, can achieve a high degree of immutability.

But here, too, there are major differences, which are most likely the result of diverse starting constellations that at some point are created or establish themselves. Whatever one chooses to adopt from the outside, the decisive factor is inevitably what forces (or what sort of forces) eventually prove decisive in determining which rules apply. This is true not just of constellations of power, but of attitudes, forms, and habits of life, and ways of behaving in the world as well.

In world history, cultures were usually determined by monarchs. To a greater or lesser degree, in conjunction with religious authorities, they were able to shape societies, even their thinking and mentality, to their own ends. This means, not least, to anchor their own rule so firmly that ultimately the only alternative to be perceived was chaos. Monarchs may put themselves in a position to achieve large-scale military or administrative successes. They may be crucial to increasing wealth, collecting knowledge, attaining insight, inspiring miracles of technology, and facilitating the creation of great works of art, architecture, and literature. But shaking the foundations of the social order will no longer be easy. Social dissatisfaction and rebellion will aim, not only in their legitimation, but also in their goals and effects, at reducing power that exceeds accepted limits to what is considered normal and at re-establishing justice. If the unity of a regime breaks apart, new and smaller ones will arise to fill the vacuum. If an Egyptian pharaoh such as Akhenaten tried to introduce radical innovation by replacing polytheism with a more monotheistic faith, his successors were quick to revert to the original tradition. Dynasties may change, and conquerors may replace previous rulers, but society and culture essentially continue along the same well-worn track—unless they are completely destroyed.

Much less commonly, it can be an aristocracy that forms and main-tains itself and the world according to its own needs and purposes. That at least was the case in Rome, where initially the Etruscans seem to have established a powerful monarchy that, however, was soon toppled. Although several hardly insignificant institutions of this period survived, the decisive impulse for the subsequent development of the Romans' thinking (and perhaps their emotional universe), religion, and system of law came from the republican aristocracy. That class also determined the forms of political order, politics, and warfare, social organization, and finally the ways in which conquered territories were integrated, so that the aristocracy—with its specific forms of social relations and dependencies—mediated everything and, as a result, became more and more indispensable. The opposition that gradually emerged only con-tributed to stabilizing the regime by providing relief from tensions and helping, initially, to discipline, then to augment and strengthen the aristocracy itself.

The Republic, the aristocracy ruling it, and the entire Roman social and political order therefore succeeded in achieving such stability that they not only remained unshakeable for centuries, but could also serve as the basis for the founding and administration of a global empire. Even when the Republic was finally hit by severe crises, when tasks and responsibilities proved too challenging, and the rule of law and domestic peace could no longer be maintained, there was no immediately appar-ent alternative. Although Augustus was able to establish a monarchy and put an end to a large number of Rome's troubles, the source of legitimacy remained the Roman Senate and the Republic. Conditions were very slow to change. That was due to the extent to which the early and still deeply rooted aristocratic order had conditioned all of Rome and its world.

But there is one case in which things took a different course. In ancient Greece, it was not a monarchy nor an aristocracy that was ruling, but a relatively broad class of men and free citizens who shaped themselves and their world, spread as they were across hundreds of autonomous communities known as *poleis*. Admittedly, members of the upper class, aristocrats, were initially influential among them. Nonetheless, those aristocrats attached great importance to living freely and independently in relatively small communities, and they were not interested in making conquests. There were no clear and permanent boundaries between them and other property owners. The perspective—and problems—that dominated were thus those of communal life among equals, and not those of ruling over others.

It is difficult to fathom what this meant. For the ancient Greeks, freedom was not defined in terms of rights vis-à-vis a monarch within a state, or as a private sphere in which one could do as one wished, but rather as a fundamental characteristic of property holders in numerous communities. Freedom bound people together; it was a duty when it needed to be maintained and secured in increasingly complicated circumstances, and, ultimately, it was both a challenge and an opportunity to live in a completely novel fashion. For what we now call the culture of the ancient Greeks was their very element.

If these Greeks, then, from very early on wanted to be their own masters, that is, to be autonomous and avoid dependence on others, to the largest extent possible they had to be able, to provide for themselves and to do everything they needed on their own. That was true in both their households, in their private spheres, and increasingly also in their communities. General consensus and rules which arose from the centre of society were needed for those tasks that could only be dealt with communally, tasks that affected the ability of communities to live together. Public tasks were to be delegated to individuals only minimally, where it was unavoidable, since that tended to result in an increase of power, which was not in the interests of the community.

Initially, communal life in such communities may have functioned more or less successfully over extended periods or even as a general rule. Difficulties arose whenever it came to more serious sorts of confrontations. Although conflicts happened every once in a while, they became decidedly more frequent and intense as the *polis* societies grew more differentiated. Therefore there was an increase in, on the one hand, demands (and arrogance), on the other, poverty and misery, resulting in uprisings.

Because of the lack of strong and superior authority, in such situations there was a great need for finding a balance among members of the community. How could parties in a conflict be reconciled? How could their demands be weighed against one another? Practical procedures had to be introduced, and mediators had to emerge; it is hardly a coincidence that the sources from that time reflect a remarkably high valuation of *charis* (grace). The idea of justice had to be thought through. Whereas in other cultures people's emotions are domesticated and imaginations and intentions are restrained and internalized by pressure from above, in ancient Greece this had to be achieved time and again within the circle of the community members. The Greeks never, for example, succeeded in eliminating or controlling people's desire for revenge so fully that only a few still openly proclaimed it. But that was part and parcel of the fullness of the personalities involved and the corresponding richness and diversity of human experiences the Greeks enjoyed.

All this brought about political difficulties. Some of these could be alleviated by creating institutions, but these by no means sufficed, especially since they were often no match for the expanding ambitions of the most powerful members of society. In communities in which so much has to be settled between so many participants, the burning issues were always those of how to coexist—of conflict, balance, and reconciliation, of the creation of rules and self-assertion. Those issues must have extended deeply into and dominated the whole broad realm of language, poetry, and art that people in early, uncertain circumstances always utilize to find their way in the world and towards justice and order. Where no power is easily able to gain authority, poets, bards, and other specialists face particularly high expectations. The more they pick up on the tensions that exercise their audiences, playing through the problems of communal life in imaginatively roundabout, artistic, and vivid fashion, the better they are able to meet those demands. This is precisely what we find in the *Iliad*.

Where people are so free and conditions are in such constant flux, one logical step forward is to seek modes of expression that facilitate certainty and self-assertion, mourning, but also agreement and understanding.

One such mode of expression was the wonderful lyric poetry of Greece's archaic period, in all of its bold, sharp, but amazingly light forms.

When cities face the greatest emergencies and extreme conflict, but still want to avoid autocratic forms of rule, political thought is an absolute necessity. Such thinking must aim at discovering the relations between the powers active in the community and, as it were, the rules by which they interact with each other. Cities that want to be free must maintain themselves by finding a balance within themselves. Yet when there is so much at stake, questions concerning communal order cannot be restricted to politics. They also have to be directed at the cosmos as a whole. People in such a situation have no choice but to take up the challenge of philosophy and science—and they find their answers in the sort of thinking that can probably only arise in a free society.

When things are in constant flux, but no one absolute authority is allowed to dominate, people have to find objective criteria that govern how everything functions and must be divided —in every respect, not only in the *polis*. This kind of thinking results in theories about numbers and musical intervals, the quest for correct proportions in the construction of temples and the planning of cities, hypotheses about equilibrium in medicine, calendars, and politics, and later the pursuit of a canon concerning the human form. All these intellectual searches are expressive examples of how Greek society, stimulated and driven by its problems, was forced to find solutions—wherever they seemed to be available.

Since, however, the members of the leading class were so insistent on their liberty (and often arbitrarily), eventually the power of broader classes had to be enlisted against them. And this entailed conditions and brought consequences whose significance again went well beyond just politics. When special circumstances finally led Athens to become a great power in its pursuit of policies against the Persian Empire in the eastern Aegean, and, as a consequence, to transform itself into a radical democracy, the problems of responsibility, knowledge, and self-certainty seemed to be endless. Every aspect of tradition came in for increasingly radical questioning—all the more so since clarity about its own condition was a basic characteristic of this society. Tragedy, the intellectual culture of the Sophists, and the newly invented art of writing history dealt incisively with these experiences. In the end, the questions became so fundamental and doubts so pervasive that Socratic, Platonic, and Aristotelian philosophy had to come up with a completely new basis for understanding the world, the *polis*, and humanity.

However much power aristocracies may have accrued at various times and places, they had never been able to control people's access to their gods. Hence, certain secret cults notwithstanding, theology generally remained a matter of myths and poets, who projected onto the divine sphere what they observed or postulated on earth. Soon, though, philosophers saw themselves compelled to look for the divine in the world itself, since they believed that matters in the world had to proceed according to the right order. Thus, even later, it continued to be philosophy—whether of the Stoics, the Epicureans, the Cynics, or others—to which all Greeks turned in their search for justice and meaning—until Greek philosophy finally merged with Christian teachings.

It remains something of a secret how everything that was at that time dared, experienced, and suffered eventually found its classical shape. But wherever we look in ancient Greece, we see the imprints of a culture formed for freedom's sake, of a grand experiment in living life, under difficult circumstances, without a single ruling force. In order to achieve this, the Greeks had to both make it possible and to secure it, producing themselves everything they needed for it. If the nineteenth-century French philosopher Ernest Renan called this the 'Greek miracle', this means only that what happened was completely exceptional. Unlike most miracles, a lot of it can indeed be explained.

Homines maxime homines—human beings in the highest sense. That was how the Roman senator Pliny the Younger referred to the Greeks around 100 AD. By then it was two hundred years since the Roman upper classes had opened themselves up to Greek insights, philosophy, art, and ways of life, and allowed their own world to be gradually penetrated by Greek culture. Roman society, however, remained structured and determined by relations of power and rule that were part of its own specific legal—and originally republican—framework. This framework included relations of superiority and subordination, and various sorts of dependency and statuses relative to others. Every Roman had his own specific functions, fixed position in the hierarchical order, and duties (unless he entirely or partially withdrew to his villa to devote himself to private life in more or less Greek style). All this was not comparable at all with the life of the Greeks—neither of those of the past to whom the Romans devoted so much intellectual attention, nor of their Greek contemporaries.

The Greeks' defining characteristics were that they were first and foremost human beings, and not emperors, consuls, or senators; that they refused to be constrained by the rules of a class-segmented society;

that they were not accustomed to delegating responsibilities so that, even if they attained power (as many Romans did), they still depended on others and on whole clusters of relationships and were thus condemned to live a somewhat mediated life. Regardless of who a given individual was, the Greeks—or at least the upper classes of which Pliny was thinking—were parts of a collectivity that hardly reached beyond their group, made few demands upon them, but of which they all constituted an important part. They were as responsible as much to themselves as to this collectivity (but not, as a rule, to any higher authorities).

Even in the early days it had been typical of the Greeks that they were required to meet a great variety of demands of life. Those who want to live autonomously must depend on others as little as possible (except for those over whom they have full control). Nonetheless, if people live together in small circles, concretely and directly, largely free of the demands of specialized political or economic tasks, they have to measure themselves against each other—for example, in sporting events. Moreover, if social cohesion is not ensured by a political centre of power, other institutions— for instance, religious festivals—have to provide it. For the Greeks, music and the arts had a political dimension, which explains their significance in their society. Here too, Greeks were constantly competing with one another. Greeks not only had to provide for themselves, therefore, they also had to be able to sing and dance, to master the rules of compromise no less than the art of warfare. The end product was a type of people who, instead of dividing themselves into specialists and losing themselves in particularity, had to become all-rounders, physically, mentally, and spiritually. This is what we encounter, albeit in idealized form, in Greek statues. Every individual was expected to be a total person, who had developed and refined in himself what was generally valid, while everything in society was concentrated strongly on the everyday problems.

Perhaps it is the inherent appeal of this culture, developed for freedom's sake, that is evident in the whole spectrum of its legacy, which explains at least partially why time and again medieval and modern Europe was so fascinated by it, and why, over the course of centuries, it was always trying to reappropriate it. Yet, no matter how close antiquity and medieval and modern Europe may seem in some respects, there still is a significant rupture that separates them. Moreover, much suggests that medieval and modern culture was fundamentally different from that of antiquity and that from early on the distance increased—not least in terms of the sort of people that gradually, and in various ways emerged in Europe.

3

A Most Unusual Case II:
The Early Conditions of the Formation
of Medieval and Modern Culture

The formation of medieval and modern culture is characterized by the impact of a number of diverse and starkly divergent forces that operated either simultaneously or subsequent to each other. These were not power-wielders, i.e. monarchs or aristocrats, who succeeded in making themselves the focus of their society and world, shaping them according to their own interests and without an alternative. Nor was there a broad-based class of independent property owners, guided primarily by the desire to pursue and secure a more or less equal way of life. That had happened among the ancient Greeks, in various ways, in great freedom, and with substantial shifts of power among parts of the citizenry, which could even culminate in democracy. Ultimately, though, this process still lacked alternatives because various fundamental aspects of ancient Greek culture were never called into question: the concept of the *polis* as the only possible form of political community, the stratification of society, slavery, the inferior rights of women, a low regard for labour, the restriction of science to theory, an emphasis on leisure, and with all this the basic homogeneity of the Greek citizen communities.

Such a lasting lack of alternatives was unthinkable in Europe. The Germanic kings who carved up the Roman Empire usually did not have the means, in the form of a powerful administrative apparatus, for example, with which to gain complete control over the broad territories they found there or conquered. They never succeeded in making all the important forces in those territories dependent on themselves and in creating an order in which everything was properly interlaced, which would have allowed the monarchy to become the cornerstone and guarantor of the entire system—and thereby to direct the thinking and mentality of its subjects entirely towards itself. To be sure, for a long time medieval Europe knew nothing but monarchies. But there was little consensus as to how they were to be constituted. Kings had to court the aristocracy and were unable simply to integrate them into their systems of rule through concessions. Rather,

European monarchs repeatedly found themselves confronting aristocracies in independent institutions such as imperial and regional diets. Their ability to imprint themselves on entire societies remained limited.

Cities, as well as market and rural communities, also gained significant rights of their own, which they were forever trying to secure and expand. They drew up their own laws and conditions, and sometimes sent their own representatives to diets and assemblies. Within cities, non-property owners and skilled specialists achieved the sort of status as citizens they would never have been granted in antiquity. Specific sorts of thinking and attitudes emerged among such groups; thanks to their own ethos, and not least to a higher valuation of professional skills and labour, they were able to stand up to the aristocracy. The first republics arose.

Parallel to such secular power, there was religious power as well, and both were mutually dependent on one another—even if they also aroused considerable tension and conflict. Within the Church, contradictions between the commandments of an otherworldly god and the everyday practices of the clerical regiment, with its religious rites and faith, could turn virulent at any time. Orders of monks who had retreated from the world produced powerful movements advocating change. The Reformation and division of the Church prompted bitterly fought struggles. Typically, many of these confrontations called forth new ideas, attitudes, and demands, and thus contributed to processes of long-term development.

It was not just comparable powers—one monarchy, for instance, against another—that clashed with one another. Nor was the result of confrontation a matter of the one side winning what the other had lost. What was being fought out time and again was the structural relationship between kings and aristocrats, lords and country, secular and religious authority, bishops and civic communities, popes and clerical orders. Creative tensions arose between them. New freedoms were constantly being granted and then expanded. Many of the numerous uprisings of the period caused not only temporary trouble or improvements in the conditions that had inspired them, but resulted in new rights and legal spheres. Defeats often set the stage for renewed rebellion.

In short, a variety of diverse and potentially opposing forces with their own legal status were asserting themselves—and that over a vast territory, in which there were both drastic differences from country to country and close connections that were difficult to sever, fostered by the upper classes' use of Latin as a lingua franca. Even in the so-called Age of Absolutism, when monarchs tried use the state to monopolize the political sphere, they were never able to establish their rule as the only long-term option. Their very efforts to do so unleashed new intellectual and then also social forces. In the end, they turned out to be dispensable. Whatever they had created could be continued by a republic.

It is an open question exactly when, to what extent, and why European science, invention, and technology surpassed those of other high cultures, past and present, including those of the Greeks and Romans. It would seem that every culture develops the technological capacities it needs in accordance with various necessities and demands, whether self-created or externally imposed. In medieval and above all in modern Europe, however, technological progress and scientific advancement gradually took on such an intensity and dynamism that they soon surpassed anything that had previously been considered possible or even conceivable. Europeans began to experiment more intensely and systematically than the Ancients were ever able to—or indeed wanted to.

Universities were founded and achieved a great degree of autonomy. Theology and philosophy developed side by side and in competition with one another, drawing on the Bible, the Church Fathers, and pre-Christian ancient sources, but also on dialogue with Jews and Muslims. A quickly developing legal profession, based on the study of the *Corpus Iuris*, accrued great influence and authority.

It was difficult to harness all these different developments—particularly because of the numerous rivalries between empires and countries. Essentially, the rulers were too weak and the world that was emerging far too varied for this to happen. Censorship could be applied here and there, but it could never be enforced universally. Anybody, and especially minorities that were open to change—for instance, Jews—could escape repression by emigrating, and that eventually in turn hurting losses to those who had oppressed them. Individual countries could, for a time, isolate themselves from many changes, but the entire European continent could not. The different pace of change in different places encouraged differentiation and the development of different forces in different locations.

Various forces in medieval and modern Europe repeatedly proved too ambitious. Resources were always scarce—but the potential existed for augmenting them in new ways. In order to confront rival powers, both internal and external, societies had to support and encourage material and intellectual production: trade, the economy, and science. Not only were people dependent on innovation, but innovations could also be induced. It was often the case, in the short or long term, that those who were especially qualified were dissatisfied (not least with the status quo) and forced through improvements, and that those who were disadvantaged not only rose up, but also organized themselves in order to offer new alternatives. An ever-increasing multitude of forces stood ready to push forward comprehensive, indeed incisive transformations.

There is no need to trace this development as far as the Enlightenment, the French and Industrial Revolutions, the rise of the bourgeoisie and the proletariat, the emancipation of women, and so forth. What matters is that medieval and early modern Europe produced a dynamic of change that was completely foreign to antiquity. Quite possibly, incompleteness, inevitable in conditions of constantly unsatisfied yet insistent demands, is the single most important, long-term characteristic of European history in the period after the age of migrations: everything that seemed finished or complete carried within it the seeds of further change; no one social order or condition was able to satisfy everyone—except for a short time; new, unfulfilled and potentially virulent demands constantly arose and prevented the collectivities from merely reproducing the basis of their own existence. In the end, programmatic demands focused even on the transformation of society and the creation of a New Man (if only in a totally functionalized form). Only there and then was history perceived and understood as the comprehensive transformation of all conditions.

The German political scientist Peter Graf Kielmansegg has called Europe 'the continent of the separation of powers'. This, generally speaking, is how one could describe the constellation of forces at work in the creation of medieval and modern European culture. The rise of this culture was a long and never truly finished process, which simultaneously produced both fixation and change, and increasingly encompassed the external world, until in the end the most important motors for change were displaced outside Europe (while within Europe, in fact, much came to a standstill). All other qualities that might be called specifically European were only partially and intermittently present in European history.

'Solely by concentrating the entire energy of our intellect on a focal point and mustering our entire being in a single force, do we give wings to this force and lead it artificially far beyond the barriers that nature would seem to have imposed on it', wrote Friedrich Schiller. These words vividly describe the extraordinary possibilities that opened up in modern European history thanks to the way in which a vast number of individuals and groups concentrated on extremely specialized approaches and capabilities. The reverse side of the coin was, to quote Schiller once again, that man became 'the mere imprint of his business, his science ... instead of developing the humanity in his nature'.

Is medieval Europe, then, not the beginning of something entirely new in history? Is it not a culture fundamentally different from antiquity? Structural change was at best a central aspect of ancient Greece and Rome for short stretches of time. But how then can we explain the unusually strong and persistent tendency of medieval and modern Europe to orient itself after antiquity and constantly to adopt ancient sources? Did the impulses generated by antiquity have such a powerful impact simply because they fell here on a very different terrain? Or did these impulses serve as compensation for all the changes and one-sided-nesses as a pool of calm in an age of time pressure and haste? Were they a source of self-reliance and autonomy in both large and small respects? An anchor in a world that had derived many questions and certainties from the Christian faith but for this very reason needed more?

Or was there more continuity between antiquity and modern Europe than initially meets the eye? If so, it was not like the flow of a river—too much had disappeared. But it was also far more than a thin trickle. Much of the ancient legacy was passed on by Christianity—a religion originating in Jewish Galilee, whose testament was written in Greek, transmitted in Latin, and interpreted with the help of ancient philosophical concepts. During the Roman Empire, especially since the third and fourth centuries, Christianity had increasingly met the needs of a society that could no longer be satisfied by pagan religions and traditional forms of attitudes and interpretations of the world; a society whose intense search for philosophical orientation ultimately tended to merge with its theological quest for meaning. Finally, the Church was organized on Roman models; it used Roman law and the Roman language (insisting above all on Latin as the Bible's language at the expense of more recent ones). From the very beginning, antiquity was thus deeply rooted in the foundations of medieval Europe, and the more of its legacy was rediscovered, the richer the fruits became. It is almost impossible to unravel how the entire multitude of factors interacted or what the consequences were. Different explanations are not mutually exclusive. Nonetheless, considerations of this sort do not give us a definitive reason to locate the beginnings of Europe in antiquity.

In one concrete respect, however, it does seem that Europe started with the Greeks. According to Herodotus, writing in the fifth century BC, it was the Greeks who caused Europe to be 'broken off' from Asia. This involved far more than merely a new way of geographical division and categorization.

4

The Constitution of Europe as a Continent

The reason that Europe is considered a continent is historical, not geographical. Europe probably owes its name to the Greeks, as was also the case with the division of the earth into continents and the additional significance that accompanied such a conceptual division. Without the Greeks, Eurasia would never—and certainly not permanently—have been divided into two separate continents.

We do not know where the Greeks got the names Europe and Asia. The word Europe could be of Semitic origin (*eref* = evening = the West) and might initially have been used as an outside designation for a (far-off) western land. But it is unlikely that the word reached the Greeks as a term for 'occident' for they seem to have used it first for smaller regions in central and northern Greece and only later extended its meaning to refer to increasingly vast stretches of land. The situation is similar with the word Asia, which originally designated a stretch of coastline together with the adjoining inland areas in western Anatolia.

It happened repeatedly throughout history that, when they came to be viewed as a whole, larger areas were given the names of smaller ones that had long been known beyond the immediate frontiers (or the sea). In this manner, the Greeks eventually began referring to the entire Anatolian peninsula as Asia and to all territories to the north of the Aegean as Europe. But it was another matter altogether to divide the entirety of the known world into two—or, if we include Africa, three—continents, that is, to combine very different and often hardly contiguous countries into an entire continent. This conceptual leap was by no means self-evident. How can it be explained?

Herodotus provides the first evidence of maps in which the earth was divided up into Asia and Europe. Many authors, he says, had produced such maps; hence the mid-fifth century BC represents a *terminus ante quem*. Anaximander—the pre-Socratic philosopher from the city of Miletus— is usually credited with having drawn the first Greek map of the world, which brings us to the second half of the sixth century. It is entirely possible that he conceived the land masses into which he divided the earth as discrete continents. This is even more likely considering the primarily theoretical nature of Anaximander's work. But it is unclear whether Anaximander gave names to those continents. His disciple Hecataeus is said to have refined the map admirably, perhaps by drawing the coastlines more precisely and by adding rivers. He also composed a description of the world starting from the Pillars of Hercules in Gibraltar and following first the northern coastline of the Mediterranean and the Black Sea until it turned south and, eventually, in more or less the opposite direction, ended back in Gibraltar. The work of Hecataeus was divided into two parts, presumably for the practical reason that it did not fit on a single animal skin or roll of papyrus. Sources that have been passed down to us from later periods call the first book 'Europe' and the second 'Asia'. But there is no good reason to assume that Hecataeus used these terms. Librarians first began giving books titles in the fourth century BC, so there is no reliable evidence that the names of the continents were used two hundred years earlier.

The division between Europe and Asia in the Aegean, between the Greek peninsula and the mainland of Asia Minor, might have seemed as logical to those who lived there as it appears problematic for us today

Figure 1. Early map of Europe and Asia by Hecataeus.

with our access to modern maps and globes. In any case, this distinction definitely referred to the mainland on both sides, while Herodotus, our earliest witness, considered the Greek islands in between separately (although he once counted Samos as part of Asia). That led him to suggest that the mythical Princess Europa had not ridden on her bull all the way to Europe, but had stopped in Crete, from where she then proceeded on to Anatolian Lycia. But since the Greeks' geographical horizon reached much further and they developed a strong desire for division, classification, and conceptual order of knowledge, and for the drawing and organization of maps, the line of demarcation of continents was likely soon extended from the Aegean westward to the Pillars of Hercules and northward to the Black Sea. That was where the border between Europe and Asia had to have run.

Two possibilities were mentioned. One was the River Phasis (today the Rion) originating in the Caucasus and flowing south-west into the Black Sea, at the point where it extends furthest east, in the ancient state of Colchis. Incidentally, one famous product of the region is the pheasant (*phasianos*), which first appeared in Greece probably in the fifth century BC and was considered a great delicacy from the Hellenistic period on. The other theory maintained that Asia extended to the Maiotian Sea (Sea of Azov) and that Europe began at the River Tanais (Don). Hecataeus may, however, have come up with a third answer, at least if the dividing line between his two books was identical to that between Europe and Asia. His first book went beyond the River Tanais to somewhere near the River Hypanis (Kuban), which flows into the Black Sea south of the Cimmeran Bosporus (the Strait of Kerch).

The main criteria for placing the European–Asian dividing line were presumably various opinions about whether the rivers connected the Black Sea with the Ocean that was thought to encircle the world. With the Phasis, this was quickly proven not to be the case. Nonetheless the border of the Persian Empire did run from approximately there to the Caspian Sea. Little was known about the origins of the River Don. It would not be until modern times that the border of Europe was moved to the Urals.

The territory to the south of the Mediterranean could be been seen as the third continent. This is first attested in a poem by Pindar from the year 474 BC, and by that time, the Greeks had quite possibly already named this area Libya after a tribe that lived there. They drew the border between it and Asia either along the isthmus between the Mediterranean and the Red Sea or along the Nile—unless, as happened often enough, they neglected this distinction and simply merged Libya with Asia. What was most important for the Greeks was the contrast between Europe and Asia, the division of the world into two halves.

Wherever on the Black Sea one chose to locate the European border, and whatever one's views about Libya, the unmistakable and in the present context crucially important fact was that Greek scholars at some point began to subdivide the earth and to look for objective geographical criteria to justify corresponding borders. The empiricist Herodotus may have scoffed at the maps for being schematic constructs that distorted true proportions so that the continents appeared roughly the same size; while he said he did not understand why the earth should be divided into three parts, he still used the division because it was familiar. Even so, such divisions must be considered a great initial achievement, not to be underestimated; it holds up well among various Greek attempts to understand the world.

Remarkably, the world—so divided—had no centre. The perspective was not that of someone looking out from his own palace, city, or empire, in every direction and dividing up the various countries (and people) from and towards that central position. Instead, the overall picture was determined from the point of view of someone well travelled, who was not tied to one location or ruler. The point of departure was the sea or, as Plato called it, the pond around which the Greek cities squatted like frogs—a universal element belonging to everyone and no one. This view of the world captured the multitude of countries existing side by side, privileging none of them. By contrast, the ancient Egyptians viewed all non-Egyptian peoples (though not the world) from a central, self-focused standpoint in the middle of their country, dividing them into three parts: the South, the West, and the North-East. The Israelites followed suit (albeit including themselves in the picture) by tracing the groups' genealogical roots to the sons of Noah.

On the surface, the situation was similar with Greek maps. Greece occupied the centre of the earth, which was conceived as a circle. That might have accorded well with the idea that Delphi was the exact middle-point of the world, where the *omphalos*, a stone artefact regarded as the earth's navel, was venerated. According to Pindar, who was the first to relate the story, Zeus had sent out two eagles from the extreme west and east of the world to determine where the middle was. They supposedly collided directly above the *omphalos*. Yet if the world was seen to stretch from Gibraltar to a somewhat truncated East (in India), Greece almost by necessity happened to be in the middle. Moreover neither

Figure 2. A map of the world etched in clay with Babylon as its centre from the sixth century BC (presumably based on a model from the ninth or eighth century BC).

Delphi nor Greece was a centre of power, and the world was neither understood nor divided from a perspective of Greek centricity.

If one assumes, as was the case for instance also in Babylon, that to most peoples an ethnocentric division of the world is an obvious choice, then the Greeks' distinction of continents radically broke with custom. Not only did they attempt to make geography objective, they also made the Aegean the border between Europe and Asia—the very sea that was, for them, far more a connecting than a dividing element. Greek cities were located on all its coasts, and the Greek islands were distributed throughout it like the pillars of imaginary bridges that led across in various directions. Greeks usually travelled from place to place much more easily by sea than by land. Moreover, according to this division of the world, Hecataeus' own home town was located in Asia. The fact that the Greeks themselves occupied the periphery of Oriental empires may have made it easier for them to understand the world objectively.

The drive to understand the world better by segmenting it is a geometric approach featuring a prominent capacity for abstraction—that very capacity which Greek philosophy applied to the interpretation of the cosmos, which Greek political thought used to distinguish rationally between concrete conditions and abstract order, and which Greek historiography would soon turn to the understanding of sequences of events. The idea of Europe as a continent thus owes its existence to a scientific approach, an inquisitive means of finding one's way in the world, that arose at that time and contributed so much to placing the Greeks onto such a special path in world history.

If this is more or less correct, then the concept of Europe would have originated in Miletus, a city in Asia Minor that was a centre not only of wealth, trade, and far-reaching connections, but also of philosophy and science (including geography). We cannot determine precisely when the continents were first given the names of Europe and Asia; these are first attested with certainty in 472 BC. But by then, these terms were already embroiled in the political confrontation between the Greeks and Persians in the early fifth century, when the Greeks began to consider themselves no longer one people among many, but, in contrast to the Asian world empire of the Persians, as something wholly and radically different. The basis of that distinction was the Greek idea of freedom.

5

Greeks and Persians I:
Freedom and Rule—Atossa's dream

The conflict between the Greeks and Persians, which unfolded in the first decades of the fifth century BC, was one of the major events in world history, and its significance can hardly be overestimated. For the first time, a new group of people with an entirely novel form of social organization appeared on the stage of great politics, which until then had been dominated by continental empires centred in Egypt, Mesopotamia, and neighbouring regions. They belonged to a few small cities that had thus far led a modest existence on the shores of the Aegean. And this conflict, the first confronting in this way the East and West, ended with victory for the Greek David over the Persian Goliath.

This strikes us as something of an irony of world history. In the mid-sixth century, the Persians succeeded in unifying a massive territory, previously home to a variety of coexisting empires, into the gigantic Achaemenid Empire. Persian rule was extended from Egypt to Central Asia, and from the Indus River to the Aegean. It was also the first time that the west coast of Asia Minor was governed from far away, from the Persian royal residences east of Mesopotamia. The Persians had even managed to bring some of the Balkans under their sway. Then, a mere half century later, a novel force—one difficult even to notice at first—appeared on the western frontier of this enormous empire. This new-comer was neither an empire in its own right nor some threatening mounted warrior people galloping in from the depths of an impenetrable territory, but a group of small communities that had brought forth a very different type of people and an entirely new culture.

For all this to be possible at all, the Greek poleis—above all, the largest of them, Athens—had to attain a certain level of political organization, mobilization, and capacity for action. The process by which Athens achieved this was completed at precisely the right time, a few years before the outbreak of hostilities with Persia—and indeed, it could very well have provoked this conflict.

The Greek victories at Salamis (480) and Plataea (479) hit the Persian Empire all the harder because the Persians had sent a huge army to suppress the troublemaker to the West, in Europe. These initial Greek victories also resulted in the formation of an alliance of Greek communities under Athens's leadership to liberate their sister cities in Asia Minor, which Persia had subjugated in the mid-sixth century. Yet although such defeats were certainly hurtful and humiliating, we do not know how intensively they continued to occupy the minds of Persians; as it turned out, they certainly did not cause any serious challenge to their rule.

For the Greeks, however, and especially the Athenians, these victories changed the coordinates of their world, putting them in an entirely new position. In the proverbial blink of an eye, Athens had risen from a provincial canton to a global power. No matter how well it adjusted practically to this new role, its thinking and orientation were temporarily disrupted. However the Persians may have reacted to their defeat, victory became a big problem for the Greeks. How could and should it be understood? How had it come to pass that a handful of Greek city-states had bested Persia's empire? How had the much weaker side prevailed? Was it due to strategy? Bravery and skill? Chance? The gods? Questions like these pertained not just to the Greeks' past, but to their present and future as well, since the answers were crucial to the Greeks' further prospects for prevailing. After all, the threat from the East had not fully disappeared. The Persians might return at any time, better prepared and having learned from their mistakes. Was the outcome of the initial battles merely a temporary victory? Or had a higher will shown the Persians their limits, which were embodied, for example, in the natural division of the earth, the separation of Asia and Europe? Correspondingly, even in smaller dimensions, the Greeks tended to see justice as being anchored in the soil: the Greek goddess of the earth (Gē), and the goddess of divine order, law, and custom (Themis) often appeared as a single figure.

In any case, finding themselves confronted by immense new possibilities, the Greeks were far more deeply disturbed and had to reorient themselves far more radically than the Persians, and the reorientation had to be comprehensive. When what was previously valid in the world is suddenly no longer in force, when relations of power have profoundly been shaken, and when people do not just have to endure such experiences, but try, with an open and an active mind, to derive new energy from them, it is not sufficient to rethink politics alone. Ultimately, the Greeks had to reconceptualize the world and their place in it—no longer as one people among many, but in stark contrast to the Persians and, by extension, to the entire Orient, to which they suddenly found themselves opposed. Luckily, the historical record has preserved an equally

Figure 3. The theatre of Dionysus on the southern slope of the Acropolis, which was in use from the early fifth century BC. The steps were added later.

enlightening and beautiful testimony of how people in Athens—by now the centre of the Greek world—dealt with these challenges. It is the oldest of the surviving Greek tragedies.

Athens in late March. As is its custom, the city is celebrating the Great Dionysia, a religious festival devoted to the god Dionysus. The year is 472 BC. For more than six decades now, the festivities have culminated in a competition between three poets. Each of them is given a day to perform three tragedies and a satyr play. One of the poets is familiar with this role: Aeschylus, son of Euphorion. And one of his three pieces is *The Persians*, based on events from scarcely eight years earlier, events that were so extraordinary and difficult to comprehend by traditional means that they continued to send out aftershocks: the Persian defeat had simply thrown up too many questions.

The Athenians seated in the audience on the southern slope of the Acropolis on that day find themselves transported to the Persian capital Susa, more than ninety days' journey from the Aegean. In the play, the year is 480. The chorus in the orchestra consists of a group of old men to whom King Xerxes has entrusted his city and empire when he set off to wage war against the Greeks. They have not had word from the front for a long time and are growing concerned. Queen Mother Atossa, having had a nightmare and received a number of dark omens, visits them to get their counsel and reassurance. Before she leaves to offer a sacrifice to the gods, she asks them where the city of Athens is located. The question seems arbitrary. The name simply seems to have been running around in her mind. Far, far away in the West, the old men answer. And what is her son doing there, Atossa asks. He who possesses Athens possesses all of Greece, comes the answer. Atossa asks then about Athens's military strength and wealth, but when she wants to know who the shepherd, the ruler, is, she is told that the Athenians are no man's slaves or subjects. Atossa is dumbfounded. How can they hope to resist the attacking enemy? In the same way that they destroyed Darius' magnificent army, the chorus tells her.

No sooner have the old men reminded Atossa of the defeat of Xerxes' father ten years previously, during the Persians' first campaign against Greece at the Battle of Marathon, than a messenger enters and announces that the king has been vanquished. The entire army of the barbarians (the word is here used in its old, neutral sense) has been destroyed. But how? The old men think it must have been in a land battle, as was usually the case in Persian tradition. The defeat, however, has come in a sea battle at Salamis. Then follows a description of what many Athenians experienced at that time and what had been constantly retold ever since: the cunning with which the Athenian commander Themistocles lured the Persian king into the narrow Straits of Salamis; the paean, the song of praise to the gods, which the Greeks began to sing and which echoed from the opposing cliffs; the trumpets, the commands, and finally the course of the battle itself, which took such a devastating turn for the Persians.

Atossa asks about the size of the Greek fleet. The Persian fleet was three times its size, the messenger explains, and Greek victory can only be explained by their having a *daimon* on their side: 'The Gods have rescued the city of the goddess Pallas Athena.' So Athens was spared from destruction? That is how the messenger's words must be understood to elicit Atossa's question and the further answer: 'Where there are men, there is a secure defence.'

Men and not walls are what defend a city—that is one interpretation, which in fact accords well with a long-established Greek idea. In any case, men are much more crucial than walls when a city is under siege. Except that during the Persian invasion the men of Athens had not defended their city. Instead, surprisingly, they and their families had chosen to evacuate it and had left it for the Persians to destroy. Hence, in consequence, the city was saved because the Athenians had sacrificed it in order to concentrate all their resources on their fleet. Thanks to their fleet's victory, they were then able to reclaim their homeland. Their daring gamble, the risk they had taken, shines through in a single sentence. Instead of losing their heads and senselessly digging in where they were, or simply fleeing, they had calculated their best chance, fully aware of their numerical inferiority, and put all their faith in their newly built fleet.

Much of the story is merely alluded to in the tragedy. For example, Xerxes' father Darius had conquered the Greek cities on the west coast of Asia Minor as well as some of the islands in the area, and the chorus mentions this among Darius' great deeds. But there is no need to dwell on the fact, well known to the audience, that in the meantime the Athenian fleet had liberated those cities and islands. When the chorus laments the demise of a long list of fallen Persian generals from all parts of Asia, the all-encompassing size of the army the Greeks, and especially Athens, defeated at Salamis becomes clear. The play scarcely mentions the fact that another great battle, on land, in which the Spartans played a much more prominent role, was required for the Greeks to secure ultimate victory.

Nonetheless, while the proud memory of Athens's great victory is a major subtext, the play as a whole is composed as a tragedy of the Persian Empire. It is a remarkable testimony for Greek respect for their enemies, their sympathy with the wives and parents of the fallen. In sheer desperation, the chorus summons from his grave the spirit of Darius, who had died several years previously. He is able to analyse what has happened. Xerxes has overstepped his bounds and placed the entire Persian Empire at risk, blinded by hubris. There is no way he could have conquered Greece. Even the geography of the small, fragmented country worked against him. How did he think he could take advantage of his numerical superiority in such a country? Yet the greatest example of his arrogance is the bridge he had constructed across the Hellespont. Where the gods had drawn a boundary, he tried to unite two countries into one, joining Europe and Asia under a common yoke. The spirit of Darius warns the Persians to steer clear of Greece.

At the end of the play, the defeated Xerxes returns, alone, without his retinue, his regal dress in tatters, the very picture of a man who has lost everything. His quiver, the symbol of his power, is empty. The old men treat him with disregard, invoking the names of Persian generals, one by one, so that Xerxes is forced to repeat, time and again, that they are all dead. In Albin Lesky's words, a *furioso* of lament follows. Earlier, Atossa had claimed that the king was not accountable—quite wrongly, for in the court of the theatre in Athens he is called upon to answer the penetrating questions put to him by Aeschylus' choir. The poet forces Xerxes to wallow in the memories of his defeat. Even so, it is clear that Persia and Xerxes' rule will continue in Asia. It is Xerxes' generals and soldiers who have paid the price for his hubris. He himself has escaped, humiliated, with merely a black eye.

By making Xerxes' hubris, his impious violation of divinely set limits, the true cause of his defeat, Aeschylus' tragedy explicitly refers to geography, seeking in its structure, in the pre-existing and preordained natural order of the earth an explanation for why Greek victory had been in accordance with the higher order of the world. The Greeks' triumph was justly deserved because the Persians' defeat had been. It was a powerful and soothing argument—one connected to a very interesting reflection on the new relationship between Greeks and Asia.

The word 'Asia' occurs in various places throughout the play, mostly in conjunction with the phrase 'all of'. It is 'all of Asia' over which the Persian king rules, and 'all of Asia' follows him into the war against the Greeks and suffers defeat. At times, Aeschylus speaks of 'the entire race of barbarians' (as if these all came only from Asia), as well as 'the entire people of Persia' or 'the entire expanse of the continent'. The conflict, in Aeschylus' view, thus involved the entire continent.

The geographical counter-concept 'Europe', on the other hand, crops up only once, referring to the continent from which Xerxes and his army have just retreated. 'Greece' (Hellas) likewise only appears once as an entity, describing the object of the Persians' desire to conquer. And indeed, only around thirty of the hundreds of Greek city-states had risen up to resist the Persians. The play refers most often to 'Athens, hated by its enemies' or 'the Ionians', the group of Greek cities to which the most important ones in Asia Minor, but also Athens, belonged.

Yet, for the first time, we find here a clear reference to the political split between the two continents, over which Greeks and barbarians seem to be distributed. They no longer exist beside, but in contrast to and in conflict with one another. Not that the Greeks should be understood as part of a larger whole: they fight for themselves and themselves alone. But the difference between them and all the barbarians is clearly demarcated; for the Greeks there are different rules from those that apply to all Asia; they not only live (for the most part) in a different continent, but they live their own, very specific sort of life as well.

In the play, this point is embodied vividly in the dream that so frightens and disturbs Atossa. It features two women who are 'in terms of size far mightier than women are now and of a flawless beauty, sisters of the same tribe'. One wears Persian, the other Dorian dress. The lot has given Hellas, the land of the Greeks as a homeland to one, to the other the land of the barbarians. The two women begin quarrelling, and when Xerxes notices this, he takes hold of them and tries to yoke them together in front of his chariot, just as he had tried to do with Europe and Asia. One woman yields proudly, but the other frees herself from her tethers and breaks the yoke in two. The king falls to the ground, with his father lamenting at his side, and rips his regal garments apart. Since the two women appear to be sisters from a single tribe, their separation represents the dissolution of what once was one family, what in terms of origin belonged together. Without overemphasizing this—could it be a symbol for humanity itself?

The chance of the lot has determined where various peoples lived, and at first they coexisted peacefully. There may have been differences, of which the Greeks had no doubt always been conscious, but there were no fundamental contrasts. But now the situation is different. A quarrel has arisen, and Xerxes intervenes, trying to impose his rule to quell the conflict. But when an attempt is made to establish a single rule over Greeks and barbarians, one of the two resists, and the king's disaster is sealed. He has tried to unify two entities, each of which was supposed to remain separate, by itself, and one of a kind. Retribution followed immediately, both in the dream and in reality.

Atossa is only concerned about the fall of the king. But the crux of the matter for the world and its future, as Aeschylus interprets them here, is that at the moment when Xerxes attempts to incorporate Greece into his empire, he learns that he cannot succeed. His father Darius may have had little problem subjugating the Greeks of Asia Minor and 'the islands neighbouring this country', but the same proved to be impossible for the Greek mainland, and specifically Athens. Something had arisen there alongside and against Asia, and this meant that the boundary of Asia had been cut much more deeply in so far as it presented an insurmountable obstacle to the man who tried to bridge it. Aeschylus had no way of knowing what the consequences would be for the coming years and decades, to say nothing of subsequent centuries, although a lot had already changed in the eight years since the Battle of Salamis was fought: the Greek poleis around the Aegean had formed an alliance, Athens had gained hugely in power and, not least, the Greek islands and the poleis of the west coast of Asia Minor had been liberated.

There were many answers to the question why, to speak in the language of the play, a falcon had bested an eagle. But perhaps the closest one could come to understanding such an event was by anchoring it in the order of the world, by seeing it not as the result of individual factors but of the nature of the whole, not as the work of individual gods but of divine justice itself. More than a generation later, Herodotus, repeating words attributed to Themistocles, the victorious general of Salamis, would claim that the gods and heroes had not wanted one man to rule both Europe and Asia.

Why were the Persians prevented from ruling Greece? Aeschylus spends a great deal of effort enumerating the differences between Greeks and Persians. He starts with weaponry: the bow versus the spear. Moreover, the gods seem to have assigned land warfare to one people, naval warfare to the other. The chorus of elders in Susa say explicitly that in earlier times the Persians had always achieved their military superiority on land with the help of the gods. True, they also mention that the Persians had learned the art of naval warfare and, after all, they had among their subjects seafaring peoples such as the Phoenicians and the Greeks. But the chorus fears that this will end badly. Is war at sea too unfamiliar and untried? Or is it simply too much, since no one people can expect to be given everything?

Ultimately, and crucially, the Athenians, like the Greek sister in Atossa's dream, are not subject to any man. They are free and want to stay that way. 'Rise up, you sons of Greeks, free your fatherland, free your children, your women, the seats of your familiar gods and the tombs of your ancestors—all this is what the fight is about!' That was the Greek battle cry at Salamis. Aeschylus recalls this battle cry, and the freedom evoked here refers to more than independence from a foreign ruler. The Greeks also wanted to be free within their communities. It was precisely at that time that they became aware that this sort of freedom was one of their distinguishing characteristics. Thanks to this ideal, and in contrast to all of Asia, the Greeks fought for themselves, not for someone else— and for this very reason (as they believed and experienced in reality), they fought with particular bravery. That was how men (and not walls) could be a secure defence for the city.

If the lot had assigned to the Greeks, as it is said of the two sisters in Atossa's dream, the right to their homeland, did that not also imply that they were supposed to live in their own particular fashion? The Greeks liked to think in terms of contrasts and polarities: war and peace, age and youth, day and night, land and sea, Greek and barbarians—all then complemented each other. Perhaps despotism there and freedom here was also one of those polarities.

It is highly doubtful whether these explanations sufficed to quell completely the unease Greeks felt about their victory over the Persians. Thoughts about this issue were still very much in flux in 472 BC. But that is not the point. Rather, for the first time, we encounter here traces of an ethos of self-determination, which claims for certain inhabitants of Europe a specific characteristic that was not part of the culture of all of Asia.

In this context the border that separates Europe and Asia where the two continents come closest to one another, at the Hellespont and the Bosporus, became especially significant. The water there clearly divided Europe from Asia, but that was not the main point. Darius had, after all, crossed it to achieve conquests in Europe, and Aeschylus mentions this in his play: it is only Greece, and not all of Europe, of which Xerxes must steer clear. Instead, the Hellespont is centrally important as a boundary because Xerxes tried to bridge it, contrary to the laws of nature and the will of the gods. (Interestingly, Darius had also constructed a pontoon bridge there, even if across the narrower Strait of the Bosporus, but Aeschylus is wise enough not to mention this.) The specific form of the violation of this boundary, and the hubris it revealed, was what gave it a sacred status in the tragedy and condemned Xerxes to his preordained failure. Again, the poet speaks only of the Persians' injustice. Still, it would be easy to assume that not just the European Greeks but all of Europe was to remain off-limits to the Persians. Admittedly, Aeschylus does not say this, but the contrast he builds up between Europe and Asia does contain some inconsistencies. Asia is an empire ruled by an individual will, whereas in Europe there is space for a multitude of peoples and ideas. And the border between them meanwhile no longer ran through the Aegean, but further east, beyond the Greek poleis—beyond a zone of several miles, as it were, not from the land out to the sea, but from the sea in to the land.

Distinctions between the Greeks and the Persians now had to be based on the difference and contrast between Greeks and barbarians. The main point was that the Greeks were very different from the Persians, and that the gods apparently did not want both to be ruled by one man. Aeschylus anchored these concepts in deeper distinctions: between land and sea warfare, despotism and freedom, (Asian) barbarians and Greeks. The incompatibility in each case of the one with the other justified the right to existence of that which was so different and so opposed to the other. The world was supposed to encompass this *and* that. Freedom was not just a factor of strength. It was most of all a characteristic that was apparently worth preserving, at least within a divine world order. And that applied, too, to the Greeks in Asia Minor.

6

Europe and Asia in Antiquity

Wherever borders are drawn in enmity, what is proximate is often driven far apart. Small differences become big ones, and difference itself becomes opposition. Distinction and alternatives replace transitions and variety. Differentiation gives way to generalization.

There is no reason to assume that the Greeks always considered themselves fundamentally different from others, from the barbarians. The word 'barbarian' was primarily an onomatopoetic reflection of the foreignness of non-Greek languages. It was not at all pejorative. After all, Egyptians and other members of ancient high cultures in the East were just as much barbarians as all the hardly developed peoples around the world. On the scale of particularity, the Greeks were closer to some people than others, in one respect or another, regardless of the extent to which they differed from each other. The result, in so far as anyone bothered to think about it, was a picture that stressed variety and transition.

But with the Graeco-Persian wars, the Greeks began to conceive of themselves in opposition to both the barbarians and to Asia—two oppositions they often conflated in view of the Persian Empire. The world was divided in a novel fashion. Things took on new meanings, as did the understanding of the continents.

Some time shortly after 449 BC, the lyric poet Simonides composed a song of praise for the victory the Athenians achieved over the Persians in a double battle at sea and on land near Salamis on the island of Cyprus. The event was unprecedented, sang Simonides, 'since the time when the sea divided Europe from Asia and raging Mars began visiting the cities of men'. This can hardly be an arbitrary poetic paraphrase with no further significance than to indicate an unthinkably ancient time. It is more likely that these lines are an indication of how the contrast between the Greeks and Persians was increasingly being perceived as a contrast between Europe and Asia. In any case, at that time, a local self-conception focusing on individual poleis was yielding to a new perception of the world.

Around 430, we find Herodotus stating that Asia and Europe had always stood in contrast to one another. At the beginning of the *Histories*, Herodotus relates some strange stories that he claims to have heard from Persian scholars. According to them, the cause of the war between the Greeks and Persians had its roots deep in the past, centuries before the founding of the Persian Empire. The Phoenicians had abducted the Greek princess Io, and the Greeks had in turn kidnapped the Phoenician Princess Europa. The Argonauts then stole Medea from Colchis on the Black Sea, and the Trojan Paris abducted Helen a short time later. This could have been the end of it. Such abductions were not to be taken too seriously since 'obviously women would not be abducted if they themselves did not wish to be'. But the Greeks had overreacted, taking revenge on Troy with their army, and from then on the Persians thought that the Greeks regarded them as enemies. 'The Persians rule over Asia and the barbarian peoples living there', Herodotus concludes. 'Europe and the Greeks are, in their eyes, separated from it.'

At the same time, we read in Herodotus of the possibility of Sparta subjugating 'all of Asia'. Xerxes was allegedly even of the opinion that either all of Persia had to be ruled by the Greeks, or Greece by Persians. There was no middle ground, given the level of enmity, just as he himself had wanted to conquer 'all the Greeks and the other people living in the west', becoming the ruler over all peoples from the rising to the setting sun. Was this the characterization of a deep-seated, irreconcilable opposition?

No matter who conceived of the possibility of global domination by the Greeks and placed words to that effect in Xerxes' mouth, and no matter how much their victories may have gone to the Greeks' heads, the Persian king's attempted conquests had made what had been previously separate political realms into a single world. And given the Greek desire not to be ruled by any one despot, the question arose for the king: who should rule, he or the Greeks? That was the logic of a would-be lord over the entire world. Yet, once the conflict had been defined globally, symmetry demanded that not just Hellas, but Europe be seen as the opponent of Asia.

Around the time when Herodotus was writing his *Histories*, an unknown author in the school of the great physician Hippocrates was composing the treatise 'Airs, Waters, Places' on the island of Kos off the coast of Asia Minor. The author examines the effects of the physical environment and the change of the seasons on people in various parts of the world. The treatise starts with general observations, but quickly proceeds to discuss differences between peoples. For this purpose, distinctions between Europe and Asia become important. The way in which the author orders and interprets his material is often contradictory and schematic. Yet the ideas that he apparently wanted to confirm are all the more significant. Asia and Europe, the author proclaims, differ from one another in every respect; not least as far as the physical appearance of peoples is concerned, he writes, the two 'have no similarities at all'.

Asia, at least in its central part, he says, has a relatively constant climate. Because of the absence of dramatic changes of weather, people there do not experience the mental challenges and constant bodily adjustments that produce passion, boldness, and liveliness of spirit. For that reason, the author concludes, the Asian peoples may be handsomer, taller, and more highly cultured, but they are also weak. Moreover, because they are usually ruled by kings, they do not perform well in war. They are unmotivated because they are called upon to risk life and limb for their rulers and not for themselves—thus they lack bravery, toughness, initiative, and liveliness of spirit. The emphasis in Asia is 'by necessity on enjoyment'. The author underlines the importance of political constitutions by writing that in those parts of Asia not ruled by monarchs, where people live 'autonomously' according to their own laws, they are braver—whether Greek or barbarian. This is the only mention of Greeks (typically those living in Asia) in the little treatise. Otherwise, the characteristics the author enumerates are valid for *the* Europeans or *the* Asians. Special traits are reported only for isolated peoples who live in remote parts of the world.

In contrast to Asia, the author states, people in Europe are exposed to extreme changes in weather and are consequently more spirited, flexible, and warlike, and they live under different political conditions, although these vary by region. Therefore Europeans were superior to Asians. Presumably, the questions raised by the Greeks' victory over the Persian Empire were the backdrop against which the much-travelled physician formulates his various hypotheses. He attempts to find an explanation in nature. We do not know how widespread such views were. But they recur in Greek literature: from that time on Europe is privileged. That Asians were spoiled and effeminated by luxury became a popular topos (even if it initially did not apply to the Persians—and may have seemed appealing to some). 'Greece', however, Herodotus writes, 'has for ever been home to poverty. But manly excellence (*aretē*) is a matter of upbringing, effected by wisdom and strict laws.' Views of this sort, expressed in a wide variety of ways, have been a centuries-long tradition in the West, with commentators stressing their own quality over Asian quantity. Moreover, in time, the word 'barbarian' became a synonym for lack of civilization and savagery.

Increasingly, Europe and not only Hellas appears as the antithesis of Asia. For the Attic orator Isocrates in the fourth century BC, 'expanding Greece' is basically the same thing as 'making Europe stronger than Asia'. He thinks it fitting for the Greeks, the Europeans, to rule and settle Asia Minor. By that time, military technology and boldness in calculating military possibilities had developed far beyond the mental limits of the *polis* so that such conquests came to seem perfectly conceivable.

In keeping with this general trend, the Trojan War was interpreted as a fight by one side for Asia, by the other for Europe. Before crossing into Asia, Alexander the Great offered a sacrifice at the grave of the mythical hero Protesilaus, who was believed to have been the first Greek to step onto Asian soil or, at any rate, to have died upon it. The sacrifice that the king of Macedonia offered in the middle of the Straits to Poseidon and the Nereids referred back to that made by Xerxes at roughly the same location (although from his pontoon bridge). Before Alexander, in full armour and at the vanguard of his troops, stepped off his ship, he threw his spear into the Asian mainland, symbolically taking possession of it as 'conquered by spear'. He then set off for Troy in order to offer further sacrifices, following the example set by Xerxes in his crossing to Europe.

Through a whole series of symbolic acts, the Macedonian king at this crucial contact point between Europe and Asia thus placed his own undertakings into a significant web of meaningful connections, linking it with both Greece's war against Troy and Xerxes' campaign against Greece. He appointed his general Antipater, who was responsible for maintaining order on the other side of the Aegean, as the 'Governor of Europe', and he too equated the Persian Empire he conquered with all of Asia, aspiring to be the king of Asia. He did not replace the Persian Empire with a Macedonian one. Instead, the name of the continent became the name of his empire.

Aristotle distinguished between three types of peoples: those who lived in the colder regions of Europe, those residing in Asia, and the Greeks. The first are very courageous but lag behind in intelligence and methodological capabilities, which is why they are able to defend their independence but have trouble forming communities and are unable to rule over their neighbours. Asians, on the other hand, have intelligence and methodological capabilities but lack courage, which is why they let themselves be ruled and enslaved by others. In keeping with their geographical position in the middle, the Greeks possess both types of qualities: they are both brave and intellectually gifted. 'For that reason', writes Aristotle, 'they are able to maintain freedom and are strongest in their political constitution and capable of ruling over all—if they succeed in forming a single political unit (*mia politeia*)'.

Aristotle here posits a marked difference between Greeks and the peoples of northern Europe. In another passage, he equates the barbarians and the Greeks with the peoples of Asia and Europe, concluding that the former group in each pairing is by nature more slave-like than the latter.

The grammatical way in which this thought is formulated does not make clear whether Aristotle really believes that the Greeks were capable of forming such all-encompassing political unity. But had he been of that opinion, he would have had to contradict his entire political dogma of the *polis* as the only form of community that was worth living in. We can understand his statement only as a comment about the extraordinary power residing in courage and intelligence under the conditions of politically constituted freedom. One logical consequence of this view could be that precisely this constellation might enable the Greeks to conquer the Persians. It remains unclear, though, how Aristotle thought the Greeks would subsequently rule and administer such a global empire. But his statements show the extent to which Greek political thought had begun to exceed the boundaries of the *polis*.

When Aristotle was making his statements, his former student, the Macedonian king who would later be known as Alexander the Great, might well have already been on his way to achieving 'rule over all' by conquering, with a relatively small army, 'all of Asia'. The Macedonians, whom Aristotle described as very brave and free, but weak in the forming of communities, were able to achieve some of the things the Greeks could not. They did not live in *poleis* but formed a single political entity under the leadership, though not really the rule of the king. They were courageous, well-armed warriors, trained above all for battles with their less civilized neighbours and for whole wars instead of just single battles, as was the case with the Greeks. Whereas the Greeks tended to feel somewhat lost away from the sea, the Macedonians were capable of conducting far-reaching military operations. They were adept at handling wide open spaces, at least when it came to conquering territory. 'Alexander's greatness resides less in his ability to conquer the Great King himself than to overcome great stretches of space', wrote the

German poet Ernst Jünger. 'What is more amazing than his breaking of Babylon is the fact that he made it back from India.' The Macedonians provided the core of the extremely efficient army with which Alexander made his conquests—the conquests of a monarch who did not have much in common with the Greeks, despite being educated by Greeks and fond of Greek culture. In fact, the Greeks considered Alexander's Macedonians to be barbarians, although the latter's language was a Greek dialect; we have no idea how well they were able to understand each other.

According to a poem by Choerilus of Samos from the late fifth century BC, under Xerxes 'the great war had come from the soil of Asia to Europe'. Roughly a century and a half later, the opposite was happening. All of Asia (as far as it was known or, to be more precise, as far as Persian rule had extended) was being subjugated by a conqueror from Europe, although Alexander no doubt soon learned that he could not rule over such a huge empire without integrating Persians and other native peoples into his administration, on a large scale and in leading positions.

Nonetheless, Alexander's victories and conquests were also Greek victories and conquests. Greek influences had largely been responsible for Macedonia's rise to major power. Now cities were being founded on Greek models in conquered territories from Egypt to deep within present-day Afghanistan. Greek ways of life, festivals, sports, theatre, philosophy, and science spread to the East, where they took root, produced new shoots, and also attracted new forces. Greek became a lingua franca. In this respect, the Greeks really did prove superior to the whole world. True, the process of Hellenization at the time may often have remained superficial, but Greek culture came to dominate the regions east of the Mediterranean and far beyond. For centuries, it would be the only common culture these parts of the world would know. Wherever it advanced, Greek culture prevailed.

On the other hand, in the wake of Alexander's conquests the division between Europe and Asia quickly lost its significance. Political power and a host of relationships crossed the border between the two continents in a great variety of ways.

The difference between the two continents played no significant role for the Romans, especially since they had politically united the Mediterranean. Differences with the barbarians, which the Romans adopted once they could no longer be considered barbarians themselves, were much more important than geographical classifications. To be sure, the situation changed again when the Western Roman Empire split from the Eastern half and then dissolved completely due to the migration of peoples. The centre of power now switched from the Mediterranean to northern Europe, and the border between East and West was no longer located in the Aegean but ran from south to north through the Balkans. Greece itself was by then part of the Eastern Byzantine Empire.

Medieval Europe defined itself far more in terms of Christianity than any specifically European idea. Yet, the Greek conception of Europe and all the significance it had accrued remained present, thanks to the preservation of ancient texts, and this eventually allowed the geographical distinctions to be revived. But the gulf between the first blossoming of the concept of Europe and its later revival is much wider than the gap between the decline of ancient culture and the gradual renaissance of its legacy.

Thus, it makes little sense to search for the origins of Europe along this particular path—nor, for that matter, from a perspective that simply oscillates back and forth between antiquity and medieval and modern Europe. In order to decide upon a more promising approach— and indeed a decision is necessary here—we have to tackle this issue in a broader, world-historical context.

7

Antiquity as European Prehistory
or Early History

In Hegel's view of world history, first one, then a select few (among Greeks and Romans), and finally everyone was free. But, Hegel adds, the one who was free in Asia at any given time was 'not a free man, a human', but a despot. The freedom he enjoyed consisted of the arbitrary exercise of power. Within this threefold development, there was at least one major threshold: because the Greeks—even if only select groups, the citizens, not everyone—did not develop their culture from a centre of ruling power, but from the people and for the sake of freedom they placed themselves on the nearside of that threshold. This is precisely the conclusion Hegel draws from a comparison between the Greek world and youth: 'The European spirit spent its youth in Greece.'

In a similar vein, Jakob Burckhardt wrote that the Greeks were 'different . . . from the ancient Orient and the nations that emerged since then' and represented 'nonetheless the most significant point of transition towards both sides'. Burckhardt emphasized the importance of exposing the 'world-historical position of the Greek spirit between Orient and Occident'. Moreover, he added: 'Whatever they achieved and suffered, they achieved and suffered *freely* and differently from all previous peoples. Whereas others were ruled by mind-numbing necessity, they appear as original, spontaneous, and self-aware.' Thus, while continuing, in the same context, to write about the 'continuity of world development', Burckhardt moves the Greeks far more closely to medieval and early modern Europe than to the Orient.

Today we know far more than Hegel and Burckhardt did about the monarchic high cultures not just in the ancient Orient, but also, for example, in India, China, and Central America, as well as in the Arab, Persian, and Ottoman spheres. We are only too well acquainted with the arrogance and will for power of Europe and its descendents, and suspect—if indeed we do not know—how Europeans recklessly and brutally exploited, if not annihilated and enslaved, other peoples—to say nothing of destroying the foundations of civilization that supported those peoples' ways of life. The question whether or not what those peoples eventually received in turn from the Europeans was a blessing should probably be better left unanswered.

In any case, we have no reason to underestimate the worth of other cultures or declare European culture to be the ultimate goal of world history, in so far as we can even speak of such a thing today. At the same time, it is undeniable that on the European continent there gradually emerged immense and previously unthinkable possibilities and a unique capacity for action, insight, and knowledge, for shaping, discovering, and changing things. It is hard to contest the fact that Europe took—and for a long time pursued—a path that differed markedly from the world's other cultures.

It is precisely this aspect that has a prelude among the Greeks—for the very reason that they were the only ones who formed a culture for the sake of freedom and not domination. As much as the Greeks may have learned from the Orient, they only adopted what they found there for the sake of their own bold and daring purposes. Greek culture was decidedly less a continuation than a new beginning, not built upon what had gone before, but totally new. Hence, in many respects, both technologically speaking and in terms of the formation and administration of empires, the Greeks lagged far behind the Orient. What mattered to them was something different.

From today's perspective, it is difficult to comprehend what it meant to be responsible for the whole, without higher authorities, without blinkers, everyone together and working for themselves rather than everyone in his proper place guided from above—free and thus vulnerable, extending feelers in every direction, constantly posing new questions, and testing themselves and their words imaginatively, artfully, and always as if for the first time. The Greeks' basic problem was nothing less than this: they had to enable their freedom to meet all the challenges they faced under increasingly complex conditions. For this reason, besides the well-known long-term revolutions in world history (the Neolithic and the Industrial), the political revolution realized by the Greeks deserves it own prominent place.

Without doubt, the ancient Greeks owe their lasting impact to the fact that Rome saw the rise of a great aristocracy, which both knew how to create and rule a world empire and succumbed to the fascination of Greek culture. Ancient Greece's centuries-long influence depended on the dissemination of Graeco-Roman culture west and northward and its translation into a new language and different context, from which it was then able to derive new vitality.

At any rate, it was not just the Greek legacy that continued to exert influence in medieval and early modern Europe. Roman law and political forms, together with all the memories associated with the fame of Rome, initially even stood in the foreground. Even more prominent was the Roman Church, the Gospel, and the teachings of Jesus, which found their voice built on the foundations of centuries of Jewish tradition. But ancient Greece was where the new impulses originated, and in the symbiotic merging of disparate elements, Greek elements continued to play a decisively important role.

There are no hard-and-fast rules about where to locate historical ruptures. To a large extent the choice is a matter of how one understands history. Scholars can only veto senseless divisions. There is nothing significant, however, that would argue against seeing Greek history and culture, including the history of Rome and early Christianity, as an early part of European history and culture. On the contrary, in my opinion, a lot speaks *for* this view. Are not freedom and everything it caused to blossom—along with a broadly accessible rationality that is directed at what is general and concerns all aspects of order and the world—more important than technology and dynamism? Is not what connects antiquity with medieval and early modern Europe more important than what separates the two?

Even if one does not want to follow this line of thought and prefers to classify antiquity as the prehistory of a Europe that first fully emerged in the Middle Ages or even later—even then this undoubtedly must be considered an especially privileged kind of prehistory. The French Arabist and philosopher Rémi Brague speaks of a process of 'inverse adoption' by which Europe appropriated the ancient Greeks and Romans as its ancestors. Europe has connected itself with them so closely and melded with antiquity to such an extent that, even if Greek and Roman history is considered distinct from European history, any history of Europe must still begin with the ancient Greeks and Romans.

Thus any history of Europe must start with the question how the Greeks came to be, how this highly exceptional, unusually strong, and broadly influential culture could arise, survive, and flourish, and how it was constituted.

PART II

The Rise of the World of *Poleis*

Introduction

The culture that etched itself as 'Greek' into man's collective memory grew out of the ruins of an earlier civilization that was also produced by Greek-speaking people, and which we call 'Mycenaean' after its pre-eminent site, which originated around the middle of the second millennium BC. Both cultures were strongly influenced by the earlier and superior civilizations of the Orient. But only Mycenaean culture—and the Minoan civilization of Crete that preceded it—were part of the orbit of the Oriental empires.

As far as we can tell from the numerous and often grandiose remains, Mycenaean culture was monarchic in both organization and character. It was a palace culture, and Mycenaean kings seem to have ruled over large territories. These are two of the major differences between Mycenaean and post-Mycenaean Greek culture.

There is no road that leads from Mycenaean to *polis*-based culture. All the fundamentally new aspects of this latter culture, which turned world history on its head, could not have arisen easily, had the foundations, forms (and limitations) of the preceding epoch not been destroyed, and, notwithstanding a small and on the whole insignificant number of continuities, had the post-Mycenaean Greeks not had the chance to begin again from scratch.

8

A Post-Mycenaean New Beginning: Origins of Greek Particularity

How the Mycenaean world collapsed is unknown. Much of the evidence suggests that—together with the mighty empire of the Hittites, for example—it might have been overwhelmed by the devastating invasions of the eastern Mediterranean by the so-called Sea Peoples around 1200 BC. But epidemics, natural disasters, and internal conflicts could have already weakened and rocked the Mycenaean kingdoms. They depended in every respect on a small ruling class that in the end might have been fatally exhausted. In any case, the Mycenaean world was so thoroughly destroyed that there was no hope of rebuilding it. Large parts of the Mycenaeans' sophisticated arts and crafts disappeared, and the script used by palace administrators was forgotten because it no longer served any purpose. Destruction, poverty, and uncertainty spread where magnificent fortifications had once towered above the country, where armies of chariots, fleets, and a refined system of coastal guards had protected the king's rule and guaranteed security from foreign threats, where a network of roads had been built and maintained, and where trade, based on settlements in Asia Minor and Lower Italy, had once flourished. Everyday life now was paralysed by danger; people's desires and demands became increasingly basic. The Aegean lay fallow like a wasteland.

Waves of immigrants poured into the region from the Balkan areas to the north, perhaps contributing to the destruction of the Mycenaean world. In any case, whole stretches of land changed hands. Some were newly settled by immigrants who were perfectly willing to tolerate the remnants of previous native peoples in their midst. In other regions, though, the immigrants came as conquerors, subjugating and exploiting the natives. Many Mycenaeans fled to Asia Minor, probably especially those from the ruling classes, where they founded new settlements, often on sites of former trading posts. Others took refuge in Cyprus. In isolated locations, Attica, for example, the natives were able to maintain themselves. For a long time, much turmoil, insecurity, and constant change must have ensued before the old and newly arrived Greeks could live peacefully alongside and ultimately with one another. In time, the differences between natives and immigrants disappeared. Although both groups wished to retain some of their own particular characteristics, actual distinctions were soon far less prominent than the people's desire to maintain them. In any case, relations were determined more by current situations than by peoples' origins or traditions. Even the memories of Mycenaean Greece's long-lost golden age, celebrated by bards, became common cultural property.

We know very little about the early, 'dark' centuries of Greek history (1200–800 BC). What light archaeological finds can shed on the period is dim and flickering. Graves or the remnants of walls reflect only in extremely fragmented fashion the conditions and changes that interest the historians. But be it in isolated farms, scattered hamlets, villages, or even small towns the Greeks of this period seem to have lived in small, loosely organized units, and from cultivating pastures and farms, from hunting and fishing, and a bit later from piracy and sea trade.

People took care of matters of common interest in collaboration with their more or less immediate neighbours. The task of governing, in so far as it was necessary, fell to the *basileis*, a word usually translated as 'princes' or 'lords'. (later on the word designated 'kings'). In essence they were like village elders or leaders, whose status was inherited, little more than *primi inter pares*.

Wherever (for example, because of migration) larger associations or 'tribes' are thought to have stretched across a number of small areas, broader forms of community were usually weaker than narrow ones; indeed, broader communities soon lost any function they may once have had except for periodically maintaining certain cult rituals. At least that was the situation in many places on the coast of the Aegean Sea. Things may have been different further inland and in the west of the Greek peninsula.

It is not known when more stable forms of political organization began to emerge, but the process certainly varied from region to region in terms of when and how it took place. The needs for security, law and order, and roads or walls were as unevenly distributed as the means to achieve them. Random factors surely played a leading role in determining the size and borders of what were to become the *poleis*.

Nonetheless, by the eighth century BC at the latest, in many places property owners began to separate themselves from others as political units, focused on settlements or groups of settlements. If the core settlement of such a community was not determined by topographical conditions (which it usually was), the community chose one, and the leading families moved there. The term *polis*, which originally designated a hilltop fort that usually protected such a core settlement, eventually came to describe an urban centre and then the entire political unit.

On the whole, the *poleis* that arose in this way were small, but there were differences. Large stretches of Attica, where the native population survived, seem to have maintained a degree of connection over time. In Sparta, immigrants could well have taken over—at first partially (because of stubborn resistance), then completely—the former territory of a Mycenaean ruling family. Something similar may also have applied to Argos, the third Greek city with a relatively large territory.

Attica was roughly as large as Luxembourg (*c.*2,500 square kilometres). Argos was only half as large, while important communities such as Corinth (880), Chios (826), and Samos (468) were only a third to a fifth of that size, and even they were bigger than average. Boeotia, roughly the same size as Attica, was divided into ten *poleis*; Crete was said to contain a hundred. There was also more than one politically autonomous community on medium-sized islands such as Lesbos and Rhodes, even on tiny Keos. After the conquest of Messenia, Sparta stretched across 7,400 square kilometres, but its citizens actually occupied only part of that territory.

Athens was by far and away the most populous city-state, with 35,000 to 45,000 adult male citizens in the fifth century BC. Otherwise, at that time few *poleis* had more than a thousand citizens, and the numbers must have been considerably smaller at the start of the millennium. It took less than a day to cross a normal *polis* by foot or on a donkey. It may seem curious that for a long while Athens was not able to take advantage of its numerical superiority in military conflict against its neighbours. Was it too focused on itself? Were there too few common interests? On the other hand, what did Athens stand to gain by threatening others? In any case, the size of this *polis* did not offer an example that others tried to emulate.

Landscape and climate encouraged the formation of small communities. In many places, mountains stretch all the way to the coast, with only a scattering of small, isolated fertile patches of level ground in between. The autonomy of the islands was fostered by nature anyway. But geography alone cannot explain why Boeotia contained ten independent, only loosely associated *poleis*, or Rhodes three. Already in the Mycenaean period, topography had not proved a serious obstacle to the formation of larger political units. In that era, however, neighbouring territorial powers—Minoan Crete as well as the Hittite Empire in Asia Minor—seem to have provided the impetus for the formation of larger centrally ruled kingdoms. This may be part of the solution to the puzzle: in this sort of landscape, external impulses were necessary to stimulate the development of larger political units. In the centuries after 1200 BC and the collapse of the Hittite Empire, however, no Oriental power took an interest in the Aegean region. Nor were there threats by mountain tribes against whom the coastal communities would have had to defend themselves, as was the case later in the areas around Rome, which eventually prompted the beginning of Roman expansion.

It is certainly worth asking whether there could also have been impulses within the Greek world to form larger political entities. Individuals or groups might have tried to make others dependent on themselves, and yet others could have resisted such efforts, successfully or unsuccessfully, so that over time one or the other could have gained more power. But if there were such efforts, they did not get very far, at least not in the long term. Something must have hindered them, whether the difficulty of forming large groups of followers, the lack of organizational skills, the strength of resistance, or natural, geographical obstacles. Perhaps, too, people's energies and interests were diverted too much towards the outside, into projects undertaken by small groups, which might have been encouraged by their location along the Mediterranean. Or perhaps such changes would have gradually come if there had been more time. In fact, though, the Greeks did not remain forever entirely isolated in their own world, but came to encounter the Orient, though from a very specific situation, and that may have prompted them to consolidate and further develop what had begun to evolve earlier.

The Greeks became what they were in the course of their history. Max Weber once famously wrote that any reference to an original character of a people is merely an 'acknowledgement of ignorance'. Likewise, the idea that the Greeks created their culture only makes sense if we conceive of 'the Greeks' and 'their culture' as being broken down into an infinite variety of elements that formed one another, time and again, as part of a long process, or to paraphrase the Austrian novelist Robert Musil: it's the clothes that make the man, and such a man always makes such clothes.

The question, then, is how Greek landowners established themselves alongside and against one another on the Aegean coast between 1200 and 800 BC; how they formed their environment and mastered or adapted to a whole host of challenges; and how in time they learned to avoid doing what did not work and to do and even enjoy what was possible and appealing, so that customs, aspirations, and ideals crystallized among them.

The particular traits that had been established and had become even more prominent by around 800 BC would persist for many centuries despite constant changes of detail. Many of these characteristics are already evident in the works of Homer, and to some extent we can retroject later, well-attested indications of such characteristics back to earlier periods, since it is rather unlikely that any of the major traits we are discussing here had not crystallized early on.

A prime example is the remarkable Greek desire for independence. Greek landowners were their own masters, and because they wanted to remain so, they joined together with their peers. Their community was thus based on the independence of its members, just as, to follow Marx, their independence resided in 'their mutual relations as members of the community'. The members of this community, especially in so far as they were relatively wealthy, wished to have access to everything necessary to live an orderly life and to represent themselves adequately. Such necessities included an estate, herds of livestock, and servants, also followers, on whom they could rely at least for self-defence and military forays. The typical estate was probably not very large by our standards. Arable land and pasturage were limited, and conditions were probably rather modest, even if raids and piracy might add something. Obviously, economic self-sufficiency was never absolute, but it was extensive enough that people were able to forget its limitations.

Property and livestock were owned by individuals who generally do not seem to have been closely tied into networks of clan or patron–client relationships. The Greeks took great pride in being self-reliant and managing very much by themselves, and the necessity of doing so was also one of their main hardships and challenges. They were thus adept at working in the fields, and mastering many crafts (that would quickly fall into disrepute among aristocrats). According to the *Rhetoric* attributed to Aristotle, a free man was not supposed to exist 'for the sake of another'. People who thought highly of themselves preferred to work for themselves rather than labour for someone else, even when the former was more taxing than the latter. In declaring self-sufficiency (*autarkeia*), especially of the philosopher, to be the highest goal and in asserting that things should be done for their own and not another's sake, Aristotle was later merely pushing to an extreme what had been a long-standing ideal.

Greeks wanted to live independently not only as individuals but also as communities. That was undoubtedly because they formed communities directly with one another, just as they were, and then insisted with increasing emphasis that they wanted to keep it that way. They resisted the idea of being ruled, whether by the 'kings' they initially may have had or the officials who soon replaced them. Greeks preferred to discuss and resolve issues amongst themselves. They were neither inclined nor had much opportunity to delegate tasks or to separate communal aspects from themselves in a way that these could have been transferred to representatives or persons of power and might have evolved into institutions with their own legal authority, above and beyond the community of men.

On the small scale of Greek social relations, citizens were an immediate part of the collective. They interacted with one another on an eye-to-eye basis, person to person, as is usual among equals, not in the mediated form of relations that are indirect and carried on through representatives, a system which is necessary when one is part of larger associations, and often lost in them if not integrated in a hierarchy (and thus again dependent). Tonio Höscher has drawn our attention to the great importance of the human body in Greek art, arguing that it was part of a 'culture of unmediated action'.

The 'presentness' of a culture of being together and encountering one another without mediation was complementary to the Greek ideal of independence, and it played a huge role in determining Greek concepts of community. Community was very concretely the sum total of all its members, and it did not extend further than the eye could see. Greeks lived in direct contact with each other and placed great emphasis on knowing one another. Hence they needed the *polis* to stay small if it was to maintain the specific quality of life that must have been established among them, their ideas of a man's dignity and of justice, of property and social interaction, ambitions and goals, present and future. These were not just values or wishes. They were aims, intrinsic to and inseparable from Greek realities, ways of life, and conditions. Because everything was interconnected, everything constantly renewed itself and fitted together.

From their very beginnings, these communities had to be highly exclusive. Landownership was a condition of membership. Even much later, foreigners were prohibited from possessing landed property, in order to build a house, for example. Nor did Greek society ever give up the idea that landownership and belonging to the community were inseparable. The *poleis* arose and continued to exist only as associations of property owners. Marrying into families and acquiring property must have been possible early on, and for practical reasons the requirements for community membership would have to have been relaxed, for instance, for men who had lost or failed to inherit an estate. But such citizens always lacked something, particularly if they became artisans and thus made themselves dependent on customers, so violating the Greek ideal of autonomy. Much as the Greeks valued seafaring and trade, at best such activities merely modified the original criteria of communal belonging. Moreover, the exclusivity of such belonging was only augmented by the Greeks' conception of themselves as a community of cult.

Together, individual independence and direct participation in the collectivity must have constituted the elementary force that exerted pressure to maintain the tiny autonomous *poleis*. While this force did not universally or always achieve its goals, it remained constantly vibrant. People who have their property and their roots in one place and wish to stay where they are in their own communities have little incentive for conquest, let alone to incorporate others. The ways in which the *poleis* were internally attuned allowed communal coexistence to function. It was far too risky to share this with others who had their own ways of living together. On the occasions that other cities were conquered, their inhabitants were usually killed, driven off, or (in the case of women and children) sold into slavery.

Rarely did fully fledged communities join together into what were called *synoikismoi* (literally: joint settlements). But literal joint settlements were only one option. Another possibility was for settlements to remain spatially separate but unite politically; in this case the aristocrats usually took up residence in the *polis* centre. Still, even in the Peloponnese, where some communities did merge into more powerful joint units and caused others to follow suit, limits were soon reached, since living together in unmediated closeness is only possible in societies of modest size.

From the beginning and increasingly so with time, the openness of the sea corresponded to the lives people led in the closeness of their own estates or small neighbourhoods. Travelling the expanses of the seas and living together closely within individual communities complemented one another. For many people, the sea represented freedom and mobility. What was separated from place to place by the rules of community membership was, across broader spaces, connected in many ways: by acquaintance, hospitality, intermarriage, and joint undertakings. Within both their immediate and especially in more distant surroundings, Greek men engaged in piracy, sought adventure, and captured booty. A kind of entrepreneurship seems to have arisen in those vast areas of the sea that were difficult to control.

Moreover, because Greeks everywhere were in more or less the same situation and had more or less the same needs, they developed the same sorts of particular characteristics. They all had to be equally adept in managing an estate and in waging war, in giving and judging political advice, and in excelling in dance and the chorus as well as in sports. In the words of Homer, one had to be 'a speaker of words and a doer of deeds', someone with prowess in communal fighting as well as 'at the assemblies, where men distinguish themselves'. One person might be better at one thing, another at something else, but everyone was ideally supposed to possess all these skills. We can speak of the Greeks' advanced sense of individualism in so far as strong, ambitious, and independent personalities tended to flourish in Greek society. But the variety of individual characteristics among them was rather restricted.

If there is one word to describe the particular character of these early Greek communities, it is freedom. Though the Greeks at the time did not have the word itself, freedom was a matter of course for them, a characteristic of property owners and community members. It meant freedom from domination, the freedom to establish one's own existence, in the sense of independence, and mobility too. Freedom was simultaneously a way of being oneself and being the community, and this under established customs but in a largely unregulated world. People had to keep this world in balance amongst themselves and with great risks—to say nothing of the challenges and opportunities that would present themselves in more turbulent times.

Admittedly, this sort of freedom only applied to those who participated in the community in its fullest sense. It was a freedom of men much more than women, let alone slaves. Moreover, before long differences could be observed between large and small landowners, the freedom of the latter being curtailed in a variety of ways. But that, too, would change with time. Freedom at least applied to a lot of people in a lot of communities, and it was from their midst—truly from a foundation of freedom—that Greek culture was to arise. What evolved over time was by no means predetermined. Much of it remains puzzling—just as we have to reckon with the possibility that among these Greeks much was very different from what we find elsewhere. The question was what would happen when the original Greek characteristics were subjected to major trials and challenges.

This is more or less how we must envision the Greeks establishing themselves in their environment during the early centuries, all the more so since roughly similar tendencies arose and manifested themselves wherever Greeks settled. Under these circumstances, it was difficult for anyone to establish personal rule over the others, and it is no wonder that periods of such rule were brief or indeed never came to pass at all.

Those who appreciate the value of freedom will understand what drove people to aspire to such ideals of independence and broad self-reliance. Perhaps where such qualities are present, something like a law of inertia causes people to hold on to them. The same could also apply to the notion of unmediated coexistence. Nevertheless, as a rule in world history, the potential of such qualities is usually closed off when societies begin to differentiate themselves, take on higher tasks, and develop specific, seemingly necessary and typical hierarchies and categories of specialization. At such historical junctures, the freedom even of the members of the upper classes will be restricted. This is usually the case when larger political units are formed—powerful monarchies, for instance, which break with, indeed shatter, what has been inherited from the past.

So why did this not happen to the Greeks? In the early history of the Aegean region it is relatively easy to see why, people founded small, manageable communities, continued to prefer them, and placed such emphasis on self-sufficiency. It is also no great surprise that the Greeks were able to keep the power of their early monarchies limited. The small *poleis* did not offer enough opportunities to establish any sort of larger political dominance, and the possibilities for expansion were very limited. The small size of the *poleis* and weakness of their central institutions were mutually self-reinforcing factors. But why did that situation persist in times of major changes and challenges? Is not the usual tendency then to rely on the ability to organize and act—a capacity that is more easily provided by energetic individuals and conventional monarchs with their supporters, or even usurpers, than by wider circles of people? Do such times not usually favour the establishment, augmentation, and extension of rule from above?

Having an original multitude of small communities was not an exclusively Greek characteristic. Early Mesopotamia also featured independent villages and small cities coexisting side by side. Together with the Mesopotamian kings, councils of elders and popular assemblies helped make decisions about matters such as war and peace. But over time, major Mesopotamian communities and their kings began to subjugate larger stretches of territory. They did not usually last, but sooner or later one empire was followed by another, and all were ruled by powerful monarchs or castes of priests. The result was a sequence of specific cultures formed by and serving centres of power. Qualities like organization, thinking, and imagination were harnessed, encouraged, and developed further to serve those interests. Their purpose was to stabilize central rule. Much of what had long existed had to be thrown overboard. Those who remained on the outside—as was the case for those on the margins of the Mesopotamian empires—had to accommodate themselves to this fact. That further restricted the scope of possibilities.

The Greeks, however, seem to break with this historical pattern in that they preserved much of the past, so that their culture was formed by more fully developing and extending their original particularities. While 'ruptures' did occur over time, these usually affected relations between classes and between the individual and the collective, and not the *polis* itself with its innate, fundamental forms of life and customs. Thus the Greeks remained remarkably true to their beginnings, however much they might have developed them further in many aspects. The tasks of the community too were gradually expanded but remained rather limited. The political organization and strategies for survival and success that crystallized in the early centuries after the fall of the Mycenaean kingdoms thus apparently proved adequate to meet the greater perils that came later. The question is: why? How—given the constantly increasing challenges of an ambitious culture—could such early, unusual, small communities of landowners continue to develop in such a way as to remain sustainable and able to function? How were they able to produce their very own type of culture that made this possible, even in the long term, so that they were even capable of holding their own against the Persian Empire?

9

The Dawn of an Era: The Eighth Century BC

The eighth century BC is the first period for which we have information about specific events in Greek history. It is sparse but still suffices for us to recognize that the Greeks had to adjust to a host of new developments, and that they did so successfully.

It is risky to make generalizations about entire epochs of a century or even fifty years. What may appear in a concise summary to be compact breaks down under closer scrutiny into a multitude of often nearly invisible impulses. Still, we can say that new energy must have been unleashed around the middle of the century. Rather suddenly, as if a spell had been broken, the Greeks seem to have become aware of entirely new possibilities and began to exploit them in various areas.

The circumstances were unusually favourable. People were both compelled and enabled to explore new ways. There was much to be learned. Challenges and people's attempts to meet them opened up previously unimagined possibilities for action. The ways in which the Greeks took advantage of these opportunities, however, allowed them to preserve their original forms of life, the small size and unmediated nature of their communities, together with their self-sufficiency and freedom. It became clear, therefore, that the Greeks would continue on the original course defined by the *polis* culture—at least for the time being.

From the very beginning, a certain flexibility had probably been built into the forms of settlement and life of the post-Mycenaean Greeks. But now a whole movement gained momentum that required the Greeks to further develop and refine their forms of life in most challenging ways, provided nothing intervened.

What we hear or conclude from archaeological sources of this age points towards issues that continued to be significant; it also gives us some insight into the troubles, needs, and predicaments the Greeks had to confront. But we are in the dark about most of the disturbances and failures they had to master, the wars they had to wage, and the conflicts they had to pursue.

Land became scarce. The population had grown. It became difficult to keep everyone fed. The cultivation of grain had already been expanded here and there, thanks not least to internal colonization. But this was not enough. Among the upper classes in particular, there was not enough land to go round. Laws of inheritance stipulated that in the case of multiple male heirs, a man's estate should be divided among them. At the same time, others were amassing property, not least through marriage. Alternative means of making a living—piracy, trade, or mercenary service—were insufficient. At any rate, the growing number of people who were inadequately provided for, or not at all, seems to have become alarming.

In such a situation, one probable outcome would have been for able men to take command of those who were lacking resources, and with their support to usurp power within their *poleis* and/or conquer land from neighbouring communities. Perhaps attempts of this kind were made—and not infrequently. Evidence of novel fighting formations might support this hypothesis. But such actions rarely had lasting success. True, Sparta conquered neighbouring Messenia, but history would show that this was the exception to the general rule. Because the Messenians were not integrated into the Spartan citizenry, Spartan rule was so difficult to maintain that in the long run Sparta was forced to become a permanent military camp—even in peacetime. If a significant number of conquests had been successful, power formations with larger territories would have arisen. Rivalling powers would have fought to eliminate each other, and the victorious power would have expanded further.

Instead, what happened was rather different. Internal pressure was redirected outward. No path towards the formation of larger power units opened up. The monarchies proved too weak and were sooner or later toppled. They were unable to prove themselves indispensable in the new, changed circumstances.

People founded colonies. Whole groups left their homes, for the most part for ever, to found new *poleis* hundreds of miles away. Some preferred to continue their customary *polis*-based life at home, while others decided or were compelled to establish a similar existence elsewhere. The traditional social structure, consisting of a multitude of small communities, was never questioned. On the contrary, the number of Greek communities increased substantially, and that strengthened the *polis* way of life. The Greeks expanded far beyond the Aegean. Instead of becoming agents of power within their own region, the under-propertied—probably primarily sons of the upper classes—became founders of a Greek diaspora; while they did not turn the Mediterranean into a Greek sea, they did lead the Greeks to become the most important mediators between East and West.

Individuals led this movement, but they acted—temporarily—like entrepreneurs without holding or establishing power to rule. Thus Greek communities remained broadly speaking in the hands of a plurality of members. As before, they more or less *were* the community, the aristocrats in a narrow sense and property owners in a broader sense, although the superiority of parts of the upper classes would continue to be bolstered for a variety of reasons. In short, the new problems, which could have changed the typical Greek form of political organization more drastically, were simply exported.

Why did it happen this way? Had the Greeks already had too much negative experience with attempts to conquer neighbours' land? Did they choose the path of least resistance? Or did the new opportunities electrify the entrepreneurial spirit of many aristocrats? The reasons may have varied. One decisive factor seems to have been that the political organization of Greek society, the idea that a community was directly made up of its members, was already deeply rooted in the Greeks' thoughts and aspirations. They might have been prepared to wage war but not to exceed their limits as a community. What, so the logic would seem to have run, was the point of communities that got too large to handle? Even if a would-be ruler had nothing against such expansion, most of the people he would have had to rely on did not want to have anything to do with it

As a result, acquiring distant land probably seemed like the only option. And the Greeks were fortunate that the broad coasts of the Mediterranean offered vast sparsely occupied spaces that helped relieve the pressure.

The beginning of the Greeks' colonization efforts around 750 BC was the most significant event of that century. At the same time, the Greeks increasingly sought contact with Oriental cultures. Having earlier encountered the Orient in the form of travelling Phoenician tradesmen and their wares, the Greeks themselves had by then reached the Levant via Rhodes and Cyprus. They founded a trading outpost at the mouth of the Orontes (Al Mina); a second one, further south, was soon to follow. What fascinated the Greeks about the Orient was what they could learn from it and use as a source of inspiration. Hence they did not just seek to increase trade and perhaps see astonishing new sights; they sought to build up close contacts.

Once Greeks had departed from their traditional, accustomed activities, they embarked on a period of increasingly intense experience of the world. And in so far as reality did not limit what was possible and thinkable, they also began to reconsider their own ways and, where necessary, change them. The Greeks' forms of life began to take on sharper contours. The many new problems they faced at home must have made them far more open and receptive to the fascination exerted by the culture of the Orient.

This other world quickly ceased to be merely foreign and baffling and offered itself up as a model for imitation in a number of respects. One of the most famous examples is the Greek adoption of writing, as is evident on Greek vases from the mid-eighth century BC. But that was by no means all that the Greeks learned and adopted, or which otherwise inspired them. Once they began exploring the Orient, the Greeks operated within dramatically expanded horizons. At the same time, encounters with the Orient also caused them to develop new, broader ambitions.

The new opportunities that had opened up presumably undermined old privileges. All sorts of advantages stood to benefit the most entrepreneurial and imaginative members of the aristocracy, who had long been used to ply the seas. The riches they accumulated are apparent from archaeological artefacts reflecting public self-presentations: the monumental amphoras and kraters that wealthy people began to place on their graves, the grandiose dedications in sanctuaries, and the luxurious burial rites depicted on vases.

The kings lost their pre-eminence, at least in the most populous cities. But the same scenario repeated itself everywhere. New opportunities were realized here or there. Some followed those opportunities, while others were left behind.

Paradoxically, close contact with the largely monarchical cultures of the Orient strengthened precisely that class of Greeks, in opposition to monarchs, who attached such importance to freedom and exploited the new opportunities to serve their own interests. The idea of founding colonies, for instance, could well have been inspired by the Phoenicians. But what people make of foreign influences depends on those people themselves, especially if they are adopting knowledge originally specific to particular social groups. Thus, the Orient could well have been one of the factors that enabled the Greeks to develop a culture for the sake of freedom.

In fact, it was probably only their intense contact with the Orient that allowed Greeks to jump immediately, almost without any transition, up to the next rung of the ladder of civilization without drastically changing their original nature. That was the likely cause of 'the remarkable luck' that, in the words of Jacob Burckhardt, 'the rich fullness of the Hellenic myth, born in an age of complete naiveté, extended into a literate and later indeed a very literary age'.

None of this means that the Greeks in the eighth century BC could afford merely to continue to live together according to tradition and custom. On the contrary, they had to try to reorganize both their community and the space of the *polis*.

Reorganization was often manifested concretely by the demolition of houses and excavation of grave sites to create an open space, an agora, in the middle of the city, for a public sphere, which was soon to assume unparalleled importance for the *polis*. Such spaces were kept empty except perhaps for trees to provide shade. They belonged to no one and everyone and served to facilitate both communal politics and daily life. It was in such spaces that the *polis* began to emerge, as if from its cocoon, and its realm was distinguished more clearly from the private sphere of the households. In so far as the agora was the men's domain, it also contributed to differentiating the spheres of gender. Its function as a marketplace only arose later. In many parts of ancient Greece, the establishment of *necropoleis* (cemeteries) outside the cities seems to have taken place at the same time. It is reasonable to assume that the number of (wealthy) landowners living in the city increased during this period. They dominated the newly formed public sphere, and the creation of new public spaces was surely their work. One consequence was that, over time, the divisions between high and low became sharper.

Roughly simultaneously, the cults and religious topography of the *polis* were also rearranged. Individual sanctuaries had served for some time as cult centres for broader circles of people who lived in surrounding areas. Others were maintained by individual families or villages. Now, the collectivity began to appropriate and expand various cults. Sacred precincts devoted to individual divinities were walled off from the rest of the city. From around 750 BC stone altars were built, followed by stone temples by about 700. The increasingly dense *polis* communities began to gather at specific sites and at specific times of the year to perform certain rituals. It was a collective attempt to ensure the protection and favour of the gods. Apart from the sanctuaries in the centres of the city, others that were especially prominent in the *polis'* periphery emerged as destinations of large processions, along roads that were laid down and maintained for that very purpose. At the same time, such sanctuaries served to demarcate and protect borders. Tombs belonging to heroes of the local past received special attention through sacrifices and funeral games. Such rituals, like other festivals, were intended to strengthen the community's cohesion.

Song and dance were two common elements to enhance sacrificial rites and other ceremonies that were gradually being established or expanded. Choruses staged competitions and recited poems newly written for each individual occasion. Poets and singers, who were also expected to perform on such public occasions, had to meet high expectations—not least because of the relative weakness of the political and priestly authorities. Poets were therefore constantly reinterpreting the myths that were the main subjects of their songs. Not only because these myths extended from an earlier age into a literary one, but also because they needed these myths the Greeks developed them as richly as they did. As the importance of festivals and ceremonies grew, so did the significance of the arts in both Greek education and daily life.

The eighth century quite possibly also saw the reorganization and subdivision of citizenries. That may have resulted from a tendency to enhance exclusivity, but we are unable to determine the specifics. The same is true of the establishment of offices and the formalization of political procedures, two things one would expect at this juncture. But there is one piece of evidence: starting in 754, Sparta began keeping lists of *ephors*, or overseers (presumably newly created officials), who were responsible, at least in the long term, for representing the community vis-à-vis the kings and eventually were among the most important officials in the city.

As of 776, lists were kept of the winners at the Olympic Games, and the competitions were reorganized, although this was not yet reflected architecturally. Vase painters began to depict animals and human beings in entirely new ways; the previous long period of geometric painting came to an end.

It is probably characteristic of the new spirit, the mood of departure, and new beginning that towards the end of the eighth century a poet tried to use the myths of the Trojan War to compose a giant epic and fix it in writing. This strikes us as little short of a miracle. Even if the work did not initially consist of all the fifteen thousand lines it comprises in its extended form, in comparison, the longest epic poem we know from the Orient, *Gilgamesh*, has only three thousand five hundred. But, of course, it was not just the length of this work that makes it stand out in world literature. The *Iliad* would soon by followed by the *Odyssey*. Many things thus began to change more or less simultaneously, and stimulate one another.

In all this, the Greeks benefited from the political situation in the wider world, especially from the fact that the Oriental empires continued to ignore the Aegean. A unique combination of distance and proximity was at play. The Orient remained as distant politically as it was easy to reach economically and culturally.

Thus, the Greeks were able to appropriate an incalculable number of things from the Orient, without having to pay the usual price for coming too close to a foreign empire: submission to foreign rule or the need to invest hugely in military preparations in order to resist unwelcome advances. The examples of both Sparta and Sicily show what might have happened. Wherever the Greeks were permanently confronted by a powerful enemy they either had (and learned) to bend to the will of a tyrant or subject themselves to stricter laws.

In the short term, the *poleis* preserved and even extended and secured the self-sufficiency and freedom of their citizens. Yet the question soon arose of how the ambitions of the leading aristocracy, born of new possibilities, aspirations, and standards, could be contained. The more the new chances were exploited, the more freedom—originally an opportunity—became a problem.

10

The Greeks and the Orient

It has always been apparent that the Greeks owed a lot to the Orient. A treatise published under Plato's name, for instance, states this and emphasizes that everything the Greeks adopted they made more beautiful than the barbarians. In Nietzsche's view, Greek culture was 'for a long time a chaos of foreign Semitic, Babylonian, Lydian, and Egyptian forms

Figure 4. Greek sculptors were inspired by Egyptian statues of this sort when they conceived of the *kouroi* (see p. 135).

and concepts'. Continuing archaeological discoveries allow the Oriental influence on Greek culture to emerge with ever greater clarity. But numerous questions remain. The sources of information are unevenly distributed. Greek appropriation of some items is relatively easy to observe, of others less so but reasonable to assume. Much is debated, with good reason. Chronology is particularly problematic.

Phoenician tradesmen already appear in the Homeric epics, and there is archaeological evidence of Greek journeys to the Orient. Trade was initially concentrated in Chalcis on the island of Euboea, which was also heavily involved in Greek expeditions to Italy. The city established a trading post in Pithecousae on the island of Ischia, on the margins of the Etruscans' sphere of influence.

Traders learned to calculate weights and measures and use weighted metals as means of payment. Craftsmen learned entirely new arts. There is no doubt that significant numbers of specialists came to Greece from the Orient. They included builders of stone temples, sculptors, goldsmiths, and ivory carvers. Greeks learned from them, but also in the Levant. Griffins, sphinxes, and fighting lions began to appear in the Greeks' pictorial universe. Borrowed words for things such as lime, plaster, and bricks also suggest the influence of the Orient. Egypt, for example, inspired the form of the temple as well as the famous statues of male youths, the *kouroi*. Sacrificial practises reveal similar influences.

One unique group of specialists were the learned male (and perhaps female) miracle workers, who transmitted magical practices from the Orient to Greece, including expiation or purification from bloodguilt and insanity, which promised a way out of frighteningly pressing situations.

Other evidence indicates how much the Greeks adopted in terms of Oriental wisdom, myths, forms of music, and literary motifs and figures. Some of this, too, may have been transmitted by learned miracle workers, many of whom seem to have possessed considerable cultural knowledge. The Oriental myth of the succession of divine dynasties not only helped Hesiod around 700 BC to order the world of the Greek gods, but seems to have aided Aeschylus, much later, in interpreting the abrupt rise of democracy.

According to Herodotus, the Greeks obtained their alphabet from the Phoenician variety of West Semitic script. This was a uniquely crucial development. The Greek alphabet, with its twenty-five letters, was accessible to all. Wherever it was introduced, people were no longer dependent on professional scribes. The Greeks were quick to adapt the script to their own language, and this was done simultaneously in various places, so that a number of different local alphabets arose. Letters that stood for consonants unknown in Greek were used to represent vowels.

Without doubt, the inspiration for writing down the *Iliad* and the *Odyssey* is owed to the Orient, where scribal schools had long copied and recopied ancient epics such as *Gilgamesh*, the *Atrahasis*, the *Enuma Elish*, and many others. Most of them were only rediscovered in recent decades, but Greek poets must have been familiar with at least parts of them from at least the mid-eighth century on. In any case, both the works of Homer and the *Kypria* (another epic about the Trojan War from around 650 BC) contain scenes that are unmistakably based on Oriental models and in part can only be understood with reference to the latter.

Aphrodite interferes in the battles at Troy, is wounded, and complains to her father Zeus and her mother Dione on Olympus. Nowhere else does Aphrodite, the goddess of love, born from the foaming waves after the castration of Uranus, the oldest god. The name Dione is almost unknown otherwise, but is clearly the feminine form of Zeus (Dios in the genitive). The appearance of this goddess in this particular passage can only be explained by a precisely corresponding scene in the *Gilgamesh* epic, where the goddess of love, Ishtar, flees to her parents, Anu and Antu. There, too, the name of the mother is the feminine form of the name of the father. Furthermore, in Homer, we only once find an interest in cosmogony: Oceanus and Tethys appear as the creators of the gods, indeed of everything, and are mired in conflict with one another. The same story occurs in the opening lines of the *Enuma Elish*.

A number of Oriental myths revolve around the concern that the earth is suffering from human overpopulation. Some gods think that the destruction of mankind is the only solution to this problem. Moreover, gods often complain that human noise disturbs their sleep. Enlil, the highest of the gods, therefore tries to destroy humanity through disease, drought, and flood. In the *Kypria*, Gaia complains to Zeus and asks to be relieved of the burden caused by the human race. Here the god seeks a solution through war: the campaign of the Seven against Thebes and above all the Trojan War. These are rather limited means, considering the ultimate aim, and as an explanation it is pretty far-fetched. The god who advises Zeus is called Momus, which means censure. This was always a puzzling detail until a comparable passage was found in the *Enuma Elish* featuring an adviser named Mummu. This is the origin of Momus and most probably of the entire scene in the *Kypria*. Motifs such as the flames that issue from Diomedes' sword or the description of 'flame-surrounded Hector' in the *Iliad* can also be traced to Oriental models. Many other examples could be cited.

The Greeks obviously pored over the narrative treasures of the Orient, appropriating elements at will. The same was true, over time, with science, whether the discipline was astronomy, geometry, or medicine. The division of the circle into 360 degrees and the duodecimal system are two examples. The Babylonians' divine names for the planets were translated into Greek (and later into the Roman forms which are still used today). Around 600 BC, the Athenian statesman Solon supposedly journeyed to Egypt and gained knowledge from local priests that could have influenced his own political ideas, although he carefully adapted them to the very different Greek conditions. If this was indeed the case, it would have been typical. For the Greeks did not just learn, adapt, and then adopt from the Orient. They also used it to understand what they already had and to apply it in a new way.

The result was an expanded West Asian–Eastern Mediterranean cultural sphere (a cultural *koinē*) with common elements that concentrated on practices, insights, wisdom, and intellectual and artistic approaches. Customs such as reclining at symposia were also adopted, although all participants at Greek symposia reclined whereas in the Orient only one of them did. It is hard to evaluate the extent and significance of the Greek adoption of various secret cults from the Orient. All this amounted to a lot in quantity, even more in significance. At times, Oriental influence prompted not just individuals to be inspired by Oriental models but Greek artistic production in general to strive to imitate them. The best example is the Oriental style on Greek vases from around 700 BC. Nor can we rule out the possibility that individuals may have tried to copy the lifestyles of wealthy Phoenician trade magnates or even Oriental governors and lords. In later eras, examples exist of Greeks succumbing to the temptation of such aspirations. The fairytale royal residence of the Phaeacians, as described in the *Odyssey*, could reflect an imaginative attempt to describe the palaces of the Orient.

Nevertheless, no matter what individuals may have dreamt of, or even tried to achieve, very little of it could become reality in the world of the Greek *poleis*. The life and customs there remained fairly constant. Indeed, the influx of Oriental influences seems to have anchored such customs even more firmly. On the whole, the new possibilities that had opened up rather served to help the members of the upper classes develop themselves and their own individual ways.

One question that repeatedly crops up is whether the small Greek *poleis* owed anything to Phoenician models, especially the powerful, affluent cities on the Levant, which, while at times being required to pay tribute, had for centuries asserted their independence from the monarchies further to the east. The most important of these cities, Tyre, which was located on two islands (later combined into one) off the coastline of today's Lebanon, ruled over a significant stretch of territory on the mainland. For a short time, it brought Cyprus under its power, and its influence, thanks to trading and colonies, stretched deep into the western Mediterranean. 'Would it lessen the honour of the Greeks', Jacob Burckhardt asked, 'if one were to assume that this model did not remain without influence upon them?'

But distinctions need to be made. Much suggests that by the eighth century the Greeks had begun on their own to live in small, independent communities. This was not a matter of choice, let alone an intellectual question. At any rate, the conditions under which they lived were far too different from those of the Phoenicians to allow for wholesale imitation. On the other hand, in the course of learning about Phoenician cities, Greeks may have become aware that they could and had to introduce better measures for their own communal life, and they may occasionally have adopted an idea from abroad. One example might be the custom of resolving problems by passing laws and setting these up in public. Another perhaps included the institution of a central public square, an agora, in which citizens could convene; at least there is evidence for such a system at a later time in Carthage, which had been founded by Tyre. Yet another example could be the monumental elaboration of sanctuaries.

We know next to nothing about the political organization of Phoenician cities. At the top were kings, whose power was likely somewhat restricted by strong oligarchic advisory councils. For a time during the sixth century, elected magistrates, called *shofets*, seem to have taken over this function. Presumably there was a popular assembly. And uniquely in the Oriental world, the Phoenicians also had broadly based citizenries, characterized by equal membership in the community despite differences in wealth and status.

Aristotle, in fact, included Carthage in his discussion of the *polis*. He even praised it, along with Sparta and the Cretan cities, for its 'mixed constitution', while other cities he reviewed were far inferior in this respect. But that was what already characterized the majority of Greek cities in the age of Aristotle and, *mutatis mutandis*, even earlier:

they were simply not able to have mixed constitutions of the sort found in Carthage, Sparta, and later Rome, in whose political system Polybius discovered numerous parallels with that of Carthage. As far as we know, the constitution of these cities centred on a highly disciplined oligarchy, whose task it was, on the one hand, to pay respect to, rely on, and control powerful office holders. On the other hand, significant rights were also given to popular assemblies, although the people, dependent as they were on the oligarchy, made seldom, and at most, limited use of them. In all known cases of mixed constitutions, the rule of the oligarchy was strengthened by the fact that external dangers and problems demanded a high degree of cohesion from the community.

It was precisely this form of moderate but stable oligarchy that the vast majority of Greek cities were incapable of maintaining. While they did feature the three components—officials, aristocratic council, and popular assembly—relations between these institutions were rocky, and the aristocracy in particular was difficult to discipline. (In the long term, this was to become a *sine qua non* for the possibility of democracy.) Thus, the Greeks lacked the preconditions that would have allowed them to copy the Phoenician political system in any wholesale way, beyond a few details; it is thus not surprising that we have no evidence that they did. Travelling Greeks were hardly able to transfer what they had experienced in the Orient to their own cities. Moreover, there were worlds of difference between the well-developed cities in the Levant with their sophisticated civilization and the rather modest communities maintained by the Greeks. How could the latter have adopted, for instance, the advanced administrative skills of the Orient? How could they have even comprehended the particular nuances of their organization?

Aside from knowledge and techniques, the influence of the Orient on Greece was less a matter of imitation than inspiration. Flexibility and the acceleration of change was what made Greek interactions with the Orient so fruitful. The decisive factor was not the nature of what Greeks adopted, but the wider effects it had on the completely different soil of the *polis*. The key was not what was received, but the unique character of the recipients.

No matter how much Homer borrowed from the Orient, and no matter how much Oriental models made his works possible, he was still continuing an established Greek poetic tradition, and he related the new traditions he created to specifically Greek problems. Hence it is Greek ways of shaping personalities, Greek questions about what a person was supposed to be and be able to do, and Greek notions of social life that persisted despite and because of Oriental influences. (On a side note, Greek products and artisans—to say nothing of Greek mercenaries—also quickly became very coveted in the Orient.)

The coherence of the eastern Mediterranean cultural *koinē* (mentioned above), seems to have begun to dissolve in the course of the sixth century BC. Apart from certain specialists, the Greek world had learned what it could from the Orient—although, apart from tradesmen or mercenaries, that would not have precluded individuals from travelling to the Orient to learn from the wisdom and science of the ancient cultures, and to marvel at their wonders.

While the Aegean Greeks were moving into the periphery of a culture centred in the Levant, Mesopotamia, and Egypt, they were also beginning to undertake colonizing expeditions to the west and later the north and south.

At the same time as the Greeks discovered an Old World, they created a new one. Just as they were located geographically between East and West, they would come to find their place historically between the old empires of the Orient (with the Phoenicians on their periphery) and the new Roman Empire—in a transitional phase that, however, opened up entirely new perspectives for the world.

11

Colonization

The astonishing process by which the Greeks once again expanded into new territory, this time from Cyprus to the coast of southern France and from Cyrene in present-day Libya to the Crimea, began shortly after 750 BC with the founding of the colony of Cumae just north-west of Naples. That, at least, is what we can gather from the historical record. The city was located opposite the island of Ischia, then called Pithecousae, an outpost for Greek trade with the Estruscans, which had been founded by people from Chalcis. The settlers came largely from there as well as from neighbouring Eretria. Possibly some of them had previously lived on the island.

If our information is correct, for a century and a half Cumae remained the most remote Greek colony, before around 600 BC men from Phocaea in Asia Minor founded Massalia (today's Marseilles), the town of Emporion (Empúries/Ampurias in Catalonian Spain), and Alalia (Aléria on Corsica). The Cumaean settlers thus must have spent weeks sailing past many coastlines and numerous sites suitable for settlement and with plenty of arable land, even landing here and there—in places where others would soon found their colonies. Still, they kept pushing onward until they stopped at the border of the Etruscan sphere of influence, which stretched from Tuscany to Campania. Beyond that line, it was hardly possible to establish a settlement. Apparently these settlers had from the beginning aimed at Cumae or Pithecusae, and the interests of the traders on that island and those in search of new land presumably complemented one another.

The idea of founding new colonies may have been 'in the air' at the time. The Phoenicians had shown the way. In any case others were quick to follow their example. It must have been tempting for many to migrate in search of those elements of daily existence that were normal but unavailable to them in their homelands—chiefly their own farms in their own *poleis*, located, wherever possible, in landscapes that resembled home. Soon after the establishment of Cumae, colonists were sent out to Sicily, to Naxos (734 BC), Syracuse (733), and somewhat later to Leontini (720), Catane, and Megara Hyblaea. Thucydides records the dates, and archaeological evidence has confirmed their basic accuracy.

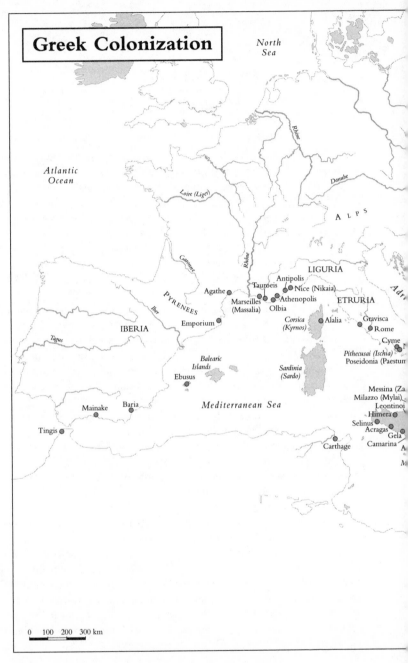

Map 3. Southern Italy and Sicily showing Greek colonies.

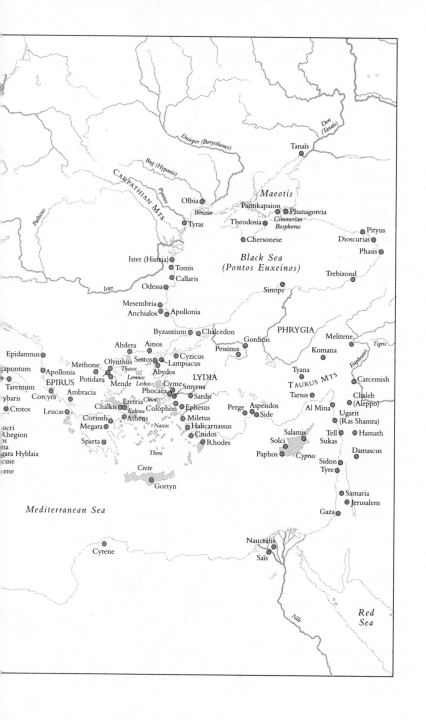

Don
(Tanaïs)

Dnieper (Borysthenes)

Bug (Hypanis)

CARPATHIAN MTS

Prutos

Tanaïs

Pathisus

Olbia

Maeotis

Pantikapaion

Phanagoreia

Berizan

Tyras

Theodosia

Cimmerian
Bosphorus

Pityus

Dioscurias

Phasis

Chersonese

Black Sea
(Pontos Euxeinos)

Ister (Histria)

Trebizond

Tomis

Callaris

Ister

Odessa

Sinope

Mesembria

Anchialos

Apollonia

Byzantium

Chalcedon

PHRYGIA

Melitene

Tigris

Gordion

Abdera

Ainos

Pessinus

Komana

Euphrates

Epidamnus

Olynthus

Sestos

Cyzicus

Tyana

Carcemish

aponum

Methone

Lampsacus

TAURUS MTS

Apollonia

Thasos

Abydos

LYDIA

Tarentum

Potidaea

Lemnos

Cyme

Smyrna

Tarsus

Chaleb
(Aleppo)

ybaris

Corcyra

EPIRUS

Mende

Lesbos

Sardis

Al Mina

Ambracia

Phocaea

Chios

Perge

Aspendos

Ugarit
(Ras Shamra)

Crotos

Leucas

Chalkis

Eretria

Colophon

Ephesus

Side

Tell

Hamath

Euboea

Corinth

Athens

Miletus

Sukas

ocri

Megara

Naxos

Halicarnassus

Salamis

Damascus

Rhegion

Cnidos

Solci

Gaza

Sidon

os

Sparta

Thera

Rhodes

Cyprus

Paphos

Tyre

ara Hyblaia

cuse

Crete

Samaria

ene

Jerusalem

Mediterranean Sea

Gortyn

Gaza

Cyrene

Naucratis

Saïs

Nile

Red
Sea

The settlements of Zankle (Messina) and Rhegion (Reggio di Calabria) were to follow; they possessed little arable land but were profitable because they controlled the Strait of Messina.

The exact details are not particularly significant. What is certain is that the Greeks established a whole row of colonies beginning in the middle of the eighth century, in Sicily probably earlier than on the southern coast of Italy (Sybaris, Siris, Croton, Tarentum, among others) and at Cumae and Pithecusae before Sicily. In any case, the Greeks preferred to sail westward for weeks at a time, rather than send their ships to the Chalkidike and Thasos in the northern Aegean or the Sea of Marmara, which they could have reached in a matter of days. Kerkyra (Corfu) was also among the oldest of the settlements. It was an important stopping point for voyages to Italy and up the Adriatic Sea. A Greek attempt to settle in Cilicia, on the mainland across from Cyprus, was unsuccessful. There, the Greeks were defeated by the Assyrians, who in the mid- to late eighth century extended their rule to the Mediterranean. Even so, later there were a number of Greek colonies on the southern coast of Asia Minor, while the Phoenicians blocked settlements on broad stretches of the North African coast and in western Sicily.

By the end of the sixth century, Greeks had founded some 150 cities, and the number of failed attempts must have been far greater. Some of the failures were registered in the historical record; the unrecorded cases would have been more numerous. In any case, sources from the period are full of lamentations for those lost at sea. Some simply went to re-enforce already existing colonies.

The average colonizing expedition probably comprised only a few hundred men or even fewer, but Greek history is full of examples of great things being achieved by relatively small numbers—a few hundred every year (especially in the early decades), then also some larger contingents: the total number of settlers probably quickly swelled to many thousands. It would have been impossible for the Greeks, who were originally confined to the small region of the Aegean south of an imaginary line from Euboea to Lesbos, to have taken possession of land in so many areas unless a significant part of the population participated in this venture.

The coastlines in question were hardly unknown. Piracy and trade had led the Greeks through distant areas. For example, a Greek sanctuary, presumably for traders, was discovered in Gravisca, the harbour of Etruscan Tarquinii. Tiny settlements or trading posts were probably set up initially on islands and promontories. A passage from the *Odyssey*, which was composed around 700, demonstrates how keen Greek eyes were when it came to discovering habitable locations. Odysseus' men arrive at a low-lying deserted island, whereupon the poet writes: 'There are meadows that in some places come right down to the sea shore, well watered and full of luscious grass; grapes would do there excellently; there is level land for ploughing, and it would always yield heavily at harvest time, for the soil is rich. There is a good harbour where no cables are wanted, nor yet anchors, nor need a ship be moored, but all one has to do is to beach one's vessel and stay there till the desire of the sailors pushes them on and the wind becomes fair for putting out to sea again. At the head of the harbour there is a spring of clear water coming out of a cave, and there are poplars growing all round it.'

The Greeks were choosy and sought out the best locations, regardless of how distant they were from their homeland. Arable land was important, as was a harbour so that the colonists remained in contact with the Greek world, keeping up with the latest tales (as was expected of the poets) and taking part in the prestigious exchange of gifts and trade. Ideal spots for settlements would entice passing seafarers to stop for supplies or take shelter from storms. Only later did Greeks begin to settle for what was left over, for instance the island of Thasos in the northern Aegean, which the seventh-century poet Archilochus describes as 'no beautiful place, neither gentle nor friendly like the land in Siris [in lower Italy]'. Thasos was settled at the beginning of the seventh century by an expedition from Paros, allegedly consisting of 'the scum of all Hellenes'.

Sometimes the success or failure of a colony depended on how much resistance the natives put up and whether there was a suitable place for a fortification, if possible, an Acropolis. The Greeks were probably seldom—and certainly not invariably—received or invited with open arms. They must often have acquired land through force or deceit and deception, as is attested by various traces of destruction in the territories occupied by Greeks. In this regard, Greek military prowess stood them in good stead. Alfred Heuss writes of 'politically empty spaces' in which they took hold. And the poet Mimnermus of Colophon says around 600: 'In lovely Colophon, we settled with overwhelming force, the instigators of harsh aggression.' Mimnermus was describing the experiences and feeling of guilt of his own times, transferring them to the conquest of his home city in the immediate wake of the Mycenaean epoch.

Entrepreneurship, a talent for organization, optimism, and daring are some of the hallmarks of Greek colonization. But not all of the settlers left their homes voluntarily. Often, pressure had to be exerted. When the founders of the first Greek colony on the island of Corfu (Kerkyra) were

driven off and tried to return home, they were refused permission to land
in their home port Eretria on the island of Euboea. They had no choice
but to find another site, which they finally did in Methone in the
northern Aegean. On the island of Thera (Santorini), a seven-year
drought left inhabitants with no option but to send one of every two
brothers out to search for a new home. The Oracle of Delphi drew Libya
to their attention, and explorers went to the unknown territory to find a
suitable location. Eventually, a hundred men were dispatched on two
ships. When they had difficulties establishing themselves there and tried
to return to Thera, they were received by a hail of arrows. In the end,
they founded Cyrene, which soon became a flourishing city. The population was bolstered by further immigrants, from other Greek cities as
well, and within a relatively short time the colony was able to field an
army of well over seven thousand heavily armed men.

It was no accident that these developments began in Chalcis. This city
was located on the sea route between Euboea and the Greek mainland,
which was popular as it was safe from storms, but which was also difficult
to navigate because of the currents. Ships often had to lay anchor, and
thus Chalcis, a city that also derived its wealth from agriculture, quickly
became a centre of Greek commerce. Parallel to and sometimes together
with Chalcis, neighbouring Eretria organized colonizing expeditions as
well. The island of Naxos cooperated with Chalcis in the founding of
a colony bearing its name on Sicily. Corinth was the mother city of
Syracuse, and later Megara, Rhodes, and others also sent out colonial
ventures, not least the Achaeans from the northern Peloponnese, who
lived in *poleis* but were politically organized as a tribe. The larger communities of Athens and Sparta, on the other hand, hardly engaged in any
colonization, and the men of Argos did not take part at all.

From the middle of the seventh century, the large and wealthy city of
Miletus on the coast of Asia Minor founded a series of colonies at prime
spots on the Black Sea. In this case, comprehensive plans must have been
drawn up, and projects organized on a large scale, based on commercial
interests. Something similar, if on a much smaller scale, was done
by Phocaea a *polis* north of Miletus. In contrast to the Milesians, the
Phocaeans did not possess much tillable land, but they did have a well-
sheltered harbour. They were daring seafarers, who, as is explicitly
attested, specialized in using the extremely manoeuvrable warships.
They are perhaps an example of how quickly the transition from piracy
to trade could be made. They were allegedly the first Greeks to discover

the Adriatic and the western Mediterranean, and they pushed through the Strait of Gibraltar to Tartessos in modern-day Spain, which had relations with Brittany and Britain and was a source of important raw materials. Together with Massalia, which it had also founded, Phocaea was probably involved in the establishment of numerous colonies stretching from Nice to northern Spain.

In the mid-sixth century, as the Persians began to take control over western Asia Minor, the Phocaeans took their women, children, and statues of gods and abandoned the city, sailing first to Chios in the hope of purchasing a group of islets, the Oinoussai, between Chios and the mainland. The Chians refused, so they set off for Corsica. Along the way they stopped at home and sank a piece of iron in the sea, vowing not to return before the iron had resurfaced. Nonetheless, half the expedition soon preferred to return. The other half settled in their colony of Alalia on Corsica, where they terrorized the surrounding waters as pirates, until the Etruscans and Carthaginians banded together to put an end to the nuisance. The Phocaeans in fact won the decisive sea battle but suffered such heavy losses that they were forced to withdraw from Corsica. They then founded the city of Elea (Velia) in southern Italy, which lived not least from fishing and the export of pickled fish. It was best known as the home of the Eleatic school of pre-Socratic philosophy.

The initiative to send out colonial expeditions came mostly from individuals, whose home city became the mother city of the colony. A colony always considered one individual its founder (or two, if two cities were involved), and they were revered as heroes. Among the honours they received was burial in the centre of the *polis*. The Greeks believed that the graves of great men were a source of strength and blessings.

We know nothing about how colonial expeditions were financed. The settlers were likely the younger sons of fairly affluent families. They would have had the necessary capital, equipment, and livestock, and would have been able to make the contributions required for a successful colonial undertaking. Others may have been able to take out credit from colonial founders, so the poor could have been able to participate in colonial activities as well. Colonies usually consisted of men from a single city, although in some cases, others joined them. But when whole groups from different cities came together in a colony, there were often conflicts and other difficulties.

Expeditions must have known in advance where attractive locations were, and in some cases those spots had to be conquered. There had to have been specialists to draw up geometrical city plans and to measure and divide up the land. The initial settlers ideally received land equal in size and equally far from the city centre. Later arrivals had to make do with less attractive or smaller properties. Whether women from the mother city followed the settlers varied from case to case. The historical record of female names suggests that many settlers simply married native women.

Colonists followed the mother city's customs in their cults and festivals and also in weights and measures. The same was basically true of laws and constitutions, although the colonists probably took the opportunity to eliminate flaws, and much was deliberately replaced in new ways. Older people could not be included, so the colonies lacked their advice and experience. The founding of colonies, which political theory would later posit as a fictional background for devising ideal constitutions, must have prompted at least the beginnings of political thought.

The founders of colonies got support from the priests and citizens of Delphi, who took an abiding interest in colonial activities. It was customary to ask the oracle for advice before sending out an expedition. And while the Pythia's pronouncements were often vague and required bold leaps of interpretation, they did at least frame the points of reference when people were faced with difficult decisions. They also legitimized the colonial enterprise. If necessary, since Delphic oracles were considered indispensable for such foundations, they were invented with hindsight. Equally important was the extensive knowledge that accumulated in the homes of leading citizens in Delphi, where foreign ambassadors stayed. The hosts learned about their problems and were able to suggest possible solutions. It was also customary for cities to express gratitude for good advice received from the god and to send representatives to offer dedications at the sanctuary. They were in turn able to answer many questions. In this way, the chain of trial and error that was unavoidable in colonization could be shortened.

Even at Delphi, though, there was no overarching plan. The oracle only issued prophecies concerning individual settlements. Miletus' comprehensive colonial policy was the exception to the rule. There was no higher authority pushing for the expansion of Greek territory. At most there could have been agreements reached with settlers who already occupied land near a potential location. In some cases, colonies founded cities of their own in order to expand their sphere of influence: Syracuse established Kamarina in south-east Sicily; Gela, together with its mother city Rhodes, founded Agrigento; Zancle (Messina) settled Himera on Sicily's northern coast.

But it was generally impossible, if only because of the distances involved, to keep daughter cities under control. Yet close relations continued. Colonies were required to send representatives and sometimes sacrificial animals when the mother city celebrated major festivals. Corinth was the only mother city to provide the highest officials for some of its colonies, since these had been founded as dependencies by its tyrants.

Colonization had significant effects in a number of different directions. It diverted so many forces that the world of the *polis* could survive in the Aegean. The lessening of the internal potential for conflict delayed impulses to strengthen the structures of the *poleis*. Aristocrats were free to develop their entrepreneurial spirit and set a model for others. In the longer term, though, a 'boomerang effect' on many cities was unavoidable, causing even more intense conflicts and longer periods of unrest— which, in turn, were the precondition for broader classes in a number of cities to improve their status. Meanwhile, the founding of colonies in general and the increase in Delphi's experience and authority in particular promoted the development of Greek political thought.

Cicero likened the coastlines occupied by Greeks to 'a hem around the lands of the barbarians'. This was crucial for the development of a unique diaspora that enhanced the Greek way of life. Greeks became more conscious of their own particularity vis-à-vis their various non-Greek neighbours and strove to preserve and intensify it. The experience of commonality bridged great distances. Greeks, as Herodotus once put it, had the same blood, the same tongue, common sanctuaries and sacrifices, and the same customs. Greek cities, squares, and temples were distinct from those of others. Now too the common name 'Hellenes' came into use, and there was a growth in the influence and importance of common institutions such as the Olympic Games, which athletes from throughout the Greek world began to attend. The sort of cohesion among Greeks that was impossible, indeed undesirable in the political realm, became a lasting and effective reality in other areas. Hence those areas that formed what might be called the common cultural sphere were seen as especially important and promoted accordingly.

The extent to which the Greeks spread themselves out between East and West unleashed much energy in the Mediterranean, and feelers were extended even further. By the end of the sixth century, Euthymenes of Massalia passed through the Strait of Gibraltar and explored the West African coast all the way down to Senegal. Incidentally, approximately at the same time, a Phoenician expedition starting in Egypt succeeded in circumnavigating Africa. They took more than two years, had to land for long stretches of time to raise crops, and were surprised to find the sun to their right when their journey turned westward.

Surrounding peoples imported Greek wares and art objects and adopted aspects of Greek knowledge, techniques, and myths. They also took in Greek specialists and exiled Greek aristocrats. This phenomenon is especially apparent among the Etruscans, although it is difficult to specify exactly how open they were to impulses from the Greek world. In any case, the hierarchical tendencies of their political organization were hardly influenced by the Greeks. The Romans, however, may have learned from Greeks to appreciate the strength that institutions could have, *mutatis mutandis*, for securing plebeian power. In the fifth century BC, as the Romans were facing problems similar to what the Greeks had gone through, they were said to have taken an interest in Greek laws. The question is indeed to what extent the presence of the Greeks freed the Romans and others from their narrow provincialism and introduced them to new possibilities. It seems entirely possible that the Greeks on their periphery—in Italy as earlier in Macedonia—helped advance and accelerate the development of powers that eventually proved capable of achieving something that was alien to the Greeks themselves: the formation of large empires. The ironic upshot would be that this would end the period in which relatively small, independent communities could play such a significant role in world history.

The zenith of Greek colonization lasted into the first half of the sixth century. By then, the good locations were all taken, and it had become possible to support more people on mainland Greece itself. Moreover, the Greeks had begun to reorganize their communities—but only after a long phase of great unrest.

It is not just progress, however great or unprecedented, in this or that area that characterizes the dawn of a new era. It is the dynamism that takes hold of a whole society, encompasses all of its members, and allows them to look at the world with greater clarity, comprehension, and confidence— while distinguishing between what is decisive and what is not. The eighth century could well be considered such a new era for the Greeks: if so, colonization, as well as the development of Greek cities and sanctuaries at home, would figure as signposts, together with the composition of the Homeric masterpieces. The immense achievement of Homer would then be part of that dynamism that set so much in motion at the time.

12

Homer and Hesiod

It had long been customary for Greeks (or Greek men at least) to gather within their communities for feasts and festivals, at which they listened to poets singing of the great deeds and suffering of past heroes. The art of poetic song was handed down through the generations. Many singers travelled from place to place, while others were engaged permanently in courts of wealthy leaders; the roles might have changed frequently. On a variety of occasions—for example, to mark the death of a leading member of society—poets would assemble for competitions. Their subject matter ranged extensively, and poets were constantly coming up with new combinations and interpretations, revising their stories, expanding them, and relating them from different perspectives. Greek encounters with the cultures of the Near East could have been a decisive impulse for further innovation.

The transmission of lore entered a new phase towards the end of the eighth century BC, when one of the singers decided to compose the stories of the Trojan War in writing, concentrating on one specific plot element. The Greeks knew the poet by the name of Homer and credited him—probably wrongly—with two epics, the *Iliad* and the *Odyssey*. It is even unclear whether the two epic poems we possess today each originated in one single composition. There could have been an original, written or perhaps dictated, ur-*Iliad* that was later expanded. On the other hand, both epics contain long passages that initially seem to have been transmitted in other contexts. However this may be, the written compositions went far beyond any that preceded them. This is true not least in a technical sense in that they involved thousands of verses being written and copied on animal skin or perhaps already papyrus. We do not know if any other written versions of epic subject matter had preceded those of 'Homer'.

The fact that new problems (or perhaps, more accurately, more intense and consciously acknowledged problems) encountered by eighth-century Greeks are reflected in these epics makes them—the oldest surviving examples of Greek poetry—an important source for the archaic Greeks themselves. In addition, both the *Iliad* and the *Odyssey* are still seen today as two of the greatest works of world literature.

Because these epics were recited and copied to such an extent, over and over again, the cycle of stories that coalesced around the Trojan War was henceforth privileged vis-à-vis others concerning, for instance, Oedipus, the Seven against Thebes, the adventures of the Argonauts in search of the Golden Fleece, the hunt of the Caledonian Boar, the labours of Heracles, or Zeus' battle with the Titans. Even so, the poet of the *Iliad* combined heroes from various backgrounds (Greece, Thrace, and Asia Minor, among others) in the two armies that fought the 'man-slaughtering war', and thus established connections between them and other cycles of myth. If other written versions of such epics were produced at all, they have been lost.

The epic tradition we encounter in Homer contains vestigial memories of the glories of Mycenaean lords, and such memories were perhaps refreshed by Greeks' experience of monarchic power in the Orient: Agamemnon, for example, is in a position to give away whole cities. Homer is well acquainted, too, with Mycenaean arms such as the leather helmet of Meriones, consisting of boar tusks. Of other matters, such as chariot battles, only traces survive. Generally speaking, earlier and later elements are mixed together and difficult to distinguish. For example, numerous Homeric similes make reference to iron, while the battles described in the plot are fought with weapons made of bronze. And though the heroes rise far above the masses of combatants, they still worried about their livestock like any good farmers.

'Anger be now your song, Goddess, Achilles' anger doomed and ruinous', so the *Iliad* begins. The goddess, the Muse, the daughter of Zeus, guarantees that the singer will be able to tell accurately how things were in the past. She speaks through him. This may be a traditional storytelling formula. But could it not also be a sign that an alert age, which was developing a new consciousness of itself and a new appreciation of reality, did indeed sense a divine power at work, just as the heroes of the epics are often unable to comprehend actions, unpredictable decisions, fear and triumph in solely human terms?

The Trojan War supposedly lasted for ten years. The *Iliad* only spans some seven weeks, with much else being included by flashes forward and back. This is not about the long story from the judgement of Paris and the abduction of Helen all the way to the departure of the Greeks after a decade of war, with forty of their best warriors left behind in a wooden horse, which the Trojans, blinded as they were despite Laocoon's warnings, then dragged into their city. Rather, it is an excerpt from this story, or perhaps more precisely a theme, that determines the shape of the *Iliad* and gives it unity. That theme is Achilles' anger. As the epic begins, the great Greek hero is upset because King Agamemnon has taken away Briseis, a woman captured in war with whom he fell in love. Achilles subsequently withdraws from battle and makes his divine mother, Thetis, ask Zeus to cause the Greeks to suffer a series of defeats. A great number of warriors die as a result.

The axis around which the plot revolves on the Greek side is thus a political struggle that plays out within the army as if in a *polis*. The Greek army is by no means just a fighting unit. Agamemnon may be the commander-in-chief, but he is little more than a *primus inter pares*, and he repeatedly has to call the Greeks to assemblies, as is also the case among the Trojans. Great detail is included in describing the verbal fights and decisions made there. The king has serious difficulties with the others and seldom displays a happy hand in dealing with them. The decisive role is played by a small circle of self-assured heroes who, together with the king, occupy centre stage., In the words of Bruno Snell, they 'always have to be ready for action to preserve the necessary quantum of honor, which renders order precarious but sharpens the wits'.

We can see how current such issues were in Homer's day in Odysseus' judgement: 'It is not good to have a rule of many. Let one man be king.' This statement seems to have come directly from the reality of the *polis*. There, it was not necessary always to have just one 'king'. Often there were many rivals. But even when this was not the case, by the eighth and seventh centuries monarchs were being toppled from their positions nearly everywhere, and that in turn caused significant conflict—as we see in the *Iliad*.

The *Iliad* enacts dramatically the difficulty of balancing the turbulent relations and conflicting interests of the aristocrats: the excessive anger of a great man who feels insulted and is obsessed with restoring his honour; the arguments, placating gifts, and 'flattering words' used (in vain) to try to reconcile him; and the crisis of how to get individuals pushing in different directions to pull together towards a common goal.

There is also the problem of legitimation. A leader whose rule is supposed to derive from Zeus himself is required to demonstrate his prowess and bravery in battle and is constantly being compared with others. The privileges of the aristocracy, too, require justification. 'They are no common men, our lords who rule in Lycia', the poet of the *Iliad* says in a dialogue between Sarpedon and Glaucus. 'They eat fat lamb at feasts and drink choice wines, but the main thing is their fighting power, when they lead in combat.' On occasions, the poet invokes the dangers of civil strife. Both the *Iliad* and the *Odyssey* feature vivid depictions of turbulent popular or army assemblies. A prime example are the disrespectful speeches of Thersites, a deformed braggart, who articulates the dissatisfaction of the common soldiers, but upon whom the Greeks turn their backs, laughing, when he receives a series of blows from mighty Odysseus. Moreover, the poet is especially skilful in depicting the responsibilities of the *primus* towards his *pares*. Not only does he, like Zeus, desist from actions of which he is actually capable because they would rankle others, but he is required both to talk and to listen, and to help others articulate what they want to say. He is the one who ultimately makes the decisions, but in the process, he has to know every argument and to take each one seriously. The perennially difficult problem politicians have with listening was a topic that continued to move Greek audiences; it will be taken up again in describing King Creon in Sophocles' *Antigone*.

Only when the army's situation becomes extremely dire, and Achilles is forced to yield to the entreaties of his friend Patroclus at least to let him take part in battle, does the course of the story change. The pre-eminent Trojan hero Hector kills Patroclus in battle, and Achilles takes to the field to seek revenge. When Hector falls, according to a prophecy Achilles' own death is near. Were the *Iliad* just an epic about a hero, the story would end here. But two full books follow. Funeral games are held for Patroclus, and final respects are paid to a beloved friend. Achilles' mourning and anger are out of control. For eleven days, he drags Hector's body three times a day around Patroclus' grave. This is too much even for the gods, and they seek a solution. This is the theme of the twenty-fourth book of the *Iliad*. We do not know when it was added to the work, but, in any case, here the problems of human nature and relations come to dominate the heroic and martial aspects.

Apollo refers to the hero as 'murderous Achilles . . . a man who shows no decency, implacable, barbarous in his ways as a wild lion'. The hero, Apollo continues, 'has lost all mercy [and] has no shame'. In other words, Achilles has transgressed against the convention that prevents people from doing what is inappropriate. Hera contradicts him, but Zeus decides to take matters into his own hands and sends Thetis to her son. Achilles agrees to relent. Hector's father, King Priam, accompanied by Hermes under the cover of night, is told to go to Achilles and pay a handsome sum of ransom for the return of his son's body, which, thanks to divine intervention, appears largely unscathed. In a short scene, in the light of the certainty of death the common fate of humanity shines upon the bitter enemies. Priam reminds Achilles of his own father. Both lament old age and death, until Achilles says to the Trojan king: 'Come, then, and sit down. We'll probe our wounds no more but let them rest, though grief lies heavy on us. Tears heal nothing, drying so stiff and cold. This is the way the gods ordained the destiny of men, to bear such burdens in our lives, while they feel no affliction.' It makes good sense that an epic about the anger of Achilles ends with the burial of his great foe, who has defended his city to the last. Unexpectedly, with the help of the gods, Achilles reveals his true greatness: the victor in so many battles at last defeats his own self.

The event would not be nearly so moving, however, if Hector were not Achilles' near equal, a hero in his own right who is depicted with great or even greater sympathy. Hector has no divine mother, and he is not fated, like Achilles, to achieve the highest fame. He is a man who possesses a strong sense of responsibility for his city, a loving husband and father, and burdened by all the problems besetting Troy, which has been plunged into injustice and now faces destruction. It is both part of the greatness of this epic and perhaps a specifically Greek characteristic that the poet divides his sympathies between Greeks and Trojans, allowing his audience to identify with both. Even students of the 20th century could still feel mixed sympathies for the two sides.

None of the aesthetically far less ambitious epics of the Orient enjoyed a status comparable to the *Iliad* among the Greeks. Only the epic story of Gilgamesh (and his friend Enkidu) occupied a similar cultural position. The two heroes in that work struggle to overcome terrible, overwhelming natural powers, challenging the gods in the process. The only slightly comparable story the Greeks had was that of Heracles. The Greeks were obviously much more interested in fights and other conflicts among humans; they were disposed to be concerned with each other much more than with nature. In the *Odyssey*, the hero encounters various monstrous forces, but he never tries to do battle with opponents like the wild, inhuman Cyclops, preferring instead to use deception to ensure his men's safety. Homer was also almost completely uninterested in the creation of the cosmos, the battles between the primordial gods, and the succession of divine dynasties that occur in great myths in many cultures of the Orient. It was only Hesiod who takes up parts of these myths—though we do not know whether he was the first to do so.

Gilgamesh's great motivating fear was death. He refuses to acknowledge and rebels against the fact that he and Enkidu have to die.

Individuals such as Utnapishtim or Atrahasis may have succeeded in escaping this fate; others must console themselves with the idea that their fame will outlive them. Only at this point does the *Epic of Gilgamesh* overlap with those of Homer, although the concept of fame in these works is quite different. Does Gilgamesh see human mortality as an especially tortuous problem because he is a regal, indeed superhuman hero? The reason, in any case, that Homeric heroes do not exceed normal human proportions by very much is that they are closely embedded in society, surrounded by their equals. The *Iliad* and the *Odyssey* are not about the inevitability of death; rather, it is questions such as the when and how of their deaths and what will happen to their bodies that excite these heroes.

The world of the *Iliad* is entirely concentrated around the real-life story of Troy, that is, the human world. Everyone involved, including to some extent the gods, is directly present at the scene. True, the war is terrible, full of suffering and tears, and Ares, the god of war, is the most hated of the gods even to his father Zeus. But the Greeks are less concerned with the horrors of war than with how to fight it. As fiercely as they fight about Troy, it is mostly in the desire to prove themselves that their humanity reaches its peak: the greatness to which they are able to rise and which shows what human beings are capable of achieving. 'Only the common man withdraws from the battle,' reflects Odysseus in the *Iliad*, when he is tempted to do so himself. 'The man who is first in battle has to hold out, whether he is hit or another.' The fight is never in vain, even if the battle fails to achieve its end, as long as one does what one is supposed to. The heroes are thus involved in an *agōn*, a competition. They must demonstrate *aretē*, or excellence, not least for the sake of posterity. One individual measures himself against others, Greeks against Trojans, and the heroes amongst themselves. The idea is 'to be preeminent and to prove oneself the best of all'. That is the goal and the cause of the Homeric heroes' ambition, suffering, and pride. The heroes know that they are responsible for taking care of their people, yet this concern seldom comes to the fore.

'If I remain to fight at Troy, I lose all hope of returning home, but gain unfading glory', Achilles concludes in the *Iliad*. And one of his comrades opines that if one were able to avoid ageing, one would not be among the first in fighting. Since that is impossible, he reasons: 'Let us go and win glory for ourselves or yield it to others.' Fame and glory in Homer are the result of dying a hero's death, and conversely, in the words of Jean-Pierre Vernant, 'true death is being forgotten'. As a result, falling in battle—in the blossom of youth and unscathed if possible—was considered a good way to die. The Greek conception of human life was thoroughly intertwined with death. As Karl Reinhardt has remarked, the human element seems only to be released fully in funeral lamentation, to become pure song. Achilles and Hector both know they are fated to die in battle, and Hector anticipates the fate of his wife Andromache, his small son, and his home city: Homer shares this with his audience in a moving scene of leave-taking. The heroes gain in tragic stature because they do battle despite this knowledge.

Homer's heroes may not try to resist their fate, but they do lament it. Indeed, they seem to feel an urge to do so. This is not an expression of resignation. On the contrary, in lamentations they gloat, soothe themselves, and try to pick up their spirits. Lamentations have a liberating quality; they are in fact *the* liberating element in Homeric song. The way in which Homeric heroes endure the frailty, weakness, indeed the piteous state of humanity shows what matters to them: they aspire to do whatever they are destined to do with excellence. There is something both humble and self-humbling in this attitude. Homeric heroes want nothing more than to be themselves in their world, albeit in heroic proportions. They do not seek answers to ultimate questions or any meaning beyond themselves. 'People come up against their limits,' Reinhardt wrote about the *Iliad*, 'but these limits do not point, directly or indirectly, to anything beyond themselves. The limit lacks any double sense; it remains one-sided in the here and now.'

Yet many elements of their victories and defeats, even their power and energy in battle, are incomprehensible both to Homer and to his heroes without recourse to the idea of divine intervention. The author constantly sees the gods at work. They are active parties in the battle for Troy. Sometimes they change sides; sometimes they are committed to one cause because of deeply rooted enmities. Homeric gods, just like men, act on passion and the desire for revenge, unfairly and with deceit and deception. What the Greeks in the eighth century actually believed and feared of the gods, and how they worshipped them in their cults, was another matter entirely. Max Weber has written that the disrespectful treatment of gods and spirits is often associated with warrior societies that are oriented towards the here and now, and delight in raids and spoils.

Even in antiquity, some people found this offensive. It is indeed easy to regard the way the gods in Homer behave as beyond the pale—if one insists on moral judgements. But Greek gods, as Kurt Latte has put it, were neither good nor evil, but simply powerful. Their arbitrariness was an expression of their frightening power; because everyone was dependent upon them, one had to offer them sacrifices. This belief was mirrored in cult, and the idea was also expressed in the epics. Yet, how one imagined those gods was left up to the individual poet. No censoring control applied to myths, all the more so because Greek priests had little influence, except in the performance of rituals. Moreover, cults were local phenomena, whereas poets moved about in the broader pan-Hellenic community.

Gods were not only essential for understanding events, they were, in the words of Hermann Fränkel 'counter-images of mortal, wretched human-kind, limited and tied to the earth'. They were the foil against which it became clear what it meant to be human. But whereas the gods, who were immune and invincible, could be passionate about something one minute and lose interest the next, humans had to take everything bitterly seriously. In contrast to the divine conflicts in Oriental myths that would later be imitated by Hesiod, Homeric gods had little investment in their fights. The fact that humans are exposed to all dangers at the potential risk of their existence also entails the potential for their greatness.

It has been said of the Mesopotamian gods that they needed human beings to work in their stead. The Greek gods only needed people in order to amuse and annoy them, and to watch the drama of their struggles. Moreover, Greek gods were not omnipotent. Zeus might have declared that he was the strongest of the gods, that all other immortals could pull on a golden cable hanging from heaven without ever being able to drag him down. 'But let my hand once close to pull that cable—up you come, with you earth itself comes and the sea', Zeus boasts, 'by one end tied around Olympus' top I could let all the world swing in mid-heaven.' This vivid image, however, is little more than idle bragging. In the end, Zeus has no choice but to hold the scales on which the weight of the death lots is revealed. Before that, his own preferences vacillate. He even considers whether he should save the life of Hector, dear to him, who had sacrificed many thighs of cattle in his honour, at which point Athena answers, 'do as you wish, but the other gods will not approve of your action'. As Reinhardt puts it, 'One of the most sublime of Homer's thoughts is that the most powerful god is also the most indecisive.' The greater context or, if we may use the human equivalent, the larger order is more important than any monarch, even the father of the gods.

The gods' decision finally to do something to stop Achilles' exaggerated thirst for revenge is not entirely free of personal interest. But even if

Apollo always supported Hector, Zeus and the majority of the immortals decide here. And that is precisely the point. Interested parties always take one side or the other on a question. The important thing is that the majority wants to prevent Achilles from continuing his revenge on Hector's body (and that he eventually thinks more about the tragic destiny of humankind than about vengeance).

Why did audiences take such pleasure in works that were so full of sorrow? Why did the Greeks seem to have *needed* such works? 'Indeed I think life is at its best when a whole people is in festivity and banqueters in the hall sit next to each other listening to the bard, while the tables by them are laden with bread and meat, and the cupbearer draws wine from the mixing-bowl and pours it into the cups', the poet has his hero proclaim in the *Odyssey.* 'That, I think, is the happiest thing there is.' But why then these songs that did not mince words when it came to the horrors and brutality of war? On the contrary, they went into almost anatomic detail, as this passage from the *Iliad* shows: 'Meanwhile Meriones killed Phereclus, son of Harmonides... Running behind and overtaking him, Meriones hit his buttock on the right and pierced his bladder, missing the pelvic bone.' Homer's audiences had experienced such scenes on the battlefield. But why do they consider it the height of enjoyment to hear such descriptions while they are eating a festive meal? The singer, in any case, does not spare any gory detail; his songs are full of lamentations about the suffering of men. Whenever he relates the death of a warrior, he usually describes the sadness of the man's father or even his mother. Nothing is glossed over here.

'Why did the Greek world exult in the images of battle in the *Iliad*?' Nietzsche asked in his essay 'Homer's Contest'. 'I fear we have not understood these scenes in a sufficiently "Greek" way, and that we would shudder, if we did.' Indeed, how can anyone account for the popularity of the Homeric epics, which were recited over and over again and which eventually became required reading in schools? Might perhaps these works have been so essential for Greeks because they mirrored their own experience of the brutality of life, the helplessness and vulnerability of man, the vast burdens that had to be borne, and the possibility of overcoming everything with glory? The audiences might have drawn encouragement from the greatness of the heroes, and from the art of the singer, who knew how to describe them so wonderfully.

Jacob Burckhardt stressed the basic pessimism of the Greeks, who felt compelled to stare the ferocity, suffering, and vulnerability of human existence straight in the eye, pragmatically and without illusions. Seeing this world through the lens of heroes and poets may have helped them. Like their heroes, they did not want to despair of this reality, but rather to confront it. They wanted to make sure of human destiny for themselves. Misery and arrogance, suffering and bravery, anxiety and triumph that could arise from all of these conditions were part of the Greeks' relationship to their world. The singer's audience must have enjoyed lamentations in this vein.

Confronted with mortality, Greeks reminded themselves of stubbornness in the face of death; confronted with the futility of much human endeavour, they summoned up the possibility of human greatness. In their heroes, who were forced to rely and concentrate on themselves, with all the blind spots that entailed, Greeks saw larger-than-life versions of themselves, in a hypothetical reality. Homer leaves no doubt that his contemporaries did not measure up to the heroes of yesteryear. But the distinction is only one of proportion. What happens in the epics does not go greatly beyond present-day conditions. The intervention of the gods only augments qualities like courage and strength (or even grace), as well as fear and terror, notwithstanding occasional instances of miracles— when, for instance, someone about to die is whisked from the battlefield. There are worlds of difference between Homer's epics and, for instance, the claims of the Egyptian King Ramesses that, after praying, he defeated an entire enemy army single-handedly when his troops had fled to a man. As is usual, he not only obscures his army behind his own self but this self is simply an extreme version of his own personality.

In their epics, the Greeks also found ample and heroically enlarged reflections of the problems they encountered with one another: the excessive demands of certain individuals for honour; the stubbornness with which such demands were pursued; the collisions they caused; and the strategies of asking and forgiving that could have helped them, if they had wanted to choose them. It is nearly impossible for us to comprehend all the things the Greeks had then needed in order not just to enjoy themselves, but to understand their lives as part of a larger context beyond the concrete tasks they had to perform. Seeing one's own existence projected onto someone far greater was a means of making one's own life more significant and tolerable and a way of not having to suffer alone.

It is interesting to observe how the world of the heroes and gods overlaps with that of the poet and his audience. The poet's present audience hears of how other singers recited before an auditorium. At one juncture, they even learn that one of the heroes in the song being performed is himself sitting among the audience. They also hear heroes speaking of the fame they hope for in the posterity that they, the poet's audience, themselves represent. The poet and the audience delight in depictions of the bloody battle that is carried out for the enjoyment of both Zeus and Agamemnon, who are not just characters in the plot but, like the audience, take pleasure in it. While the audience eats their meal, they hear descriptions of how others in the fictional world of the epic are doing precisely the same thing. The world of human beings is reflected by the world of the gods—only the divine world is even less restrained than the mortal one. The pinnacle is 'Homeric laughter', irrepressible and reserved for the gods, since when humans, such as the suitors in the *Odyssey*, come close to it, it appears ridiculous and is an unmistakable sign of their imminent demise. Concerning Troy's downfall, Homer writes in the *Iliad* of 'our portion, all of misery, given by Zeus that we may live in song for men to come'.

It is probably mistaken to see Greek singers primarily as 'educators' of the Greeks. On the other hand, Greeks undeniably learned from their epics, for example, when they vividly depicted Agamemnon and Achilles' delusions as well as the ways in which others tried to deal with them. Homer's works were central to the education not only of ordinary Greeks, but also of Alexander the Great, who studied Homer with Aristotle and who recognized himself in these works. In so far as they were the most important works within a culture, the epics were comparable to the Bible. Painters and sculptors adopted numerous Homeric motifs. All of this contributed among the Greeks to a sense of belonging together; it helped shape their common way of life.

Many of the things left out of the *Iliad*—overwhelming natural forces and fairytale elements, including monsters like the Cyclops, Scylla and Charybdis, and Circe the sorceress—appear in the *Odyssey*. But the final books of that work also revolve around struggles between human beings. Twenty years have passed since Odysseus set off from his homeland, Ithaca, for Troy. No one knows whether he is still alive. Suitors have gathered in his house to woo his (as they presume, widowed) wife Penelope. There they live a life of luxury at the expense of the missing husband.

Whereas the *Iliad* was about a battle between two armies of comparable strength, in the *Odyssey*, first the hero's son Telemachus and then the hero himself are left practically on their own to confront and ultimately overcome the superior power of the suitors. It is an uneven competition played out with deceit and deception. Only at the very end is the hero able to prove himself as a hero. The turning point is a demonstration of superiority: Odysseus alone is able to draw the mighty bow and shoot an arrow through twelve axes. What sounds like a miracle can be explained, upon closer examination, as a product of a much distorted narrative tradition, at the beginning of which stood an athletic achievement performed by the Egyptian pharaohs. They were able to shoot arrows through copper plates that were concave in shape and thus thin in the middle, similar to the Greek double axe, or *pelekys*, which replaced the copper plates in the Greek tradition.

Unlike the *Iliad*, the *Odyssey* does not allow its hero many opportunities for glory. Whereas Achilles constantly tries to gain honour, risking countless lives in the process, Odysseus is solely concerned with saving his and his men's skin. He endures great hardship in the process, but he is only called upon to demonstrate a hero's courage at the end of the tale. Before that, he has to be flexible and wily, qualities for which he was often despised in later times but which also made him appear—for example, in Sophocles' *Philoctetes*—as the embodiment of clever modernity. Above all, Odysseus needs to be able to handle frustration. He is often referred to as 'the much-enduring', that is, he is capable not only of surviving external threats but also of bearing up under insults to his honour. Odysseus has to be patient and deal with the frustration building up inside him.

'Of all things that breathe and move on earth, nothing is more frail than man', . . . 'The father of gods and men makes one day unlike another day, and earthlings change their thoughts on life in accordance with this.' Men are sometimes happy, sometimes downcast, and masters of nothing. These are the lessons Odysseus, disguised as a beggar, has for Penelope's suitors. It was a moral already familiar in the ancient Orient, and it was continually repeated in the centuries that followed the *Odyssey*. Those who aspired to independence were probably all the more aware of it. Odysseus' lamentation is accompanied by the lesson that humans should not respond to tribulations, but rather silently endure the fate meted out to them. On the surface, his comments may be directed at the injustice committed by the suitors. But they also fitted in a new, much broader context.

The *Odyssey* explores a new theme that in the *Iliad* cropped up only on the margins, in a simile, in the *Iliad*: justice and the guilt of those who violate it. Right from the start, Zeus complains about the mortals: 'They accuse the gods, they say that their troubles come from us, and yet by their own evil deeds they draw down sorrow upon themselves that outruns their allotted portion.' The poet returns repeatedly to the question of how injustice exacts its own revenge until finally Odysseus' bloody acts of vengeance upon the suitors appear as just deserts for their transgressions. 'These men have perished because the gods willed it so and because their own deeds were evil', Odysseus says. 'They had no regard for any man, good or bad, who might come their way; and so by their own presumptuous follies they brought on themselves this hideous end.' In one passage we even hear of how men landed on a foreign coastline and carried away booty with the help of no less than Zeus, but still felt 'a powerful fear of the retribution of the gods'. Kurt Latte has remarked: 'What was heroic daring in an age of heroes now becomes a transgression against the rights of others and the violation of a sacred order.' Here, for the first time, we encounter sensitivity towards the injustices one has committed oneself. Moreover, for the first time, the gods are held responsible for maintaining order. 'Father Zeus, now I am sure that you gods still reign in high Olympus', Odysseus' father Laertes exclaims, 'if indeed the suitors have paid the price of their monstrous insolence.'

The question is also raised of how the inferior or defeated can get justice. Telemachus calls an assembly, seeking support from the people. 'You should feel self-reproach, shame for the reproach of your neighbours, of those who live all around you here?' Odysseus' son asks the crowd. 'You should shrink from the anger of the gods; the gods in their indignation may bring your misdoings down on your own heads.' The threat is that divine retribution will be visited not just on the culprits, but the entire city. Telemachus' ally, Mentor, does not blame the suitors as much as the rest of the people, 'to see how you all sit there dumbly, instead of rebuking them and restraining them; you are many; the suitors are few.' There is no indication, however, of how Telemachus' words can lead to action. Even if the 'neighbouring people' share his point of view, the question remains how they 'all' can be deployed as a collectivity against a group of arrogant princes. Yet their problem, which was obviously of deep concern to the poet, was not laid to rest easily.

The *Odyssey* is probably only a few decades younger than the *Iliad*, but the poets involved could have been born further apart in time, and they could have had very different ideas and agendas. Audiences, too, of course, wanted to hear a variety of things. Yet the differences between the *Iliad* and the *Odyssey* might also be an indication of how quickly things were changing at the time. The *Odyssey* is concerned on the one hand with a household (albeit a noble one) and the *polis* and on the other with the wide, wide world that had opened up to Greek seafarers and colonial founders. As such, it reflects experiences and challenges from a more recent past than the *Iliad*. It also seems to include more elements and details taken from the Orient. Odysseus' journey to the realm of the dead, for instance, is obviously based on Oriental models.

In this epic, too, the gods are directly involved in the human world, and here too they quarrel with one another. Poseidon pursues Odysseus, while Athena and other gods protect him. In the end, after Odysseus has exacted his revenge, and the citizens of Ithaca, from among whom the majority of the suitors come, threaten violent revenge in turn, Zeus forces everyone to forget. This is the first recorded case of a general amnesty in world history. Odysseus' revenge is justified but bad, because it could have provoked further acts of vengeance. The forgetting Zeus brings about not only gives closure to the plot, it also establishes something of an example—even though it remains unclear how people in Homer's day could have followed it. The gods are pulling the strings here, but their actions are in effect less arbitrary than the mortals would have deserved. It is the mortals' transgression and responsibility that begins to assume centre stage against the backdrop of justice, in which Greeks are starting to believe. Does this mean that the audience had changed? It was in any case a new theme, which carried with it new worries.

A third poet, Hesiod, took up and developed the theme of justice. Composing his poems not much later than the Homeric epics, Hesiod was inspired by a new need for Greeks to orient themselves in the realm of the gods and in time, and he too would become required reading in schools. Hesiod wrote didactic poems, not epics, and his two main works were *Theogony* and *Works and Days*. Unlike 'Homer', Hesiod was unquestionably a historical figure who gives his name and place of origin and reports how the Muses visited him while he was tending sheep on Mount Helicon. His father emigrated from Cyme in Asia Minor in search of a better life and acquired a farm in Askra, a small and, in Hesiod's opinion, rather depressing hamlet in Boeotia. The farm was probably not all that small, and Hesiod's father might have married into a local family.

The *Theogony* is concerned with all dimensions of cosmogony, starting with the gaping void of chaos. In keeping with Hittite and other mythologies, this work spans three generations of divine rulers, from the original god of the heavens, Uranus, to his son Cronus, to the weather-god Zeus, Cronus' son. It also describes the genealogical connections between countless gods and major forces that dominate the world. Zeus, for example, has three daughters from Themis, goddess of justice: Eunomia, Dikē, and Eirene (good order, justice, and peace). Nyx (Night) bore miserable Old Age and Eris (Strife), who in turn brought forth Toil, Forgetfulness, Famine, Tearful Sorrows, Combats, Lies, Delusion, and Transgression. Hesiod's poem combines a number of different narratives and is thus inevitably full of contradictions. But in the end, the centrepiece of the narrative aims at the new order of Zeus.

That order is determined both by the cleverness of the most powerful of the gods and by the fact that the primordial powers, Heaven and Earth, are always at his side making their superior knowledge available to him. These advantages allow Zeus to emerge victorious in his battles against Cronus and the Titans, whom he banishes to Tartarus. He guarantees the privileges of all other gods, older and younger, who put their services at his disposal. Zeus' victory is lasting because, as a victor, he is conciliatory. He avoids the danger of being deposed by one of his own sons, who is prophesied to be more powerful, by devouring his wife Metis, the wisest of the goddesses. She is given a place of honour inside him, as his adviser who 'shows him right and wrong'. The rights of the gods and the rule of Zeus thus support one another. That is how the new ruler of the gods creates a just and lasting order. All power now serves his purposes.

The attempt to imagine new and comprehensive connections among the gods and other supernatural powers may have been inspired by encounters with the East. It could also have been the necessary result of increasing communications among the Greeks themselves, who were confronted with a greater variety of ideas that were, at various places, connected with the same names of divinities. For this the Greeks needed a more or less orderly system. Homer had done the preliminary work. No matter which deities were worshipped by individual communities, no matter what exactly they were called or which realms they were thought to rule, they were subsumed into the Homeric family of gods. At the same time, all this reflected an effort to secure for oneself the justice, represented by Zeus, that would triumph in the end.

A special place inside this new pantheon was given to the nine Muses, which Zeus conceived with Mnemosyne, the goddess of memory. Hesiod can hardly praise them highly enough. The Muses know of the past, present, and future and give pleasure to both gods and men. They also grant forgetfulness to those who have suffered terrible misfortunes. In Fränkel's words, they are an instance of old wisdom drowning out young pain.

Hesiod's muses are able to tell many falsehoods, but when they want, at least so they say, they tell the truth. Is this a barbed comment at Homer, or just Hesiod's way of staking a claim upon the truth? Whatever the case, Hesiod must have experienced how much the poetic word and even more, what grace—both gifts of the muses—can achieve; and he saw it not only in himself but also in the leaders. Everyone upon whom the muses gaze at birth is revered because he is able to diffuse conflicts by rendering wise judgements and protecting citizens from harm—it seems to be the most important skill expected of leading aristocrats. People wanted to live in peace. In Homer, for example, we find a scene in which a prize is given to the man who passes the straightest judgement. Here too the muses may be involved because finding the right words was crucial. This idea seems to articulate what Greeks experienced and expected from the agora—and also from song, for which they like to gather so much. All this reflects the enormous value the Greeks attached to poets, singers, and language itself.

Hesiod's *Theogony* may seem rather clumsy when compared to Homer. It did not have a long tradition to build upon, and the Greek language had to discover new territory for this sort of work. No matter how wide the gates that had been opened for Eastern myths and teachings, the Greeks themselves first had to work through their own challenges.

We do not know to what extent Hesiod was writing for the same audience as Homer. In any case, his second major poem, *Works and Days*, took a different direction that cannot have pleased everyone. Here, the poet addresses his brother Perses. After the death of their father, the two have become involved in a legal dispute concerning their inheritance. Perses had emerged as the winner thanks to some well-placed bribes and seems, in Hesiod's account, to be bent on doing further harm to his brother. He has also put on airs and graces and has mingled with the aristocracy, although he is out of his depth among them. In his poem Hesiod advises his wayward brother to concentrate on doing his work and not to waste his time with matters related to the agora. Labour, argues Hesiod, is the only way for a man with limited means to get by or even to become wealthy. In fact, Hesiod adopts for the farmer an old elite point of view, that a man is only worth as much as he achieves: through sweat and effort one can attain excellence (*aretē*) and even fame and honour. Hesiod points out that Eris (Strife) occurs in two guises, an evil one that causes quarrel and conflict and a good one that encourages competition; one only needs to observe successful people, be they farmers, potters, or singers, and imitate them.

Hesiod offers numerous recommendations about how best to cultivate and keep up one's farm, many of which are reminiscent of the wisdom of Solomon as well as Egyptian and Mesopotamian wisdom literature. It is unclear from where Hesiod derived his faith in the great opportunities to attain wealth through labour. His proclamations on this score are astonishing. 'Toil is no source of shame; idleness is shame,' he admonishes Perses. Hesiod lived around the time when the aristocracy began to shun working themselves. Yet here he seems to direct his remarks primarily at those who lived on the margins of subsistence. He also proclaims that the industrious are far dearer to the immortals than the idle. This view is unique in surviving Greek literature. Might Hesiod have borrowed this piece of wisdom from the Orient? Or was he influenced by the vast opportunities for action discovered in his time? Did the plethora of insights at his disposal give him a sense of confidence and courage, despite all the uncertainties and worries such new opportunities engendered?

But Hesiod went far beyond his own situation and horizons. Like Homer, he saw human destiny—albeit in a novel sense—as his central theme and concern. To him the main issue was not how to survive war but how to master the countless difficulties in securing a living. Remarkably, he considers such problems not as simple givens that had always been part of life. In the beginning, he writes, there was a time when people could produce enough in one day to survive for a whole year. In those days the horrific suffering that causes humans to die did not exist either. Conditions, in fact, were similar to biblical paradise.

In two stories, Hesiod tells how things came to be as they are in his present day. One narrative concerns Prometheus, who tried to deceive Zeus by teaching mankind a trick by which to withhold the best parts of their sacrificial animals from the gods. Zeus punished mankind, by withholding the fire, for allowing themselves to be taught such deception. When Prometheus then stole the fire and gave it to mankind, Zeus decided to visit them with 'an affliction in which they will all delight as they embrace their own misfortune'. This was a woman, Pandora, decked out in the most enchanting fashion. She carried a jar containing every sort of evil imaginable, and when she opened it, they all escaped into the world, all except Hope, which remained inside the jar. Did Hesiod mean to imply that hope, too, is an evil? Possibly, since delusions are, after all, the source of much ill. Or did he just want to draw attention, for the first time, to the ambivalence of hope? Prometheus had repeatedly warned humans never to accept a gift from Zeus, but his warnings were in vain.

'If you like', Hesiod immediately proceeds, 'I will summarize another tale for you.' This second narrative concentrates on what Hesiod calls the five races, or generations, of man. The golden generation, under Zeus' father Cronus, lived free of want, like the gods. To the subsequent series of generations (silver, bronze, and iron), which Hesiod took from his sources, he added a fifth one, based on Greek myth, the age of heroes, as the penultimate stage of the development. Each generation was created from scratch, only to be eventually eliminated. Even the last one, living in utter misery, the generation of iron, which honours those who do evil and perpetrate violence, will be swept away, when it pushes its evil ways too far. It is in this age that Hesiod sadly is condemned to live. It is a time when the guest is not kind to his host, a friend not good to his friend, and when fathers and children, children and fathers have nothing in common.

Whereas the *Theogony* tended to stress the increasingly just and lasting rule of Zeus, in *Works and Days* Hesiod confronts his audience with a continual, if not necessarily permanent, deterioration in the human condition. Zeus' punishment of mankind, and the declining succession of ages are both examples of mankind's fall from grace. These two narratives offer two interpretations of Hesiod's own age, and both stretch far beyond the present. What is striking most of all is the latter's misery, or perhaps Hesiod's priority was precisely to explain human misery. In any case, we perceive a new sensitivity to misery, which demands explanation—and which encouraged Greeks to cling all the harder to their faith in justice.

Hesiod continues with the well-known, bitter fable of the hawk and the nightingale. It depicts contemporary society as troubled by the hubris, transgression, arbitrariness, and violence of the powerful. A hawk holds a nightingale in its talons. The nightingale cries out, whereupon the hawk says: 'Why are you screaming? You are in the power of one much superior, and you will go whichever way I take you, singer though you are. I will make you my dinner if I like, or let you go. He is a fool who tries to compete against the stronger; he both loses the struggle and suffers injury on top of insult.' This tale certainly does not mince words about the realities of human life. Nonetheless, Hesiod sets against this an image of hope and belief: justice will in the end triumph over hubris. Dikē (the goddess of justice) is Zeus' daughter. She 'howls when she is dragged about by tribe-devouring men,' Hesiod writes, 'at once she sits by Zeus, her father, Cronus' son, and reports the men's unrighteous mind, so that the people may pay for the crimes of their lords who balefully divert justice from its course by pronouncing it crooked.' In addition, Hesiod writes, Zeus has thirty thousand 'watchers' among men to uncover their injustice.

Homer's Telemachus suggested that an entire city might be called to answer for the sins of a group of irresponsible noblemen. Hesiod contrasts the images of the poorly governed city with the well-governed one. In the case of the latter, peace protects the land's young people, the citizens celebrate festivals and have enough to eat, even the oak trees on the mountains bear acorns and have bees in their trunks. People do not need to take to the seas because the farmlands yield enough food. Zeus, on the other hand, punishes the inhabitants of the bad community. 'Often a whole community together suffers in consequence of a bad man who does wrong and contrives evil', Hesiod warns. 'From heaven, Cronus' son brings disaster upon them, famine and with it plague, and the people waste away. The womenfolk do not give birth, and households decline, by Olympian Zeus' design.' Zeus destroys the army, the walls, the ships. Again, jurisdiction is the key—something that was so very crucial in the early Greek communities. Yet it is unclear how straight justice, and the lack of it, can be the causes of the effects Hesiod describes—at least in merely human terms. The connection between cause and effect is Zeus and Zeus alone—as if it corresponded to a triangle with the bottom missing, leading from human society up to Zeus and from Zeus back down to earth again.

Hesiod clings desperately to his belief both in justice and in Zeus. On one occasion, he remarks bitterly: 'As things are, I cannot wish to be righteous in my dealings with men, either myself or a son of mine, since it is bad to be a righteous man if the less righteous is to have the greater right.' This is a brutally harsh statement of reality, but Hesiod immediately softens it somewhat, writing: 'Only I do not expect resourceful Zeus to bring *this* to pass yet.'

One of the most difficult questions is how to square Hesiod's expectations of Zeus as a guarantor of justice with the hostility the god shows towards humanity in the Prometheus story. But justice, too, is at the heart of the solution he finds. Humans chose to follow Prometheus and thus deserve punishment, just as the entire city has to do penance for the unjust decisions of its unworthy judges.

In any case, Zeus blessed mankind with a different order from what he gave to the animals, who devour one another because there is no law among them. 'To men he gave Right, which is much the best', Hesiod proclaims. 'For if a man is willing to say what he knows to be just, to him wide-seeing Zeus gives prosperity.'

The concept of 'right' (*dikē*) was new. The word originally meant pointing in a particular direction, which is why Greeks distinguished between straight and crooked paths of justice. It also designated what is innate to a group of people or a thing, be it kings or servants or even the sea. (And, as with our term 'human', the ideal often disguised reality.) The sea is 'just', in the Greek sense, when it is calm, not whipped up by storms. (The same was true of a sober person in contrast to a drunken one.)

The question then became how to realize such justice. In Hesiod's view, everything depended on the kings, the aristocratic leaders. Hence they needed to be told that punishment follows injustice. The castigating sermons of the Israelite prophets contain much the same message; passages similar to Hesiod can be found in Hosea and Amos, and appeals to the sense of justice of kings are a prominent feature in Oriental societies. It is difficult to determine whether criticism of the aristocratic leaders in Greece aimed only at individual cases of injustice, or whether they signalled a general crisis of their leadership. But one thing is clear: injustice, misery, and suffering were no longer seen as givens, no matter how much the manifold Oriental traditions and Greek experiences failed to meet, and no matter how unchallenged the superiority of the aristocracy may have seemed. A new horizon began to emerge. Hesiod's faith in justice was to spread and bear new fruits.

Accelerated change can cloud a society's senses. But it also tends to be liberating, if new forces drive that change and succeed in directing it towards a new form of human existence and a new understanding of the world. This may very well have been the case with the Greeks.

13

Gods and Priests

Hesiod and Homer brought order to the world of the gods for the Greeks, describing their genealogical connections, allocating honours, powers, and areas of responsibility among them, and giving them distinct appearances. This is how Herodotus put it.

Every city revered its own particular divinities. Most gods are attested already in the Mycenaean period, while others were 'discovered' in the fields and woods or via encounters in the Orient. In emergency situations, the oracle at Delphi might recommend that communities establish cults devoted to this or that divinity. The power of the gods could be experienced, and they needed to be honoured everywhere. Although we have no way of reconstructing the precise details, even the priests at Delphi made a great effort to show proper devotion to Dionysus, who represented the exact opposite of Apollo.

Many of the gods were common to all Greeks: countless communities, for example, considered Athena Polias the protectress of the city. But other gods appeared only in specific places. One of the most stunning of the surviving Greek temples is the one of the otherwise unknown goddess Aphaea on the island of Aegina.

Homer described the small circle of Olympic gods, which consisted of Zeus' immediate family, and Greek communities tended to adapt to them their own divinities, which often had marked peculiarities. These might be expressed in the gods' epithets. In addition, there were more than a few other deities that were often also common to many Greek *poleis*. They include Hestia (the goddess of the hearth) and Themis (the goddess of customary law), who was honoured in close conjunction with the goddess of the earth, her mother Gē or Gaia.

Just as Poseidon controlled the seas, Zeus the weather, and Hades the underworld, Artemis was responsible for hunting, Zeus' wife Hera for marriage, Aphrodite for love, and Hephaestus (together with Athena Ergane) for handicrafts. Hermes kept a protective watch over trade although he was also the god of thieves, Demeter over grain and harvest, and Dionysus was the god of wine and, later, the theatre. But divine 'responsibilities' often exceeded the boundaries of the gods' core identities. Among other functions, Apollo brought assistance and health, and his son Asclepius was the god of medicine. Special characteristics were often indicated in the ancillary names (epithets) many gods were given. Zeus Xenios was the god to whom Greeks could pray when abroad and appealing to the rules of hospitality; Zeus Hikesios was the god of suppliants, and Zeus Agoraios the god enabling agreement in the political arena of the agoras.

The Greeks saw or at least suspected the influence of higher forces everywhere, and they sought to identify, name, and characterize divinities in order to ask for favours, to swear oaths, make vows and sacrifices, and express their gratitude as well. Poets honoured the friendly muses. Impulses and effects were credited to divine forces. The attic community of Rhamnus in the fifth century BC devoted a grand temple to Nemesis, who represented retribution and just anger (in reaction to inappropriate actions). Themis stood for custom and enactment. She regulated Greek social life and ordered the popular assemblies where citizens deliberated and made common decisions.

The entire uncertainty and difficulty in understanding what people experience seems to have led to the postulation of forces that soon coalesced into easily visualized images of divinities. And because the gods were conceived as real beings, in the words of Richard Harder, they had 'to contain within them also deep-seated experiences of real-life cruelty and crass deception'.

We do not know to what extent people in real life believed in the supernatural powers of the gods as conceived by the poets, but it is likely that Greek literature, with all its vivid imagination, mirrored the tangible everyday Greek reality of a world subject to incalculable external factors, comprising everything from the weather to poetic grace and the success of political order. They experienced such factors, for instance, in the surprising energy of men going off to battle, as well as the utter desperation in which people, for whatever reason, occasionally find themselves. Greeks could not even be certain of how they themselves or their friends and enemies would behave. Their tendency to say that people's dispositions depended on the type of day that Zeus brought forth was probably more than just a colourful way of suggesting that people sometimes get out of bed the wrong way. Rather, it expressed the experience of being subjected to imponderables which could neither be controlled nor avoided, but which one wanted to confront in order to articulate it.

By the eighth century at the latest, the Greeks found all aspects of life beyond the procurement of basic necessities (and sometimes even there) to be influenced by a high degree of flux. Happiness alternated with misery, profit with loss, rise with fall. There was only a limited amount of security to be had, and life was particularly fraught with danger for those who did not restrict themselves to living within certain limits.

Political authorities and priests were hardly able to make people feel that conditions of life were steady and reliable. Nor were they capable of controlling and regulating access to divine powers. Greek ideas about the gods were formed not by them but by the poets and singers, respected men who travelled freely among cities, followed specific pan-Hellenic and broadly accepted standards, and thus were able to shape and expand Greek myth—independently of whatever happened to be the rituals of any particular place. But the fact that the divine cosmos they depict is the only one that remains accessible to us does not mean that individuals and communities did not have their own ideas about the gods.

In any case, the dominant and undeniable impression of the unpredictability of the gods could not be limited or pushed aside; rather, it was openly—one might even say, realistically and humbly—accepted and captured in words and images. As concrete and direct as their social life in small *poleis* was, the Greeks still had a keen sensitivity for all that lay beyond what they could see, touch, and form. The divine world was a realm of fantasies, wishes, and fears, but also a sphere of free thinking. Precisely because Greeks had every reason to be keen observers, they must also have been very conscious of the boundaries of what was perceptible and calculable. Hence, their fundamental questions had to be directed beyond such limitations.

New hopes for justice could be expressed not just through the ancient and venerable goddess Themis, but also through Dikē, who was thought of as the daughter of Zeus and Themis and who also confronted men as a goddess. To some extent, for example, the Egyptian goddess Ma'at may have influenced this figure.

The increasing intellectual penetration into human affairs eventually led to the development of a political theology that was connected with Zeus and the idea of his innate justice. Around 600 BC, when Solon of Athens set out to define 'good order' (*eunomia*), he saw it as not just an idea, but as a goddess. That was because no mortal authority was thought able to guarantee it. It consisted of the appropriate balance between diverse powers: who else but a god or goddess could have stood for such a principle?

Since certain tasks were attributed to specific gods, the immortals in Homer could also be the source of moral behaviour on earth. The gods themselves may not have been especially good or strict at setting moral standards, but the responsibilities with which they were entrusted required them to be concerned about adherence to certain norms. The gods, for instance, were seen, with considerable passion, as guarantors of oaths that were crucial in many spheres of life, and breaking one's word was considered an offence to the gods. Likewise, it was an insult to Dikē when someone committed an act of injustice. Behaving like any good father, one might say, Zeus then took revenge for the affront by punishing the perpetrator. The situation was similar with Apollo if someone violated moderation, for which he stood. The goddess of hunt, Artemis, had long been thought to be concerned that hunters should spare young animals, and to be ready to intervene if they did not. 'Her delight is the bow,' reads the Homeric *Hymn to Aphrodite*, 'killing wild beasts on the mountains, lyres, dances, piercing shouts, shadowy groves', but also 'a city of just men'. And no matter what the individual conflicts of interest among the gods, Homer describes repeatedly how the majority comes together, if things go too far, to ensure that justice is done. Accordingly, fear of divine retribution was an incentive for people to behave properly. Odysseus, landing on an unknown shore, asks himself whether the inhabitants 'are cruel, savage, and lawless, or good to strangers, and in their hearts fear the gods'.

The Greeks did not recognize any dissonance between the egotism, moodiness, and malice of their gods, attributes which were modelled on the image of mighty lords, and the idea that those gods were also responsible for justice and moderation. Nor did they see a contradiction when a person who had done wrong sought to avoid punishment by gaining the gods' favour with particularly opulent sacrifices. 'I give so that you reciprocate' (*do ut des*) remained the dominant principle. The gods kept an eye on most things. But they had not created morality. Even between the *Iliad* and the *Odyssey*, we perceive an increasing belief that the gods were concerned about their reputation. However one conceived of them, piety and justice were closely connected.

In the case of Apollo, it is apparent that the priests at the oracle of Delphi propagated what were considered to be his teachings. In the case of Zeus, this was probably done by those who were in a position to express general aspirations. Zeus' name was supposed to stand for the totality of what the Greeks were seeking (unless people went so far as looking for it in the cosmic order).

As Burckhardt noted, the Greeks did not place religion 'above and apart from the *polis*; instead, cult and life were *one*', intertwined at the deepest level. Every meal, symposium, or battle began with a sacrifice, every public assembly commenced with a prayer, and religious issues stood at the top of its agenda. The subdivisions of citizens met at altars, performed cult rituals that served, among other purposes, to accept newborn children into their ranks, made sacrifices, and ate the meat in a festive setting. People consulted seers to discover the will of the gods. Men and women, fathers of the household as well as communal officials, were constantly aware of the gods and tried to earn their favour, whether because something special demanded it or just because that was the general order of things.

The Greek calendar was sprinkled with festivals devoted to various gods. Along with sacrifices and prayers, such rituals consisted of processions, song, and dance. Choruses staged competitions and performed texts composed especially for the occasion, and there were sports events as well. Apollo's heart swelled with joy, it was said, when 'Ionia's sons in flowing garments, together with their children and chaste wives' turned their thoughts to him full of grace, and when 'competition commences with dances, songs, and fighting with fists'. Solemn hymns praised the god. Mostly, the same things were pleasing to both gods and men.

Greeks made images of their gods, built temples to them, and bestowed upon them more or less valuable dedications. When there were too many offerings, the older or less valuable ones were buried within the temple. The sacrificial altar was located in front of the temple, where there was also a communal space. Stelae, inscribed with a community's laws, were often erected in a city's sacred precinct, and suppliants could seek asylum there. The Greeks were hardly unique in depicting their gods in human shape. Nowhere but among the Greeks, though, did these figures change over time to depict the human aspects of the gods increasingly realistically and their nature ever more ideally.

During sacrifices and festivals, the citizens experienced themselves in a particularly intense way as a community. 'Together and with all on the same level', writes Walter Burkert, 'people stand around the altar, experiencing and causing death, honouring the immortals and affirming life, with all of its brevity, in their feasts. The shock of death, present in the form of the hot blood draining away, makes a direct impact. This is not an ancillary, embarrassing rite. It is the centre upon which all eyes are directed. And yet in the feast that follows, the encounter with death is transformed into a life-affirming sense of satisfaction.' Cities were associations of cults, and membership, as well as the very autonomy of the community, were based upon them. But that did not prevent associations between them, such as that between the twelve Ionian cities, from maintaining their own cult-based connection. On the Mycale peninsula across from the island of Samos, there was a sacred altar to Poseidon Heliconios, at which the Ionians gathered for both religious ceremonies and political consultations.

But there were also other ways in which Greeks sought to gain access to higher powers. The mystery cults that had spread from the Orient were one way, as were secret cults and sects with their own teachings, such as Orphism. They seem to have had no more difficulty fitting in with the usual ways of honouring the gods than some of the more excessive forms of the cult of Dionysus, about which we know precious little.

Politically, what is most striking about Greek religion is what it was not. Greek aristocracies did not use it as an instrument of power. To be more precise, Greek aristocrats did not organize and control access to the gods, and specifically to the discovery and interpretation of divine will, in a way that would have made it possible to develop, on that basis, priestly and ultimately political authority. Priests were not thought to possess any superior knowledge beyond how to carry out cult rituals correctly. This resulted from the orientation of the upper classes within the world of the *polis*, and being embedded in it. They lacked both the ambition and the ability to seek lasting rule. This probably encouraged the wild growth of a pluralistic pantheon as well as the distinction between rituals and myth. The authority that the priests lacked fell to the poets, and there were no restrictions upon the imaginations of the latter. Theology, on the other hand, was left primarily to political thinkers and wise men.

When the priests at Delphi or seers and interpreters of the entrails of sacrificial animals or other omens provided information about the will of the gods, they were merely acting as specialists. As such, they were in great demand. In return, as a sign of gratitude, they were given gifts, as the archeological evidence at Delphi attests. That was also true at other oracular sites such as Dodona and Didyma. Therefore priests had to do their job as well as possible. Thus, over time, the oracle at Delphi developed close relationships with the wise men, but the plurality of *poleis* never allowed Delphi to assume a significant political role. However, its advisory role that had crystallized during the age of colonization, based on something like a 'third position', was far more significant.

Nietzsche wrote that the Greeks 'knew and experienced the shocks and horrors of being' and that, in order to survive at all, 'they had put the glorious dream birth of the Olympians' before themselves. If that is correct, it was prepared in a long process. It was the written form into which this 'dream birth' was put in the eighth century, Homer's epics, that secured its survival for posterity—in close connection with the heroes of the Trojan War. Along with everything else that emerged from the eighth century, it attests to the immense opportunities that could arise from Greek freedom.

14

Crisis and Consolidation: The Seventh and Sixth Centuries BC

There are two sides to every coin. Greek expansion into broad areas of the Mediterranean, together with the founding of so many colonies, offered relief for a number of social tensions. But in the long term, the opening up of such vast spaces and the intensity with which they were exploited made it difficult for the Greeks to preserve their tradition of freedom. The knowledge, abilities, ambitions, and arbitrariness of many elite citizens grew faster than society's capacity for containing them.

Standards of affluence rose quickly. By 600 BC, Solon maintained: 'Nothing in the way of a visible boundary has been set upon people's wealth; those of us who already possess the most are doubly greedy.' 'Who can satisfy them all?' With demands like this in play, there was never enough to go round. Solon concluded by reminding his audience that money always changes hands. 'Money makes the man' soon became a Greek motto, and it applied both to members of established families and to upstarts. Since the legitimate means of acquiring wealth—agriculture, piracy, and trade—often lagged far behind individual aspirations, traditional restraints upon what people could do to satisfy their desires were frequently ignored—perhaps not quite to the extent sources suggest. Yet, as these same sources make clear, people were sensitive to such transgressions and this exacerbated the situation. It was unavoidable that the political ambitions of some rose and began to collide with those of others: competition was no longer about honour and status, but about power, indeed the power to rule over others.

The *poleis*, lacking any dense institutional framework, were not equipped to deal with these kinds of problems. Once the will to get along and keep one's goals modest became weaker than the drive to acquire power and get one's way, Greek society had few means for limiting conflict. Who was entitled to set such limits? What good were courts, which themselves often lacked impartial judges, when the struggle for power was fought by unscrupulous means? And how could mere opinions, even when widespread, stand up to would-be or actual holders of power? When associations or factions of the aristocracy fought tooth and nail among themselves, advisory councils and officials became part of the problem rather than the solution. In fact, offices and other public functions were often handed out to this or that faction as rewards for loyalty. The more they were fought over, the higher their value, since they provided access to public and sacred property, to which officials helped themselves. They also offered opportunities for exploiting those who were weaker. In circumstances like these, power tends to run unchecked, and people who are daring enough can reshape it by taking things into their own hands. Indeed, struggles between aristocratic factions often became violent and ended with the losers being banished or having their property confiscated. Such conflicts seriously threatened the already loose cohesion of Greek communities and proved a continual source of deep concern and fear.

But competition at the top was only one problem. As the wealth, power, and demands of the upper classes grew, so did the misery and poverty of society's lower echelons. We do not know the precise cause and extent of such poverty or the exact chronology of how it developed, but there is no doubt that farmers in numerous communities became heavily indebted (because of bad harvests or perhaps investments in olive or wine production). Many of them were forced to mortgage their farms—or they themselves and their families were even sold into slavery. For they had to provide security with their own bodies, and neighbourly assistance was soon exhausted. Aristocrats who initially might have been helpful, often became impatient, could demand exorbitant interest, and used brutal means to collect what was owed.

Thus, ever sharper contrasts arose between rich and poor, and these conflicts were sometimes intertwined with struggles between aristocratic factions. The historical record reports rebellions, civil wars, and incidents in which ambitious noblemen placed themselves at the head of the desperate masses and took over whole cities, establishing what the Greeks called a 'tyranny'. This was the case in several communities, especially larger ones near the sea that were more intensely involved in trade and other enterprises. Boundaries which had been maintained by the *poleis* and upon which the *poleis* depended for their continuing existence were thus crossed.

Given that tyrants ruled various cities, often for two or three generations, it is legitimate to ask to what extent Greek freedom from ruling power was generally endangered. The tyrants were very efficient by Greek standards and were able to guarantee internal peace and order. In the face of increasing social differentiation, serious conflicts, violation of laws, feuding, and civil strife, the basic and easily abused freedom in Greek cities was put to the test. It is very difficult to imagine how Greek communities of the archaic period could have maintained a balanced, peaceful coexistence—especially considering the frequent moments of crisis they endured. Even if we grant that the Greeks regarded a variety of open conflicts, indeed outbreaks of violence to be inevitable and perhaps even natural (even if they complained about them), how did they eventually succeed in reconciling themselves with each other, time and again? Did majorities, either instinctively or consciously, intervene between quarrelling parties and get them to accept limits? Did communities develop a general awareness of when things had gone too far, had exceeded the bounds of permissibility, and become too dangerous? Did moral authorities raise their voices, as Nestor does in the *Iliad*? Or did solutions lie in offers and appeals such as the Greeks extended to Achilles? The challenge at the time was to develop new strategies for suppressing the abuses of power and injustice, to restore a functioning social order, and to do so from the middle of society. In other words, the community itself had to be able to accomplish something that otherwise only a tyrant was capable of.

The only way for Greeks to stay true to themselves was to change, and astonishingly, they largely succeeded in doing this. Tyranny remained a temporary, transitional phenomenon, albeit a very significant one in a number of cities for the restoration of order and economic consolidation. These were two preconditions for the *poleis'* continued existence as free communities—and in some cases for the realization of the early stages of democracy. There is historical evidence of tyranny in thirty city-states, but the actual number was surely higher.

With the benefit of hindsight, crisis and consolidation appear to be the two most significant trends in the seventh and sixth centuries BC. But at the time, they occurred only for short periods and only here and there— no matter how often or how long crisis may have overshadowed the rest of life, and no matter how many attempts were made to achieve consolidation.

In order to come to a better understanding of this historical period, it is useful to distinguish between two overlapping phases, the second of which commenced around 600. This division de-emphasizes tyranny, whose approximate heyday was from 650 to 550 BC. (Only in Athens, where a tyranny was set up relatively late, did this political form exceed those historical boundaries by about four decades, until 510.) This division is determined by the time when various communities began to be able to rectify crises on their own. In the seventh century, the ability to take political action and make political decisions seems to have been restricted to details and small-scale problems.

By around 600, however, it became possible to subject the social order of the *poleis* itself to fundamental reconsideration and comprehensive reform. Citizenries were able to transform themselves. In many cities, especially smaller ones, this meant little more than the restoration of good relations between the leading class (in so far as its members had indeed committed abuses) and the rest of the community. In other cities (and these are the more interesting and exciting cases), people seem to have come to realize that only the build-up of a strong counter-force could restrain the arbitrary exercise of authority and the ambitions of the leading class. If the *polis* was to do without a ruler, and elected officials were not to be allowed to gain too much power, then the community as a whole would have to flex its muscles. Broad segments of society—or to use an expression from the time: those in the middle—would have to become more involved in the running of the *polis*.

In the archaic period, the 'middling citizens' were primarily seen as those who occupied a politically centrist position between two quarrelling parties. They were not involved and tried to avoid having to enter the fray. The amount of property they owned varied. Solon, for example, placed himself between the quarrelling parties, but that does not tell us anything about his (presumably substantial) wealth. At the same time, those who occupied a middle position politically could only achieve long-term results if they allied themselves with broader classes of people, who socially stood in the middle, for example, owners of medium-sized farms. This was the sense in which Aristotle would later use the term. For him, the middle ones were normally the people best suited to care about and for the city. Affluent artisans and traders may well have felt a sense of connection with them. Even if they did not enjoy the same prestige as property owners, they did not necessarily have to be excluded from politics.

But whether we define the term politically or sociologically, those in the middle had the potential of developing into an alternative to the often failing regimes of the aristocracy. The foundation of the community could thus be expanded, and the common interest in restricting the arbitrary exercise of power and establishing balance could make itself heard. Various forces seem to have pushed in this direction. We can recognize the phenomenon, albeit without being able to trace its development in detail.

In any case, arrangements often arose in which the members of these classes of people achieved greater opportunities to participate in decision-making. Such arrangements were the precursors of democracy. As of the early fifth century, a term emerged for them: *isonomia*, which can be roughly translated as 'order of equality'. The earliest surviving instance of this order (though not yet the word) occurs on the island of Chios early in the mid-sixth century. There a new type of council was instituted, elected by the people and apparently juxtaposed to a council of aristocrats. Aristotle would later write that, where popular assemblies could not be frequently convened, the council was 'the most democratic organ'.

The process that led to these new arrangements had in a certain sense been set in motion previously. The social boundaries between aristocrats and other property owners were fluid, aristocratic pride notwithstanding. Within communities that were virtually closed to outsiders, as many factors bound people together as divided them. People sat together in popular assemblies and fought side by side in the phalanx. What could have seemed more logical than to compensate for the weaknesses of aristocratic leadership by giving others a major say in politics? Yet it was not enough for citizens to participate in voting occasionally, whenever opportunities arose. If community was truly to receive a new foundation, they would have to be regularly engaged in politics, and more was needed for this to come about than just suitable institutions. To put it succinctly, a new type of citizen needed to evolve. Men who did not have the same amount of leisure as aristocrats and who were not used to operating in the public sphere had to become citizens in the more demanding sense of the word, with all the duties and expectations the term 'citizen' came to imply among the Greeks. Such men had to reorient their lives and rededicate a not insignificant amount of their time. They also, among many other things, had to acquire new knowledge and abilities, cultivate a good sense of judgement and community, and see the *polis* in an entirely new light. This was only possible thanks to an intense process of political thought, in which such men themselves had to take part.

The Greek intellectuals were here challenged in a specific way. With few exceptions, there was no monarch to engage their services. That left them free from any dependencies, and they came to play a very significant role that went beyond mere insight and institutional understanding. Wherever power was largely disconnected from authority, a vacuum arose, and there was a great need for individuals who could offer convincing words of warning and advice without being influenced by personal interests. They could be poets or priests at the oracle at Delphi or simply elders whose wisdom had proved itself over time. Such people occupied a third, neutral position, and thus they were called upon when tensions or stalemates seemed to yield no other way out than violence or tyranny. Sometimes, they were given special authority as *katartistēres* ('bringers into order') to resolve crises. On some occasions, the results even included radical redistributions of wealth.

And that was not all. Since the ultimate goal was to make the community capable of maintaining order on its own, a balance needed to be found for the diverse forces within it. Or to put it a different way: a concept of the proper order of the *polis* was necessary. This was an urgent issue, and no energy was spared in finding a solution, which, after a long period of experimentation and effort, the Greeks in fact did.

A problem this fundamental must have occupied people's minds to an extent that exceeded the narrow realm of politics. After all, the issue of order as the proper relationship between diverse forces could also be observed in other realms, and the Greeks began to look for analogies. They took a new interest in the cosmos, and philosophy and science began to emerge as disciplines. They could draw upon the wealth of knowledge, for example, which had been collected and processed over centuries in Babylon. Still, the questions that were asked now were specifically Greek. This was the genesis of pre-Socratic philosophy.

Political thinkers had to prepare broad segments of the citizenry if they wanted to enlist them against domineering and often power-hungry aristocrats. Such thinkers had been accustomed to making their ideas public anyway, but now they had to convince a wider audience and to make themselves understood more broadly. In order to attain the necessary support, they had to awaken in previously uninterested middle classes a sense of responsibility for the community. They had to call them to action, pass on knowledge, and show them how to convert dissatisfaction into demands. What helped them was the appeal of the public sphere, which had previously been occupied by aristocrats. Getting involved in politics was the only way for members of small communities of property owners to improve their social status.

Starting in the seventh century, and coming to fruition in the sixth, a substantial change in mentality must have taken place, more or less everywhere in Greece, even in those *poleis* still led by aristocratic oligarchies. It was a process of learning that went deeper than just intellect with all its irritations. Historical evidence suggests that the Greeks' story in this period was not least one of fear.

Chester Starr has written that the time around 700 was conditioned by 'general stresses', the widespread experience of excessive psychological pressures, and he cites the sudden appearance of various monsters in Greek art. Starr draws a connection with E. R. Dodds's observation that a culture of guilt was beginning to spread. For a long time Greeks had emphasized their own personal rights and honour; now the question of guilt pushed itself to the fore. Worries about guilt and pollution, suggested already in the *Odyssey*, now became more prominent. For example, the presence of a murderer whose crime had gone unpunished caused pollution that threatened entire cities. The *polis* began to be perceived as a community of fate, more urgently than even for Hesiod, and that was reason enough to find and try such a murderer, if he refused to leave voluntarily. It was a way of showing everyone that murder was a crime not just against the victim and his surviving relatives, but against the whole citizenry. Hence the city also became a community of collective responsibility. It is possible that the oracle at Delphi encouraged this belief, but it also offered potential solutions to communities seeking advice so that people would not be paralysed by desperation. Experts emerged who knew the rituals of cleansing the polluted. In a sense, the general feeling of unease was a correlative of the development of so many new possibilities that exceeded so many boundaries. If Greeks at the time had the opportunity of adopting mythical beasts from the art of the Orient, the broader context that had opened up this possibility made them seem topical as well.

Ultimately, the sum total of the experiences Greeks had with tyrants, factional quarrels, and civil strife—with the various failures easily suffered by persons and groups with lofty ambitions—must have gradually encouraged a reorientation within and between the small, face-to-face communities. They stood by themselves, and yet they were not alone, being embedded, as they were, in a pan-Hellenic public sphere. Were such activities really inevitable? Was there no choice but to suffer them? And was it worthwhile? Did one have to take part? Might it not be more reasonable to choose moderation and trust in Zeus' justness?

Indeed, might it not even be possible to determine what such justice consisted of? The Greek search for the golden mean in so many different areas was, no less than their interpretation of the cosmos, an index of how seriously Greeks took such questions to heart. They also began to appropriate the *nomoi*, a term that describes a variety of concepts, including conventions, customs, and laws—concepts that could be derived from what was generally customary and considered proper. Often such concepts needed to be shaken up in the face of new opportunities, and warnings about the need to keep one's feet on the ground and stay moderate must gradually have found clear resonance. People lived in close proximity to one another; escalations of conflicts were dangerous.

In order to discover the proper order of things and restore equilibrium, people turned, as they almost always do, to the past. There was no source of authority that could have embraced innovation as such. Disappropriated and heavily indebted farmers, in particular, had to argue in terms of restoration, and indeed the possibility of restoring a good old order represented the only serious hope that things would get better. Such beliefs offered support to the *katartistēres*, who promised 'to straighten things out'. As the middle classes in many places came to grow more politically active, this change likely followed a similar expectation. The challenge was to find a political way of securing the restored order of the *polis*.

Yet in communities where a great number of things needed to be balanced among the citizens themselves, it was also necessary to be very clear about ethical principles and their relative importance. New standards had to replace traditional prejudices, according to which the leaders, who had superior experience and knowledge, were supposedly also morally excellent, the 'good' or the 'best' (*aristoi*) in every respect. Justice, moderation, and perhaps even wisdom needed to be added to the idea of *aretē*, excellence. We perceive exactly such a process of reconceptualization in the rich lyric poetry of the time. The social form of the symposium, which had been adopted from the Orient, served as a forum for such rethinking through song.

It was primarily in lyric poetry, too, that the concerns of the autonomous members of this society of free men found expression—and a means of maintaining their position. Lyric poetry publicly articulated annoyance and anger, self-assurance and confidence. It was an enterprise that resonated in many ways and probably contributed, through the highest artistic means, to the Greeks' ability to cope with their difficult existence.

Much speaks for the idea that ambition and energy were redirected, and one phenomenon that had always played a large role in Greek society blossomed even more: the so-called 'agonistic impulse', or competitiveness (from *agōn*, competition). The many sporting and performative contests (in music and dance) already in existence were expanded. In the sixth century, the Greeks added competitions similar to the Olympic Games on the Corinthian Isthmus, in Nemea and Delphi, as well as the Panathenaic Games in Athens. The latter were established by a tyrant, and a tyrant could also have turned an older competition on the isthmus into a pan-Hellenic contest. A variety of new disciplines were also introduced, including boxing in 688 and chariot races in 680 BC. On the margin of such sporting events, poets and singers also had the chance to compete with their songs before ever wider audiences.

Hoplite or phalanx warfare, which emerged in the seventh century, was also carried out as a competition, virtually in the form of tournaments, which were admittedly very bloody. These events probably also absorbed energies that could not be used elsewhere, given the Greeks' general lack of interest in conquests.

The cultivation of everyday life can probably also be considered a way in which Greeks relieved the pressures of political conflict. Apart from social gatherings, architecture, sculpture, and vase painting engaged people's attention, money, and passion. It was around this time that the *kouroi*, the marvellous statues of male youths, appeared. Their artistic form had been borrowed from Egypt but was significantly modified.

Figure 5. Remains of the Temple to Apollo at Corinth, *c.*540 BC.

In general, society succeeded in preserving what had long been nearest and dearest to Greek hearts: autonomy, freedom, and the division into numerous small-sized *poleis*. What the Greeks produced in this period was part of a unique process. We have no reason to suspect that a single directing force was behind this development—where would it have come from, given the hundreds of Greek cities? Nonetheless, a lot of impulses seem to have proceeded in the same direction. The basic traits of the world of *poleis* apparently had such solid foundations that they could not simply be broken up. As strange as it might sound, something about the Greeks made them averse to autocratic forms of rule. It is hard to say whether that was truer of those who would not just have endured but would have borne such rule, or of those who would have had to devote all their energy to maintaining it. In any case, too much in Greek society was based on presence, directness, concrete straightforwardness, and homogeneity in the formation of character. No one wanted to become a means to an end, let alone a distant one—even if the end was one's own. The Greeks had a low tolerance of those aspiring to power. Thus the tendencies that could have led to a build-up of power were stopped short. Even if such power might have arisen here and there, the 'communicating pipelines' in the system would elsewhere have brought forth forces to oppose it.

Nonetheless, if there ever was to be an end to crisis, the citizens would have to be enabled to restore equilibrium in the *polis* despite all the upheavals. Citizens were required to develop a type of reason that was not just a means to an end but able to set norms, and for this they needed to understand the basic principles of a just order—until those in the middle could eventually play their proper role. The Greeks obviously succeeded in this, and as a result redundant sources of energy sought outlets causing less resistance: in festivals and competitions, art and social life. All in all, Greek culture found the means to continue to develop for the sake of freedom.

By the sixth century BC—and in some places, depending on local circumstances, already in the seventh—the Greek world also experienced economic consolidation. Those most affected were the farmers. They seem to have profited from better protection by tyrants and the intervention of mediators. But the exact details cannot be reconstructed.

The artisan class also flourished. The circles of those practising a trade expanded. People learned new techniques, became more specialized, and worked less at the behest of individual families and more for a competitive market. The desire for luxury goods stimulated production. On the Acropolis in Athens, a number of offerings attest to the affluence of artisans. We do not know how quickly the use of slaves spread, the earliest evidence for large-scale purchase of slaves (and thus for 'chattel slavery') refers to the island of Chios in the sixth century. And the income that Greeks earned as mercenaries in the armies of the Orient could hardly have been insubstantial.

Partly as a result of the founding of colonies, trade increased. Most of the profits went to the aristocracy. They or their sons often went out on diverse expeditions, but they were also involved in the financing of ships and the costs—and gains—of long-distance trade. Long distance enterprises overseas must also have been the source of the well-attested wealth of some nouveaux riches. We should not underestimate the extent and significance of these activities but, on the whole, the aristocracy pursued them without a great deal of effort. No matter how rich trade and piracy may have made some individuals, social status was still primarily a matter of owning landed property (as the basis for self-sufficiency) and of proving one's worth in politics, battle, and competition with one's peers.

By the second half of the sixth century, public squares in towns were being used for commercial purposes. The agora partially became a marketplace. Roads and harbours were improved, and measures taken to protect against piracy. At the beginning of the century, Corinth built

Figure 6. A tetradrachm, worth 4 drachmas, with an image of Athena on the obverse and an owl and the first three letters of the word 'Athenian' on the reverse (*c.*525 BC).

the Diolkos, a paved track for ships to be moved across the isthmus between the Corinthian and Saronian gulfs, allowing seafarers to avoid the dangerous circumnavigation of the Peloponnesian peninsula. Courts and government buildings, aqueducts and fountains were also constructed.

In the first half of the century, *poleis* such as Aegina, then Corinth and Athens began minting coins. Their worth was based on varying systems of weight. The idea may have come from the Lydians in western Anatolia and perhaps others. Previously livestock had been the Greeks' most common measure of value. In practice, they often paid for goods and services with small skewers called *oboloi* or *obeliskoi*, rings, and other pieces of metal. Six *oboloi* made a handful, the original meaning of the word 'drachma'. Bars of metal were used for larger sums. Solon wrote of much silver and gold being in the hands of rich men. Now, in the early sixth century, Greeks began to produce drachmas and other types of coins. They were made of silver and stamped with images and often the names of communities (in the genitive).

Such coins were too valuable to be used in retail transactions, and archaeological evidence suggests that they seem to have been seldom used in long-distance trading. (Athenian coins were the exception, but Athens was so rich in silver that this was probably a case of silver being exported rather than used as a means of payment.) The most plausible assumption is that the coins served to pay tribute (for example, to the Persian king) and contributions, duties, and taxes to temple and government treasuries. Conversely, governments used coins to redistribute surpluses to citizens as well as to cover the cost of public projects and the salaries of mercenaries. The imprinted names of communities probably originally referred not to the issuers, but to the owners, who worked with coins and for whom they soon became an expression of pride. In any case, the practice of minting coins spread like wildfire—even if people only gradually discovered the many advantages of using money for trade. Thus, Carthage, another commercial powerhouse, only began minting coins in the fourth century BC, and they too seem to have been used mostly for paying mercenaries. How intense relations to the East were at this time is impossible to determine.

There is no doubt that differences between Greek cities increased in the seventh and especially the sixth centuries BC. There were uneven concentrations of both ambition and wealth, and larger *poleis* might try to make smaller ones dependent on themselves. Those who were on the periphery were less affected by the spirit of the times. Sparta had already achieved great power by the eighth century, but by the end of the sixth it had a serious rival in Athens. The colony of Sybaris in lower Italy was said to have dominated twenty-five *poleis*, and the tyrant of Samos, Polycrates, to have ruled portions of the Aegean. Still, the plurality of small *poleis* survived.

The political framework in which they were embedded remained largely untouched, and serious external challenges never materialized. For example, when a tribe of horsemen, the Cimmerians from southern Russia, raided and plundered Asia Minor (*c.*675 BC), destroying the Phrygian Empire, they sacked a number of Greek cities. But they then withdrew as quickly as they had come.

Nonetheless, during the sixth century, conditions on the periphery of the *polis* world began to shift. In Asia Minor, the ascendant Lydian Empire began to exercise more and more control over most of the Greek cities on the coast. There was no joint resistance. The philosopher Thales suggested that the cities unite to form a single *polis*, but that idea fell on deaf ears. Only Miletus was able to fend off the Lydians. On the other hand, the Lydians seem to have been content with exacting tribute and took little interest in the internal affairs of the Greek *poleis*, which, therefore, were generally able to come to terms with them without making huge concessions. Their capital Sardis was a day's ride away from Ephesus, and Lydian kings made generous gifts to Greek temples and sought advice from the oracle at Delphi. Greek aristocrats married into the Lydian royal family. The leading Attic family of the Alcmeonidae was said to have owed much of their wealth to the Lydian King Croesus. Overall, Greeks and Lydians seem to have enjoyed a fairly close relationship.

When the Persians defeated the Lydians soon after the middle of the sixth century and subjugated the whole of Asia Minor, the Ionian Greeks suddenly found themselves confronted by an entirely foreign power. It was then that the inhabitants of Phocaea and Teos simply left their homes. The philosopher Bias of Priene, one of the Seven Sages, even advised all Ionians to emigrate and take possession of Sardinia, where they could live as free men and rule over a large area. But they refused. Once again, only the Milesians succeeded in escaping subjection by the Persians—by forging an alliance with them, however one-sided. Yet the Persians, too, seem to have been content with indirect rule, via Greek tyrants, and the exacting of tribute. The conquerors had no interest in choking the life out of the Greek *poleis*. And they had few ambitions to expand their power beyond the coastline. These conditions only changed when the Greeks of Asia Minor decided to shake off Persian domination in 500 BC.

In the West, the Phoenician colony of Carthage seems to have tightened and expanded its power during the sixth century. One of its goals was to limit Greek influence in western Sicily, another to seize additional parts of the North African coast. By conquering Sardinia, Carthage could have tried to hinder Greek access to Massalia, just as it was an alliance between Carthage and the Etruscans that led to the failure of the Phoecaean colony Alalia on Corsica. Nonetheless, although foreign powers were increasingly making their presence felt, the Greeks still had ample space in which they could act freely. They also had internal problems of their own and were hardly cut off from the rest of the world.

Our information about the events of the period is piecemeal, and we only have a vague idea where the individual pieces fit in the overall mosaic. The dates, even of Athenian history, are no more than approximate. The only certain chronological dates before the late sixth century are the solar eclipses of 648 (mentioned by Archilochus) and 585 (predicted by Thales of Miletus); the latter happened during a battle between Persians and Lydians.

Our knowledge of the seventh and sixth centuries BC is thus very limited. Fifth-century historiography hardly reached back that far. Our most important sources are contemporaneous poems, including those of the great Athenian reformer Solon. The rest of the historical record consists of scattered fragments. With the exception of Sparta, Athens, and Corinth, none of the many hundreds of Greek city-states left behind a record that would permit us to write at least an outline of its history. All we can do is draw some general conclusions and try to tie them in various ways to our sources.

In general, we can assume that the seventh and sixth centuries were a period of extreme change and volatility. In *Works and Days*, Hesiod saw this as an expression of Zeus' will: 'Mortal men are unmentioned and mentioned, spoken and unspoken of, according to great Zeus's will... For easily he makes strong, and easily he opposes the strong; easily he diminishes the conspicuous and magnifies the inconspicuous, and easily he makes the crooked straight and withers the proud—Zeus who thunders on high, who dwells in the highest mansions.' Solon must have been of a similar mindset when he wrote that one should be content with his 'god-given wealth', that is, probably, one's own honestly earned or inherited property. The elegiac poetry of Theognis of Megara is full of eloquent laments from people who were among the losers. Where there were opportunities to profit, there were also huge risks of losing even what had been invested. Everything was up in the air and subject to change. Greeks had many reasons to feel dissatisfied, even despairing. Try as one might, one would perhaps have success, perhaps not. And people were essentially unscrupulous, though perhaps diminishingly so. The sage Pittacus of Mytilene is said to have placed ladders in the temples of Lesbos so that citizens would have a concrete image of the ups and downs of human fortune. The lesson to be learned was modesty and humility.

Thus, however we look at it, it seems hard to comprehend that the Greek world gradually succeeded in reordering itself even at a time when massive changes were still stirring everything up and causing great confusion.

15

Polis Individualism and the Pan-Hellenic Context: The Agonistic Impulse

Greeks everywhere had a number of things in common: more or less the same gods, the same language, the same ways of life—and the fact that they wanted to live in small, independent cities. But the small size and tight nature of Greek communities was only possible because of the wide open space before and between them. Everywhere Greek land opened onto the sea, beyond which other coastlines were visible. What could have been more natural than to take to the waves during the spring and summer, when the weather was good? In the *Odyssey*, Homer says, every Phaeacian had a boat of his own and a shed in which to keep it dry. Greek reality was no doubt somewhat different from this fantasy island. Still, when writing of 'sea-surrounded Ithaca', Homer speaks of 'many ships, new and old', so that Odysseus' son Telemachus has no problem borrowing one when he sets off to try to learn something of his father's fate. The ship he procures was easy to man as well, and this was probably no exception. The ownership of boats thus seems to have been quite common.

Aristocrats could increase their wealth relatively easily by engaging in foreign raids. The danger of being robbed by strangers is a constant element in Homer's works. The aged King Nestor of Pylos even boasts about how much livestock he stole as a young man. In the underworld, Odysseus asks the spirit of Agamemnon whether he was lost at sea or in defense of his own town. 'Or did hostile men strike you down on land as you drove off their flocks and herds?' Greek raiders overran and burned down unfortified cities and villages, killing the men and distributing the women and goods among them so that, in Odysseus' words, 'as far as I could determine no man lacked an equal share'. According to the historian Thucydides, the most ambitious among the Greeks led these raids, either for their own profit or to provide for the weaker members of their communities. So the spoils could also be divided unequally. In any case, robbery brought fame, not shame. Among the Attic laws of the sixth century BC, associations of people 'voyaging for plunder' were listed directly alongside merchants and associations concerned with matters of burial and sacrifice. All of them were subject to the same rules.

But the Greeks probably also took to the seas to secure raw materials and acquire fashionable items in exchange for goods they had previously brought into their possession. The more trade increased, the more active Greeks became in combating piracy, at least in parts of the Aegean.

It was common practice in both the Greek and non-Greek worlds to conclude relationships of mutual hospitality (*xenia*, 'guest friendship') and marriage alliances. Guests and their hosts typically exchanged gifts, and the rooms where such gifts were kept were the pride of every household, proof of their owners' far-reaching connections. There was a story to be told about every one of these treasures. Relations of *xenia* were passed down through the generations. Pure curiosity was probably another reason behind the Greek propensity for travel, and before long a certain knowledge of the world became a must for members of the upper classes. That accorded well with the prevailing entrepreneurial spirit.

Large numbers of people regularly convened in particular cities, most prominently Chalcis and later Miletus and Athens, to make acquaintances and swap information. Travellers who spread news back and forth concentrated on major population centres, which in turn gained in interest. A number of cities sent representatives to the festival of Apollo on the island of Delos. Another important meeting place was Delphi. At more or less regular intervals of two to four years, a growing number of Greeks congregated at Olympia and other sacred sites. There, they took part in athletic contests to honour the gods or merely watched and exchanged views with the great number of other spectators who were eager to make new contacts. The significance of athletic and other competitions and the need for meeting places in this extremely polycentric world were mutually reinforcing. Perhaps as early as 600 BC, a general truce was in force throughout Greece while the Olympic Games were under way, granting safe passage to all who wanted to participate. Indeed, the first common chronological measure—generally acknowledged throughout the Greek world—was the Olympiad, counted in units of four years and beginning in 776 BC.

Life in the *polis* would have been inconceivable without the relief and enhancement offered by connections with faraway places. In other words, the *polis* depended upon the pan-Hellenic context, especially for the aristocrats. Near and far complemented one another like land and sea, winter and summer, just as, in different ways, freedom and dependence, the household and the *polis*, and, in yet another way, ritual and myth. While cult rituals with more or less established forms for honouring the gods were a matter for local *poleis*, the poets' play with the gods seems to have flourished in the free atmosphere of a pan-Hellenic public that was not limited to specific cities.

Within their small communities, Greeks had their estates, their families, and their self-sufficient basis (as far as was possible). One needed to be at home somewhere, in a circle where one's own status and actions were recognized, where one could participate in discussions and decisions, and where one was also part of a cult community. 'There is nothing dearer to a man than his own country and his parents,' Odysseus proclaims, 'however splendid a palace he may have in a foreign country.' The lyric poet Alcaeus of Mytilene on Lesbos, who had been forced to flee from his home town, longed for the cries of the herald and the consultation among citizens; although he called them *allalokakoi* (nasty with each other), they were still his fellow citizens. His father and grandfather had participated in all aspects of their home community. Hence those in exile missed a major component of what made life worthwhile: living as an equal among his fellow citizens, participating directly in a collectivity. It was not homesickness per se or material need, but the truncation of a sense of self that caused such pain to the many exiles. Greeks who wanted to count for something were not private individuals, but citizens tied into a city as if it were a familial setting— including all of the quarrels that arise and often escalate, especially among relatives.

As Aristotle later put it, the *polis* was not supposed to exceed certain dimensions; it had to remain *eusynoptos*, or easy to survey. How else could the voice of a herald be heard throughout it? How else could citizens know one another well enough to reach just decisions and avoid mere chance when assigning offices? 'A very populous city', Aristotle wrote, 'can rarely, if ever, be well governed.' Greeks were well attuned, indeed trained to live in *poleis* of such limited size. They wanted to be closely associated with one another, on an eye-to-eye level, in direct contact, despite the constant alternation of attraction and repulsion. By contrast, they had no desire to become anonymous parts of a larger whole. One major component of living in communities in which people directly coexisted with their equals was the common discussion of all-important matters and the balancing of interests. No matter how abstractly they came to conceive of other matters, the Greeks could not ignore the *polis*—which virtually meant themselves. Yet the need to maintain the autonomy of *poleis* that were located so close to and related so intimately with each other required the precise limitation of the circle of membership in the community.

We do not know how many Greeks regularly moved beyond their home cities. A larger radius of action could indeed have been the basis for or a manifestation of prominence. At any rate, it is difficult to imagine how everyday Greek life was divided among various spheres. Changing constellations certainly were significant when someone visited another city, when he was both foreign and familiar, and viewed his own city from the outside. One met, conversed, played, and drank with men from the most diverse areas. Access to the sea also allowed Greeks to bypass their immediate neighbours. Regional public spheres arose and gradually expanded into a pan-Hellenic context. Hans Schaefer wrote of 'a delicate and intricate mesh of internal Greek solidarity'. The rise of 'Hellene' as a description for all Greeks is an expression of that feeling.

Only Greeks—and not, for example, Macedonians—were admitted to the major competitions; members of the ruling dynasty were the only Macedonians considered to be of Greek descent. A clear boundary ran between Greeks and non-Greeks (barbarians), even if it was possible to cross it in many ways (for example, through friendship and intermarriage), and despite the respect that Greeks felt for cultures such as Egypt.

The common Hellenic public sphere was a forum in which individuals and cities could achieve fame and earn honour or, alternately, embarrass themselves. In the *Odyssey*, for example, the Phaeacian King Alcinous wants his visitor, Odysseus, to receive the best possible impression: 'So come, you finest of the Phaeacian dancers, and play your parts before the stranger, so that when he has come home again he may tell his kinfolk how much we excel other men in sailing and running and dance and song.' The Phaeacians, Alcinous says, were not good at everything, but in general they loved 'feasting, and the music of strings and dancing; changes of garments, warm baths, and the pleasurable sofas'. The king wanted others to know this, although he had no interest in attracting visitors.

Even Telemachus' complaint that the people of Ithaca should fear the blame of their neighbours and be ashamed for deserting his father's family in its misery attests to the emphasis Greeks placed on their reputation in the eyes of others. Because of the relative proximity of others and the many channels of communication between communities, other people's judgements did indeed make themselves felt. People regarded their honour to be besmirched if they came from a city with a bad reputation. In an almost familial sense, one felt responsible for one's fellow citizens. This was almost literally true: when abroad, one could be held accountable for the outstanding debts of a member of one's *polis* and be forced to offer property or even one's own liberty as security until the debts were paid. Solon wrote that he would rather come from an obscure village than to be subjected to the talk Athens incurred because in a war it had yielded Salamis to the much smaller Megara. Cities were constantly competing with one another. But what, precisely, was at stake?

The story of the wooing of Agariste shows both how widely Greek relations ranged and the extent to which the pan-Hellenic public was fascinated by spectacular events. Around 560 BC the tyrant of Sicyon, Cleisthenes, having just won the chariot race at Olympia, announced that he wanted to marry his daughter to 'the best of the Hellenes'. Those who considered themselves worthy were to present themselves within sixty days. The wedding was to take place a year later. Herodotus, whom we have to thank for the story (which seems reliable at least in its basic outline), reports that thirteen suitors arrived, all of whom were very proud of themselves and their home cities. They came not just from the Peloponnese and Athens, but from Italy (Sybaris and Siris), from the Ionian Sea (Epidamnus), and elsewhere. Herodotus lists them by name.

The first thing Cleisthenes did was to ask about their families and native cities. Afterwards, individually and collectively, he tested their bravery, temperament, education, and character. To this end, he had built a racetrack and a wrestling ring (*palaestra*). The most important tests, though, were how they behaved at meals (and presumably at the symposium) and festivals. The emphasis, of course, was not just on table manners, but on dancing, singing, and the capacity for intelligent conversation.

In the end, the tyrant sacrificed a hundred cattle and invited both the suitors and the entire city to a banquet. Megacles of Athens was chosen as the winner. He would go on to be the father of Cleisthenes of Athens, who would restructure his city through comprehensive reform near the end of the sixth century. One of his nieces, also called Agariste, was the mother of Pericles. As a gesture of consolation, the other suitors, losers in the competition, received generous quantities of silver.

Herodotus reports that the clan of the Alcmeonidae, to which Megacles belonged, owed its 'fame throughout Greece' to this event. Megacles' father, by the way, had also won a chariot race at Olympia, and, according to another popular anecdote, he owed his wealth to the Lydian king, who, out of gratitude, had promised him 'as much gold as he could carry on his person'. Megacles stuffed gold into the puffs of his tunic, his broad-cut boots, and his mouth. Even his hair was full of gold dust. 'He resembled anything other than a man,' the anecdote ran. The Lydian king found that amusing and gave him even more gold. Although Cleisthenes of Sicyon had set out to find the best man among the Greeks, another suitor, Hippocleides, almost won the day thanks to his political connections. He was related to the ruling house of the tyrants of Corinth.

In the close confines of the *polis*, people were politically engaged, making decisions and occupying offices. In the vast space of the pan-Hellenic public sphere, by contrast, they were part of a larger society, free and not bound beyond relations of friendship. In the *polis*, politics was potentially serious; elsewhere, one appeared in front of an audience and was oneself a spectator. In the *polis*, one was confronted with the lower and middle classes, abroad one lived among the aristocrats of other *poleis* and those who emulated them. As a result, there one attracted attention not so much through political achievement in the service of the *polis* as through sporting triumphs, extravagance, adventures, luxury, and the display of wealth (not least in raising horses), as well as beauty and grace. All this contributed to the enhancement of nobility, to the all-round qualities that constituted good style. At the risk of simplification and overgeneralization, here the spectacular and not the political occupied centre stage.

Of course, friendships could have political consequences that crossed local boundaries. Networks of mutual support criss-crossed the world of *poleis*, and *xenoi* (guest friends) facilitated diplomatic interaction between the *poleis*. The worse the internal fighting within the *poleis* became, the greater the number of exiles and refugees who often tried with the help of their hosts to force their home cities to allow them to return. We know of cases from the sixth century in which usurpers such as Peisistratus of Athens came to power with the help of allies from other cities. Once, when the city of Argos rejected such a request from the island of Aegina, a private initiative among Argive aristocrats organized support for the Aeginetans. Communities had their hands full trying to prevent their members from waging private wars. The communities themselves could be held accountable for any damage caused by their members, and they seem to have used this responsibility as leverage to acquire a monopoly on the waging of war.

It is difficult to measure what role the pan-Hellenic public sphere played in consolidating the world of *poleis*. Did it pressurize the cities to exercise the sort of moderation necessary to overcome the crises of the archaic period? One may indeed, like Telemachus in Homer, have felt ashamed of neighbours who tolerated injustice rather than resisting it. But how could the situation be changed? Warring factions within cities or tyrants who ruled with an iron fist would hardly have been bothered by public disapproval, let alone the disapproval of other cities. External support for quarrelling parties would only have made things worse. Or perhaps were broader circles of disinterested parties capable of offering impartial judgements about what was acceptable and what was not? Did something of this nature emerge over time? After all, communities suffered from others' conflicts, when exiles and refugees turned up on their doorsteps.

For all their autonomy the *poleis* were intimately connected; hence the broader public beyond the *polis'* borders must have been concerned with questions of justice and the right order—questions that always emerged when problems of civic coexistence became urgent, as is already vividly evident in the *Iliad*. In invoking *nomoi*, one could not restrict one's perspective to one's own home community. On the contrary, people had to look around to see how things were done elsewhere, perhaps even how they were done generally. What was widely established was most easily considered to be standard practice.

The more critical the situation became and the more Greece became a field of experimentation for the creators of institutions, the more people needed to compare their own customs with those of others, and those again with yet others. Why did something work in one place and not another? People asked for and offered advice, and enlisted mediators from abroad to help solve serious conflicts. Was it then perhaps not unavoidable that, in the face of the numerous conflicts within individual *poleis*, the pan-Hellenic public would form views about how to maintain extensive freedom while preserving the ability to coexist? Would not discussions among politically experienced men in such a wide public have tended to produce general insights into what was required in the political sphere? This was after all a period in which one still needed to discover and formulate what was right, before one could think of enacting laws. Moreover, the disruption caused by many conflicts and widespread economic misery set a high priority on restoring the previous social order (at most with some modifications to secure it). If, for example, tyrants never succeeded in establishing their own rule permanently as something that was obvious and as a given, would not experiences of cities that were not ruled by tyrants (whether no longer or not yet) have seemed particularly helpful? The search for a just order and the golden mean, for laws that ruled political life as well as the cosmos, must have been very resonant here. The pan-Hellenic public was probably one major source of support for the political thought of an era that was constantly concerned with finding a third position or a generally accept-able middle course between conflicting parties.

The 'customs of the Hellenes' also had to be maintained when *poleis* dealt with one another. Treaties needed to be reliable, and there had to be limits on raiding expeditions and the violence of warfare. Ideas about what was acceptable and what not in relations among *poleis* must have developed over time. The phalanx form of warfare was probably one instance that satisfied such needs. The Greek commonality—although allowing many Greek cities to wage wars amongst themselves, without considering these as civil wars (as happened only in the fourth century)—must at least have caused the avoidance of certain excesses, such as the razing of cities. The diversity and multitude of *poleis* was also a part of the Greek world that needed to be preserved. Wars themselves must have served an important function in holding the larger Hellenic community together.

If Greek cultural development was moving in a specific direction, then pan-Hellenic processes of forming opinions and changing mentalities must have been among its driving forces, based on common, agreed-upon conditions and established modes of exchange between the *poleis*. In short, the decisive factor in early Greek history was not just the small size of the *poleis*, but their general grounding in a pan-Hellenic context.

The pan-Hellenic public sphere was not marked by political unity—far from it. Accordingly, a general tendency of Greek character and society flourished in it that Burckhardt and Nietzsche tried to define as the 'agonistic impulse'. While legitimate objections to this concept have been raised, it does reflect a particular characteristic of the Greeks. Sports and contests occurred in other cultures, of course. In ancient Egypt, for instance, the pharaoh Amenophis II boasted that his skills as a horseman and a runner were second to none. Ingomar Weiler has written of 'an innate human disposition toward testing one's strengths in competition'. There is ample evidence of this disposition among so-called 'primitive peoples' in cultures such as Mesopotamia and elsewhere—there are even occasional indications that the competitors were naked, as they were in Greece. But many aspects of Greek compe-titions, starting with the way they were staged, are unique to the Greeks.

Greek competitions were open and offered equal chance to all, high and low, which could hardly have been the case with contests involving the Egyptian king, assuming these did, indeed, take place. Specifically Greek, too, was perhaps the fact that sporting events took place in the middle of the cities, in central squares or in *gymnasia* and *palaestrae*, and under the eyes of a general public. Unique as well were the pan-Hellenic games and the extent of the honours bestowed upon victors by their home cities. Those who triumphed were showered with glory—even city walls were sometimes torn down to construct a special entrance for them since it was considered beneath their dignity to enter the city through the usual gates. In Athens, they were given a lifelong invitation to the daily meal in the old city hall (*prytaneion*) at which the most important members of the community, holders of office representing the collective, convened. By 500 BC, intellectuals like Xenophanes were already mocking the excessive emphasis placed on sports, claiming that athletics were less useful to the city than what they themselves, the leading minds, could have contributed.

We might also see as typically Greek the extent to which religious festivals integrated agonistic elements. Both sporting and performative contests were held to honour and delight the gods, and the latter featured not just one, but several choruses. There were even preliminary contests to determine who would be allowed to compete in the final event. Many songs, and later tragedies and comedies, were composed uniquely for a given occasion. Each performance was supposed to spur others on to new heights, in line with Hesiod's idea of Eris, the 'good' goddess of competition. In any case, one typical characteristic of the Greeks was that athletics had a decisive influence on shaping the image of masculinity in their sculpture. The *kouroi* depicted naked men as well-toned, self-controlled, muscular human ideals without any indication of their social status or function. They represented only themselves, were nothing more than the best examples of young, ideal persons, and yet, precisely for that reason, stood for far more than even kings or officials.

Wherever we look in Greek society we find contests. On the level of daily life, we find it in the agora, where citizens came together; the less they were concerned with discussing objective problems, the more the agora became an arena for determining the rank of individuals. In a typical Greek symposium a topic was chosen for discussion or poetic elaboration so that one could see who was the best in illuminating it. Likewise, in his descriptions of the battles in the Persian Wars, Herodotus never fails to mention which warrior was the bravest or even the most

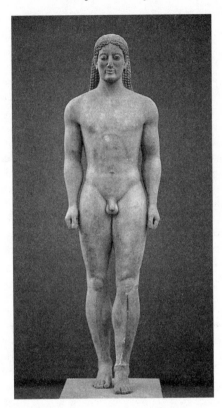

Figure 7. The *Kouros* of Anavyssos in Attica. The inscription underneath the statue reads: 'Halt and mourn at the monument of fallen Kroisos, killed by violent Ares while fighting in the front line' (*c.*530 BC, see also above, p. 68).

beautiful. In the sanctuary of Zeus, Hera, and Dionysus on Lesbos, a beauty contest was held for young women. The Greeks developed intricate procedures for determining who was, for instance, the best sculptor or the best general in the war against the Persians. They waged their wars much more in the spirit of an agonistic comparison than according to the theory of Clausewitz, who defined the objective of war as dictating one's own will to the enemy (provided that such a will even existed at the time). This tendency is already visible in Homer's epics that emphasize the heroes' *aristeia*, their effort to excel far beyond all others. The Greek inclination constantly to compare themselves with others could have been the result of the intensity of their social life. More precisely, it could have been triggered by the fact that the (friendly or inimical) interaction of people who were all supposed to be universally well developed was based on the principle of equality (in whatever circle), rather than that of superiority or inferiority within a hierarchically or functionally segmented society. That was true both of the *polis* and the larger pan-Hellenic sphere.

Additionally, and perhaps decisively, the agonistic impulse—especially during the archaic period—was characterized by a specific accentuation of individual ambition, which in turn was probably connected with the Greeks' special reliance on autonomy. In other words, the relative weakness of their social ties was a major factor in encouraging competition. We can distinguish between the desire to best others and the desire to rule over them. In many areas, the two can be synonymous. Even control of power or the power struggles resulting in tyrannies can be understood as a kind of contest. Nonetheless, victory in a contest remains something different from acquiring and securing political rule.

The Greek aristocrats could only become powerful within the relatively narrow confines of their own *polis*. But in the pan-Hellenic public sphere, before diverse spectators, they could only excel and try to be the best (in whatever discipline they happened to compete in).

In fact the Greek way of dealing with power offers a key to understanding the agonistic impulse. Much evidence suggests that, in general, the Greeks had little interest in forcing the power role on themselves, despite their often uninhibited struggles. They had difficulty providing the sorts of services needed to establish ties of obligation with many others, to keep them motivated and organized, to continually justify and re-establish their own power. They scorned, in Schiller's words, 'submission to those restraints which he, who would hereafter rule, must bear'. Personal autonomy and the corresponding desire to be self-sufficient were not just qualities of those who might have been dominated by others, but also of those who would potentially have established their domination. Where ties were difficult to form, and each individual primarily fended for himself, directly and (at least ideally) among equals, the concept of competition had to take centre stage again and again. As a result, the Greeks related to one another in a unique way. Situations of crisis, when major factional struggles came to a head, could undermine this form of interaction, but only temporarily. Thus, when the members of the broader classes sought a more central role in politics, they were less concerned with gaining power to advance their own (for example, material) interests than with attaining status within the city.

Some scholars have suggested that the moral ideas of the Greeks in this period were far more competitive (agonistic) than cooperative. Hence, when things became critical, struggles temporarily increased in intensity. At the same time and more significantly in the long run, much energy and ambition were diverted into the sphere of pure competition. The agonistic impulse was able to relieve pressures and provide a specific sense of meaning to Greek coexistence in both larger and smaller respects.

16

The Diversity of the *Poleis*: Sparta and Other Cities

Greek particularity manifested itself in very diverse forms in individual political units. Not all Greeks lived in *poleis*. Some, especially in western Greece, were organized into tribes (*ethnē*). In addition, among the several hundred *poleis*, many simply existed in their own small worlds. We know very little about either the *ethnē* or these sorts of *poleis*. Yet in contrast, other communities underwent a rapid process of change, although despite all commonalities they shared, each moved in an individual direction.

Sparta was a special case. The Spartans' ancestors who had founded and defined the community had immigrated from the north and eventually taken possession of Laconia, or more precisely, large parts of the Eurotas river plain. There they enslaved the original inhabitants. Something similar happened in a number of other places, for instance, Argos and Thessalia.

By the end of the eighth century BC, at the dawn of the period of colonization, the Spartans had also conquered the fertile neighbouring region of Messenia and subjugated those inhabitants who had not fled. Sparta thus controlled a third of the Peloponnese. Its rule, however, proved to be anything but secure. The Messenians rose up in the second half of the seventh century, and could only be re-enslaved after a long and difficult war that resulted in many casualties. This is almost all we know about conditions in early Sparta; the historical record is highly unreliable. Initially, though, the Spartans undoubtedly participated fully in Greeks customs and culture. But later there must have been major internal conflicts and a series of fundamental reforms aimed at ending both inner strife and the Second Messenian War. The Sparta that would play a leading role in Greece was different and is visible only from the mid-sixth century.

The exceptional situation in which Sparta found itself after the conquest of Messenia determined its further history. The original inhabitants of Laconia and especially the large area of Messenia—now enslaved and called helots—maintained relatively close ties among themselves. There was no comparison between them and slaves in other cities, often quite numerous, who were bought over the years at slave markets. Such slaves were too diverse in terms of origin, abilities, and status to be able to join together to take action or even stage rebellions. The helots, on the other hand, had lived together for a long time and had formed a relatively homogeneous population. They were not owned by individual Spartan citizens (Spartiates), although they were assigned to work for them. Instead, they were communal property. Every year, Sparta formally redeclared war on them so that they could be killed, if necessary, without causing problems. Young Spartans also spied on, attacked, robbed, and sometimes even murdered them. The Spartans had expanded old rites of initiation to include new functions so that young elite teams formed themselves into something resembling a police force. Despite such constant supervision, however, whenever Sparta's situation turned critical the threat of rebellion was always close at hand. Hence Sparta owed its existence primarily to the solidarity and superiority of its fighting forces.

We also know hardly anything about daily life on Spartan estates, which must often have been run by womenfolk and where perhaps some helots were privileged to supervise the others. At any rate, the Spartans took helots along as servants during campaigns, where they also fought as lightly armed troops. In the fifth century, Spartans even recruited hoplites from their ranks, who were later freed and occasionally given some citizen rights. In general, there must have been some differences among the helots, or at least the Spartans encouraged differing expectations. It is further possible that Laconian helots were better off than those in Messenia—although, on the other hand, it was once said of the former too that 'they would love to eat the Spartans, preferably raw'.

The Spartans had fewer problems with the communities of so-called *perioeci* who lived in the hills and mountains surrounding the fertile Spartan plains and along the coastlines. They managed their own affairs, were subject to tribute and conscription, and had to help secure the Spartan borders, but were otherwise not incorporated into the ruling community.

However the necessary changes might have unfolded in early Spartan history, by the sixth century Spartan life had become strictly regimented. The Spartiates, as those with full citizenship were known, tended to reside close to each other in five architecturally rather modest villages in the centre of Laconia, which were collectively called Sparta. They featured the men's rooming houses, where the twenty- to thirty-year-olds communally ate and slept. To spend a night hunting was acceptable, to spend it with one's wife less so, but impossible to prevent, as long as one did not get caught. Otherwise the men had to be constantly ready for war. Their daily lives were consumed with drills, sports, and hunting—and with choral song, dance, and social activities. Pindar praises Sparta for the wise council of its elders and the skill of its youth in handling the spear—both equally excellent—but also for its artful choral dancers and the spirit with which it celebrated festivals. Spartans do not seem to have been especially talkative. Instead, they favoured a 'laconic' brevity, though apparently peppered with ridicule and wit.

Young Spartans grew up in close community with their peers. At the age of seven, they were required to leave their parents' houses and were educated in 'herds' by older adolescents. Their education was extremely harsh, aimed at developing resistance to heat and cold, beatings, and various sorts of pain. Reading and writing were also part of the curriculum. All parts of this training were intended to produce men who were capable of a high degree of achievement for the community and were fully oriented towards it. Spartan education was not about individual autonomy, but rather subordination to a whole that was, in this case, much more than the sum of its parts. Incidentally, the girls' education too was entirely aimed at rendering them able to do what the community demanded of them, for instance, bearing healthy children. Unlike everywhere else in Greece, Spartan girls also participated in sports. It was part of their education, and like the boys, they did so naked.

Although older Spartiates were allowed to spend nights in their own homes, even after their thirtieth year they were still subject to demands of the community and spent much of their time going through drills, taking part in sports, and participating in social activities. According to Aristotle, Sparta was the only *polis* that trained its hoplites systematically—which presumably means constantly—for war. It was customary for older and younger Spartiates to develop intimate relationships. The fact that friends fought together in war boosted their will to fight. In any case, life in a community of peers was probably more interesting and fun than out in the countryside.

As a result, compared with those in other Greek cities, women in Sparta enjoyed a highly unusual degree of independence and permissiveness. Spartan women, no less than men, could commit adultery without impunity. Their clothes tended to be revealing, and they were said to delight in showing off their thighs. At least in Aristotle's day, they possessed large sections of land, which they were able to pass on to their heirs.

Originally, every Spartiate had been assigned a share (*klēros*) of land, and land was not in short supply. But inheritances changed the distribution of wealth. Some people became too poor to be able to contribute their share to communal meals. They were therefore excluded from full citizen rights, and that—together with fatalities in war—meant that over time the number of full citizens declined substantially. There were an estimated ten thousand Spartiates in the sixth century; by the fifth, there were only eight thousand, and by the end of that century, the number was down to approximately three thousand. The birth rate does not seem to have been high. Was this a consequence of the power of Spartan women? In the fourth century, we even find talk of women ruling Sparta. It is hard to understand that the Spartans were unwilling or at least unable to counter these trends. But perhaps the necessary measures would have encroached too drastically on the identity and rights of Spartan citizens.

Little as we really know about it, it is clear that in Sparta possibilities of development were able to unfold that were usually unreachable to other Greeks. In many respects, the Spartan community, by being an exception, illustrates the way in which so many things were usually connected in other Greek communities. It tried to cut itself off from the outside. Its citizens were not allowed to leave Spartan territory without permission, and foreigners were frequently expelled. The Spartans were famous for their unusual money. It consisted of iron bars so large that one needed a small wagon to transport any sum of significance.

The Spartans themselves traced their order back to a lawgiver named Lycurgus and believed that it had received the approval of Apollos's oracle at Delphi. In historical times it was considered divinely ordained and sanctioned by age-old traditions. True to their pious, exact ways, the Spartans followed it strictly. In a number of famous cases, the Spartan army was not able to leave the city despite an emergency because custom dictated that the festival of Apollo Carneius had to be celebrated on a specific date.

What we read in the oldest surviving Greek constitution, the 'Great Rhetra', usually attributed to Lycurgus, is most probably the result of reforms enacted in the first half of the seventh century BC. It focused on the political order, although it is difficult to see how it worked in practical terms. Uniquely, the Spartan state was headed by a pair of kings, whose office was hereditary. Next there was a council made up of the kings and twenty-eight other members, who had to be more than sixty years of age, held office for life, and were chosen by the assembly via a curious mixture of election and acclamation. Acclamation was usually used to signal approval of a single candidate, but among the Spartans it was applied in order to choose between several. The one who attracted the loudest cries of support was 'elected'. A group of men posted in a building at the far end of the city square, where they could hear everything but see nothing, decided the winner. They did not know in which order the candidates would be presented before the assembly—presumably this was decided by lot shortly beforehand—and were thus intended to judge objectively what number in the sequence had attracted the loudest shouting. The decisive factor here was the strength and decisiveness with which the citizens expressed their preference, and not, as was elsewhere the case, a majority of votes after corresponding counts or estimates.

Like the later 'popular councils', this 'council of elders' had directly elected members, although the latter held their posts for life; in addition, the minimum age requirement was very high, and the council's size was conspicuously small. The intention was obviously to concentrate in this council, aptly called *gerousia* (council of elders), as much experience, power, and capacity for action as possible. We do not know whether Sparta had leading families and whether perhaps their members enjoyed an advantage in elections. Later evidence attests that Spartans thought of themselves as equals (*homoioi*, literally peers), and they likely arrived at this self-conception much earlier in their history. The ideal of equality was behind the demands for a redistribution of land in the seventh century. (The point became moot once the conquest of Messenia was fully secured.) On the other hand, the oligarchic component of the Spartan order was probably already well established at that time.

The Spartan popular assembly was intended, as we read in the 'Great Rhetra', to have the decisive power (*kratos*)—presumably in those cases where the kings and the council were unable to agree. Otherwise, the assembly, whose members were neither allowed to speak nor to make proposals, were to 'respond in straight words', that is, more or less to give its approval to the council's decisions. It was not permitted to make 'crooked resolutions', the 'Great Rhetra' stipulated; otherwise the council had to make them invalid.

Along with the council members, five overseers or *ephors* were chosen. They held office for one year and are not mentioned in the 'Great Rhetra'. Whatever the original purpose of the office may have been, the *ephors* gradually came to represent the community, initially in opposi-tion to the kings. We do not know to what extent they had to act in unison or whether they could also block each other's actions. In any case, their influence was significant. As of the mid-sixth century, they largely determined Spartan policies. Every month, the kings and the *ephors* renewed an oath—the kings to use their office in accordance with the law, and the *ephors* to support the kings' authority as long as they did so. At the end of their year in office, the *ephors* had to render account to the popular assembly. Incidentally, in the realm of foreign affairs, the kings enjoyed much independence; for example, they were able to mobilize allies to wage their private wars.

But what was likely more important for Spartan politics than the city's political institutions was the fact that fixed principles very largely guided political activity and both obedience and a close focus on common interest limited people's room to manoeuvre. As a rule, there were few opportunities to develop independent opinions; rather, people were very willing to sign on to whatever crystallized as the general opinion, espe-cially among the group of leaders. One thought the way one did because one thought everyone else thought that way. Consensus was made all the easier because differences of opinion were—if possible—resolved in small circles of leaders. Hence the Spartans do not seem to have set too much store by debates. They commented that when speeches were held, one had often forgotten the beginning before the speaker had come to an end.

This community achieved an excellent reputation among the Greeks and became their leading *polis*. It was commonly referred to as *prostatēs tēs Hellados*, Greece's protector and advocate. Sparta's army was the finest in the land and considered invincible. As a result of the difficulties they had encountered in the Second Messenian War, the Spartans had been forced to introduce the highest degree of discipline into their ranks. Heroic individualism, supposedly cultivated in the past, was now frowned upon. The hoplites fought with the burden of the entire com-munity on their shoulders. To return either with the shield or on the shield was their credo. Anyone who had displayed cowardice was not going to find life very easy within the closely knit Spartan community.

In the face of constant threat from the helots, Sparta had to ensure that it concluded and maintained stable alliances with its many neigh-bours. The resulting system is often called the 'Peloponnesian League'. Sparta's diplomatic connections extended even further. Its conservatism

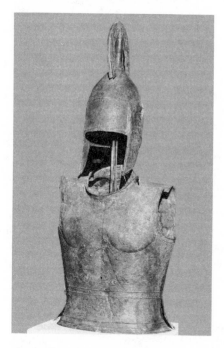

Figure 8. Helmet and cuirass from Argos (*c.*720 BC).

made it a coveted ally for aristocrats in a great number of cities. And on the whole, Sparta made moderate use of its power.

Yet, over time their concern with preserving tradition made the Spartans inflexible and reluctant to act. Because they placed such emphasis on their own special way of life, much that should have been a matter of mere technique and skill was tied to their identity. For example, for all their prowess in war, the Spartans never learned how to besiege enemy cities: this was simply contrary to their nature.

Argos, Sparta's great rival in the Peloponnese, also seems to have expanded in the mid-eighth century BC, under the rule of King Pheidon. The expansion was short-lived, but the city retained control over a relatively broad stretch of territory. Nonetheless, its political horizon did not usually extend beyond the Peloponnese and was fixated on neighbouring Sparta, against which it conducted a number of mostly unsuccessful wars.

Other cities rose above the others as centres of trade, points of origin for colonial expeditions, and specialists for specific types of artisanship— although, of course, they too essentially remained communities of property owners. They included Chalcis and Eretria on Euboea, Corinth, the 'charming sea-side metropolis' of Miletus, and the smaller but very active city of Phocaea on the western coast of Asia Minor. Led by Miletus, the cities of Asia Minor founded Naucratis in Egypt, which soon became a flourishing commercial site. Miletus and Phocaea were also unique in erecting a series of outposts according to a master plan that allowed them to control access to and effectively take possession of long stretches of coastline.

The island of Aegina was 'famous for its ships'. The city's power resided in its large fleet, whose might made itself felt more than once on the coastline of Attica, which lay across the waters on the mainland. For this reason, Aegina was a constant source of irritation for Athens. Owing to the island's lack of fertile land, the leading families could not depend on agriculture and turned to trade and piracy—with great success, as historical evidence of their wealth attests. At home, they maintained an exemplary aristocratic lifestyle.

Things were different again with Megara, which began sending out a wave of colonial expeditions after losing a significant portion of its fertile land to Corinth. Although it was constantly being squeezed between Corinth and Athens, remarkably—and in contrast to its defeat by much smaller Corinth—it won a war against Athens and was able for decades to maintain control over the disputed island of Salamis.

The inhabitants of the island of Chios are thought to have been the first Greeks to import slaves. The city lived from its flourishing trade. And an inscription dating from the mid-sixth century attests that broad segments of the citizenry enjoyed relatively far-reaching rights to participate in political decisions.

Further to the south, the island of Samos, according to Herodotus, possessed three of Greece's greatest architectural wonders. The first was the sanctuary of Hera, where in the course of some two centuries the Samians built four temples in sequence, all of which were among the largest and most splendid of their time; the temple built by the famous tyrant Polycrates was 20 metres tall. The second was an aqueduct, for which Eupalinus dug a tunnel of more than a thousand metres through the hill behind the city, and the third a huge breakwater that protected the city's harbour. The island also maintained a powerful fleet, with which Polycrates controlled parts of the Aegean Sea.

Figure 9. The tunnel and aqueduct of Eupalinus on Samos.

Unavoidably, wealth and knowledge accumulated in certain locations, most prominently in well-visited port cities, and as a result people there were more flexible and open-minded than elsewhere. Nonetheless, there are some curious peculiarities as well. For example, we do not know why the island of Lesbos became a centre of lyric poetry, or why early Greek philosophy, the thoughts of Thales, Anaximander, and Anaximenes, originated in Miletus. Perhaps it was easier in Miletus than elsewhere to learn about the scientific knowledge of the Orient that inspired the earliest philosophers and to apply it fruitfully. Or perhaps it was a matter of unique personal constellations, the length and intensity of encounters with the Orient, or the fact that a relatively large number of men from divergent backgrounds came together there—probably more than anywhere else. Or maybe it was the size, power, self-confidence, and appeal of this trading city that allowed the earliest Greek science and philosophy to flourish there. Another of the famous learned men from Miletus was Hecataeus, who was known not least as a geographer. Strangely enough, the other earliest Greek philosophers also came from the western coast of Asia Minor, from the cities of Ephesus, Samos, and Colophon. Some of them later emigrated to Italy. In any case, nothing comparable initially emerged on the Greek mainland.

In general, the Greek *poleis* developed at varying speeds. As of the mid-seventh century, Corinth had progressed far beyond the majority of Greek cities, and Chalcis and Miletus had likely done so as well. Overall, the impression is that a city's zenith was a singular experience; once experienced, it did not repeat itself.

Whatever the cause of the differences that arose between the cities, they would have been expressed in dialect, perhaps hairstyles, clothing, and jewellery—and probably considered larger than they actually were—so that people could better distinguish between places. In colonies whose citizens came from a variety of cities, it became apparent how complicated, at times impossible, it was to maintain an orderly coexistence.

It is difficult to say anything definitive about seventh-century Athens. The historical record only begins yielding a somewhat clear picture in the century that followed. Athens was certainly significant as a centre of art—we see this specifically in its painted pottery—and the city was no doubt wealthy and well connected in trade. But it does not seem to have made much use of its potential as Greece's largest and most populous *polis*—as is suggested by its military defeat by Megara, a city with only one-sixth of its citizen body. What prevented Athens from winning this war? Did the leading circles of the city only partially or half-heartedly support this endeavour? Was the relatively large community too politically divided to mobilize its power effectively? Did the city still lack competence and specialist expertise? Clearly, Athens diverged far more than even Argos, Corinth, or Miletus from the model of the face-to-face society of a small Greek *polis*. Or did internal tensions block the path to success?

Among the colonies, those in Sicily and southern Italy take centre stage in the historical record. Thanks to the size and fertility of the land they possessed, they were usually rather wealthy. Gains from trade were also hugely important, especially in Syracuse, Tarentum (Taranto), or Sybaris; the last controlled the overland route between the Gulf of Taranto and the Tyrrhenian Sea and was known for its extremely luxurious lifestyle. It was completely destroyed in 510 BC after being defeated in battle by its rival Croton.

At the end of the sixth century, Pythagoras left Samos and settled in Croton where he founded a (short-lived) aristocratic order that was strictly based on his philosophical teachings. The philosopher Parmenides made his home in Elea, another southern Italian colony.

Many of these western cities were generously laid out and featured large city squares. Metapontum even had a building for popular assemblies. Wars of conquest were rare in the Greek motherland, but in Italy Greeks spread out—sometimes at the expense of other Greek colonies. The 'corset' of a clustered world of *poleis* that held everything together and restricted ambition in the motherland did not apply to the Italian colonies. No matter what customs and expectations the colonists had brought from home, the circumstances where they settled opened up whole new possibilities. Different political constellations arose, and in time opportunities emerged for colonial Greeks to rule over others. An initial impetus was provided not least by the need to defend themselves against the constant threat emanating from Carthage.

17

The Wars

The ten-year war Homer depicted between an army levied from a great variety of *poleis* and a distant city that was eventually destroyed was only remotely related to reality. Achilles' justification for temporarily refusing to fight against Troy reveals the reasons that normally drove the Greeks to war: 'I have no quarrel with Troy or Trojan spearmen: They never stole my cattle or my horses, never in the black farmland of Phthia ravaged my crops.'

In the Greeks' early history it was the norm, and even later frequent enough, that they had to contend with being attacked by marauders from near and far, and many of them undertook plundering raids themselves. Those under attack united to mount common defences, taking revenge on hostile neighbours and deterring them as effectively as possible. Attackers who came from greater distances, often by ship, were harder to tackle or pursue, and it was difficult to combat piracy, even in one's home waters. The men of Ithaca were said to have joined forces, probably for this very purpose, with those living in the Thesprotis on the opposite mainland. Indeed, they nearly ripped the heart out of one of their fellow citizens (and plundered his estate for helping pirates from the island of Taphos attack the Thesprotians). In time, the Aegean *poleis* seem to have succeeded in limiting piracy by forming coastguards and, as is recorded for the Corinthians, sending out naval patrols. Pirates were allowed to do as they wished on the periphery, especially in the Tyrrhenian Sea, although our sources make a point of mentioning it when Greek pirates refrained from attacking Greek vessels.

Armed conflicts also arose when one *polis* tried to take land away from another. Attackers and defenders, as already depicted in the epics, might encounter one another along a battle line. In some cases, cities were besieged and destroyed, the inhabitants expelled. Argos, for instance, obliterated Asine, a rival city on the Argolic gulf; its citizens were lucky that the Spartans allowed them to settle in their territory. Otherwise, those expelled usually became exiles, wandering from place to place. It was, as the elegiac poet Tyrtaeus wrote, 'ghastly when a man flees planted fields and cities and wanders begging with his dear mother, ageing father, little children, and true wife... scorned in every new village, reduced to want and loathsome poverty.' Women and children of vanquished peoples were often sold into slavery as well. But the continuing existence of the *polis* world as a whole suggests that the destruction and annexation of foreign cities was the exception and not the rule.

Because the evidence is so scarce, we know of little that actually happened—not even whether or not wars were frequent in the archaic period. It is telling, though, that the oracle at Delphi stipulated that members of the league founded for its protection were forbidden to destroy cities or cut off water supplies to the besieged.

The most common and typical form of fighting armed conflicts among Greeks of the archaic and later periods was what we might call phalanx warfare. It seems to have become the norm in the course of the seventh century and entailed a short war between two *poleis* that was fought in early summer, just before the harvest. Such wars tended to be decided in a single battle in which phalanxes (tight formations) of heavily armed soldiers, several men deep, clashed with one another. Whoever controlled the battlefield in the end was the winner. To signify his triumph, as well as to express thanks to the gods and perhaps to reconcile them after the bloodshed and killings, the victor erected a trophy (*tropaion*, literally, a sign of turning). It symbolized the turn on the battlefield when the enemy fled, and took the form of captured weapons arranged on a wooden stake—similar to the hunters' habit of hanging the pelt, skull, and horns of a dead animal from a tree, thereby symbolically restoring the prey. As a rule, the vanquished were not pursued beyond the battlefield. They confirmed their defeat by asking for their dead to be returned.

These wars were usually announced by heralds and often commenced with raids that devastated the enemy's territory. Horsemen and light infantry had their roles to play in this phase. They could also be deployed in initial skirmishes or to cover the army's flanks. The main fighting, however, was done by hoplites, heavily armoured foot soldiers, who carried a round shield and were protected by a cuirass, helmet, and greaves, as well as strips of leather below the waist. Slaves usually carried this armour during the march to battle. The hoplites' main weapon was a sturdy spear, but they also carried a short sword.

Each hoplite had to provide his own set of equipment (called the panoply), but because it was partly made of iron it was considerably cheaper to produce than the all-bronze weapons of earlier eras. Many

(a)   (b)

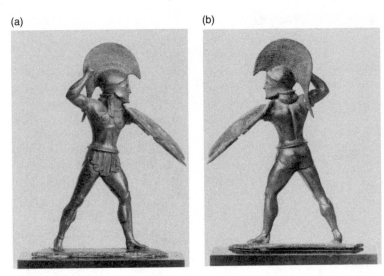

Figure 10. A hoplite in full armour (bronze statuette from *c.*500 BC, Antikensammlung Berlin).

farmers still had to spend beyond their means to own a panoply or could simply not afford one. Still, the panoply—and participation in battle—were a great source of pride. Every member of the community who was physically and economically capable of doing so was expected to fight, even if only as a light infantryman. There must have been military drills and exercises, although the Spartans were the only ones to truly train their hoplites. Training one's body, incidentally, was the citizens' private responsibility.

Hoplite fighting required an enormous degree of discipline. The phalanx advanced step by step, each soldier close to his neighbours and (with the exception of those on the right flank) partly protected by his right-hand neighbour's shield. Sacrifices (and promises concerning booty) were made to specific divinities in advance, as a ritual start to the killing. Seers consulted various omens (if time allowed). The generals briefly exhorted their troops, and there might have been some flute music and singing before the warriors donned their helmets and advanced against the enemy with as much determination as they could muster. Meanwhile, enemy light infantry might try to bombard the phalanxes with arrows, javelins, and stones.

Figure 11. Phalanx as depicted on the so-called Chigi vase *c.*650 BC (Villa Giulia, Rome).

Death, according to Tyrtaeus, the seventh-century Spartan poet, avoids those who 'stand fast, supporting each other, hold the front line, coming to grips with the foe'. This was the warrior ideal, constantly impressed upon each soldier. No one was allowed to yield or rush ahead; otherwise the ranks could easily break. Each soldier was expected to repress his fear and serve as an example of courage and bravery to his comrades. The rear rows exerted pressure on those in the front. Moreover, Greek armies tended to be arranged according to civic subdivisions. One fought side by side with the same men today with whom one would associate tomorrow, if one survived the battle.

When the armies clashed, spears were capable of piercing enemy shields and armour. Greek armour offered little protection for the neck or groin and, unlike in duels between swordsmen, in dense phalanx fighting there was little chance to evade or parry an enemy blow. When soldiers fell, the warriors in the next line simply stepped up over their dead or wounded comrades. Sometimes, the two sides locked shields in a kind of clinch until the fight resumed. Here and there, breeches opened up in the ranks, or the battle might dissolve into individual duels. When one side fled, they often threw away their shields—their other armour was more difficult to throw off. In one case it was said that more equipment than bodies were left on the battlefield. When flight had commenced, the light infantry and cavalry of the victors might take over, pursuing the defeated enemy at least for a while. The hoplites with their heavy armour were usually too exhausted for this and anyway, at that point the battle would have been long decided.

Whether the victors then looted or burned their vanquished enemies' territory varied from case to case. But sooner or later, the victors always had to return home to bring in their own harvest. Mutual sacrifices accompanied the end of a war. Treaties for ceding contested territories might be drawn up, although such land often had more symbolic value than real, and few of the soldiers stood to profit. On the other hand, extant poetry preserves a defeated *polis* lamenting that its borders were now visible from the agora. Sometimes, defeat sealed a relationship of dependence. Peace was usually defined as temporary, lasting from any-where between five and thirty years. Both sides, and especially the vanquished one, needed time for younger generations to replenish their ranks. Indeed, the Spartans once inflicted such heavy losses upon the Argives that Argive women took up with slaves in order to produce new offspring.

According to Herodotus, the Persian general Mardonius expressed his astonishment at Greek customs of war: 'When they declare war against each other, they choose the most beautiful, level field of battle' rather than the site at which each side considers itself the most difficult to defeat. Accordingly, the casualty rate is high, especially on the losing side. This indeed begs a series of questions: why did the Greeks not try to take advantage of the terrain? Why did they not launch surprise attacks from ambushes—or aim, right from the beginning, to encircle the enemy? Why was battle totally concentrated on close man-to-man fight-ing? Some of these strategies were utilized from time to time, but they were anything but common.

Naturally, it is rare that all the rules of war were followed. For example, it was not self-evident that the victors would not pursue the vanquished after battle—otherwise there would have been no need for occasional agreements insisting on precisely this point. And entirely different types of war were also waged, for instance, against non-Greeks in the colonizing period or by utilizing mercenaries. The wars in which the Spartans in the seventh century needed to save their control over Messenia and perhaps themselves against rebellious subjects were certainly fought by any means available: here the question clearly was either Us or Them! Tyrtaeus proclaimed that one should regard life as hostile and greet as one's friend the gloomy fate of death like the ray of the sun. Other wars also deviated from the norm, and not only those involving sieges and the conquest of cities or ports; it all depended on the purpose. In the early fifth century BC, for example, the Spartan King Cleomenes attacked his Argive enemies while they were eating breakfast. After the battle was won, he encircled the remaining Argive army in a forest and enticed his enemies to come out, one by one, with the claim that ransom had been paid for him. When the remaining survivors realized that this was a mere ploy to have them killed one after the other, and refused to leave the forest, he ordered his troops to collect wood and set fire to the forest. In a war between the Phocians and the Thessalians, the former broke a siege after six hundred of their bravest soldiers painted themselves and their armour white and went on a night-time sortie, killing everything in their way that did not glow white. The terrified Thessalians, it was said, lost four thousand men in that encounter.

Nonetheless, phalanx fighting seems to have established itself as a norm in wars among Greek cities. That was probably because it suited the circumstances. Greeks were generally not interested in wars of conquest or in threatening their neighbours' survival. On the contrary, they favoured short wars that demonstrated their superiority according to well-established rules. This was a matter of honour, which required the same starting conditions for all, and of proving *aretē*, excellence, as the heroes of the Trojan War had done. 'For no man ever proves himself a good man in war unless he can endure to face the blood and the slaughter, go close against the enemy and fight with his hands', Tyrtaeus wrote. 'Here is courage, mankind's finest possession, here is the noblest prize that a young man can endeavour to win.' Tyrtaeus' formulation of the ideal was especially designed to meet Sparta's particular difficulties. But on a slightly lower scale this ideal is likely to have been valid throughout the Greek world: 'And he who so falls among the champions and loses his sweet life, so blesses with honour his *polis*, his father, and all his people, with wounds in his chest, where the spear that he was facing has transfixed that massive guard of his shield, and gone though his breastplate as well.'

Phalanx warfare represents what the Dutch historian Jan Huizinga has identified as 'agonistic warfare'. It was a tournament, though bloody and for many fatal. Accordingly, warring parties sometimes agreed to have selected contingents of soldiers, perhaps three hundred on each side, to fight the battle instead of entire armies. This is hardly surprising since the Greeks were all too well acquainted with the 'baneful works of grief-bringing Ares and war's harsh temper' (Tyrtaios). But usually such efforts at limitation offered no final solution, and whole armies still engaged one another in battle.

Whether all hoplites made themselves available for every battle remains an open question. If that had been the case, Athens—with its vast numerical superiority—should have been more or less invincible. It is possible that, for example in the war against Megara, only part of Athens's hoplite force was actually involved. Or were there perhaps other ways of compensating for stark differences?

The typically Greek form of phalanx warfare offered a means by which the innate Greek penchant for life in autonomous small communities could work its way through a variety of thorny problems. The founding of distant colonies starting in the mid-eighth century BC had temporarily taken pressure off the Aegean world. Still much more needed to happen to ensure that the multitude and diversity of small *poleis* survived and continued to develop. Everything would have been called into question, if individual city-states had routinely and ruthlessly exploited military superiority, pressed victories to the bitter end, and tried to make major conquests and permanently eliminate enemies. Somehow the Greeks may have been aware of this.

The customary short but intense wars that emerged under the specific conditions of the *polis* world served to contain the Greeks' desire to demonstrate their own strength also in the form of military prowess, and did so by ultimately reinforcing these very customs and conditions. The only goal in such wars was to achieve a result that was not only clear, but, thanks to the horrific nature of the clashes, most impressive and resonant. Except for some rare occasions (when, for example, one side removed the winners' victory monument and replaced it with their own), the results of this sort of warfare could not be corrected *ex post facto*. The vanquished could, however, initiate a new conflict, once a sufficient interval of time had passed. Walter Burket had speculated that the usual truces of between five and thirty years were intended to give every generation a new chance to fight in battle and thus have the ultimate experience of *polis* solidarity. If this was the case, phalanx warfare may have contributed importantly to the eventual consolidation of the *polis* world. The Greeks' uniquely agonistic way of thinking also played a role in determining relationships between city-states.

Herodotus wrote that the Persian general Mardonius was unable to understand why the Greeks could not resolve their conflicts peacefully, especially since they all spoke the same language. The historian thus seems to emphasize the Persian's utter lack of understanding of the Greek character and the particular conditions under which Greeks lived. In fact, it turns out, the Greek style of war was a means of relieving pressure and creating stability essential to the survival of the *polis*.

The establishment of phalanx warfare also had significant consequences for the domestic histories of many *poleis*—and not just in terms of encouraging solidarity among their citizens. Men's willingness to risk death in battle further stabilized male domination in society, especially vis-à-vis the women. The phalanx also contained an element of equality for all (as long as they were reasonably wealthy property owners); after all, phalanx warfare did not reserve any special role for aristocrats. To be sure, officials in charge had to decide when and where to fight, including whether to wait for a few days if the omens seemed temporarily unfavourable. They also decided how many lines of the phalanx would be deployed in the middle and on the flanks. Finally, they had the important job of motivating and inspiring the warriors with speeches. 'Fear not before the masses of enemies and be not intimidated—hold your protective shield against the front ranks', exhorted Tyrtaeus. 'Persevere with a courageous heart, bite your lips, spread your legs powerfully, and dig your feet into the soil.' But initial decisions and exhortations like these were about as far as leadership went. Prominent citizens in the Greek *poleis* otherwise had no other task but to fight alongside everyone else as equals among equals. Although such equality did not extend directly into the political realm, it did elevate the status of the 'middle classes' and thus may have helped, after a long transitional phase, to facilitate the emergence of egalitarian systems that would prove to be the precursors of democracy.

At the same time, a decidedly martial component was inserted into the Greek concept of citizenship. The extent to which serving as hoplites influenced the self-image of Greek men is evident in art, which loved to shape or paint hoplites, most often wearing only shield, helmet, and spear, and otherwise depicted naked—to emphasize their heroism or perhaps an allusion to the popular discipline of *hoplitodromos*, or hoplite race in sports. The equation of citizens and hoplites would play a major role even in fifth-century Athens, although, or perhaps precisely because, the lower classes by then fully participated in 'radical' democracy, and although they, or rather the fleet in which they served as oarsmen, achieved their *polis'* most glorious military triumphs. But naval warfare was not a matter of man-to-man combat but a contest of collective skills and technology, and non-citizens were also hired to serve on warships. These new conditions contradicted the traditional idea of the *polis* to such an extent that, despite their military successes, Athenians had difficulty going any further in drawing comprehensive consequences from them. 'Ideology' was definitely more powerful, and the political interests of higher social circles may have played a role too.

The phalanx proved a very effective instrument, in other types of fighting as well. It was superior, for example, to cavalries, whose riders did not have saddles and stirrups. Although we have a report from the final days of Athenian tyranny that a thousand Thessalian cavalrymen defeated a Spartan force of hoplites, we do not know how large that force was and whether it had time to form ranks before the battle commenced. It is perhaps no accident, after all, that a phalanx army defeated the Persians at the Battle of Marathon.

It was perhaps the Spartans who first demonstrated on a large scale the superiority of this new technique of warfare in the years of bitter fighting during the Second Messenian War, when they eventually succeeded in putting down a rebellion among the people they had subjugated in the eighth century. It was during this war, with its many changes of fortunes, that Tyrtaeus composed and recited his martial verses.

Thucydides describes an interesting case of unusual restrictions placed on the means of fighting in his account of what was in his view the one major conflict of the archaic period, the war between Chalcis and Eretria on Euboea around 700 BC. The object of the conflict was control of the very fertile Lelantine plain, which lay between the two cities that belonged among the wealthiest and most powerful at the time and dragged others into the conflict as well: Chalcis was allied with Samos and Thessalia and received support from its colonies in the Chalkidike and likely from Corinth as well; Miletus, probably Megara, and perhaps Aegina took Eretria's side. The two sides reached an agreement, which was engraved on a stele in the sanctuary of Artemis Amarynthia, forbidding the use of long-distance weapons such as bows and arrows, javelins, or perhaps slings. The war, which was presumably renewed,

Figure 12. Two Greek warships, second half of the sixth century BC.

perhaps in a single battle, every year, made a deep impression on the memory of subsequent generations. We do not know which side won the conflict; we only know that, in the aftermath, Chalcis and Eretria were no longer major trading centres. They must have exhausted themselves in this war.

According to Thucydides, the first major Greek naval battle took place around 660 BC between Corinth and Kerkyra (Corfu). Another was fought in the second half of the sixth century between Phocaean immigrants in Corsica and the Carthaginians and Etruscans, who wanted to end Phocaean piracy. The trireme had been invented in the seventh century, most probably by the Phoenicians. Among the Greeks, Corinthians were reportedly the first to build this sort of vessel, which featured three rows of oarsmen half sitting next to and half below one another. The design allowed for the concentration of a great amount of oar-power in a relatively short and highly manoeuvrable vessel. In the second half of the sixth century, the tyrant Polycrates of Samos and the island of Naxos came to dominate the seas. We do not know to what extent this was due to naval victories, but it seems likely that the use of force and violence would have played a major role.

'No one is so foolish as to prefer war to peace, in which, instead of sons burying their fathers, fathers bury their sons', wrote Herodotus in the last third of the fifth century BC. 'War is sweet for those who have not tried it', sang Pindar, several decades earlier. 'But anyone who knows what it is is horrified beyond measure in his heart when it approaches.' The lamentations in the Homeric epics were similar in tone. Such insights, however, were of little use to people who were not mere spectators, but actually challenged to take part in wars, whether wars of defence or attack, or simply contests of strength against rival cities. Greeks knew that war was an evil. But they still instigated and fought wars—even if not at every possible opportunity—as long as wars could not be avoided and also because they were taken for granted as a normal part of life. After all, it is the same with many other evils, then and throughout world history. Lessons learned, assuming they are not too traumatic, tend to fade over time.

18

Polis Structure: Public Sphere
and Institutions

An inscription from around 600 BC has been discovered in the small Greek city of Dreros on Crete stating that a law was passed 'by the *polis*'. By that time the word had long served as a term for the body politic. But as a rule it was the *demos*, the popular assembly, which was responsible for ordinances of this kind. And treaties between city-states usually do not mention a city name in the singular (such as 'Athens'), but rather, the collectivity of citizens (for example, 'the Athenians') who approve the agreement.

Accordingly, later on Aristotle wrote that the city was the citizenry, and indeed, the citizens were participants in the *polis*, virtually in the sense of its shareholders. Like the booty from hunting and warfare, the surpluses from *polis* revenue were shared out among them; so too, citizens gathered, often at great feasts, to consume together the meat of sacrificial animals. Thus, as Aristotle was later to explain, whether it was an advantage or disadvantage to allow people to hold political offices, if there was to be equality (in democracy), all citizens had to take part equally in them, on a rotating basis. An individual's level of political participation was a measure of his significance in the *polis*.

If small communities of property owners, living in close proximity to other basically similar communities, wanted to maintain their political independence, they not only had to create clear separation and distinctiveness but also develop a feeling (or consciousness) of belonging together, almost a sense of kinship. That was all the more true when their unity was derived directly from the members themselves rather than being concentrated in or even personified by a king.

The familial nature of such communities was reflected in an almost paradoxical combination of great openness of movement towards the outside and strict exclusivity as regards non-members. The *polis*, like a home, had a hearth at its centre, usually located in an official building. The highest city officials would eat there—sometimes together with especially honoured guests or foreign ambassadors. In a symbolic sense, the entire community came together during these meals. There was even a special god for the hearth, Hestia.

If the *polis* was made up directly by the collectivity of its citizens, their community had to be distinguished from their individual households. The latter were the province of the individuals, the foundation of their independence. Men were the lords (*despotai*) of their own homes. The home was a place of work, of earning a livelihood, mostly by agricultural means, since the estate was part of the home. The home was also the sphere of the woman, the place where she bore, raised, and educated her children, and where, it is said, many fairytales were passed on. Women also worked in their homes, for example as weavers. Servants, maids, and later slaves also belonged in the home, and not in the *polis*.

In the public sphere of the community, which extended beyond an individual's immediate neighbourhood, however important that remained, each citizen was one among many. The public sphere was defined as the arena of free men. Its establishment most probably contributed to deepening the separation of the genders. Women had no business in the political sphere of the agora. The *polis* drew clear distinctions internally as well as externally.

If the lords of the households wanted collectively to embody the *polis*, as independent persons, which probably by necessity also means directly and with their full personality, they had to show a high degree of presence within it. They had to be able to compete, offer council, help make decisions, and balance various interests. On the other hand, politics could always represent only one aspect of their immediate way of living together. The function of the *polis* as a political association was only one side of what created community among the citizens.

This became tangible on a city's central square. There, the men of the community would meet every morning—the bigger the *polis*, the greater the proportion of members of the upper classes. Morning, for the Greeks, might be called 'the time when the agora is full of people'. Boundary stones demarcated this space—as communal property. Part of it served as an orchestra, a place for dances and other performances, sometimes with temporary or permanent stands for spectators. Often there was also a special track for racing, which should be as long, as it was once described, as a pair of mules could plough without stopping. The popular assembly convened in the agora proper; that was also where the council met. 'Polished stones', sometimes arranged in a 'sacred circle', offered city elders comfortable seats and underlined their status. In later periods, buildings were constructed there for the city council and for civic officials.

The agora was where people kept up with the latest news, where they had the feeling of 'being part of it' and where they discussed the affairs of the city and of anybody who offered cause for talk, in whatever way. Burckhardt characterized all this 'as people standing around and strolling together, doing business, conversing and pleasantly passing the time'. Everybody wanted to be where there was talk.

Odysseus was a man of both words and deeds. For Homer, the ability to offer wise council was on a par with skill in battle—a powerful testament to the power of speech—whether in the council, in the assembly, or within the various circles of people that gathered in the agora. According to Burckhardt, without the centrality of conversation it would be more difficult to imagine the development of the mind in Greek culture than in any other. The agora and the symposium—another meeting point for men, albeit in smaller circles and in private homes—were the two primary locations where conversations took place.

Aside from speech and conversation, it was a person's self-presentation that was noticed and might be admired. Since some of this could be learned, the agora was the place where men practised these skills, and it was a school in how to walk, move, and control one's body.

The agora was also the space for a number of competitions—between judges over who rendered the straightest verdicts, between citizens over the best council and most conciliatory words, between choruses at festivals, and between athletes in various disciplines (before *gymnasia* and *palaestrae* were built specially for them). In the agora, the young grew up under the scrutiny of their elders, and the first distinctions in rank among the former were made here. Yet the elders, too, were ever mindful of who among them was worth what, which place he occupied in society, how gracefully he moved, how well he dressed, and how 'beautiful' he was. Where there was only a limited amount of official business that was to be determined by objective criteria, personal factors acquired huge importance. As Homer's Odysseus already made clear, even if not everyone could excel equally at everything, one still had to try to do so in as many ways as possible.

Despite the prevalence of freedom, and indeed probably precisely for the sake of maintaining such freedom, there were strict rules governing public conduct, and people followed them. The sixth-century poet Theognis of Megara wrote: 'Show not how hard you have been struck. For if you show the force of the blow, you will hardly find allies in danger.'

No pity could be counted on. Aside from practical considerations, this was a matter of style. Pindar cautioned: 'Let foreigners not see what trouble we bear', and exhorted: 'What of beauty or joy falls to our lot, one should display openly to all the people.' There could well have been a culture which disapproved of public revelation of private matters, especially private pain. Pindar calls those 'fools who are unable to bear pain with dignity', while noble people actively display what is beautiful.

A great number of varying opinions were formed in the agora, and a lot of criticism was advanced there. Yet what people in villages took care of through blame songs had to be articulated differently in the city's agora. The 'flare-ups in the city', which Hesiod describes in the wake of unjust verdicts, are one example. When things came to a head, disagreements could get intense; fights and direct confrontations with adversaries could break out. If the citizens were split more deeply, the community's divisions became manifest in the agora.

This also meant, however, that the Greeks had to develop numerous skills for reaching compromise and reconciliation, and this talent had to prove its effectiveness in the public sphere. Homer's assertion, in a world of warriors, that men distinguished themselves in the popular assembly suggests the extent to which participants in the agora did not just decide but actively debated the issues.

Yet even if all men were expected to contribute at least something towards reaching agreement, this task was reserved in particular for a special few who rose above the others. In the *Iliad*, this role of offering conciliatory council fell to Nestor, who is depicted as the archetypal mediator. 'Speech', Homer writes, 'sweeter than honey rolled from his lips.' Many others followed in Nestor's tradition.

The importance of mediation created a special need for a quality whose importance is therefore particularly emphasized by our sources: charm or grace (*charis*). In the *Odyssey*, the hero proclaims: 'A man may seem in outward aspect unworthy of much regard, yet heaven crowns his words with grace, and those who hear him gaze at him in delight while he speaks unfalteringly and with winning modesty; he stands out among those assembled there, and as he goes his way through the city, men look at him as if at a god.' In the *Theogony*, Hesiod says of the leader who is favoured by the Muses: 'Upon his tongue they shed sweet dew, and out of his mouth the words flow honeyed.' 'With unerring firmness and wisdom he brings a great strife to an end.' Solon, the great Athenian reformer, also prays to the Muses that they grant him respect and acknowledgement among his fellow citizens. A visual expression of charm or grace is the 'archaic smile' typical of archaic Greek statues.

For all these reasons it is hardly an exaggeration to say that the great circle of those who regularly visited the agora developed the sorts of skills and competences in speech and action that complemented those of the officials, council members, and the popular assembly.

But the agora must also have been an especially significant forum for taming passions, for the general, civilizing implantation of those restraints in contemplation and expression which were elsewhere initiated by rulers, their courts, and religious and other institutions, including the 'police', that were intended to impose social discipline. In the Greek *polis*, discipline had to result from the cooperation of large numbers of people and emanate from their midst. The process was difficult and never complete, when we think, for example, of the desire for vengeance that had to be quelled continually and in every case, and always in communal

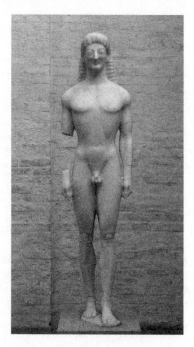

Figure 13. *Kouros* of Tenea, showing 'archaic smile' (now in the Glyptothek, Munich).

collaboration. The point was never reached when the Greeks became reluctant openly to profess this desire.

Greek culture was to a large extent a matter of personal development in a great variety of aspects that were important to the Greek ideal of the human being—even if this only applied comprehensively to the male half of the population and especially to the upper classes. While other members of the citizenry may have had power and the desire to participate in politics, they had no culture of their own as an alternative. Thus, the aristocratic way of life, including the ideals that determined it, became the norm for everyone. The aura of this world retained its fascination and found expression in art. That was because, in Burckhardt's words, man is not just 'what he is but also what he sets himself as an ideal, and even though he may not conform to this ideal fully, the sheer will to do so determines a part of his being'.

Other members of the community, most notably the middle classes, were by no means excluded from the agora, which was, after all, the site of the popular assemblies. But they would hardly have had the time to congregate there regularly. And we have no way of knowing whether they felt at home there outside larger, more general events or meetings. In other words, their place may very well have been on the margins. Yet, however this may have affected each individual, the agora must still have exerted some sort of fascination upon them—which later became a not insignificant reason for their readiness to become politically engaged.

The word 'aristocratic' is commonly used for Greek families who over time—for example, thanks to particular successes, profitable marriages, and less division of property—rose above others. This is a practical and not really inaccurate term—as long as we do not imagine the Greek aristocracy as overly grandiose. They were proud and certainly put on airs, but their circumstances had significant limits. The total area of many Greek *poleis* was hardly larger than an estate owned by the landed gentry of modern times, and an aristocratic class never distinguished itself sharply and definitively from the rest of society. The only hard-and-fast distinctions were between citizens and non-citizens.

The historical sources use a number of terms to describe those who had risen to the top in Greek society. Some of them seem to refer to specific, local aristocracies, while others signified the upper class more generally. We hear of the 'good' and 'best' (*aristoi*), the 'nobles' (*esthloi*), and the 'leaders of the people', but also of the 'rich', the 'fat ones', the 'property owners' (*geōmoroi*), and even the 'horse breeders'. Names that describe family qualities, such as *eupatridai* ('of good fathers') and *eugeneis* ('of good descent') were less frequent. Nonetheless, it is likely that there was continuity within family lines.

Wealth and excellence (*aretē*), Greeks believed, were more or less hereditary within certain social circles, whose members tended to inter-marry. Having been thoroughly and carefully educated, they maintained a particular lifestyle that distinguished them from others and soon excluded physical labour. Even among men, hairstyles, jewellery, and expensive clothing may have demarcated social difference. The practice of holding symposia was initially reserved for aristocrats. So too, perhaps, were athletic triumphs, extensive hospitality, and guest friendships, cos-mopolitanism, and perhaps, in a certain sense, even wisdom. At the same time, there must always have been successful social climbers: on a small scale farmers whose successful management allowed them to expand their holdings, and, on a larger scale, traders and adventurers who were lucky enough to gain riches. They perhaps married into better families— much to the dismay of those whose fortunes had declined. Their wealth may have compensated for the lack of property. They were probably slightly handicapped in the area of social graces, but it might have been possible to overlook or correct that deficiency.

It was members of the upper classes who typically occupied public offices and served on the council. It is an open question what role fell here to the remaining segments of Greek society, who were citizens and some of whom took part in phalanx fighting and the popular assembly. Most likely, things varied a lot from place to place and over time.

When a few aristocratic families rose further above the rest of their class, the results were violations of rules, abuses, power struggles, and, ultimately, the crisis, beginning in the mid-seventh century BC, that rocked Greece for more than a hundred years until it was finally over-come by new arrangements and reforms. When the dust settled, the aristocracy was still around. But often the distribution of power no longer exactly followed social divisions.

Henceforth, even in democracies, the aristocratic ideals remained in force, hardly mitigated, and at most applied in somewhat more moder-ate forms since now they could no longer be brought to bear politically. Nonetheless, the middle classes and, by the fifth century, partly even the lower classes gradually succeeded in gaining the political upper hand in various *poleis*. This was an unusual situation and a source of very fruitful tension that led to solidarity between the middle and lower classes and also to their social assimilation. Chester Starr has referred to the Greek middle classes as semi-aristocrats, and the term is certainly not entirely false. Another good description might be notabilities.

The familial nature of how the *poleis* came together virtually seems to have usurped the role actual family relations usually play in comparable situations. One of the special characteristics of the *polis* societies was that people's relationships with family members hardly had significance beyond obvious issues like mutual support in times of crisis. For instance, we do not find any family or clan associations or heads of clans who might have steered politics together with their peers. The small size of the communities and the interrelatedness of their members perhaps did not allow for such cliques. The community was instead directly comprised of men who stood for themselves and were based in their own households.

Accordingly, the community was segmented into larger and smaller subdivisions, which were understood in a familial sense. There was a division into three, four, or more *phylai* (often translated as 'tribes'), and they in turn were comprised of still smaller groups, which Homer and others referred to as phratries ('brotherhoods'), and which could in turn contain even smaller sub-groups. These subdivisions served, at least in the long term, a variety of practical purposes, for example, for the distribution of obligations and rights such as being drafted into military service. Armies were often divided into tribal units, and members of the same phratry commonly fought side by side. In the case of taxes and other obligations, the subdivisions were able to ensure a fair division of the burdens, and they had the important task of keeping lists of citizens. In Athens, for example, the phratries decided whether newborn children were legitimate and eligible for citizenship. According to the Greek idea of community, that was a task not for offices or official representatives, but for the groups of which the community itself consisted. Members of these groups also shared the same cult practices, which demanded infrequent but regular sacrifices, and this both manifested and strengthened their sense of connection. Aristotle referred to them as 'common, familiar contexts'.

Within these subdivisions, especially the smaller ones, the aristocracy tended to provide a kind of patronage. Their leaders usually came from the aristocratic ranks, and aristocrats owned the altars upon which sacrifices were made. They were also in a position to grant members assistance. In cases of murder, and if the victim left behind no relatives, they were in fact obliged to make sure the killer was pursued.

What did *not* emerge in the Greek *poleis* were firmly established and hereditary relations of clientage or friendship, based on mutual obligations, as were so common in Rome. Thus, while Aristotle stresses the enormous importance of various aspects of friendship in his *Nicomachean Ethics*, he never mentions obligations that arise from its long-term continuation. Apparently the individualism of the *poleis* mirrored that of the individual citizens, no matter how much the independence of both may have occasionally been subjected to practical limitations.

It is very difficult to say how and why such a differentiated system of social subdivisions arose. Some of it could have come from the period of Greek immigration, perhaps under certain circumstances as a compromise with the original inhabitants of the territories involved. Other elements may have been set up later for military reasons. At some point, probably in the eighth century BC, whatever had sprouted from various roots was apparently systematized.

In any case, it was highly significant that the *polis* was organized and integrated through its subdivisions and that no other types of ties, obligations, or dependencies interposed themselves between individuals and the collectivity. Through its small and still smaller sub-units, and notwithstanding the inequalities such units may have contained, the *polis* could be perceived and experienced directly by members of the broader classes, who of course also participated in popular assemblies. The result of all this was that the structure of the citizen body could henceforth also be changed by decision of the *polis*. In several places this began to happen in the sixth century and, in Sparta, perhaps already in the seventh. In both Sparta and Athens, old subdivisions were not replaced, but supplemented by new parallel ones that assumed some of the essential functions. But the decisive change was that they enabled new forces from the broad citizenry to express themselves more strongly, both directly and indirectly, in the political arena. In this way, solidarity among equals gradually superseded relationships of dependency. Whereas under the old systems the less wealthy largely remained limited to the small subdivisions, under the reformed systems everything was aimed at bringing smaller subdivisions via larger ones into close contact with the community at large. A prime example of such a new system is the one Cleisthenes established in Athens in the late sixth century BC.

Forming associations of property owners into political units and developing the skills needed for collective action cannot have been easy. But with many challenges, for example, providing protection from the outside by organizing arms and armed forces, Greeks had few alternatives. The same was true of securing peaceable coexistence within communities by resolving conflicts, especially by establishing courts. But there was more: the citizens also had to ensure that the proud lords of the upper classes, who were accustomed as a matter of honour to enforcing their own justice (through vengeance), would learn to accept mediation—until eventually everyone was prepared to acknowledge judicial decisions as binding. Necessary conditions for achieving this arose in the emergence of Greek legal thought and a culture of guilt. Yet, restraints also had to be put on the arbitrary power of judges, who were sometimes called, not without reason, 'gift-devouring'. Thus new courts and institutions for appeal had to be created, and this was no doubt quite a difficult and slow process. Interestingly, the *Iliad* already contains a famous scene in which a god encourages a man who is about to kill another to think of the talk and scorn of the people. Hesiod's line about how 'Justice (Dikē) howls when she is dragged about by bribe-devouring men' expresses a comparable sentiment.

In any case, it must have taken a long time to achieve communal monopolization of the legitimate use of force—both internally and externally; after all, in the latter sphere too, aristocratic liberty needed to be curtailed. Moreover, with time, the law itself had to become more detailed, especially as regards contentious issues; enacted and written law needed to replace customary norms that were passed on orally and often arbitrarily applied.

One constant, serious problem was providing appropriately for cults that were necessary for the *polis'* well-being. Gods and temples were to be given what was their due. But there was also a need for buildings, roads, harbours, and supervision at markets—to say nothing of the manifold other issues that required collective action. Elements of organization such as officials, councils, and popular assemblies usually already existed. The question was: what was their purpose? What were they able to achieve, and how did they typically work together? Such questions require different answers for periods of 'normal' life compared with crisis periods, hardly infrequent in the archaic age, when aristocratic factions appeared and fought violently over power. To put things another way: what the Greeks faced was also an issue of capacity and of the ability of early systems to contain and deal with problems and conflicts—all the more so because such systems were embedded in the circle of community members, particularly aristocrats, who were so present in the heart of the *polis* itself.

The basic idea of public office was not obvious to the Greeks, to say nothing of corresponding concepts and terms. Unlike in Rome, Greek 'kings' did not bequeath to those filling the highest public offices any sort of special status or even charisma. They had been mere *primi inter pares*, and in the majority of instances it would be an exaggeration to attribute to them any sort of sole rule or monarchic power. The sceptre which in the *Iliad* Agamemnon had received from Zeus and which the herald passed around from speaker to speaker in assemblies occurs nowhere in the later historical record. There are also no traces of special insignia, servants demanding attention (comparable to the Roman lictors with their *fasces*), or rituals of respect paid to officials. The 'gestures, forms of address and expressions of honour' Aristotle describes as being paid to officials probably emerged later, and even then it is questionable how much real power they reflected.

It is doubtful whether in early times official responsibilities were simply allocated or even formulated. Responsibility flowed from the tasks at hand as well as from customs that gradually established themselves in conjunction with those tasks. We can assume that the autonomous citizens who were so concretely present in the *polis* would hardly have transferred any more responsibilities than was absolutely necessary to their officials, especially since that would have entailed placing limits on themselves. Thus, as a rule, Greek officials were probably quite weak. That is not, however, to say that things could not be different in exceptional circumstances, when, for instance, officials formed a united front with powerful aristocratic groups or acted as their representatives and took on all kinds of further tasks. In such cases, it was not easy to prevent them from grabbing what was not rightfully theirs, and using their offices as leverage to expand their personal power. Who would have been in a position to resist an aggressive official, backed by powerful allies—except for a hostile faction, whose leader would then likely have wanted to do the same? Nonetheless, in such cases, it was not the office itself or the community, but merely ambitious parts of the community that made officials strong.

In Republican Rome, we find a unique give and take between the enormous responsibilities and power of the magistrates and a variety of potentially limiting opposing forces. Such interaction resulted from collaboration and competition between magistrates and the senate and among the magistrates themselves, with the tribunes of the plebs playing a special role. That opened up large opportunities for decisive action, while limiting abuses. But among the Greeks, with the possible exception of Sparta, we cannot expect to find anything comparable.

To subsume oneself within a role that an office demanded one play, to abstract oneself from concrete self-interest and a personal perspective was presumably quite hard for Greeks. Such a stance did not fit in with the unmediated directness in which Greeks lived together and in which they were what they naturally wanted to be. Themistocles, the victorious Greek general at the Battle of Salamis, is said to have remarked that an office that did not allow him to favour his friends was just about worthless. Whether he actually said this is doubtful; it is contradicted by another saying attributed to him—to the effect that as an official he could not favour anyone against the law. Nonetheless, the story is telling since it points out a difficulty that confronted the Greeks, especially during the archaic period. Life at that time was not marked only by the usual temptations towards partisanship or corruption, but by a strongly felt duty to help friends and hurt enemies. This was especially true for the most ambitious characters, who sought most vigorously those offices which were not only understood, but actually designated as honours (*timai*). Even the tiny *polis* of Dreros on the island of Crete was already forced in the seventh century BC to decree that a person could only hold the highest office for a second time after a period of ten years, and that violations of this law were to be subject to serious sanctions.

In a tradition that may have started under the Greek kings, often the most important functions were distributed among various office holders, who held more or less equal power. Moreover, the more complex the needs of the community became, the more offices had to be created. We know from Athens and other city-states that there were a number of archons (*archontes*, leaders). That increased the number of public honours and simultaneously reduced the power of individual office holders. Ultimately, there were nine of them. They included the head archon (*archōn epōnymos*), who gave each year its name, the *archōn basileus*, who assumed the king's religious responsibilities, and the *archon polemarchos*, who took over his military tasks. The six others had judicial functions.

Sometimes it may have been the council, but mostly it was popular assemblies that were responsible for selecting the officials. Who was allowed to participate in such decisions is an open question, as is also when elections as such began to be held, as opposed to acclamations confirming proposals by assembly leaders. Counting votes or, more precisely, determining majorities, was by no means a given. Early non-monarchic societies tended towards consensus solutions, for example, by distributing offices over the years among those who were entitled. Thus the Greek form of counting votes requires explanation, and the answer is probably that, given the intensity of competition, objective criteria were needed by which decisions could be measured. If it was not the case from the beginning it soon became the norm that terms of office were limited to one year. Moreover, to ensure that the greatest possible number of people had access to these honours, re-election was often limited.

Potential office holders had to have enough free time to serve, and they also needed to be able to afford the costs of carrying out their duties and paying for the festivals and sacrifices that were expected of them. They must have had assistants, but we do not know who paid them.

Equally obscure are the sources of public revenues in ancient Greece. It is usually assumed that Greeks paid no property or income taxes, except when tyrants imposed such levees. But there is also evidence that some free communities demanded a tenth of people's revenues. Or we hear that the income derived from a mine owned by the *polis* was so high that citizens were not required to pay any direct taxes. The rules most likely varied according to the needs of individual cities, including sacrifices for the gods (although the meat was frequently used for ceremonial meals among the citizens). Overall, Greek cities' needs must have been limited, since a large portion of what elsewhere constitutes state business was here handled by individual households or by the community as a whole—if it mattered at all. Greeks had no police force; citizens took care of their own security together with their neighbours, and the same was true for fighting fires. There was no equivalent of a district attorney. Citizens were responsible for their own health and care in old age and for the education of their children. At the most, and rarely before the fifth century, a community might provide a doctor or a teacher for elementary instruction. Market fees, customs duties, and revenues from public property could thus cover most public expenses. Still, expensive projects like the building and renovation of city walls and temples, the expansion of an agora or port, or the construction of aqueducts and fountains would usually have required some distribution of costs.

The Greeks seem to have hit early on upon the idea of binding their officials by oaths. Fear of divine retribution was supposed to keep them within their limits. Athenian archons not only had to swear to protect citizens' property for their year in office; they also had to promise to discharge their duties in full accordance with the law. If they were found accepting gifts in their official capacity, they were required to dedicate a life-sized, gilded statue to Apollo of Delphi, and a number of other fines benefiting the gods were prescribed as punishment for official violations and negligence. That was in keeping with the custom, common to the Greeks and the Romans, that communities were not supposed to enrich themselves through fines. Moreover, for the Greeks obligations vis-à-vis the gods could have been a means of ensuring that office holders actually paid the fines they had been given—something that was difficult to enforce otherwise, apparently met with all kinds of resistance, and thus was often omitted.

Particularly striking in this context are a number of legal texts enacted by various *poleis* that survive in inscriptions from the archaic period. They lay out special duties for certain office holders in exactly described, specific cases, and they consider the possibility that those tasks might not be carried out. Hence, they also determine what is to happen, if, for example, the officials fail to collect punitive payments—namely, they themselves will owe twice the amount. The laws also spell out which gods are to receive the fines. Occasionally, other office holders are charged with collecting such sums from the colleague who was originally responsible; in cases of violation they are also subject to paying double fines. Furthermore, laws might determine that if officials are unwilling to meet their obligations (for example, by executing outcasts), the responsibility will pass to their successors; in that case too, penalties are set for the eventuality that this is neglected.

In one instance, a popular assembly decided not just to prohibit second terms in a specific office before an interval of ten years, but to punish anyone who obtained such an office before that span had expired (presumably because the assembly had elected him to it). The perpetrator would be fined a sum double that of all the penalties he had himself imposed in his first year of office, forbidden from applying for an office ever again, and all his actions in office would be revoked.

All these popular resolutions were chiseled in stone and set up in sanctuaries—otherwise we would know nothing of them. Are they evidence only of the difficulties Greeks had in getting officials to fulfil their tasks? Or do they also indicate the difficulty office holders had in getting powerful (or well-protected) citizens to meet their demands? As far as the popular assembly was concerned, were such laws perhaps an attempt by individual groups to impose their will on office holders? Or was it rather the collectivity of citizens that wanted better control of the officials—and perhaps of itself? After all, if the citizens did not want individuals to hold the same office many times in quick succession, all they had to do was not to vote for them—unless, from case to case, new majorities had coalesced, which would have been especially troubling in raising individuals far above the others and strengthening factions. More generally, how did assemblies come to pass such regulations? Did the Greeks perhaps adapt a Phoenician model to fit their own needs? In any case it is tempting to assume that the Greeks copied from the Levant the idea of writing out rules and setting them up in sanctuaries. Many of these resolutions seem in fact too trivial to merit such an honour.

Communities in general have good reason to threaten officials with punishment. Republican Rome did so as well. But Roman regulations were not usually aimed at impressing upon the officials the duties to be performed, but rather at restricting areas of authority and eliminating possibilities for individuals to increase them on their own, as well as fighting corruption and the exploitation of provincials.

If the Greeks, on the other hand, saw themselves compelled to draw up exact and detailed rules concerning official duties, including penalties for non-compliance, the potential for enforcing the order seems to have been rather weak. Perhaps we should best see the popular resolutions mentioned above as desperate attempts to address, at least here and there, the negligence of officials, who tended to see their office principally as a sign of honour. The Greeks may thus have been trying in individual cases to accomplish with laws specifically what oaths of office were supposed to achieve generally (which—along with prayers and curses—were among the few means available to invoke higher powers to support communal interests).

At any rate, especially early on, the overall capacity of Greek communities was quite limited. Too much power was concentrated in the hands of individuals, especially the most powerful. Officials had difficulty holding them to account. This was true in normal conditions, before powerful factions or tyrants emerged. It may well be that at least occasionally in the popular assembly a will manifested itself to enforce common interests against particular ones.

Popular assemblies are already described in Homer, in whose epics they usually appear as meetings of soldiers or informal gatherings. But Homer also describes comparable institutions in Greek cities. In the *Odyssey*, when Telemachus calls the people to the agora, he assumes the seat of his missing father. In the *Iliad*, polished stones are arranged for judges into 'a sacred circle'. As a rule, the agora and circular space (orchestra) for dances were often dedicated to a divinity. In Homer the assembly is led by a herald, who gives permission to speak by passing around the leader's staff. On one occasion the agora is given the attribute 'many-voiced'. Over time, much of what probably began there as ad hoc practice eventually had to be subjected to more exact rules. Those rules likely concerned who was allowed to participate and other proce-dural matters, such as, who called people to the agora, when, and how often. How could it be ensured that different opinions could be voiced? What matters required a popular resolution? We can assume that rela-tively early on all men eligible to fight as soldiers—including large numbers of farmers—were entitled to speak and vote, and that they decided about war and peace. The extent to which they actually dared to raise their voices and even advocate their own interests is another matter. The brash Thersites, who speaks out in the *Iliad*, does not come off very well at all.

The communal assembly must have decided relatively early as well on treaties binding the *polis*, and soon on filling the offices. Extant written laws show that 'the *polis*' or 'the people' could decide not just on fines for officials, but also on individual legal issues concerning, for example, marriage and guardianship, inheritance and adoption, as well as regula-tions governing neighbourly relations, grazing rights, contracts, guilt, and punishment. In Athens, attempts to establish tyrannical rule were a punishable offence early on as well.

Other regulations often focused on curbing luxury and the desire to impress others, expressed particularly by affluent people at funerals. This was apparently a constant source of public anger, not least for those suffering from poverty, and their ire was possibly considered justified well beyond their circles. Greeks also took special interest in the issue of whom their heiresses were supposed to marry in order to keep inherited property in the family. Upper limits could also be placed on the size of estates. That was necessary because the number of people who could serve as hoplites depended on the number of at least moderately sized estates. Moreover, at some point it must have become clear that the *poleis* could only continue to exist as communities of property owners if there were a certain number of landed citizens, and inequalities were not too marked.

Just as citizenries could push through small-scale regulations via the enactment of individual laws, they could also insist on a large scale on the institution of whole sets of laws. The literary tradition records several well-known lawgivers, including Zaleucus of Locri, Charondas of Cata-nia, and Draco and Solon of Athens. The usual assumption among scholars has been that one of the goals of broader citizen classes was to fix the law comprehensively in written form. This seemed to make sense since the aristocratic judges who passed the judgements took the norms on which those judgements were based from oral tradition best 'known' to themselves. They were all too frequently accused of having bent the law or of remembering it arbitrarily. The enactment of written law was a way of protecting it from such capriciousness by making it visible and clear to everybody. But recently doubts, justified by the extent, detail, and density of known legislation, have arisen as to whether we should really think of comprehensive 'codification' of the law. Most likely Greek lawgivers did not do much more than bundle regulations into a written rule, combining in one step what previous legislation had achieved only in several. In each case, such laws concerned contentious questions within a legal system that on the whole continued to be orally transmitted and updated with new judgements. But such laws could also be prompted by urgent needs. The manifold traditions about the activities of lawgivers are hardly all invented.

Finally, the question of exactly who and what decisively determined actions of the popular assembly must be left open. We do not know exactly who attended (regularly or only in exceptional circumstances), or what chances aristocrats (a few, many?) typically had of getting their way. Is it possible that in cases of a scandalous nature a majority even of aristocrats collaborated with others in support of proposals to eliminate the cause of the problem? We do not even know who was allowed to make proposals. How often and to what extent did public anger prompt broad unity despite many disagreements? When and how did majorities in the assembly come to recognize their common interests—even and especially if such interests could only be realized in several steps?

Powerful aristocratic factions are likely to have used groups of their followers to establish majorities in or put pressure on assemblies. Conversely, the assemblies' ability to suppress factional fighting was surely limited. More than one assembly had itself, at some point, favoured a tyranny. Much in the historical record suggests that many men at least temporarily kept their distance from politics—be it out of caution or disgust. Thus, the range of effectiveness of popular assemblies in the archaic period was likely small. A reorganization of Greek citizen bodies, as it was undertaken several times in the sixth century, was needed in order to turn assemblies into institutions that were able to wield significant power on a regular basis.

Our information about Greek councils in the archaic period is particularly scant, although jointly convened advisers already occur in Homer. When and how more concretely organized councils emerged, with formal rules governing numbers and eligibility of members, remains obscure. In Athens, after their year in office the nine archons were accepted into the aristocratic council on the Aeropagus, and this may have been one example among many. It seems to have been the rule that membership in such councils was for life.

In any case, it needed to be determined who convened these councillors and how often he did so, whether regularly or as need demanded. There is one written record of a popular resolution, including penalties for noncompliance, stipulating that officials had to convene the council at least once a month. If, as can hardly be doubted, the most respected and powerful members of the community sat on the council, these institutions should be expected to have been influential—and perhaps they were. This would have been the case even more if, as is attested again in Athens, officials were required to render account to the council at the end of their year of service. Conversely, when making important decisions, officials were almost certain to have sought the council's support.

Yet no matter how much influence the councils may have had in small city-states and in precariously balanced political circumstances, as soon as tensions increased or aristocratic factions began fighting, the council seems to have become paralysed. It is at any rate hardly likely that Greek aristocrats would have been able to develop and maintain a system of rules needed to engage in and ultimately limit major conflicts among themselves so as to ensure that the final word remained with a majority capable of concerted political action. That is something we know was achieved by the Roman Senate, whose exact system of rank and cleverly devised, strictly enforced codes of practice imposed on its members enough discipline to contain conflicts and act in unison. By contrast, it was precisely when the council's decisive action would have been most urgently required that the Greeks failed to rise to the challenge. In the archaic period, whenever aristocrats and their associations strove to gain power in any given circumstances, there was no authority that had power over these circumstances—even if only to keep them in place.

In general, we can say that the political institutions of archaic Greece had little capital of their own, either in terms of traditionally acknowledged authority that was eventually taken for granted, or of capabilities supported by expectations and anchored in themselves. Such institutions were not separated enough from the concrete immediacy of the *polis*. Thus the structure of these institutions tells us very little about the nature of the *polis* (if indeed we can reconstruct such structures at all). There is also no reason to assume that anything like a political order crystallized at this early time. While Solon of Athens may have tried around 600 to conceptualize the *polis* order as a *eunomia*, that concept included the most diverse factors, including economic and social conditions and public morality. Solon also did not mention other factors which were self-evident—for example, the role of festivals, processions, sacrifices, and the innumerable choruses with performances in dancing and singing; both belonged together and such choruses sometimes even accompanied embassies to foreign sanctuaries. The enormous political importance Plato was later to attach to music, tonality, metre, and rhythm may in some ways reflect attitudes typical of the Greeks in general.

Whereas elsewhere religion—represented by priests or a king's close connection with a god—helped stabilize political rule, in ancient Greece it may have underpinned the cohesion of a community that was free from such rule by the way citizens were incorporated in rituals of song and dance, sacrifice and festivals. In some obscure way, what Burckhardt called 'the intoxicating exceptional times' that were part of the cult of Dionysus may have played a role here as well.

One characteristic of small communities and indeed politics itself is the rise of political groupings. The Greeks can hardly have been an exception. But just as families or their associations played no important political role, so too political associations seem to have been, as a rule, quite loose. That changed when major disputes flared up, for instance caused by desires for revenge. But before long Greeks seem to have returned to their normal situation of fluctuating positions.

Yet in a number of *poleis* the interplay between rule and exception seems to have yielded to a phase of protracted factional fighting over political dominance. As a result, in many places tyrannies were founded. That was always the beginning of a crisis, which seemed to calm down at least on the surface once someone's rule was established, but inevitably developed continuing virulence because the concept of the *polis* and the very idea of political domination stood in irreconcilable contradiction. Nonetheless, in many *poleis*, such crises seem to have been necessary for a subsequent consolidation and reconceptualization of the community that was ultimately placed on an entirely new footing.

19

Crisis: Aristocratic Rivalries, Social Conflicts, Tyranny

The crisis that many *poleis* went through in the latter half of the seventh and first half of the sixth centuries BC had its roots, at least according to the complaints of contemporaries, in the upper classes' unfettered striving for wealth, the accompanying violations of norms and acts of injustice, and subsequent factionalization and conflict. Initially, such conflicts played themselves out among the aristocrats, but those at the other end of the social scale, who suffered from them, soon came to be involved. The result in the end was popular outrage and revolt, civil war, and the usurpation of power.

Complaints about what was happening during this period harked back to the old idea of a society whose leadership was supposed to unite wealth and excellence (*aretē*). The ethical ideal of excellence referred primarily to an individual's abilities in war as in athletics and speaking at council. The Greek term *aretē* designates both these capacities and their achievement; they were essentially inseparable. For Greeks, a person who was good had success and was therefore wealthy. Wealth and power were deserved, and the members of the upper class were justified in seeing themselves as the 'good ones'. But the unity of these ideas was lost during the crises of the seventh century, as is shown by changing usages of the relevant Greek terms.

'Many bad men are rich, and many good ones are poor,' wrote Solon. Taken by itself, what he may have meant was that a number of men from the lower class (who were traditionally considered, in a social sense, 'mean' or 'bad') had risen in society, while the fortunes of numerous others, upper-class men, had declined. Such social changes elicited much criticism at the time. Moreover all categories were relative. Given the rising standards of wealth, what was once an entirely respectable estate could soon appear rather small.

But Solon in this case was referring to another aspect. He used words like 'good' and 'bad' in an ethical sense and with new imperatives. It was no longer sufficient for Greek leaders just to be brave warriors. Because it was no longer a given that they acted fairly and justly, the idea of 'excellence' now needed to be enhanced by including notions of justice, moderation, and even wisdom. That meant, in turn, drawing distinctions between goodness and high social status. Many of those who were rich were bad not because they came from lowly families but because they had sacrificed their goodness (*aretē*) to wealth. The result was that they were 'overfilled with possessions', which in Solon's view led to compulsive gluttony and a tendency to disrespect all limitations. The 'bad-rich' gave in to impulses and actions that Solon found reprehensible.

Moreover, the men who were once good but had turned bad pursued not just wealth but power, and here, too, Solon cautions: 'We will not obey you, nor will these things be favourable to you.' Since legitimate means were hardly sufficient to satisfy these men's growing demands, they resorted to illegitimate methods, such as using and perhaps even appropriating public, communal property as well as that devoted to the gods. And to do so, they needed power, sometimes even political domination.

Observations and formulations like those of Solon registered social changes without fully comprehending them. Old terms were being used to describe new phenomena that were initially considered nothing but deviations from a norm that people could not yet conceive of as obsolete. Thus, the logical conclusion was that once the deviations were eradicated, the old order would be restored. No new political categories took the place of the old ethical ones. Everything was happening very fast. The Greeks had no way of knowing that, in the face of ongoing change, they needed new institutions, new ways of thinking, and a new mentality.

Learning and rethinking were necessary, and change had to settle in gradually. Given the incipient stage in which Greek culture found itself, many an insight could only crystallize out of the very beginning of political thought. The possibilities for forming political groups, and that means, for combining power and the ability for action, were not naturally suitable for creating an entirely new basis for a functional society, beyond the realization of isolated reforms. On the contrary, the political groups of this period were themselves part of the crisis. They could neither contain nor work through the problems at hand.

Looking back from the end of the crisis, it seems apparent that in a variety of cases—in fact, the more difficult but fascinating ones—alternatives would have to emerge from the citizen body itself. A new force waiting to be activated—the 'middle ones'—had to be mobilized, and permanently so. Those who suffered most from the crisis were too much

at the mercy of the competing aristocrats to be able to help in forming
something new. Indeed, in general, Greek society first had to experience
the crisis itself in order for the forces to be awakened that were necessary
to overcome it. For a long time, therefore, there simply seemed to be no
way to stabilize conditions.

The Greek difficulty in tackling directly what was wrong can be seen
in generally human terms. History is full of examples in which political
groups in societies prove helpless in dealing with crisis conditions
because they lack (at least temporarily) the strength (and ability to
organize it) which they so desperately need. Because an alternative that
could profoundly affect current conditions did not exist. At the same
time, though, Greeks were struggling with problems specific to the
structure of their own world. When everyone *is* the *polis*, it must be
very difficult, except in specific details, to make the *polis* itself an object
of political action and reform. To do so requires transforming the whole
citizenry. As a result, fundamental changes could initially be realized
only by authorities who stood outside or above the *polis*—tyrants or
'specialists in straightening things out' (*katartistēres*), who, from around
600 BC, were sometimes charged with restoring order to the *poleis*.
Normal politics, by contrast, revolved around other things.

Everything in the class ethos of Greek aristocrats, Alfred Heuss wrote,
was based 'on the awareness of their own strength and ability'. The
worth of a man was measured by his ability to get his way and to
be of use to his friends and hurt his enemies. 'I would be a god before
men, if ... I would die as a man who could avenge what others have done
to him', sang one aristocratic poet. Even a wise man like Solon beseeched the gods to let him always be 'kind to my friends, to my enemies
bitter, held in respect by the one and in fear by the other'. That, in the
Greek view, was the only way to be secure. Every man stands alone but
he also needs his friends—depending on circumstances. After all, even
among friends, constellations shift with alarming frequency, as Greek
lamentations about unreliable and treacherous friendships attest.

The normal functioning of *polis* society and in particular the
upper classes seems to have presupposed that its members constantly
regrouped. People could agree in some cases and quarrel in others.
Even if oppositions persisted beyond individual situations, the usual
fluctuations would be restored in time. This was in keeping with the
independence of Greek men and the open way in which they dealt
with one another in small circles. It guaranteed that they would not

become permanently dependent on the same leaders and fellow faction members.

Resolution was more difficult in cases of murder, manslaughter (and perhaps the more serious instances of violated honour). Being responsible for one's own status makes one vulnerable, and Greeks were quick to resort to violence. Cycles of vengeance arose, involving friends and relatives on both sides. Already in the *Iliad* we hear of fear of 'war, heartbreaking war, with one's own people'. But this, we should assume, was initially the exception to the rule, which would eventually yield to normality.

Yet by the seventh and sixth centuries BC, new forms of factionalization seem to appear. They were no longer concerned primarily with vengeance but with power. The more intensely individuals striving to increase their honour and wealth focused on the political offices (that is, the power) in a city, the more long-term alliances were concluded between leading aristocrats. The *polis* now no longer belonged jointly to all its members, or as Theognis formulated the problem, 'distribution no longer proceeded equitably among all'. Membership in the community, in so far as one was qualified for it, manifested itself in being part of things and the recipient of whatever was distributed, including, not least, sharing in offices. The symbolic value of such sharing may even have exceeded its real worth. When distribution became unequal because a few people claimed everything for themselves, it restricted others' sense of belonging, undermined the possibility for coexistence, and poisoned social relations. Traditional means for resolving conflicts proved completely inadequate. The result was an increase in not just violence and murder but also the flight and exile of many opponents (and corresponding attempts to return by force).

'Soon at the hands of its foes will a lovely city be ruined, in conspiracies that are so dear to the unjust', laments Solon, and it does not much matter whether he means that conflicts between these factions were damaging the city or whether he declares them even to be the city's true enemies. He clearly claims—and attests—that aristocratic factions and the injustice they committed were leading Athens into ruin. Solon fears that the city will be 'enslaved', obviously by the domination of a single group. That will cause a condition of *stasis* and sleeping war. The enemies are within the gates, the city is divided, and it is only a matter of time before the flames of war erupt. Hans Schaefer has advanced the hypothesis that factions consisted of members who swore to maintain the same friends and enemies. If so, parties and their conflicts became intense and permanent, and the commonality could easily dissolve in discord. In the face of such constellations the community as a whole was essentially powerless. Egotistical interests and factional ties were more important to those involved than the sense of a community that belonged to everyone together and no one alone.

Stasis was, at the time, a neologism. It meant 'standing', or 'standing up' in the sense of positioning oneself apart from others and even insurrection. Solon's use of the word to designate a latent state of war implies that people were stepping apart and lining up in order to face each other in battle. On one occasion, he speaks of *dichostasis* (standing separately, divisiveness). Later on, *stasis* was used as a word for civil war or for the parties that could or indeed did fight such conflicts. The word may very well originally have had a literal meaning in that determined quarrellers rejected the custom of sitting in the popular assembly and instead remained standing in a front, striking hostile postures, which then prompted their opponents to do the same. The normal procedure is described in a passage of Homer, who calls the goddess of law, Themis, the patroness of assemblies of men: she seats them and (eventually) dissolves them. Since the Greek language offered a number of other words to describe intense conflict, it is probable that *stasis* was coined to describe a new phenomenon.

Throughout antiquity, not least in Rome, people were afraid that factions, which were manifestations of *stasis*, would form and that deep, virtually irreconcilable rifts would develop. The word *factio* implied both intrigue and association, and the boundaries between the two were seen as fluid since both conjured up worries of secret meetings and agreements. There were no states to offer the community a secure framework, nor were their parliaments in which various parties could productively discuss a variety of issues and in which the representation of contrasting interests might have been useful, indeed desirable. In societies where the community consisted so directly of the citizens, as was the case especially among the Greeks, factions, driving a rift through the leading classes, only had the result of dividing the community which, as a consequence, no one was able to represent any more. One part of society was hostile to the other, and where one side triumphed, the other was threatened with exclusion. In communities that were so closely knit, anything could happen when the two sides collided, if there was no third force to intervene between them—which initially seemed a very remote possibility.

With their demands for relief from debt or redistribution of land, the lower classes could be drawn into the struggle. A number of details have survived from the history of Miletus. After the fall of two tyrants, the city came under pressure from a pair of groups, the Ploutis (*ploutos* means wealth) and the Cheiromacha (or party of fists). The latter emerged victorious, driving off their foes and having their children trampled to death by oxen. When the Ploutis later regained control of the city, they smeared all members of the Cheiromacha they could detain, children as well as adults, with pitch and burned them alive. This may have been an extreme case. But violence, banishment, the razing of enemies' fields, and the slaughter of their livestock, violations of laws, and recurring acts of vengeance were common. Miletus was said to be in *stasis* for half a century.

In one of the many songs in Theognis' collection, an aristocrat laments that while his city was the same, the people were different. Those who formerly knew neither justice nor law but whetted goatskins on their backs and lived like roebucks outside the city—those bad ones, he complains, are now the good ones, and the formerly noble are now the bad ones. In contrast to Solon, this poet does not use good and bad in their ethical sense, but solely as designations of social status, describing the entire paradox in sarcastic, if helpless terms. Low descent was an easy insult. But such jibes contained a measure of truth in so far as many followers of usurpers of power were among the suffering members of the lower classes and perhaps also social climbers as well as, in some cases, reckless and worthless persons.

According to some details that accidentally survive in poetry, Mytilene on the island of Lesbos in the early sixth century had to endure a dense sequence of rule by tyrants and aristocratic factions. One of the tyrants, the sage Pittacus, was originally elected by the people as a mediator but extended his rule to ten years (on his own initiative, perhaps based on good insight). From Athens, we hear that in the mid-sixth century two factions, each led by a prominent aristocrat, fought for power. Peisistratus formed a third faction, based on circles and classes that had previously been disadvantaged. He allied himself with one of the other factions in his second of three attempts at usurpation, but succeeded only in the third one to establish his rule securely.

The historical record, though, contains less information about these factional struggles than about the tyrannies that often resulted from them. There is no shortage of reports about the deeds and misdeeds of tyrants, which is probably because they were truly able to achieve things and thus made a name for themselves. Whereas factions constantly had to consult and reach compromises, and could easily be divided by envy, individuals could pursue their goals in decisive, energetic, and sometimes spectacular fashion. Attracting followers was probably not a big problem, and tyrants tended to place their bets on one single winning card. They could present themselves as a player and could often cut through problems that left others stumped. And when they took up the demands of the lower classes, there arose that synergy, which is hardly unique in world history, where one partner in a joint struggle claimed the political reward of power, while the others reaped greater or lesser economic advantages and perhaps legal protection.

But first a city-state had to get to the stage of tyranny. Rivals were usually comparably strong, and they often neutralized one another. The successful usurpations of power preserved in the historical record are likely only the tip of the iceberg. Greek reality would have been even more colourful, with sometimes factions, then individuals, both for themselves and as leaders of aristocratic groups, fighting for control over the *poleis*. The Bacchiadae of Corinth, the Penthilidae, Archeanactidae, and Cleanactidae on Lesbos, or the Paraloi and Pediakoi in Athens are probably just a few examples of many rival aristocratic groups. And their struggles often dragged on without coming to any sort of resolution. In the end, they might result in the rule of a faction or a tyrant—but only for as long as it lasted.

The majority of *polis* members had little option but to join the followers of some powerful person or simply to endure what was happening and keep their heads down. One would have thought, given the small size of the *poleis*, that 'the people' would have been able to intervene, especially to prevent severe injustice. That was indeed Telemachus' wish when he called the men of Ithaca to the agora in a desperate attempt to prevent his father's estate from being destroyed by his mother's suitors. But what did he really want them to do? Certainly not 'to sit silently, although they were many', but obviously 'to assault the few suitors with words and to check them'. Athena had advised Telemachus to make his troubles known publicly, with the gods as his witnesses. But that would have entailed little more than uttering complaints, wishes, and perhaps warnings, with scant chance of achieving concrete results. What could 'the people' do in such situations other than to take the law into their own hands and act as a kind of a lynch mob, as indeed they did try to do on another occasion and threatened to do at the end of the *Odyssey*?

But when the city was threatened by unjust conditions and not simply by the injustice of individuals, there was no option but to take one side or the other or none at all. That at least was the case before Greeks in such difficult situations hit upon the solution of appointing a wise man as a mediator or, as they called it, a 'specialist in straightening things out' (*katartistēr*). When fronts were hardened, and things began coming to a head, that often appeared to be the only answer—whether, as was the rule, the wealthy aristocrats or occasionally those rising up against them were the stronger party. But even so, it could take a long time for peace to return to a city.

Around 600 BC, we encounter the first attempt to mobilize those in the middle on behalf of the entire *polis*. Solon tried to convince them to become politically active when their city was in jeopardy. He even tried to get a law passed to the effect that, in a situation of *stasis*, every citizen had to take up arms for one of the two sides or be punished with *atimia*, the loss of civic honour (and, in effect, citizen rights). Factional fighting, Solon thought, should not be allowed to take place on an empty stage. The majority who were likely to suffer from such fighting should be actively enlisted. Apparently, Solon expected those who were primarily interested in peace and quiet to intervene to stop the fighting rather than supporting one of the parties. Splits within the citizenry, so his logic ran, would normally be lessened if they were spread across the entire populace; enmity could be de-escalated into opposition. But we know of no case where such a law was applied, and it is difficult to imagine that the victors would have persecuted the neutrals. Hence Solon's proposed law was presumably no more than a bold intellectual experiment, and he was probably unaware of how much desperation it expressed.

There is another interesting case from around 525 BC. As the citizens of Miletus finally tried to end the long series of internal wars, they asked their ally, the *polis* of Paros, to send men who could help restore order in their city. They carried out inspections in the countryside of Miletus and wrote down the names of citizens whose estates were in good shape. They then handed over leadership of the *polis* to the men on that list, apparently concluding that they had not been involved in the political turmoil and therefore had not neglected their estates or suffered their devastation. By chance a couplet by a poet named Phocylides of Miletus has survived from around the same time: 'Much stands well for the middle ones. I would like to be among them in the middle in the *polis*.' It was somewhat naïve, however, to believe that those in the middle could just take over the government of a city, and in Miletus, things did not work out. The city was soon subjected to another tyranny.

But in other parts of Greece, people had already made more progress. Before long, Athens too would succeed in moulding such people into a class of citizens who no longer simply relied on political leaders to improve economic or legal conditions, but who developed a political will to control their city.

It is scarcely possible, given the scant number of stones we possess, to reconstruct the entire mosaic of ancient Greek life of which they were once a part. And indeed, perhaps the static metaphor of the mosaic is inappropriate for the vibrant, highly fluctuating world of the *polis*, which varied significantly from city to city. Nonetheless, one thing is unmistakable. No matter what impetus began and was translated into slow but constant change in many smaller *poleis*, wherever such changes assumed large proportions, unleashing the drive to wealth and power, and in turn bringing privation and outrage to the fore, the traditional institutional order was usually condemned to failure as soon as things came to a head.

The best indication of this is the series of tyrannies that were established at the time. They would hardly have arisen with such apparent ease, had officials and councils possessed the power, solidarity, and will to resist them, had those in the most desperate need not supported the usurpers, and had the particular ambitions of specific parties not outweighed the common interest in avoiding any kind of rule and thus failed to suppress the would-be tyrants. 'The city is pregnant', sang Theognis, 'and I fear she will give birth to a chastiser (*euthyntēr*) who will make us pay dearly for our wicked insolence.' *Stasis* and monarchy were on the cards.

The Greek word *euthyntēr* literally means someone who makes something straight, and is thus similar to *katartistēr*. But in this context, Theognis was not talking about an appointed mediator, but someone who rises from amidst the crisis of the city. Nonetheless, the term does reflect a claim apparently made by usurpers that they were restoring a lost order. When Theognis speaks in this context of a 'good deed' (in which he has no interest whatever), he does so with bitter irony, thinking of the negative conditions which such a 'benefactor' will bring forth. And in another passage, when he invokes men who are not saved, it would seem to be a serious reference to the idea of salvation coming from the *polis* and not a sarcastic jibe at salvation through the tyrant.

Ultimately, Greek tyranny tended to end the excessive power struggles from which it was born, and established a measure of calm. Strangely, it left more memories than lasting traces in Greek political orders and still fulfilled an important function. Tyranny was not just an interruption. It was a transition and effected transformation at a time when it was impossible to achieve further development of the traditional order in any other way. Tyranny was thus very useful, even if it was incapable of establishing its own legitimacy. Its very success was to render it superfluous.

The Greek word *tyrannos* was originally used neutrally to designate a lord or ruler. It only acquired its negative resonance in the fifth century BC. By contrast, in the two preceding centuries, many Greeks were uncertain about which was worse: the rule of a tyrant, the rule of an aristocratic class or clique, or even the factional struggles for power which tyranny usually ended. Only gradually did the belief grow that tyranny was incompatible with the *polis*. We encounter this conviction for the first time in Solon around 600, but he seems to have been well ahead of his time.

Tyrannies are attested in almost all of the Greek cities that had been touched by significant change. We find them from the mid-seventh century on the Greek mainland first in Corinth, later in Sicyon, Megara, Athens, and other cities, as well as on the larger islands, for example in Mytilene on Lesbos and on Samos, which was ruled by the famous Polycrates. On Naxos, Lygdamis seized power thanks to a close alliance with the Athenian Peisistratus. There were also shorter, less spectacular tyrannies on Chios, in Rhodes, and in Chalcis and Eretria on Euboea. Among the cities of Asia Minor, the tyranny of Miletus was the most prominent. In Sicily and lower Italy, we know of a series of tyrants. Because of the danger emanating from Carthage, Syracuse was the only city that virtually made tyrannical rule an office. Although in general the rule of tyrant families never exceeded three generations, and the succession of various tyrants rarely lasted longer than several decades, in Sicily the institution of tyranny maintained itself over some longer time and was re-established after an interruption in the fifth century.

Usurpation of power could happen in a variety of ways. There could be a gradual transition between the rule of a faction and that of an individual. Sometimes, an official, most often a successful general, refused to yield his office after its appointed term and used it as a basis for domination, recruiting supporters, for example, by promising them benefits such as land redistribution. Or there could be a *coup d'état*, often with foreign help, with the tyrant taking the city or especially the city's acropolis into his power. He might use armed troops to surround the council and assembly, killing or detaining a few men and ordering the others to return to their homes—quite possibly only after forcing them officially to hand over power to him. There is no evidence of any tyrant being directly elected. When Aristotle describes the position of Pittacus of Mytilene as 'elected tyranny', he is alluding to the fact that the latter was appointed as a 'straightener' and lawgiver and held on to his power for ten years. In one case, the popular assembly of Athens allowed itself to be tricked into granting Peisistratus an armed guard, which he then used in his first attempt to establish his own personal rule. Indeed, Peisistratus is a particularly instructive figure. Having come to power a second time by exploiting factional struggles and subsequently losing again, he seized control for a third time from the outside by military means, based on financial resources derived from gold mines in the northern Aegean, and supported by mercenaries and allies, such as foreign aristocrats and city states. A whole coalition came into play here.

Usurpation of power was usually followed by the banning of one's enemies, sometimes disappropriating them as well and distributing their property and possessions among those without land. The tyrant's rule was secured by armed guards and mercenary contingents, and sometimes protected additionally by alliances with other tyrants or cities. In later periods, there is evidence of surveillance systems as well. Polycrates is said to have closed the wrestling schools (*palaestrae*) in Samos because he feared that people there were hatching plots against him. He also disarmed the hoplites, as did Peisistratus in Athens. Tyrants typically struck deals with parts of the aristocracy with whom they were not already allied, assuring them of honours and privileges. It was entirely possible for a tyrant to enjoy broad popularity over a long time—and not just among the poor and miserable, but also among all those who appreciated peace and an end to aristocratic abuses of power. Apart from their immediate rivals, presumably few people were bothered by the tyrants' arbitrary exercise of power, especially since most of them at the time were hardly accustomed to living in orderly conditions.

The tyrant's rule and his policies were probably financed by taxes, which were rarely levied on property, but commonly on income from agriculture, of which Peisistratus reportedly claimed one-tenth and his sons only one-twentieth. In cases where revenues from import-export duties, mining, or similar sources were sufficient, tyrants did without taxes altogether.

How exactly a tyrant ruled depended on his relationship with various categories of people in his city as well as his own understanding of the exploitation of power, responsibilities, arbitrariness, and personal ties. One thing only remained constant: no one was allowed to challenge the tyrant's authority. There was a famous anecdote about Periander of Corinth asking the tyrant of Miletus how best to secure his rule. Thrasybulos's answer was to take the messenger out to a wheat field where he silently cut all the ears that stood out above the others. Almost all tyrants came from the upper classes, even though many of them had to endure jibes about modest parentage.

A significant number of tyrants improved conditions in their cities and of large parts of the citizenry by implementing sensible, 'modern' measures, inspired by knowledge, method, and planning that often may have benefited from Oriental models. In part, their interests could also coincide with those of the people they governed. There was no shortage of people who were happy to see the limitation of aristocratic power and arbitrary rule. The tyrant's interest in preventing aristocrats from expanding their estates and wealth helped preserve the basic character of communities of landowners; his willingness to set limits on aristocratic luxury not only made his own all the more grandiose but was welcomed by many of those over whom he ruled.

Yet many tyrannical measures infringed upon people's private lives. Corinth, for example, had a commission monitoring whether people spent more than they earned. Periander is said to have drowned prostitutes to set an example and to improve morals. And tyrants generally tried to render just legal judgements, especially concerning the lower and middle classes. They also tried to increase affluence, which in turn drove up their revenues, and used regulations banning idleness and loitering to encourage citizens to work. Cleisthenes of Sicyon decreed that farmers could only enter the city wearing their working clothes—something they were apparently reluctant to do. Similarly, Peisistratus sent judges into the countryside to decide quarrels locally so that farmers would not have to come to the city.

As much as such measures may have been motivated by fear of unrest, even mob violence, they certainly helped improve economic conditions; so did care for justice and fairness and the availability of credit. Polycrates of Samos seems to have devoted special attention to the breeding of hunting dogs, goats, and sheep, and elsewhere we hear that the purchase of slaves was prohibited. In any case, in many *poleis* crafts and production flourished under tyrannical rule.

This was in part due to the building projects dear to many tyrants' hearts. Such projects included useful facilities such as aqueducts and fountain-houses, or roads and especially public buildings that secured the tyrants' lasting memory. In addition to the projects mentioned above, for which Samos is best known, Polycrates also built a city wall and ditch, a palace that was reconstructed by the Roman Emperor Caligula, and the 'Laura', a kind of bazaar in whose niches the charming 'flowers of Samos' offered themselves for sale.

There is considerable evidence that tyrants attached great importance to securing the favour of the gods. They not only built grandiose temples and altars in their own cities, but also set up treasuries and porticoes in the sanctuary of Delphi, initiated cults and festivals, or enhanced those already in existence. These endeavours, too, served a variety of purposes. Festivals offered entertainment and pleasure to the citizens, and splendid buildings were a cause of general joy and increased the cities' pride and reputation. One prominent example is the enormous temple of Zeus that Peisistratus began (but could not complete) in Athens. Once a year, he staged a public performance of Homer's epics, and around 535 BC he founded a competition for tragic poets. That event was part of the cult of Dionysus, to which he, like all tyrants, attached great importance.

In terms of external affairs, as Thucydides emphasizes, tyrants were relatively non-ambitious. Oddly enough, they set little store by the conquests through which other historical rulers have striven to gain fame and legitimize their regimes. The wars conducted by tyrants were limited to the usual battles against neighbours. At most a tyrant might found colonies abroad. Polycrates of Samos, famous for his legendary luck, was able to subject numerous islands and stretches of coastline to his authority, but that was the exception to the rule. His success was due to his strong fleet, which he built with his wealth. (Polycrates, incidentally, initiated the construction of a new type of ship called a *samaina* that was equipped with sails and featured a broad and voluminous body; its image was struck on Samian coins.) He was an active pirate, whose forays went well beyond the Aegean; and he even pillaged his friends' estates, reasoning that he would rather return to them what he had taken than not take it in the first place. Lygdamis of Naxos engaged in similar pursuits but on a much smaller scale.

With the exception of Sicily, the limits tyrants ran up against were conditioned by the structure of the *polis* world. Not only were the tyrants Greeks who kept thinking in Greek ways, but the *polis* also gave them only limited means to achieve their ambitions. They were wary of putting their own people under too much pressure, either financially or militarily, and may well have been afraid of massing them as armed troops. Tyrants had little interest in major change and upheavals such as redistribution of land. They had no desire to found empires. They were mere aristocrats who wanted to enjoy the advantages of their class in their city alone and to the fullest, in egotistical fashion and in keeping with traditional agonistic perspectives. They did constantly compete with one another and not just in their building policies. Their wealth allowed them to maintain splendid courts. Polycrates surrounded himself with beautiful women and boys, consorted with poets, and built up an impressive library. Such habits accorded well with his pomposity and brutality. Still, it is important to recall how much intellectual potential many tyrants had at their disposal. Among the acknowledged Greek sages at the time were Pittacus and two tyrants, Periander of Corinth and Thrasybulus of Miletus. Athens, too, would later recall Peisistratus' reign as a golden age of the city.

On the other hand we have no evidence of any new institutions of civic or political organization that can be traced to the tyrannies. As a rule, they retained existing offices and sometimes councils. No alternatives were available. The institutions themselves were basically harmless. Tyrants probably allowed officials to be elected, ensuring only that their supporters filled key positions. That was sufficient. Polycrates may well have had himself named commander-in-chief of Samos's armed forces.

There were no legal experts who could have reorganized the community to fit it under the tyrant's rule, nor any civil service structure. Greek religion offered nothing to justify the rule of an individual as an expression of divine will, not to mention the idea of an individual being God's representative on earth. The tyrants had no claim to represent the *polis*. It was defined too clearly as the sum total of all its members, and membership was too closely connected with participation in the collective. As a body politic, it was unsuitable for becoming the object of the ruler's care. On the contrary, the *polis* could only belong to the tyrant in the sense of its being the object of his rule. He was its owner, not its king, which is why tyrants concluded foreign treaties in their own names, not that of their cities. Unlike the absolute monarchs of more recent history, the tyrants never founded states that were embodied by their own person—states that could have become super-personal, encompassing both ruler and ruled, and thus capable of outliving the tyrant's own regime.

As much as the interests of the tyrants and their subjects might have coincided in some areas, in the political realm they remained opposed. Aristocrats may have swallowed their pride in tough times, and support from people hoping to profit was great among broad segments of the populace. But as soon as conditions began to improve, they and others wanted to return to being what they had always been: independent and free citizens who had no ruler over them. Or, as Burckhardt wrote, they wanted themselves to be the *polis*. Even after a century of tyranny, as was the case in Corinth, stretching over three generations, or after a series of usurpers, the idea of the rule of one never established itself as self-evident. The old ideals that had been passed down not least by the Homeric epics could not simply be replaced. Connections to the outside world, to places where tyrants never or no longer or not yet ruled, persisted. Concepts of what was right and wrong depended largely on pan-Hellenic views. Aside from distributing the goods of enemies, tyrants almost never assaulted people's private property. A core of independence thus remained. And in any case, with the exception of imposing limits on the aristocracy, whose excessive desires they curbed, tyrants were hardly able to get their subjects to change their ways. If they taught citizens some industry and improved economic methods, that only enhanced the citizen's possibilities. In short, people did no more than tolerate tyranny; in the long run they never approved of it, treated it as normal, or allowed it to become part of the conception of a proper *polis*.

The tyrants' contribution to the consolidation of Greek *poleis* thus consisted only in temporarily offering a protective umbrella, under which economy, affluence, and security could develop without disturbance. The tyrants' very success undermined the need for their rule, and at some point it was abolished. The umbrella, as it were, could be folded back up. Nothing typically tyrannical lasted—except for the monuments they built and the cults they founded.

Peisistratus was quoted as saying that the Athenians should take care of their domestic affairs and leave general matters to him. That was vaguely reminiscent of Hesiod's advice to work hard and stay away from the agora. But what for Hesiod had been words of admonition for a man in trouble was now an attempt to drive a whole citizenry from the public and political sphere. The deep division between ruler and subjects that thereby opened could only be bridged temporarily by patriotism or participation in a cult community. This division led the sons and grandsons of the founders of tyranny to rule in arrogant, arbitrary fashion, enjoying their wealth and living in a grandiose style. There were no strong forces with which they could have allied. That was the reason why, apart from Sicily, where they were needed for defence against outside forces, the tyrannies all ultimately failed.

In almost all places that had happened by 550; in Athens it took until 510 BC. The demise of tyrannies most often came violently, often after a rebellion by aristocrats and sometimes with external assistance. Rebellions by the broad populace seem to have been relatively seldom.

20

Lyric Poetry, the Symposium, and a Reorientation towards Virtue

If the Greeks produced their 'culture' to the same extent that Greek particularity grew out of that culture, if those who shaped culture were simultaneously shaped by it, if those who asked the questions were also those who had to answer them because what they formed was also forming them, then Greek ways of life must have been as extraordinary as those aspects that ultimately so distinguished their legacy. Yet it is difficult to get a full grasp on what it was that was so extraordinary and it is yet more difficult to explain it. To do so, one has to be receptive to unlikely and sometimes only hypothetical connections.

What, aside from political order and the rule of law, do members of a community need in order to live in a more than very elementary sense, when their political centres are weak, their religious institutions are fit only for cult ceremonies and have authority for little more, and they themselves are relatively free and hardly burdened with ideological interpretations of the world? And how do they do so in an age of expansion, risk-taking, conflicts, and rapid changes of fortune—and in an age in which many constraints upon thinking and planning were lifted while, at the same time, social order and the rule of law were in turmoil?

What sorts of words, images, and concepts did the Greeks need to communicate and to interpret what they experienced? What tools did they need not just to be equal to, but to master what was happening and in order to emerge with their spirits and minds intact? How did they reconcile the world in which they lived with their traditional convictions and avoid losing the ground under their feet? How did they maintain equilibrium as they sought to balance all the things that were crashing in upon them? How did they replace what was obsolete with new and different ideas? Action presupposes endurance and perseverance, and in order to persevere one needs reserves. One also has to be accountable to oneself and perhaps others on many things taking one's nature into consideration.

Not everyone falls into intellectual lethargy in crisis situations. Some people always feel the need to understand themselves and the world in their own individual fashion—in thought, poetry, and other creative activities, very personally, individually, and often with great difficulty and far from fully meeting the demands, but perhaps also true to those great challenges of the time. What one man writes or creates for himself can give expression to what many people think and feel. Perhaps it can also awaken that 'capacity for endurance' (*tlēmosynē*) one so badly needs for thought and action. In a time of great upheaval, people may have developed a need to see certain things interpreted and formulated for them so that statements, poems, and images were in fact demanded from those who were capable of producing them. Understanding, after all, is often the key to mastering a difficulty.

How did the Greeks achieve that special richness, that purity and polish that still distinguishes their myths from all others? How important for all that was the freedom of the bard, whom no priest was able to restrict? To what extent did untamed imagination—that especially fertile soil, which also encourages insecurity and fear in the face of the gods—create the very space it needed by portraying the activities of those gods with particular licence? Did Greeks enjoy their unique freedom of imagination because they believed so much depended on the gods—or, to put the matter more precisely, because they felt their dependence on the gods all the more acutely because they were engaged in an often fruitless search for security and dependability? The festivals with which the Greeks honoured their gods could have provided another impetus. They featured competitions not just between singers but between various choruses, and were intended to please the gods. These competitions clearly stimulated efforts to retell old myths in ever new, better, and more beautiful forms. Bruno Snell has written that the purpose was to create a 'divine and heroic counter-image' in order 'to give sense and significance to what was impermanent'. The extant tradition begins around 600 BC with Alcman; choral poetry experienced its high point in the fifth century with Pindar.

The symposium represented another common form of festivity. It was an occasion for men to come together in one another's houses to enjoy the ceremonial drinking of wine (which was thinned with water). Symposia were preceded by the dinner of the host with his family, after which the table was cleared and the floors swept. Again we encounter a division between the genders, in this case a temporal one that ran through one and the same space. The guests were often political friends of the host, including factional comrades who reinforced one another's views, enmities, and resentments. But other factors, too, determined who was invited

Figure 14. Symposium participants. One is playing *kottabos*, a game of flinging a drinking cup by its handles in such a way that the remaining wine hit a round metal disc on a high stand; this disc in turn was to fall noisily down on another metal plate. In another variation of the game, the targets were small bowls floating in a water basin that would sink when struck in the right way.

to participate in the drinking, and other concerns were voiced in conversations, including the recent events or questions of lifestyle, morals, if not love.

The stimulus for these sorts of drinking ceremonies seems to have come from the Orient, but the way they were practised, at least in certain respects, was Greek. Whereas in the Orient the fact that one person reclined while all others sat was a signal of his superiority, the Greeks all tended to recline at symposia (at least in their most common form). It was also typically Greek that the symposium contained agonistic elements. A designated 'master of ceremonies' (symposiarch) decided on specific topics upon which every guest was supposed to give a brief and artful performance. The winner might receive a prize. A *hetaera* might open the ceremonies with some music on the flute. These cultured, often well-educated women, who were available for a variety of services, were no more excluded from this society of men than young boys were. Thus, other pleasures frequently followed the *agōn*. The

Greeks' enjoyment of symposia is evidenced in the frequency with which they were depicted on gravestones and vases. Such images show elegant, well-dressed people, with hunting dogs at their feet, surrounded by luxury. But unlike art, with its rich patrons, the custom of the symposium was probably not restricted solely to the aristocracy. There is in fact concrete evidence to the contrary from the second half of the sixth century BC.

Symposia were not the only forum in which Greek lyric poetry developed and found its resonance, but they were a very fruitful one. The word 'lyric' literally meant lyre-accompanied song, which was composed in specific metres. But 'lyric poetry' is the overarching term we use today for a broad spectrum of poems and songs; their metre was as diverse as the contexts in which they were performed. Elegies formed of alternate hexameter and pentameter couplets (which were not necessarily elegiac in tone) were well suited for public recitation. Putting words into verse made it easier to learn and repeat them. Iambic lines accompanied by the flute were a traditional form of expressing blame, scorn, and satire. Archilochus was the first to excel in these, and later Solon also used them to justify his activities.

The earliest lyric poems could not have survived unless they were memorized by other people and passed on, first orally and later in written form. They were originally intended for small audiences but soon seem to have achieved widespread recognition. Prior to the sixth century BC, poets do not seem to have collected their own works. What survived from earlier periods thus apparently expressed sentiments shared by many.

Archilochus of Paros, the oldest of the Greek lyric poets, composed his poems in the mid-seventh century. Hesiod and the poet of the *Odyssey* could have heard them at first hand. The spectrum of Archilochus' works is broad. Some take up subject matter known from the Homeric epics or from Hesiod. Some of his fables, for instance that about the fox and the eagle, were included by Aesop in a collection that is still read today. In that piece, the eagle steals the fox's young only for the meat to turn red hot so that it ignites the dry grass of the eagle's nest. 'Zeus, father Zeus!' the fox had prayed in Aesop's rendition (if modern reconstructions are accurate), 'Yours is the kingdom of heaven, and you see what people do to themselves, the violence and crime. The rights and wrongs of all creatures are your concern.'

Archilochus' poems were short and dealt with the present, in contrast to the epics, which focused on the past. While the epic poets took their listeners into the world of great heroes, here a man from the margins of society told of the things that moved him—in clear, concise, purposeful language.

Archilochus was famous for the verbal poison darts he aimed at his enemies: shipwrecked, naked, frozen with cold, his body covered with salty foam and seaweed, so shall one of them be captured by the Thracians, 'and his teeth shall chatter, as he lies there like a dog... That's how I would like to see him, who did me injustice and trampled his oath with his feet, he who once was my friend.' The harsh and often sexually explicit invectives against Lycambes and his daughters, one of whom he claimed had been promised him as a wife, became enormously popular. It is said that they caused the girls to take their own lives.

Archilochus was constantly involved in quarrels. He was a mercenary, who kept himself in bread and wine by his spear and who died in battle. 'I am a servant of lord Enyalius (the God of War) and understand the delightful gift of the Muses,' he claimed. But he also felt he was fighting against betrayal, pain, and numerous other evils sent by the gods. He was someone who knew very well how to be a friend to friends and an enemy to enemies. And he particularly lived up to one maxim, which apparently compensated for many of his feelings of disappointment and betrayal: 'to pay back him who did me ill with evil scorn.' 'The fox,' he said, 'has many tricks, and the hedgehog only one, but that is the best of all.'

His father came from one of the best houses in Paros; his mother was a Thracian, presumably a slave. Thus, he did not really fit in anywhere. Yet despite, or precisely because of his outsider background, he was able to express in splendid words what many thought and felt. He was always rethinking what people are, what they should be, and where their limits lie. His work focused on experiences typical of the time.

He was not ashamed of the fact that in flight he had once thrown away his shield to save his life. In direct violation of the usual hoplite ethos, he freely admitted: 'What cares me this shield? Let it go! I will buy me another, and it will not be any worse.' Ignoring traditional aristocratic ideals of the equally beautiful and brave hero, rather than a tall commander, with broadly planted legs, proud of the splendour of his locks and with a shaved body, he preferred a small one, bow-legged, as long as he kept both feet on the ground and was 'full of heart'. Flying in the face of the usual Greek respect for the 'voice of the people', Archilochus declared that anyone with regard for popular opinion could not rejoice in their own lives. And he had little use for fame: 'No one is respected and honoured by his fellow citizens after his death.' Archilochus' thinking paid no attention to those values which motivated and lent glory to Homeric heroes—and which were still self-evident for many of Archilochus' contemporaries. This man, one might say, emptied a whole stage because all he found there were outmoded props. Instead he filled it with a simple, unassuming reality full of need, in which the only things that counted were those that proved useful. What emerged here was a highly refreshing, obstinate, rebellious, even plebeian self-confidence.

The more one looked around, the greater the reason for uncertainty. For Archilochus, accident and fortune were what caused things to happen to men. They were like the day Zeus causes to dawn, and they 'think the way they do as reality happens to meet them'. Terrors came from nowhere. Images of bad weather, of the sea, 'when our lives lie in the arms of the waves', are as frequent as moving songs mourning the drowned. Those themes characterized the entire life.

'Give courage to the young,' Archilochus advised, for they would need it (because there was no other way to master the challenges of life). But, he continues, 'The goal of victory rests with the gods.' The gods pick the desperate man up off the ground and level him who strides along with firm steps so that 'many bad things happen to him. Hunger drives him into confusion, and his thought is disrupted'. Necessity robs the stumbling man of his reason.

The main thing in life is to arm oneself against the tides and turns of fortune. In perhaps the most beautiful of his poems, Archilochus writes: 'Heart, my heart, riled up by hopeless cares, stand up and show your chest to your adversary, standing steadfastly near the enemies, holding your ground, without relent. And if you should triumph, do not boast before the people, and should you be vanquished, don't throw yourself on the floor of the house and lament, but rejoice for glad things and don't feel too insulted in your despair. Know what rhythm holds men in its hand.'

Hermann Fränkel once remarked: 'Nothing helped Greeks more to reconcile themselves to need and misery than the clear idea of a general guiding order.' Archilochus speaks of the 'capacity for endurance' as the cure (*pharmakon*) that the gods have prescribed for all incurable suffering. One thus could always change something in oneself. What is being suggested here is a kind of control over passions as an immediate answer to the very intense experience of all emotions and passions, including love. Love, too, was heaven-sent and able to overwhelm people: 'I lie in terrible longing, bereft of soul, according to the gods' orders, and bored through with horrible pains down to my bones.'

Far removed from the great heroes of the epics, the founders of colonies, and the successful adventurers of the time, Archilochus speaks from the perspective of the vulnerable individual who is outraged at one moment and forced to remain modest at another, batted back and forth, and unable to rely on anything. Without consideration for anybody or anything, he wants to tell things how they are. Recognize the situation. Tally the circumstances: they are miserable enough. Yet there is no reason to give up. On the contrary, one can master the art of the hedgehog—in language. This is a different way of preserving independence and self-assurance. Individuals had to start with themselves and use their language to express themselves, if they wanted to master the world.

The astonishing resonance that this outsider found cannot be explained solely in terms of *how* he said it, by the form and melody of his poems and songs. *What* he said must also have attracted a strong echo. Archilochus' radicalism may have been nauseating, and a shiver may have run down the backs of his listeners, but it still fascinated, affecting the thinking of his contemporaries and later generations. *Ex eventu*, it is clear that whole groups of Greeks needed to jettison all illusions as they tried to redefine themselves in the expanding horizons and rapid changes of fortune typical of their time. They could not afford to accept any pretences. Their eyes had to recognize the essential emptiness of all forms of superficial trimming, be it the superiority of the aristocracy or indeed the lure of sole rule.

Bruno Snell has spoken of an 'awakening of personality in early Greek lyric poetry'. In any case, many Greeks had to develop a new understanding of themselves in the constantly changing conditions in which they found themselves (and others). They were confronted with the problem of finding something to hold on to, and they could only find it in themselves. Many of their efforts were groping and blind. But there was also a transgressive aspect in these attempts of a society that was free and awake, but no longer secure in its traditions, to reorient itself in the world and to take the first steps towards forming new judgements.

Music and lyric poetry experienced a great age. New instruments were built, new themes broached, and new areas opened up. Just as the martial elegiac poets Callinus of Ephesus and Tyrtaeus (who probably came from Miletus but was apparently engaged in Sparta) exhorted soldiers to battle, Solon put his political lessons and warnings in elegiac form. Anacreon dazzled listeners with love poetry and had little regard for those who sang of civil strife and war when drinking wine. What arose in one place was welcomed elsewhere. In the imaginary space of a pan-Hellenic public sphere, a multi-voiced conversation commenced and spread through symposia and other occasions, presumably including poetic contests. For the poet Mimnermus of Colophon in Asia Minor, life was without value 'if Aphrodite, the golden one, is missing', 'love in secret chamber, sweet concessions, bed'. 'If only the fate of death would strike me in my sixtieth year without illness or burdensome cares.' From faraway Athens, Solon answered that Mimnermus should have said eighty instead of sixty; he, Solon, experienced ageing by learning many new things.

The island of Lesbos proved especially fertile ground. Around 600 BC, Alcaeus and Sappho were composing songs in the Aeolian dialect spoken there. They had been preceded by Terpander, one of the great musicians of the seventh century, who had emigrated to Sparta to pursue his trade.

Politics, which also attracted much attention in contemporary symposia, are at the forefront in Alcaeus' poems. He came from an aristocratic family in Mytilene and he and his brothers had become embroiled in the heated fighting in his city. He wrote of the triumphs and defeats of the factions and tyrants competing for power. On at least two occasions, he had been forced to flee and seek refuge in neighbouring areas, where he lived like a farmer, homesick and bitter. Yet he also travelled to Egypt and Thrace. One of his brothers entered the service of the Neo-Babylonian king.

Alcaeus beseeched the gods to cleanse the earth of his enemies. He also gleefully described the fall of one of the tyrants: 'Now is the time to feast, and more than one can or will, to get drunk—Myrsilus is dead.' The poet had pledged to fight together with others in order to liberate the people from their suffering. When one of his allies, Pittacus, broke ranks and betrayed his friends, Alcaeus aimed enraged scorn at him. But Pittacus was successful. The Mytilenians appointed him as 'straightener' and lawgiver. In Alcaeus' eyes, he was no better than a tyrant. But the people's misery was desperate, as the poet attests himself, although we do not know in precisely what context: 'Poverty is an unbearable and ungovernable evil. It yokes the great people with its sister, helplessness.' It is likely that Pittacus, who was one of the Seven Sages, realized that the victor in factional strife usually did not liberate the city but rather took possession of it and provoked the revenge of the defeated. Someone thus had to break the vicious cycle and eliminate the misery caused by factional fighting. That was possible only if the citizens were enabled to govern themselves, free from a dominating power. Pittacus reportedly succeeded in this aim after ten years.

Alcaeus, on the other hand, saw only Pittacus' betrayal and tyranny, and he took both very personally. The poet was trapped by his belief in the superiority of noble blood. Pittacus, he cried, came from poor stock, as did many others who rose to prominence with him.

Alcaeus' poetry allows us to see the brilliantly burning anger of a repeatedly defeated and frustrated aristocrat, who seeks to prod his comrades to action. In a series of impressive images, including that of a storm-battered ship threatening to capsize, Alcaeus sketches out the situation of (presumably) both his faction and the whole city: 'I no longer understand the war (*stasis*) of the winds; from here comes one surge, from there another.' Later, this would prompt the phrase, the 'ship of state'. All this must be borne and (at least temporarily) forgotten—over wine and feasting. Without the latter, life is unbearable. Drinking is both a constant theme and the reason men have assembled. Despite everything, life calls men to rejoice together.

Sappho, probably a member of a noble family as well, also suffered from the fighting on Lesbos. She had to flee the island for a time, taking refuge in Sicily. Like other women on Lesbos, and presumably in other cities, she maintained a circle in her house and gardens that was dedicated not least to the Muses. Young girls used to spend time there immediately before getting married. They came both to 'form' themselves (in an elementary sense of the word) and to abandon themselves to play and joyous pursuits before being subjected to the very different serious side of life. In her songs, Sappho describes how the girls sang and danced, wove wreaths and garlands to decorate one another, perfumed themselves with oils, and served the Muses. Everything they needed to learn about being graceful is made palpable in a single detail: they had to know how to raise the hem of their garment delicately to the ankle in order to give nothing more than a hint of their charm. Similar images are depicted in statues of women from the period. Other aspects would have been included since, in the aristocratic mind, beauty was connected with goodness. Sappho sang: 'Whoever is beautiful is only so in so far as the eye can see. Whoever is good, though, will be always be beautiful as well.'

Within this circle, the girls formed close friendships amongst themselves and with the lady who was both the head of the house and one of their own number. When asked what the most beautiful thing in life was, Sappho answered: that which one loves. In her songs, Sappho asks

Aphrodite for assistance in courting, begrudges rivals their success, laments when a girl has to leave, summons memories, and tries to build a bridge in her thoughts to a friend living far away. 'It seems to me that he is near to the gods who sits beside you, close to you, listening to the sweet sound of your voice and your charming laughter,' Sappho says. Thinking of this, her heart drops, her voice breaks, her tongue is paralysed, and a fire runs over her skin. 'With my eyes, I see nothing, a drone fills my ears, I break out in sweat, a trembling overcomes my limbs and I am paler than spindly stalks of grass. I seem to be like a dead woman. But you have to accept the challenge of everything.' That task is extremely hard since 'Eros is limb-shaking, bitter-sweet, unconquerable, a snake'.

'The moon is sunken as are the Pleiades. It is the middle of the night, and time slips away. I sleep alone.' In a later poem, she sings of old age that has transformed her once so tender body, turning her hair from black to white and weighing down her soul. Her knees, 'once as supple in dance as a doe's', no longer carry her. 'But what can I do? It is impossible for human beings to become ageless.' Based on recent new discoveries, the ending of this particular poem is much debated. In one papyrus, the text quoted is followed by lines that suggest that, while Sappho's body aged, her art did not since it lived from love. Posterity later honoured Sappho by referring to her as the tenth Muse, equal to the nine divine ones.

It is hardly astonishing that in a world that revolved around men, poems by women or by men writing about women should have featured an otherwise unknown tenderness. Simonides of Ceos, who was born in the mid-sixth century BC, lived into his eighties, and continued to produce poems even after the Graeco-Persian wars, speaks of Danaë, the beloved of Zeus, whose father cast her out to sea in a wooden chest with her newborn son Perseus. Terror fills her, as a storm whips up the waters, and her cheeks become wet. 'She put her loving arm around Perseus and spoke: "My child, what misery for me, but you are asleep . . . If that which is terrible was terrible for you, your fine ear would take in my words. But I say: Sleep, my child. Let the sea and the immeasurable suffering sleep as well."' Fränkel interprets this to mean: 'Let the peace that has descended around this small, slumbering being also grasp hold of the elements.' The poem concludes with a prayer: 'Father Zeus, let a turn of fate come and forgive me if my entreaty be too bold, if it exceeds what is right and just.' Albrecht Dihle has written that the poem ends in 'that selfless mode of humility fitting Danaë as a chosen one of Zeus'.

An assemblage of almost 1,400 lines survive under the name of Theognis. It includes verses composed and edited by this aristocrat from sixth-century Megara together with a long series of other ones similar in tone and origin. It was likely a staple of ancient symposia, songs written by and for men from which the symposiasts could help themselves. Their main theme is what is typical and recurring. The focus is on daily practice and survival in the world of the Greek *polis*.

The Theognis poems celebrate wine and sociability while emphasizing the fears and misery with which Greeks had to contend. The poet laments the poverty that paralyses men's tongues. What man struck by poverty, he asks, dares to speak up, even if he has much to say, in the face of looming peril threatening the city? Here too the metaphor of the ship of state occurs. The experienced helmsman has been dismissed, and 'bad' people (the specific word Theognis uses literally means 'the carriers of burdens') have taken command. No one seems to be concerned that the ship is taking on water. The poet invokes the rise of tyrants, both in the past and potentially impending. One must not make common cause with bad men, he warns, not even out of desperate necessity. To be sure, one has to live with them, but: 'Only with your tongue give the appearance of being a friend to all.' Poor character is contagious. 'Make your hue fit the times and circumstances', but only your hue, the poet advises.

The poet sings of friends and foes, dreams of revenge and beseeches the gods for opportunities to exact vengeance. 'I would rather die', he says, 'should I not find calm before the terrible cares and should I not requite injury with injury... Would it be given to me to drink their dark blood!' This poet's strategy for taking revenge involves cunning. 'Sufficiently confuse your enemy', he counsels. 'But should he fall into your hands, cast off the disguising word and avenge yourself upon him.'

In the Theognis poems too everything happens against the backdrop of constant change. Overnight, one man can be impoverished while another becomes rich. There is no counting on anything or anyone, rarely enough even on friends. The poet repeatedly states that everything depends on the gods, but the gods act completely arbitrarily, meting out the same fate to the just and unjust alike. Thus it is hardly possible for mere mortals to understand them. In essence, and to use a modern term, the gods are but ciphers for blind, incomprehensible chance, even if in other passages the poet also asserts that people are responsible for their own destinies. On several occasions, he invokes the idea of agonizing *amēchanie* ('tool-lessness' in the sense of helplessness), a leaden feeling of paralysing powerlessness. In the end, all one can do is keep one's composure.

Curious statements mention cities and 'men who are no longer being saved'. It is unclear who or what might have saved them. Most likely, it would be the usual means by which a *polis* would try to free itself from a crisis, like a ship trying to avoid sinking. For Theognis considers whatever tyrants can achieve a social ill and not a true rescue. It is as though some people are simply innately incapable of being saved. And if that is the case, then the rule that one should always stick by what is just can no longer be upheld. 'Nothing that applies to men who are saved [or for whom there still is hope of being saved] is appropriate to us... on the contrary, appropriate is what is in line with a city that is about to be conquered.' Hesiod had once drawn a similar conclusion, if only, in the end, to go beyond it.

The book of Theognis brings together a number of voices. Some verses even feature contrasting opinions. The authors differ on various issues, and their views even seem to fluctuate. The book does not represent great poetry; nor can it be said to offer an average sample of the sorts of poems sung at symposia. Rather, it articulates the views of a specific circle of men, who are themselves the audience addressed by the poems. They were probably aristocratic but not involved in the city's power struggles—allegedly because they were too noble, but in reality because they were incapable of doing so; their wealth was precarious, they were among the losers, disappointed that other aristocrats were marrying their children into families with wealth but from poor stock; and full of resentment. And they were worn down by the constant difficulty of staying at the top of the social ladder.

The aristocrats in question have to assert themselves in all directions. They are guided by traditional moral standards, to which they continue to cling, convinced of their own essential membership in the community of 'good' men. They persist in this attitude, although their moral principles keep proving rather inadequate and the successful members of society simply ignore them. Whatever contrasts emerge are shoehorned into the stark categories of good and bad, with 'bad men' accused of being unable to distinguish between the two. Rigid protests abound: 'I will honour my father city, the glorious *polis*, and refuse either to turn to the people or to obey those who do ill.' What remains is to be stubborn and contentious, and to compensate for one's misery with desperate reassurances of one's own superiority.

One poet writes: 'Poverty is what enchains men most of all, far more than old age or feverish shivering.' Wherever possible, on land or the broad seas, the poet counsels, one should seek to overcome poverty.

The best hope thus leads far away. Things are more difficult at home. One has no desire to work, and work probably does not do much good. It almost goes without saying for Greek poetry that the author also invokes the idea that the best thing would be never to have been born at all.

In view of all this, it was enormously important that the symposium provided opportunities to put opinions, cares, worries, and protests into words. Symposia were about playing through one's own relations with others. They functioned as a kind of extended public sphere, even if those present often included only those who thought alike.

When one is only responsible for addressing oneself and one's own kind, when one is generally just an individual, has no distinction, and is no specialist, beholden neither to superiors nor to certain types of issues or tasks (to say nothing of being a woman of the house or a slave), everything becomes a matter equally of this or that person. Then one has to be a keen observer of all one's fellow men and realize how inscrutable they are (except for all-knowing Zeus). One needs to register their limitations and ultimately ask what men are—perhaps only leaves blown about in the wind.

With that, the poets of the Theognis corpus broached a specifically Greek theme, born of the situation of an intermediate class of people, in which the general experience of universal change and the failure of traditional attitudes were especially accentuated. The poets' views stood in contrast to many new forces and approaches to current problems but perhaps rather complemented the new trends. If endurance was an essential component of action, and if only those who could take pain were capable of inflicting it, then in the general flux of the era everyone could come to play first one role, then the other. Only gradually did a new social force crystallize that was capable of serving as a new basis for many Greek *poleis*. And in the process another and yet different aspect of the Greek type of person emerged.

One central topic of lyric poetry was a reconsideration of the virtues that people needed to have, especially in their capacity as citizens. This was less a revaluation of all values than a different accentuation of certain positive qualities. It was again the symposium that provided a forum for this sort of normative self-assertion. In fact, symposia seem to have been especially well suited for this task, since one of the most obvious questions to pose to participants was that of defining the most important virtue. In the Theognis corpus we repeatedly encounter comparatives and superlatives, apparently presenting answers in this social game. One poet opines: 'The most beautiful thing is the highest justice.' Similar sentiments can be found in Phocylides of Miletus. And the quotation continues: 'Health is best, but to reach the goal is the highest pleasure.'

Aretē was no longer conceived of merely as ability in warfare and athletics; nor was it the excellence of Hesiod's diligent farmer. New definitions of this concept articulated new limitations and needs: those of the *polis*. Tyrtaeus dismisses glory achieved in wrestling and running to heap praise on the bravery of those who defend the city. That was the source of 'complete *aretē*'. The philosopher Xenophanes of Colophon deemed his own wisdom (*sophia*) superior to all the strength of men and horses, and his measure of all things too was the welfare of the city, in which wisdom ensured *eunomia* and full stores of grain. Others might describe the middle path as the best course, if they did not want to flee into the private sphere and elevate love and the enjoyment of life above everything else. We repeatedly encounter criticism of people who consider wealth 'the only virtue'. Obviously, debating the ethical preconditions of communal life was one of the chief pursuits at symposia and other social occasions.

Whereas Hesiod had admonished his audiences to work hard and promised them wealth as a reward, the lyric poets emphasized the utter uncertainty of success. In a long elegy, Solon discusses what people hope for, mostly in vain, and what they try to achieve, concluding that success is not a matter of being good or evil. He beseeches the Muses for wealth such as the gods can bestow, for fame, and for the strength to prove himself both as a friend and an enemy. The gods are known, at least usually, to punish injustice, if not on the actual perpetrator then on his descendants (even if these are blameless). What one does not know is whether the gods, as Hesiod believed, will also reward people who deserve it. It is easy to accept the former, but the latter is all too is uncertain. Thus, people have to be ready for anything, and it seems good to moderate expectations. The situation is different for individuals and for the city, which, according to Solon, can count upon the favour of Zeus and Athena.

Solon also cautions that the rich are not just those who possess gold and silver, but also those who enjoy their lives in the presence of dear children, horses, hunting dogs, and a guest friend from afar. Independence can also be secured on a lower level—one only has to be constantly aware of it. Solon does not, however, think of the beggars mentioned by Theognis. Solon attests to the wide spectrum of experiences typical of the time. He can rely on 'goodness' because it is permanent, while possessions constantly change hands. He can also

level all differences between people by contrasting their fate with that of
the gods. Mortal men cannot attain true happiness; they are all *ponēroi*,
that is, plagued by misery and laden with difficulties, poor, and therefore
'bad'. Those higher up, who like to call their social inferiors *ponēroi*, are
themselves nothing but that when compared with the gods.

But there was actually no need for such comparison with the gods. In
light of changed criteria, the discrepancy between the socially superior
claims to goodness and their actual excellence was all too apparent.
Hence it was possible to play with the various meanings of the word
for 'good', using it alternately in its ethical and sociological senses. In the
conclusion that many good men were poor and many bad ones rich, the
words became interchangeable in every sense.

Simonides of Ceos, whom G. E. Lessing once called the Greek
Voltaire, adopted a saying of Pittacus: 'It is hard to be good.' Simonides
interprets the word 'good' according to the traditional ideal in which
manly excellence (*aretē*) and success more or less coincide. But how, he
asks, can one be a good man, 'square in arms, legs and reason, without a
fault?' (According to Pythagoras, the square was the perfect shape.) Yet
Simonides pursues this line of thought further. Only a god can claim the
label of goodness. Among mortals, a person is already bad, if he suffers
bad fortune that leaves him helpless. Good are those who have good
success, while the bad ones are those who suffer failure. The best people
are therefore those who are loved by the gods, arbitrary as these are.
Consequently, Simonides does not seek the impossible, the perfectly
blameless human being. Instead, he will praise and love all those who
never purposefully do anything blameworthy. After all, not even the gods
battle against the inevitable. In contrast to 'bad', the term 'blameworthy'
clearly signifies things that deserve moral condemnation. Everything,
Simonides concludes, is beautiful that is free of blame.

He is satisfied by men who possess a reasonable amount of insight and
are not entirely helpless, by the healthy who know the justice that is
useful to the city. These qualities are not merely average, but clearly
positive, for 'there are fools aplenty'. What Simonides envisions is the
ideal of a practical, reasonable, justice-oriented *polis* member and citizen—although, ironically, the poem in which he sketches out this vision
was dedicated to a member of the high Thessalian aristocracy. The poet
thus contrasts the high-flying with the possible and casts doubts upon
connections between success, prosperity, and people's actual worth.
Simonides never implies with a single word that the gods bestow favour
according to merit.

Such poems probably reflected general discussions and debates. But that does not mean that symposia and lyric poetry themselves did not play a significant role in shaping the process of which they were part—by expressing new ideas, repeating them, and formulating them in impressive forms.

'Of all things that breathe and move on earth, earth mothers nothing more frail than man', the author of the *Odyssey* says at one point. 'As long as the gods grant him prosperity, as long as his limbs are lithe, he thinks he will suffer no misfortune in times to come. But when the Blessed Ones send him sorrows, he bears these also with endurance, because he must. The father of gods and men makes one day unlike another day, and earthlings change their thoughts on life in accord with this.' These sentiments were echoed by Archilochus, Pindar, and later poets. Man is a creature who lives from one day to the next. 'What is someone, and what is someone not?' Pindar responds. 'Man is the dream of a shadow.' And Simonides: 'You who are a man should never believe you know what the coming day will bring...Change takes place more suddenly than a fly flits from one spot to the next.'

Such sentiments were certainly the expression of bitter experience, of suffering and sadness. But would they have been put so strongly or repeated so often, if they did not also resonate with extreme disappointment? Does one not, therefore, have to hear in them echoes of the great expectations and demands the Greeks maintained when dealing with themselves and others? Should merit not be rewarded? Should men not be capable of bettering their lots, planning for the future, and achieving things? Should they not be able to count on the reliability of others?

Statements like those quoted above may reflect the extreme experiences of outsiders like Archilochus, or the pent-up resentments of those who had failed. But, given especially how widespread and well-known these poems were, did they not also sum up the misery and needs of the entire Greek people, with their penchant for risk and adventure? Did they not mirror the lack of illusions, the non-ideological nature of perceptions, and the immediacy with which Greeks dealt with one another, the problems of extreme mutual dependency and those of controlling one's emotions, to be resolved only through social collaboration, and the necessity of being accountable to oneself and one's peers, and of being able to change aspects of one's own self? Did such poetry not reflect the free spirit, indeed the temerity with which the Greeks tested their destiny in the world?

An established class of rulers would neither have produced nor enjoyed such poetry. But such a class was not to be expected. Among the Greek aristocracy, however, there were always many losers, and they gave lyric poetry both its roots and its resonance. In general, these sort of men, accustomed as they were in the variety of their communities to viewing themselves not least from an external perspective, would have had a special sensitivity for aesthetic ways of perceiving and articulating reality.

Poetry should by no means be reduced to a function of social history. On the other hand, poetry can never be fully independent of what is of obvious concern to people at a particular time, of what they feel they *need*, not least from poetry. This seems all the more true for a homogeneous society that featured such a prominent and shared public sphere. Greek lyric poetry was about the difficult task of finding orientation and a just order in both the world and oneself—through observation, artistic expression, and competition.

It is worth asking to what extent the *kouroi* and *korai*—those marvellous statues of young men and women—are a comparable, if very different expression of the Greeks' essence as a people [See Fig. 7 above: The *Kouros* of Anavyssos]. The genre was based on Egyptian models, but the Greek statues stood free, without supports, possibly because Greek sculptors worked with a different sort of stone. The Greek statues were also different because the men were depicted completely naked, as 'pure' human beings, not as functionaries, and because their archaic smiles further distinguish them from the stiff dignity of their Egyptian models. [See Fig. 13 above: *Kouros* of Tenea] That smile gave the person depicted both an individual charm and an aura of personal superiority. Admittedly, the statues contain nothing of the desperation that is frequent in lyric poetry, but different artistic genres depict different things. The focus in Greek sculpture was on the ideal, on strength and self-control. Greek poetry and sculpture converged in their depiction of the human capacity for perseverance, but Greek sculptors were unable or unwilling to give expression to the lamentations and misery voiced by the poets. Moreover, the statues were but one element of widely flourishing archaic visual art, which also includes temples and their decoration (not least the freezes and metopes or relief panels) as well as the images on Greek vases and coins. Thinking about the so-called Basilica in Paestum, Burckhardt writes: 'What the eye views here are not mere stones, but living creatures... The Greek tended to make an impression not through mass, but through the *ideal* treatment of forms. The Doric order he created is one of the greatest achievements of the human sensibility for form.'

Nowhere in surviving lyric poetry is any mention made of the growing ambitions and advances of the broader classes that became noticeable from the mid-sixth century BC. This does not mean, however, that these classes did not articulate themselves in similar ways. That they in fact did so is visible in later poetry, for instance, in verses celebrating the Athenian tyrannicides. That is also where we first encounter the slogan of *isonomia* (political equality).

21

The Beginnings of Political Thought: The 'Middling Class'

There were no Greeks before the Greeks. They knew nothing of the possibility of democracy or even of an increased participation of broad classes of citizens in the community until they themselves realized those ideas. Traditional rights of participation in popular assemblies could serve as a starting point, and the small size of the communities offered favourable conditions. The appeal of the public sphere made it seem worth one's while to engage in it. Nonetheless, it must have been difficult for early Greeks even to have conceived of broad segments of the citizenry regularly appearing together with the affluent, experienced, and generally superior aristocrats and arguing beside and against them.

A usurper of power knows what he wants. The position to which he aspires is more or less predetermined, and his task is to think about ways and means of achieving his goals. But how could broad segments of the *polis*, roughly those in the middle according to wealth, come to comprehend that they could play a meaningful role in politics? How did they develop the abilities to do so on a permanent basis and not just in times of temporary upheaval? Were they even able to imagine the shape of a *polis* in such changed circumstances?

From the seventh century BC, however, the founding of colonies and frequent conflicts had encouraged the Greeks to think beyond tradition and the status quo and prepared them with increasing intensity to reconsider issues concerning the *polis* and its social order. Given the multitude and diversity of Greek *poleis*, it was useful to draw comparisons. The problem frequently was how to reconcile opposing forces, and discussions about such problems were public (not concentrated in the courts of rulers). Hence there developed an interest in observation and analysis that was at least partly informed by theory. Moreover, there was an increasing need for advice on many issues. The oracle of Delphi—where questions, experiences, and possible solutions were swapped back and forth—thus took on vital importance and authority.

This was one factor behind the spread of what soon became a typically Greek characteristic: thinking—focused on general issues and their foundations—assumed an increasingly important role in their self-orientation in the world. To take up the German sociologist Arnold Gehlen's idea that human beings, as creatures relatively poor in instinct, are inherently dependent on institutions, we might say that the Greeks, as a people relatively poor in primary, self-evident institutions (and averse to monarchy), had especially to rely on reason and intellectual communication. That applied both to how things were and how they might be. Solely pragmatic reasoning did not go far enough.

Archaic Greek sources are full of references to the Seven Sages. Opinions varied about who should be included in their number. The sages were a diverse lot. Alongside various tyrants, we find Solon of Athens, who deemed tyranny to be incompatible with a just political order. But we also encounter Epimenides of Crete, who was known as a miracle worker, specializing in the magical cleansing of cities from curses laid upon them after cases of murder. Indeed there was likely a broader circle of individuals unknown to us by name, who were also considered sages. As Burckhardt pointed out, there was 'no caste that could have claimed authorship of Greek thought as the innate protectors of knowledge and belief'. Rather, from 'extremely diverse circumstances' in the beginning, there arose the men who were considered by some sort of natural consensus to be sages.

In the historical record, the Seven Sages are credited with a series of laconic and pithy sayings. *Gnōthi sauton*: know thyself, that is, recognize that you are merely human. *Mēden agan*: nothing to excess. Both maxims were said to have been engraved on the Temple of Apollo at Delphi. Another saying was *metron ariston*: measure is best. Greek conceptions of justice might be heard in 'Do nothing by force' and 'Hate wrongdoing'. There is considerable evidence that the Greek sages, who of course had seen much of the world and were in contact with one another, were closely connected with knowledgeable men in Delphi. But such truisms, apparently current at the time and easy to remember, can certainly reflect only an especially popular and palpable expression of the influence of these men.

The Greek sages might well have adopted many of their ideas from Oriental wisdom, beginning with elementary rules on how to cultivate one's land, how to manage one's household, how to get along with one's neighbours, and, practically, how to lead one's life in general. There is abundant evidence for such rules in Egypt and the teachings of Solomon as well as in Hesiod's *Works and Days*. They would have interested all Greeks, including the tyrants.

But in time, the Greek intellectual elite must have become increasingly concerned with political problems, and this is where their path deviated from that of others. Men who rejected any form of monarchy came to challenge tyrants and their supporters. They were the ones to whom cities could turn when they could see no way out of acute emergencies. Such emergencies could take the form of destructive social tension, popular outrage and revolt, widespread murder and violence, civil war, or perhaps the imminent usurpation of power by individuals or factions. In such situations, many people, including those who otherwise preferred to stay on the sidelines, must have had an interest in preventing problems from worsening to an extreme. And they needed someone who was capable of leading a city out of a crisis. That person could be a fellow citizen like Solon in Athens or Pittacus of Mytilene. Or a city could enlist someone from abroad. By chance, we possess an oracular pronouncement from Delphi advising the men of Cyrene, who were desperate to restore order, to travel to Mantinea, where they would find someone who could help them. The person in question was named Demonax, of whom we know nothing else but that he apparently did his job splendidly. Presumably, he is one example among many.

From Herodotus, we know that men charged with such tasks were called *katartistēres*, literally, those who brought things back to order or, as Kurt Raaflaub puts it, set things straight. (Later Aristotle, probably wrongly, called them *aisymnētai*, umpires.) The word *artios* means straight, appropriate, and just. Those were precisely the qualities such men were to restore by straightening out the *polis*.

They were given unlimited authority. Their task was to eradicate abuses, which may often have made it necessary to intervene radically in the status quo. If they were convinced, as seems probable, that there was such a thing as a just social order, which only needed to be restored, then their task was not to negotiate and to bring about compromise, but rather to ensure that every member of the community got what was his just due. When, by contrast, someone like Pittacus found it impossible to leave his city to its own devices after only a short interval and thus retained power for ten years, it was a matter of smothering conflicts so completely that they could no longer flare up again. In any case, the crises must have been severe for cities to make the *ratio* (rationality) of a wise man their *ultima ratio*. The challenge simply was to avoid both the Scylla of tyranny and the Charybdis of civil war. For that, the citizenry had no choice but to accept what it might otherwise not have accepted.

The 'straighteners' must have had significant influence on the process of early Greek political thought, which began, initially within narrow circles, around 600 BC but with time must have involved the participation of ever-broader classes. For us today, the authors of this thought remain almost entirely anonymous.

We possess but one, albeit hugely informative, document in which we grasp the beginnings of such reflection and thus of Greek political thought: Solon's poem that was later entitled 'Eunomia' (fragment 4 in Martin West's edition). It was composed in Athens around 600, at a time when tensions threatened to explode into civil war. Solon's apparent aim with the poem was to encourage a large number of citizens to intervene and call for the appointment of a *katartistēr*.

In Solon's view, it is not the gods, but the citizens themselves who are responsible for the city's misery. This he emphasizes right at the beginning, explicitly referring to Zeus' and Athena's favour. The problem is that the city's leaders are unable to keep the peace. Nothing—neither public nor sacred property—is safe from their greed. They violate the very principles and sacred foundations of justice, Dikē. But Dikē, the goddess of justice, herself, will come to punish them—with certainty. The same idea had been advanced earlier by Hesiod. What is new here is that the road from injustice to punishment leads not just through Zeus, but is empirically evident on earth. For 'already an inescapable evil is approaching for the entire *polis*'. Quickly it falls into miserable slavery (which can mean here the rule of a tyrant, of an aristocratic clique, or of lords over indebted farmers). Such servitude in turn will awaken internal strife, *stasis*, and slumbering war that will cost many lives. The city will soon be consumed by the fighting between aristocratic factions. This would be a devastating, indeed hopeless message, if it were impossible to avert the process.

Yet Solon says explicitly only that inescapable disaster is approaching. Apparently, it is still possible to avoid it. Interestingly, this first document of European political thought already implies the concept of fleeting time (that can barely be grasped before it is too late). As a slightly later fragment by Alcaeus attests, this was a common fear at the time. Solon speaks in two crucial passages about the speed of the process. The citizens need to be alarmed. To increase the urgency of his appeal, he points out that the *demosion kakon*, the general ill, will spare no one: not even the courtyard gate can stop it.

Solon sums up the social evils plaguing Athens under the single term of *dysnomia*, 'bad order', in which customs, norms, and laws—that is, the entire *nomos*—are in disrepair. The whole, and not just individual parts, is in a state of crisis, and must be restored to order. How this can be done is another question. In his poem, Solon emphasizes only the concept of good order (of *eunomia*). What he states here in eight lines of verse, having devoted twenty-seven to *dysnomia*, remains entirely vague. His personified vision of *Eunomia* 'smoothes those things that are rough', 'enfold(s) in fetters those that are unjust', 'stops *koros* (extravagance) short', 'straightens crooked judgements', and 'stops the deeds of factional strife'. It is hard to interpret Solon as saying anything more than that the good order of the city will be restored when its grave problems are eradicated. Solon is not proposing a new social order according to a human plan, which he would then have to describe. Instead, he is merely calling for the old order to be re-established so that it can once more unfold all its blessings.

The city is like the sea, of which Solon remarks on another occasion that it is whipped up by storms from time to time, but when no one stirs it, it is 'the most just of all'. Solon presumably could not have conceived that Zeus, in all his wisdom, would not have provided the city with everything it needed. The way things were earlier, as far back as one could think, must have been right. Thus Solon had no doubt that the 'leaders of the people', although clearly the source of Athens's ills, should nevertheless be the ones to lead them in the future as well. As soon as the just order had been restored, this apparently would no longer pose a problem. Restoration too was the primary concern of the impoverished, the indebted, and those who had been sold into slavery. One might have to install a few security measures to make sure that the restoration maintained itself, but that was all.

History would show that Solon's assumption was wrong. He recognized very clearly which processes were threatening the city. But what should result from his intervention in the end was a sheer matter of belief, albeit a marvellous and in many respects liberating belief. His observation of the imminent necessity directing the processes involved— comparable to the laws of nature—seems to have strengthened his conviction that Zeus enforced punishment and cared for justice. Conversely, his faith in the effectiveness of divine justice confirmed to him that he had correctly observed the laws governing all processes on earth. Experiences of other cities offered evidence and examples. Vast possibilities for human understanding and action were opening up. Understanding the (unpleasant) processes implied the (pleasant) alternative that one could prevent them from unfolding. This idea may have bolstered Solon's conviction, expressed at the beginning of the poem, that the gods were in fact favourably inclined towards his city and that only humans (the citizens themselves) were responsible for its current, sorry state. This notion was backed up by what was likely a widespread belief that there once must have been a just order and that it corresponded to the will of the gods. People who assumed that the *polis* was a viable social form had to assume, at least at that time, that things there could proceed justly. This was one of the fundamental conditions for early Greek political thought.

Solon's insight represents a further step forward in that he distinguishes the political sphere from that of nature, in which Hesiod had largely placed Zeus' punishment of the judges' injustice. For Solon, what had been caused in the political sphere had consequences there and only there. And because this was the case, people could intervene. Whereas in nature everything happened according to unbreakable laws of causality, in the social and political spheres people could break through chains of cause and effect. In another poem, Solon observes that, as snow comes from a cloud, and thunder from lightning, 'the city is led into ruin by great men'. But he adds: 'The people fall into the slavery of a single ruler *through ignorance.*'

Solon's focus on the political sphere also enabled him to provide a more plausible answer to questions of guilt and responsibility. Whereas Hesiod saw the majority of people not only potentially suffering under the unjust decisions of 'gift-devouring kings', but also threatened by any punishment Zeus might send a city's way, Solon initially states only that those who do wrong are liable to suffer in many ways for their hubris. The disaster potentially resulting for the whole city as a punishment for such misdeeds, however, arises only if the citizens fail to take countermeasures in time—that is, one might continue the thought, if they assume part of the responsibility by not doing what they could do to prevent the evils.

As a consequence of such considerations, Solon discovered the citizens' responsibility for their community. Since no one could fail to care for its fate—because it was obvious that the misery of the poor, indebted, and enslaved fellow citizens was threatening to cause misery for all—the citizens had to intervene. Such reasoning might have been supported by the belief, increasingly widespread in the archaic period, that un-atoned murder stained the entire city and threatened it with ruin.

Solon's fellow citizens, however, could initially live up to their responsibility only by intervening in an extraordinary situation and appointing a 'straightener'. Further exceptional situations might be caused by future *staseis*. Most likely, however, neither Solon nor most members of broader classes, especially of Athens's large population, were able to conceive of the idea that the people as a whole could regularly play a decisive role in politics.

Solon thus unravelled the impenetrable tangle of misery and hopelessness, which seemed to leave resignation or wild rebellion as the only options, into a comprehensible process that could be countered with orderly procedures. The city could pick itself up by its own bootstraps. Due to the concept of *eunomia*, deep interventions were now possible in those social and property structures that deviated from traditional norms—by a person placed in charge by the citizens themselves. This opened up an immense range for shaping things and much freedom of action—within the claim to restore the old conditions but without the need to establish a monarchy, and even if all this did not yet succeed in taming the aristocracy.

Projects of a better future were beyond imagination. Tradition was the only source of legitimacy. Nevertheless, ideals sought in the past could affect the future by presenting an alternative to the present. A clear distinction was made between the just order and the status quo, or between aristocratic claims to goodness and their actual morals. In an era that continued to be oriented towards the past, demands could be made in good conscience that ultimately (though mostly unconsciously) aimed at change. For a long time, the Greeks had desperately sought to project their hopes for justice onto the gods. Now they began to see how they could fulfil those hopes themselves, on earth. Greek political thought had begun, and to us Solon is its first witness.

'The invisible measure of knowledge that alone maintains the bounds of all things (and keeps all things within their bounds?) is the hardest to think.' So reads another of Solon's fragments. Things have limits because this is what distinguishes them from what is unlimited. That alone determines their being. That which keeps their limits also keeps them secure and determines them. If what does the limiting is a measure, it has to keep things within a framework of what is appropriate and right for them. This concerns relations and balance between them, at least if one assumes, as Solon apparently did, that everything has something that is appropriate for it and that what is appropriate, if balanced, will be compatible with everything else. Such relations are invisible because they exist between things, yet they and only they preserve the limits of things. Things themselves cannot do this. Without such a framework, they would burst their bounds. Of course, this measure cannot be a divinity (such as Eunomia). It is probably by necessity a measure of knowledge. The fact that Solon deems it the hardest for men to think likely reflects his experience with the *polis* and at the same time with the world.

The two lines in which Solon makes that point thus are the most significant testimony for what it meant to constitute a political order among a free citizenry. What was at stake was not to reach compromises, but to ensure that everyone got what was his due: this guaranteed justice. Only when proper measure is maintained can the citizens, in turn, maintain equilibrium in their city. And that was indeed their task, of which no higher power or monarch could (or was supposed to) relieve them. The whole had to exist in the right relations between its parts. This view is perhaps paralleled in Heraclitus' famous maxim: 'the invisible order (*harmonia*) is stronger than the visible one.'

If Greeks faced the challenge of discovering new possibilities for thought and action, perhaps their only option was to do so in conjunction with the old question of divine justice and the new search for an invisible measure. The Greeks had no choice but to have considerable faith in the notion that life on earth was governed by sensible principles. Generations of Greeks memorized Solon's poems and cited him as an authority.

We have no way of knowing to what extent other political thinkers at the time shared Solon's insights and opinions, but at least there emerged a broad consensus that tyranny should not be tolerated. This is astonishing, but indeed many people saw things this way and it corresponded to the desire to restore the old order. As a consequence, if a city was to be straightened out, it was not enough to eliminate social disorder. The city itself had to be enabled to take both responsibility for itself and care of itself. That was an enormous intellectual challenge.

A reformer working in the service of a monarch operates from a centre of power and can count on an institution that is always prepared to intervene when this proves necessary. The Greek straighteners, however, had to find means somehow to balance forces within a city. They had to study a city's innate tendencies and in particular ideas about who was entitled to what, and measure them against one another.

Most probably, Greek political thinkers generally worked independently of the demands and temptations of individual rulers. It was the exception to the rule when one entered the service of a tyrant. They also had to be immune to specific political trends. Otherwise they would hardly have been able to win much trust, mediate quarrels, and reconstitute communities. Their authority was based on expertise and wisdom. It was consolidated, and the reformers' own position strengthened, by the fact that they operated as disinterested third parties, capable of keeping their focus on the interests of the whole community, whose constant protectors still needed to be groomed. The reformers' reputation, like that of an oracle or a doctor, was measured by how successful they were in coming up with solutions for a great variety of problems. In this type of men, reason—applied in the interest of all of society—got a chance. They represented a third force.

In some sense they were embedded in the pan-Hellenic public sphere. The voices of those who found the arbitrary exercise of aristocratic power and factional fighting intolerable must gradually have grown louder. The multitude of Greek *poleis* had the advantage that there was always a broad circle of disinterested, outside observers and judges of events of any significance. They stood next to the outraged and the sufferers of injustice, and they lived not on some faraway continent, but close by, in comparable circumstances and in a culture of speech and communication.

At least in the long term, however, the straighteners could not help but conclude that in many places it was impossible to rein in aristocratic ambition and all its potential consequences unless the members of broader classes, 'those in the middle', were empowered to speak up in the community regularly and freely and on their own initiative. They had to be prepared to assume responsibility not just in extraordinary circumstances, but as a political rule, whether or not there was cause for uproar. To do that, they had to be transformed, at least in part, from people affected by negative circumstances to people who set the tone.

Of course, throughout world history, despite their numerical superiority, the broader classes of societies have hardly ever had much of a say. If this general rule was to change, however, special institutions needed to be created and, more significantly, the broader classes needed to be enabled intellectually and mentally to assume this role.

Greece in the sixth century BC was a huge 'experimental laboratory' for institutions, primarily political offices, councils, popular assemblies, courts, and the maintenance of justice. Much must have been conceived, introduced, observed, copied, and developed further. Traces of institutional thinking can be found in a suggestion made by Thales of Miletus that the Ionian *poleis* of Asia Minor should join together to form a single *polis*, within which they would continue to exist as subdivisions. This idea never went beyond theory: nor did a similar plan proposed by Bias of

Priene to found a mega-*polis* in Sardinia. Even so, both projects offer fascinating examples of how far Greek thinking was transcending traditional models.

Of special interest were reforms intended to connect members of the broader classes more closely with the centre of the *polis*. The citizenry was divided into new subdivisions, and a new sort of council was conceived: the *boulē dēmosie*, or popular council, as it was known on Chios. These new bodies were juxtaposed to the traditional aristocratic councils. Seats on them, however, were not for life. They changed hands frequently, probably in most cases every year. We know this system best in Athens, where councillors were also supposed constantly to rotate. This was in keeping with the logic of direct participation in the community. Constant rotation allowed the council to be embedded firmly in the circle of those who appointed its members, and it also succeeded, indirectly, in creating a fairly direct presence of broader circles of the citizenry in the centre of the *polis*. Representatives had no chance to interpose themselves between the people being represented and the whole.

It is perhaps not all that astonishing, given the typical conditions of Greek society (including the attractiveness of the public sphere as the sphere of the aristocracy with its emphasis on leisure), that a considerable number of men were ready to devote a significant amount of their time and energy to their community, at least if economic circumstances were consolidated. Even those who did not live within the city proper or who, for whatever reason, could not easily make themselves available must have felt the allure of assuming at least temporarily a place and rank in such a public forum.

Political equality, or at least something approaching it, must have seemed like a privilege. The members of the broader classes were nothing but the less well situated among a society dominated by aristocrats. They had no ideals of their own with which to confront the nobles—other than perhaps an awareness that they felt more responsible for the *polis* because they had no personal ambitions and were thus well suited to ensure the maintenance of peace and justice and hence to care for all. Since few of them could hope to rise up the social ladder by dint of hard work, serving as a councillor was a lofty ambition in itself. Access to such service granted to the entire class raised status and importance. That must have been their motivation—especially since there was no place for them in the larger pan-Hellenic public sphere.

Both Herodotus and Aristotle later observed that in Greek democracy 'the people' did not fragment into parties. Apparently, the members of the broader classes did not make for loyal followers of aristocratic leaders. In the sixth century, this was already a crucial quality one had to, and could, count on. Amidst all the differences of opinion, participation itself was too important for members of the broader classes; it made them want to stick together, once they had been given a chance to have a say. This means that they seem to have developed a horizontal solidarity, a keen and stable consciousness of what they had in common with their peers. Their thinking became determined by general and civic concerns, not those specific to their homes and individual interests. They needed to politicize themselves rather than their affairs. Among their various senses of belonging, that of citizen must have become so central that a kind of citizen identity arose. Max Weber called changes in attitude of this sort 'fraternalization', and he characterized it not simply as people learning to help one another to pursue common aims, but as them *becoming* something different, 'allowing a different "soul" to enter themselves'.

In this sense, many *poleis* in the course of the sixth century saw the rise of a social order which was revolutionary in world history and would soon be known under the name of *isonomia* (equal order in the sense of equal participation). Isonomy was a precursor of democracy. The idea of *eunomia* was both modified by and finally fulfilled by the addition of the prefix *isos* (equal). The new concept also contained the idea of equilibrium between superior individuals and the main part of the citizenry.

Around 500 BC, Alcmaeon of Croton, a physician-philosopher from the Pythagorean school, was propounding the notion that the *isonomia* of dampness and dryness, cold and warmth, and bitterness and sweetness preserved health, whereas the domination (*monarchia*) of one element of these pairs made people ill.

No matter how much it may have fulfilled its members' own long-term wishes, the political rise of those in the middle can hardly be explained without the preparatory work of Greek political thinkers. They first had to conceive the institutional prerequisites, translate discontent into political demands, awaken ambitions, and spread political thinking to broader circles.

They also had to help create something approaching 'common intelligence'. Solon once chided his fellow Athenians for being, as individuals, clever as foxes but having empty heads when they made decisions together. Some twenty-four centuries later, the German poet

Schiller would write much the same thing concerning learned societies: 'Everyone, seen individually, is decently clever and reasonable, but when they are *in corpore*, you'll find that they turn into an idiot.' In 500 BC Heraclitus complained: 'Although the *logos* (word, reason) is common, most live as if they had their own insight.' This was not just a generally human problem, but a specifically Greek one. It required the growth of a facility of judgement based on common axioms that even Aristotle later found characteristic of popular assemblies.

The scepticism many Greek intellectuals and philosophers felt towards democracy emerged in a later period. Sixth-century Greek thinkers, by contrast, must have come to view robust political participation by the broader classes as something urgently desirable.

Greek political thinkers thus succeeded in achieving something that, to our knowledge, the Hebrew prophets, for instance, failed to accomplish. Those prophets shared with Solon the insight that men, and not (a) god, were responsible for their own misery. But their answers about what to do about it remained stuck in the realm of religion and morality. They had no political lever with which to intervene in events. They had to be content with criticizing social ills and voicing accusations, and knew only the commandment to better oneself, and not the responsibility to act politically. Moreover, Greek sages differed from their Chinese counterparts, such as Confucius, in that they did not have to direct their advice at princes. They aimed their ideas at a variety of audiences, and included the whole of the citizenry. And in the end, they changed the body politic.

22

The Beginnings of Philosophy and Science

There were conspicuous parallels between what Greek political thought gradually believed to find in regard to the *polis* and Greek philosophical speculations. There, too, people were searching in a very specific sense for general rules.

Thales of Miletus is usually considered the first Greek philosopher. It is improbable that he actually was of Phoenician origin, as Herodotus writes. He was perhaps nicknamed the Phoenician because he spent some—presumably even much—time in the Orient. In any case, he seems to have learned a lot there. Otherwise, he would hardly have possessed the knowledge that allowed him to calculate and predict the solar eclipse of 28 May 585 BC.

It had been some 150 years since the Greeks had adopted the alphabet, and roughly a century since Greek vase painters had developed the so-called 'Orientalizing style'. Only gradually, according to need and ability, had the Greeks succeeded in incorporating what they had discovered in Oriental cultures, although they no doubt registered even earlier with astonishment some of the results of those centuries-long traditions of learning. By 600 BC, however, they were certainly capable of using this knowledge—even if we only have fragmentary evidence of how they did so.

Thales was counted among the Seven Sages, and various pieces of technical and political advice attributed to him have survived. He reportedly specialized in geometry, but he also seems to have engaged in speculation about the origins of the world. What was new about his thought for Greeks was that he did not try to explain this in terms of myth but rather by positing an original element, water. In Aristotle's opinion, that insight ensured his place among the philosophers.

It is difficult to draw clear distinctions between Greek philosophy and science and their Oriental predecessors. One can by no means say that people in the Orient, especially those in priestly circles, merely collected large amounts of knowledge without engaging in science and philosophical speculation themselves. Pythagoras was not the first person to discover that in a right-angled triangle the square of the hypotenuse is equal to the sum of the squares of the other two sides. If anything, he was the first person to prove it, but even that is uncertain. Nor were Greek doctors the first to draw up detailed reports of illnesses. Such reports have also been found in ancient Egypt. Furthermore, Hippocratic medicine, incidentally also differing in this respect from other Greek schools, was not the first in the entire discipline to make itself independent of religion and magic. In the seventh century the physician Arad-Nanaï made the same distinction, as the diagnoses, instructions, and predictions he sent to the Assyrian King Asarhaddon demonstrate.

But we should expect specifically Greek approaches where questions and answers were closely related to problems of the *polis*. Since its survival depended on its ability to maintain itself while coexisting with fluctuating social forces and their inevitable conflicts, it must have seemed logical to think of and search for comparable systems of order in other areas as well. What could have been more obvious than to seek analogies in the cosmos? That is precisely what we find in the thought of Anaximander of Miletus in the mid-sixth century. Anaximander had attached himself to Thales. He was also the first philosopher we know of who wrote down his insights in a book that was still available much later.

The earth, Anaximander postulated, was not supported by anything. It simply maintained its position because it was equidistant from all points of the surrounding circle of the sky. Hence it was unable to move up or down or sideways. It did not, therefore, as Thales thought, float on water, nor did it rest on a cushion of air, as Anaximenes, a younger Milesian thinker, believed. For Anaximander, though, the earth was connected in orderly relationships to other heavenly bodies. This was thus also an attempt to understand the whole as a set of relations between parts, not least, presumably, in the sense of an 'invisible measure'. At any rate, one thing was not dependent upon another. Instead everything mutually supported everything else.

Unlike Thales and Anaximenes, Anaximander did not presume that one element, be it water or air, was the origin of the world. For him, the beginning (*archē*) was above all the *apeiron*, that which was limitless. He also called it the divine. One is reminded here of Hesiod's notion of Chaos. Everything emerged from the *apeiron*, only to return to it in the end. Anaximander's formulation of this idea survives, exceptionally, as a literal quotation: 'The original source of existing things is also what existing things die back into according to necessity; for they give justice and reparation to one another for their injustice in accordance with the ordinance of Time.'

The later author (Theophrastus), who quotes this sentence, points out that Anaximander used a rather poetic mode of expression. Anaximander may have applied experiences and postulates of legal thinking to the world as a whole—indeed, perhaps, to a succession of worlds, which he also mentioned. He went well beyond the conviction, already widespread in ancient Israel, that punishment follows injustice, if necessary in the second or a later generation. In Anaximander's view, anything that comes into existence is connected with some form of injustice. In the political realm, this would imply that every power will have to pay for the injustice to which it owes its rise, when the next power, tyrant, or empire, also unjustly seizing control, replaces it.

There was no shortage of examples of the succession of rulers, dynasties, and empires. The injustice of many a rise to power was easy to diagnose. The political experiences of people in great Miletus, which had frequently been plagued by *stasis*, or on Lesbos and elsewhere, were in everyone's minds. So, too, were events abroad, near and far, that might also have affected Greeks, sometimes severely: the rise and fall of the Lydian Empire, the emergence of the Persian Empire, and the related fall of several powerful dynasties.

Anaximander came from one of the leading families in Miletus and was involved in the founding of one of the city's colonies in the Black Sea area. Political problems could hardly have left him cold. Indeed, it would have been very strange had the cycles of political rise and fall of which Herodotus was later to write, as well as the interpretation of such events through categories of justice, injustice, and punishment—together with the relevant terminology—failed to influence Anaximander's thinking about the world. This was true no matter what other observations and speculations about the sequence of warmth and cold, dampness and dryness, and similar matters he might have connected with it.

Anaximander's basic conception differed from that of Solon, according to whom processes of increasing tension in the city could be prevented by restoring *eunomia*, which was as just as the sea when it was not whipped up by a storm. Anaximander, too, probably considered those things just that rested at ease with themselves and were mutually able to support each other. But his experiences were different from Solon's, and in his famous fragment, quoted above, the world and not the *polis* stood in the foreground. There no such order was visible that might prevent injustice. Instead, he saw instances of individual domination (as in the succession of day and night or summer and winter), but these were subjected to constant change and thus also to destruction. Overall, justice certainly ruled, but in the all-encompassing world it was realized only in the sequence of time, in rise and fall. Nor did the victims receive justice (as they did in court) and the perpetrators were not liable to pay penalties to them. Rather, the penalty for their crime came at a later point in time when others pushed them aside or overthrew them. Constant change and all-encompassing order were one and the same. Everything in the world ultimately dissipated into the limitless.

Thoughts are never arbitrary, especially in an age in which the various spheres of life are still tightly interwoven and there are no specialized forms of discourse. Ideas to the effect that ultimately every form of rule was based on injustice could hardly have been conceived in the Oriental monarchies. Among the Greeks, however, they had their place. However much the multifaceted thought of Anaximander, of which we know only the tiniest fragments, may have been indebted to Oriental knowledge and speculations about various areas of nature and the world, what he did with those influences seems to have sprung from specifically Greek claims and questions. (The same was true for Alcmaeon, writing a short time later, who used the political category of *isonomia* to distinguish between human health and sickness.) Anaximander's geography—his sketch of land masses and seas, which was made, as it were, from the third position of an observer aiming at objectivity—was presumably also typically Greek.

One member of Anaximander's circle was Hecataeus of Miletus, the most important scholar of the next generation. He not only refined and enhanced his teacher's map of the world, but energetically conducted geographical research along the Mediterranean coasts and published descriptions of those areas and their inhabitants that would later be known as Europe and Asia. Hecataeus also sought to examine mythological traditions critically and to fit them into a genealogical order. Both of these endeavours represented empirical research, and, as far we as know, he did not ever engage in speculation about the origins or essential being of the world. Other scholars were active around him who worked on systematizing and analysing various areas of knowledge. Anaximander, for example, was also credited with the construction of land-surveying instruments based on Oriental models.

Xenophanes came from Colophon, one of Miletus' neighbouring poleis. He was born around 570 BC and left his homeland when the Persians conquered it. He then took part in the founding of the Phocaean colony of Elea. He was roughly the same age as Pythagoras of Samos, who also emigrated to Italy, either because the tyrant Polycrates had driven him into exile or because he did not want to live under autocracy. He settled in the southern Italian colony of Croton, where he established a circle or, to be more precise, an order of followers. Two other major philosophers belonged to the following generation: Heraclitus, who stayed in his home city Ephesus, and Parmenides, who grew up in Elea and developed his enormously influential philosophy there.

Milesian thinkers proposed a variety of theories, but all of them ran more or less along the same lines. In contrast, with these last four thinkers, Greek philosophy began to branch out dramatically. It would take until the fifth century for comparably significant schools of thought to arise on the Greek mainland.

Xenophanes was a circumspect man of enlightenment who travelled widely, giving lectures throughout western and mainland Greece. This is presumably how he earned his living. He presented his thoughts in the form of poems, as was the case later with both Parmenides and Empedocles. It is said that he also wrote two epics. Xenophanes had much political advice to offer, which was the basis for his conviction that his wisdom was useful. For instance, he attacked the telling of useless stories at symposia and criticized excessive emphasis on luxury. The men of Colophon, he pointed out, had assembled on the agora, 'with jewellery in their long hair and drowned in the scents of artfully prepared ointments' and were promptly subjected to political domination.

Since he depended on finding audiences, his surviving fragments demonstrate how great the interest was in his ideas, at least among the upper classes in the second half of the sixth and the first third of the fifth centuries. He lived to be well over ninety.

Xenophanes disputed the idea that in the beginning, as in a golden age, the gods had shown the mortals everything they needed. 'Rather, in time, through seeking, their discoveries improve.' He himself and his contemporaries were participating in this process. People were making progress. They had to continue researching and keeping themselves up to date. At the same time, they needed to comprehend how unreliable human perception was. 'There never has been nor will there ever be a man who knows the truth about the gods and all the matters of which I speak', Xenophanes stated. 'For even if one should happen to succeed to the full in saying what is completely true, still he himself would not know it. But in all things there is opinion.'

Xenophanes found prevailing conceptions of the gods laughable. 'If oxen and horses or lions had hands', he joked, 'or could draw with their hands and make things as men can, horses would have drawn horse-like gods, oxen oxen-like gods.' For Ethiopians the gods were snub-nosed and black; for the Thracians, they had blue eyes and red hair. What was the point of all this? And how was it conceivable that gods were born or stole from, cuckolded, and deceived one another?

Xenophanes came to conclude that all such perceptions were wrong. Instead he believed in 'one (sole, unique?) god, greatest among gods and men, in no way similar to mortal men in body or in thought'. This idea was reminiscent of Hesiod's conception of Zeus as the all-powerful god of justice. But Xenophanes' one god was simultaneously the god of heaven and heaven itself. He was not just the supreme and most powerful god, but encompassed all and everything. He was all-seeing, always in the same place, and omnipresent, 'all eyes, all spirit, all ears', not bound to any one of the individual senses. If in Homer Zeus was so strong that he could lift up everything, the entire world and all the other gods, on a golden chain, Xenophanes' god 'effortlessly shakes all things by thinking with his mind'. In relation to the heavens as a whole, Xenophanes was quoted as saying: 'God is the One.' Did he mean being as such, the entirety of the universe, of which it was said that one should imagine it, as one should imagine God himself, in the form of a sphere?

Anaximander held the *apeiron* to be divine; Xenophanes thought the world was so. Whereas theology played the dominant role in Hesiod's and Solon's thinking about Zeus, Xenophanes' ideas represent a turn towards philosophy—although the term itself had yet to be invented.

Xenophanes' main concern, and even if only because his livelihood depended on it, was to spread his teachings. Heraclitus, by contrast, took an almost aggressively negative stance towards the public world. He was not at all interested in offering political advice and, even when asked, refused to formulate laws. When people noticed with astonishment that he was playing with some children, he answered that it was better to do that than to play the citizen with you. He did not expect to be listened to. He himself was not interested in 'the many'. Ten thousand of them, he scoffed, were worth but the value of one man if he was the best.

Heraclitus came from the venerable royal family in Ephesus and voluntarily renounced the family's hereditary priesthood of the Basileus in favour of a brother. He wanted solitude. He deposited the book in which he compiled his insights in the Temple of Artemis.

A relatively large number of Heraclitus' aphorisms survive, as well as some longer passages of his writings. No matter how one arranges these fragments, they are clearly interrelated in a variety of ways. Everything is connected with everything else. If Greeks regarded Heraclitus as 'the obscure', that was because his thinking contrary to all customary logic combined the extremely diverse. Individual Heraclitean sentences are as clear as it is baffling how what he is saying can be related to everyday human experience. This at least is true of many of his assertions, and especially of his most exciting ones.

What Heraclitus was ultimately trying to discover was the *logos* of the world, the fundamental law operating in everything, the reason that controlled and directed the course of all existence. 'It is wise', he pronounced, 'for those who listen not to me, but to the *logos* to agree in accordance with it that all things are one.' People were supposed to perceive the *logos* themselves. Then they would be able to experience the unity within the fathomless and extremely complex diversity, pulling in different directions in so many ways, that constituted the visible world; they would see how, on a large scale, everything was connected. This, above all, is Heraclitus' concern.

The idea of this sort of unity, one might object, is contradicted by the contrasts and opposing forces, which constantly confront human beings, and did so particularly for the Greeks, given the relatively unlimited variety of perspectives with which they perceived the world. Constant change also seems to undermine such a notion of unity. But in fact, Heraclitus argues, the opposite is the case. 'God: day/night, winter/summer, war/peace, fullness/hunger'. Indeed, not only is God all-encompassing, but 'To God', he adds in a different context, 'everything is beautiful and good and just, whereas men assume that some things are unjust and others just.' Humans distinguish and create contrasts, while God unites. Day and night are, for humans, opposites, and yet in their constant alternation, they are one.

Opposites, moreover, transform themselves into one another. For Heraclitus, what is 'living and dead, waking and sleeping, young and old', is all the same. 'For this, when it is turned over, is that, and that in turn, when it is turned over, is this.' Warmth and cold, dryness and dampness, one turns into the other.

Things also replace one another, mediated in various ways. In one passage, we read that everything exchanges itself for fire, and fire exchanges itself for everything, just as goods are exchanged for gold, and gold for goods. Yet, fire is not just a mediator between things. On the contrary, the order of the world (*kosmos*) *is* 'ever-living fire, flaring up in regular measures and dying down in regular measures'. This the world order was, is, and will be forever. Everything comes from fire. Moreover, Heraclitus asserts, 'fire on its approach will judge and condemn everything', levelling and consuming it. In this sense, the bolt of lightning, although striking suddenly, 'steers everything'.

What is opposite can, however, work together in harmony. 'That which is in opposition is in concert', Heraclitus proposes, 'and the most beautiful harmony comes from things that differ.' In another fragment, he writes that that 'which differs with itself agrees with itself—a back-turning harmony, like a bow or lyre'. The Greek word *harmonia* was a term taken from carpentry (fitting or joining together), and Heraclitus sees it operating everywhere invisibly in the background.

In this vein, war or, more generally speaking, struggle is the 'father of all things'. It is thanks to struggle that some have become gods, and others men—and among men, some have become free men while others are slaves.

Heraclitus thus intellectually unites—even if often roughly—everything that might appear at first glance to be diverse, opposed, even radically apart; he does so with all his strength and in a way that was later perceived as dialectic. He stresses the concepts of joining opposing tensions and the sequence of constant reversals. It is not that all things are fully identical, but they are all coupled most closely with each other, emerging from and disappearing into one another. In this sense, all is one, and one is all.

Assertions of this kind are impossible without constantly making paradoxical statements, such as: war is what is common and binding; justice is quarrel (in court). Thus Heraclitus writes of 'immortal mortals, mortal immortals, living the death of those dying the life of these'. Or: 'When they are born, they want to live and gain the destiny of death.' Heraclitus also tries to uncover paradoxes in language: 'The bow (*biós*) bears the name of life (*bíos*) and brings death.' Once again, what conventional notions split apart is ultimately at one with each other.

The correlative to the one that is everything is the one and only wise thing (*sophon*), of which Heraclitus writes that 'it alone is and is not willing to be known under the name of Zeus'. In another passage, Heraclitus says that this wisdom consists of understanding the thinking which steers everything through everything. What he apparently means is an intelligence somehow immanent to or determinant of various forces so that they reciprocally steer each other in the direction they are meant to go. If the one and only wise thing resists being called Zeus, it is presumably because naming it could impose limits on it. But such wisdom, which certainly is the property of the all-encompassing God, can, if people understand God's intelligence, apparently also become a property of humans.

The question is how mortals can achieve this. 'The things I rate highly are those which are accessible to sight, hearing, apprehension,' Heraclitus asserts. But, 'eyes and ears are bad witnesses for men if they have barbarian souls'. Souls without language have no way of recognizing the sense behind what they perceive as real. And they are the majority, those who are 'present when absent', deaf, asleep when awake, without reason. They do not realize what they are confronted with. Man needs his senses, but *logos* is something that cannot immediately be comprehended. Is it the task of the soul, then, to discover the *logos*? The soul, Heraclitus writes, 'has its own *logos*, which multiplies itself'. Furthermore, he asserts, 'you will not be able to discover the limits of the soul on your journey, even if you walk every path; so deep is the *logos* it contains'. This may be the proper context in which to understand Heraclitus' famous saying: 'I searched for myself.'

But the soul is not alone in its thoughts. It is embedded in what is 'common to all' (*xynon*). 'One has to follow the *xynon*', Heraclitus declares. It seems to be given with the *logos*, which is itself common to all— although most people live as if they privately possessed 'their own insight'. They live as if asleep, where everyone inhabits his own world, although the one world is common only to those who are awake. Heraclitus puts this in the form of a pun: 'One should speak with reason (*xyn nōi*) and so make oneself strong with that which is common to all (*xynōi*), as a city does with the *nomos*, and yet stronger still. All mortal laws are nourished by the one divine one, for its power extends as far as it wants. It is sufficient for all and stretches even further.'

What is common thus corresponds to the divine. It nourishes itself from the divine, and human reason has to draw its strength from the fact that it relates to and participates in it. This common element apparently is accessible not to the many but to the best in the community of those who are awake, and together become conscious of the *logos*. Heraclitus does concede that 'it is given to all men to know themselves and to act reasonably'. But few, it seems, try to achieve this—although being 'of a healthy mind' is the highest virtue (*aretē*), and the greatest instance of wisdom consists of telling the truth and acting in accordance with nature, listening attentively to it.

Without doubt, the intellectual paths Heraclitus chose to follow took him far away from the *polis* and its typical constellation of problems. But one could also perhaps argue that his thinking remains determined by those problems in so far as it begins with and is based on typically Greek sensibilities, experiences, and needs. First and foremost among these is the frequent, and so drastically felt experience of constant change. Greeks would hardly have been able to perceive this in terms of a structural transformation but in those of opposites and the struggles between them, the sequences of rulers and factions that replaced one another, the constant cycles of up and down, and the need to counter what was, in the eyes of contemporary observers, a serious irritant. Hence contrasts and contradictions had to be reconciled into a unified whole. There were various ways of doing this. One could search with Anaximander for instances of justice being served in such processes. One could follow Solon and look for general laws. One could counter the vivid confusion of change with a framework of factors that remained the same. But one could also 'sublimate' all forms of contradiction by locating them in larger contexts, seeking to identify what was identical about all the instances of reversal within the constant flux of the world. That necessarily involved seeing an active, self-driven context within the whole, the 'one and only wise thing', or the 'bolt of lightning' that steers the whole and is God, just as it is one. It does not rule over the whole—it *is* the whole. What it directs it permeates and determines. Such ideas had close correspondences in the *polis* itself.

'Into the same river we step and we do not step.' This statement is generally applicable. One is continually being confronted with the same issues in different ways.

The experience of this very truth, however, creates the need not just to recognize unity in diversity but to discover the measures and laws according to which all things happen—for example, in the process by which a fire blazes up and dies down. It is the measure, the proper relation, which had to be somehow innate in things and for which the Greeks searched everywhere, in their concepts of justice and systems of social order, in architecture, city planning, and human physiology, as well as in thought itself. This measure had to be objective—in contrast to the subjectivity of those who acted on the political stage, who held and aspired to hold power. As such, it was the correlative of freedom. As Heraclitus puts it, 'The sun will not overstep its measures; otherwise the Furies, the allies of Justice (Dikē), will find it out.' In Greek religion and mythology, the Furies were from old responsible for avenging bloodguilt. Here they appear as guarantors of the sacred order of nature. Kurt Latte has commented: 'Just as the prosecution of bloodguilt is transformed from a matter of personal revenge to a demand of justice, and the Furies are transformed into servants of Dikē, so the regularity of the movements of the heavenly bodies is subjected to the category of law. Using the example of the sun, which is not allowed to deviate from its appointed path, as it once did in Greek legend, processes of nature [are here] not just pondered as mere empirical constants, but evaluated and privileged as examples of adherence to a proper measure.'

Heraclitus must have made many more statements relating to the *polis* itself than have been preserved in the extant record. One of the three parts of his work (alongside the part dealing with the whole and the theological) is said to have taken political issues as its theme. A few isolated fragments are all that have survived. They include statements that the city has to fight for its law as it does for its walls, that it is more urgent to extinguish arrogance than a fire's blaze, and that *nomos* also means to follow the will of one man. It would be very interesting indeed to know why most of Heraclitus' pronouncements on politics were lost.

Whereas Heraclitus tried to use reason to conceptualize everything into one, Parmenides went in the opposite direction, radically distinguishing Being from all forms of change, all that is determined by emergence and decay, which is what we can perceive with our senses.

At the beginning of his only surviving work, a didactic poem, he describes with an image how he gained his insight: he is speeding in a chariot drawn by 'exceedingly intelligent mares' above all the Greek cities. The daughters of the sun god are steering his ride to the light. Eventually, the horses arrive at the 'gate to the paths of day and night'. Dikē, the goddess of justice, has the keys, and the girls persuade her to let Parmenides pass through. An unnamed deity—we do not know which one—then attests that it is not a bad turn of fate, but Themis (the goddess of traditional, customary laws), and Dikē herself who have steered him to this path that lies outside those trodden by humans. 'You must learn everything,' the deity tells the author in the poem, 'the steady heart of well-rounded truth and the beliefs of mortals in which there is no true trust.'

Similar to Heraclitus, Parmenides strongly distinguishes himself from 'unknowing mortals', who are blind and dumb, looking with their eyes but seeing nothing and hearing nothing in all the noise surrounding them. 'Helplessness (*amēchanie*) in their breasts leads astray their thinking.' Such men consider being and not being the same thing—a jibe aimed at Heraclitus, whom Parmenides thus includes among all the other mortals.

The deity challenges Parmenides not to let himself be forced by 'ordinary experience in its variety' into taking the path suggested by the senses, but instead to make a decision based on thought (*logos*). 'Only one account remains of the way, that it is', Parmenides writes. This truth is revealed to and forcibly impressed upon him in words that cannot be translated literally. Parmenides' original text contains only the words 'that is'. One can add an 'it', but the word is without emphasis or reference. What Parmenides apparently means is Being. But if so, why does he not say so? And what does he mean when he writes: 'For the same thing is being and thought?'

In any case, Being is unborn, imperishable, immune, unshakeable, and without an end. 'It was not once nor will it be, since it is now, all together, single, and continuous', Parmenides asserts. 'That is why Dikē has not freed it, relaxing the grip of her fetters, either to be born or to perish. No, she holds it fast.' The traditional personification of justice—whose task the Greeks believed was to punish injustice and even, if we follow Anaximander, to rule over rise and fall—is for Parmenides the source of stability and eternal duration for Being. Is this the insight that convinces Themis and Dikē to lead him on his way?

As something that is always the same and remains in the same, Being exists and persists for itself. It is entirely autonomous, requiring nothing, comparable to a perfect sphere, everywhere equally strong from its centre. 'Nor is there more of it here and an inferior amount of it elsewhere, which would restrain it from cohering', Parmenides writes, 'but it is full of what is. And so it is all coherent, for what-is is in contact with what-is. Now changeless within the limits of great bonds, it is without beginning and without end.'

With these words, the goddess concludes the first main part of the poem, known as 'The Way of Truth' and turns to the second part known as 'The Way of Opinion'. It is concerned with how Eros was 'conceived' as the first of the gods and how the gods, the heavenly bodies, and other metaphysical phenomena arose. Both here and in the other parts of his poem, Parmenides discusses fire and earth, warmth and cold. But his insight into Being remains the focus.

Being is the object of thought. 'You will not find thinking without what is', the goddess tells the author. This is worth further investigation. Conversely, it is 'unthinkable', and indeed impossible to put into words, that 'not is', as Parmenides puts it literally. We probably have to translate his thought as 'that nothing is'. Being, truth, and thought are as intimately related to one another as change, emergence, and decay or opinions and the simple naming of things that simulate what in reality does not exist. Much of what the goddess says to Parmenides is intended to ward him away from investigating the non-being.

Whereas Heraclitus' thought constantly reaches further out, trying to encompass everything, Parmenides draws an asymmetrical boundary, as Greeks were wont to do with categories such as free men and slaves, men and women, citizens and non-citizens, myths and rites. What is changing is not incorporated into, but excluded from the realm of Being and thought focused on Being. It seems ironic that this teaching is communicated through the poetic image of a goddess (while the description of Parmenides' ascent echoes a number of Oriental models). But what the goddess says invokes the central theme of philosophy, all divinities notwithstanding. The German philosopher Hans-Georg Gadamer called Parmenides' teaching 'one of the very most consequential intellectual events in world history'.

Incidentally, it seems that Parmenides too cared about his *polis*. It is attested that he served as a lawgiver.

Nothing survives of Pythagoras' teachings. They were reportedly kept secret so that they would not fall into the wrong hands. They were passed on and further developed by successive generations of 'Pythagoreans', an order of followers he himself founded. Still, some of these teachings were known, and increasing amounts of them became public with the passage of time. It is nonetheless impossible to determine which parts of them (if any) may have come from the master himself.

It does seem certain, though, that Pythagoras was an unusually impressive personality: he was credited with performing all kinds of miracles, and it was once related that an eagle landed on his lap and allowed him to pet it. He must have studied intensely mathematics, arithmetic, and geometry, which he appears to have first learned, among other things, in Egypt and perhaps Mesopotamia. It is in Pythagoras that we first encounter the close connection between philosophy and mathematics that would be so important for Plato.

Particularly interesting is Pythagoras' fascination with numbers. It would seem to have come from his conviction that numbers held the keys to unlocking the laws of the world order, from which one could in turn derive insights into the human soul and into individual as well as communal life that was in tune with the soul. For that reason, individual numbers each had a special significance, and certain relations between them were harmonic. Music offered especially good examples of this in the form of relations between tone and the length of strings on instruments. Octaves, fifth, and fourths were, for Pythagoras, expressions of excellent proportions. Again, we encounter a Greek intellectual searching for objective measures, guarantees and points of reference for an order that was independent of the contemporary play of forces. But among the Pythagoreans, this impulse was strangely combined with a number of other ideas about the human soul and its potential transmigration, as well as regulations for purity and the exclusion of certain foods, to name a few. Moreover, Pythagorean doctrines were connected with ideas that were heavily influenced by the Orient and expressed themselves in mystical currents among the Greeks as well.

23

Athens's Path towards Isonomy
and its Rise to Power

Athens was so large and populous by Greek standards that one has to wonder whether the city represented an extreme on the scale of small to large *poleis* or whether it belongs in a category all its own. This question defines a major problem we are confronted with when dealing with this city. Athens is the only Greek *polis* about which a lot is known. Hence we are often tempted to take it as exemplary. But Athens was anything but typical. On the contrary, it was a great exception, as was Sparta, although in different ways: the two cities had radically different effects on world history. In other Greek poleis, despite their diversity, developments usually happened virtually according to statistical probability, as part of a broad process of change common to many areas. In the city of Athens, however, which potentially had such power, a lot may have depended on whether correct decisions were reached and reforms enacted in critical situations. The fact that such decisions and reforms did occur was a crucial condition of Athens's unique rise.

The directness with which the Greeks sought to embody (or even be) their communities could not arise in a *polis* where people often needed a long and usually hot day's journey to reach the common agora in the central town. We might suspect, therefore, that attendance at popular assemblies in Athens, incomparably more than elsewhere, was a matter of chance or of the zeal with which particular forces with particular interests mobilized their supporters. The situation might have been different when serious problems arose that affected a great number of Athenians across all of Attica. But such problems would have had to have been especially grave and lasting to induce large numbers of people to make the journey to the central agora.

Moreover, Athenians hardly knew one another, and city-dwellers had few contacts and little in common with those from other parts of the large country. How could they expect to cooperate closely with one another, and what did they want to achieve? What did membership in the community or the city mean to them?

Aristocratic families from various, though probably not all, parts of the territory tended to reside in Athens proper. But they were there to advocate their own interests, not those of their fellow citizens who lived there. They were far less embodiments of the (very large) *polis* than people acting for themselves. They were wealthy, and that allowed them to live a cultivated existence, employing the best sculptors and architects, perhaps winning glory at the Olympic Games, and in general passing the time in each other's company. Athens was incidentally also a notable centre of highly accomplished artisanship.

It is questionable to what extent the collective will that perhaps eventually emerged in the city penetrated the rest of Attica, and how far the power of office holders extended. Much initiative may have slipped away like sand before it spread everywhere else. How much did people in the countryside care about what was being thought up and done in the shadow of the Acropolis? The fact that great Athens was repeatedly defeated by tiny Megara in their war over Salamis might be an indication of how little common interest actually existed, and how much the various parts of the *polis* were accustomed to living on their own, focusing on their own small public spheres and local cult communities. When an army needed to be raised, how and from how many parts of Attica were the magistrates able to levy hoplites, and how many of them were truly eager to take the field of battle? Ultimately, the only thing that would have forced them to do so might have been a sense of honour. But whose honour, that of the Athenians? People almost everywhere in Attica were well protected, unless they were attacked by sea.

Pretendedly a law was passed in Athens at the time forbidding anyone from proposing in the assembly another war to take Salamis. This bit of information might have been spun out of an elegy of Solon, which, according to his own testimony, he recited as a song and not a speech. In it, he recalls the shame the city has suffered, the scorn that the *Salaminaphetai*, the yielders of Salamis, have brought upon themselves. This was a different kind of humiliation from that which Telemachus had once invoked in Ithaca; this was not a case of tolerating injustice, but of a whole city's lamentable political and military weakness.

Solon called Athens 'Ionia's oldest land'. After the collapse of the Mycenaean culture, it had been able to stave off invading immigrants from the north and accepted refugees, many of whom were then sent on to Asia Minor, where several 'Ionian' cities were being founded. The continuity in settlement across this historical watershed had led the Athenians to consider themselves the only autochthonous people in ancient Greece, or as Demosthenes later declared: 'the only ones to live on the land from which they originate and which they pass on to their children'. The Athenians had not wrested their territory away from another tribe, and they traced the unity of Attica back to an act of their mythical king and hero Theseus. A handful of temporary setbacks notwithstanding, Athenians had been able to preserve such unity over the centuries—or rather, had perhaps essentially restored it by the mid-seventh century.

Nevertheless, the size of the *polis* was more a weakness than a strength, and Solon seems to have been first reacting to this weakness with wounded pride. He looked at his city within the context of the overall *polis* world and wanted it to be active, to live up to its (as yet unfulfilled) potential. In 591, for example, Solon urged Athens to take part in the sacred war for Delphi's independence.

The question still remained, given how atypically large Athens was by Greek standards, whether this community as a whole could ever be present in its citizens directly, concretely, and constantly, as was typical of most other Greeks.

Around 630 Cylon, an Olympic champion whose success may very well have gone to his head, tried to establish a tyranny in Athens. He was supported by his father-in-law, Theagenes, the tyrant of Megara. With his band of followers, he quickly succeeded in a surprise attack on the Acropolis. Either because he simply did not think far enough ahead or because this seemed a remote possibility in Athens at the time, he had not expected that his fellow aristocrats, feeling betrayed, would mobilize followers of their own against him from the countryside. Yet they did precisely that, besieging the Acropolis until the defenders were exhausted. Some of Cylon's followers sought refuge at the gods' altars, but to no avail. They were killed, like the others. But the man who had ordered their murders, Megacles of the Alcmeonid family, was considered guilty of having violated divine laws and therefore cursed, together with his offspring.

Towards the end of the seventh century, Phrynon, also an Olympic champion, led an Attic expedition to the Dardanelles, founding the colony of Sigeion at the mouth of that long, narrow strait. This was a strategically important location for trade to the Black Sea area. Whether the expedition was a private undertaking or one supported by the city is unknown.

Around 620, the Athenians appointed Draco as a lawgiver, to write down a number of their laws. He is mostly known for the stiff penalties he fixed for theft and vagrancy (hence we still speak of 'draconian penalties'). But he also made a very beneficial distinction between premeditated murder and involuntary manslaughter. A person who had killed another unintentionally was only to be exiled, unless the victim's relatives agreed to pardon him. The distinction was important in order to limit bloody cycles of revenge. We do not know if these laws, of which only the part about murder remained valid for a long time, were enacted in reaction to a specific social crisis.

By the beginning of the sixth century, however, there was no question but that Athens was locked in a very disruptive crisis, and a deep front line seems to have emerged across all of Attica. Economic desperation had most likely been growing, and the popular disappointment and anger that resulted came to a head. Whatever the precise reasons, rebellion and civil war were looming. This was Solon's great hour, and his admonitions fell on open ears. Popular anxiety and despair left the Athenians with no other choice but to put themselves in the hands of a sage.

Perhaps while serving his year as an *archōn* in 594–3, or perhaps a few years later, Solon was entrusted with extraordinary powers and charged with restoring equilibrium and order in the city. He had previously announced his intentions, the reasons for which he 'joined the people together', and, as he later insisted, he had realized his promises without exception.

As the basis of his actions, he mentions *kratos*, or power (on one occasion he also speaks of a goad that had been handed to him). In addition, he says, he had combined force and justice. Justice here probably refers to his unlimited authority. But force? Had he been provided with troops (perhaps mercenaries)? Did he use military power to enforce some of his reforms? The possibility cannot be ruled out. In any case he must have had a number of aids and assistants who were willing and able to get physical.

Several accounts of Solon's accomplishments have been preserved, but there are serious doubts about their reliability, at least in part. It is safest to stick to his own statements by which he renders account in relative detail, in poems, written mostly in iambic metre. He pays special attention to the 'shaking off of burdens' (*seisachtheia*), which no doubt made up both the centre and much of the periphery of his efforts. He invokes the primeval mother of the Olympian gods, the black Earth, as a witness that he carried out what he promised to do. He pulled out the so-called mortgage stones (*horoi*), making the land free where it once had been enslaved. He thus relieved debts incurred by farmers, and he restored debt bondsmen to their liberty. Indeed, Solon claims, he repatriated people who had been sold abroad or who had been forced by necessity to emigrate to faraway lands and no longer even spoke their Attic language.

He characterizes the sale of people into slavery as partially legal, partially not, but does not clarify whether mortgage stones and debt bondage were in principle in line with prevailing categories of right and wrong. Nor does he indicate whether creditors in Attica were compensated for their losses. At the very least, someone must have purchased Athenian slaves back from their foreign buyers. There is no telling, either, where the funds came from for all this, and for the practical realization of Solon's other plans. Was it already possible to use revenues from the silver mines at Laurium, which would prove such a reliable source of income a century later? Or could the city draw upon the major treasures of its temples? At any rate, Solon could hardly have asked Athenian aristocrats to make major contributions.

What is clear, though, is that Solon intervened in what many creditors considered their fundamental right, even if, at least as far as we know, he stopped short of restoring the confiscated land to the freed slaves. Not in their wildest dreams, he emphasizes, had farmers been able to imagine what they got (back) thanks to his interventions. It thus seems certain that Solon drastically expanded the range of what was normally considered possible. According to later accounts, he also abolished by law the practice of using the debtor's person as security for his liabilities. Debt bondage was common in the ancient world. The Greeks and Romans were the only ones to eradicate it fully, and, unlike the Romans, the Greeks (or at least Solon) were alone in banning the practice in a single legal stroke. In addition, Solon reportedly declared a general amnesty for all crimes except for murder and attempts at establishing a tyranny, and instituted an upper limit on the property any one man could own.

What this community was able to achieve thanks to its 'straightener' is astonishing. As weak as Athens generally was, the power it could muster in extraordinary situations was great. In its scope and capacity to act, this power was positively monarchic—but without a monarch. Nor was it based on an aristocracy. Rather, it received its mandate from an ad hoc majority, very probably including significant support from those in the middle, who seem to have been alarmed by the terrifying prospect of civil war. There were always open scores, which might be settled under the cover of armed fighting. In many cases, one's enemy lived right around the corner. It was worrying indeed to think of what might happen.

We do not know how Solon pushed through and enacted his reforms, but he undoubtedly possessed sufficient power to do what he deemed necessary and what he had promised. In any case, a broad consensus would have existed in Athens about the need to restore the previous body of citizens, and on this issue the level of agreement probably reached even beyond Athens. But no one had any concrete idea about a new and better political order. At most, it was possible to venture a little way into uncharted waters. The distinction between the 'right order' and the status quo was itself an achievement. By taking force and justice into his own hands and harmonizing them (Solon uses the verb *synharmozein*), force—which must also mean a break with what had at last been considered just—could be used to serve the restitution of *eunomia*.

The resistance Solon's reforms elicited never threw him off course, although there is no doubt that he faced strong pressure from various opposing forces. He countered it with great courage. He had to go his way alone, 'battling on all sides, twisting and turning like a wolf encircled by many dogs'. He positioned himself between the two fronts, with a sturdy shield raised in both directions, since no one side could be allowed to prevail. If he had joined one camp, he added, the city would have lost a considerable number of citizens.

Several lords believed, Solon says, that he did not take his plans and promises seriously, and that he would 'reveal his harsh intent', once he had attained power. Solon is probably referring to a handful of cynical hardliners, who could not even imagine someone relinquishing comprehensive power once he had obtained it—not to speak of loyally fulfilling his mission and believing in his cause.

Those of whom Solon talks seem to have comprised two groups. On the one side were those who wanted to keep and reinforce the status quo, and, on the other, those who strove for radical changes, advocating *isomoiria*, the redistribution of property, so that 'good' and 'bad', high and low would own equal shares of the land. This demand, which was raised frequently at the time, was intended to attract large numbers of followers. If such demands had been realized (of which there is no evidence, but our knowledge of the time is woefully inadequate), those benefiting would have been entirely dependent on, indeed at the mercy of, their leaders. We can hardly assume that such leaders themselves would have been content with smaller, equal shares of property.

Whatever may be the case, experience shows that those seeking to stir unrest are usually not exactly miserly when it comes to dispensing with the property of their wealthy opponents.

At least one and probably both of these sides sought to co-opt Solon to support their plans. The proponents of *isomoiria* advised him to retain the power he had in his hands and establish a tyranny, in which they hoped to participate. But they would hardly have succeeded without resorting to violence. Their opponents probably did not go that far, but they may have hoped that Solon would use his power to go after the other side, banishing a number of their foes (a fate they themselves feared from a victory of the others) and guaranteeing their own property. That, too, might have led to open fighting.

If Solon's assessment of the situation is accurate, factional passions must have been at a boiling point. We do not know how broad the circles were of those who were involved in the struggle or how many poor people allowed themselves to be mobilized for the cause of *isomoiria*. But no matter how difficult the two sides made life for Solon, the constellation also had an advantage. Because the two sides kept themselves in check, they could not hinder his reforms.

Without doubt, this man, the first political thinker we know among the Greeks (and indeed in the Western tradition), was an extraordinary personality—highly educated, articulate, gifted in practical matters, and strong in character. He made his assessments from a new objective distance, a new vantage point and position, free from mere considerations of power and vested interests. And he must also have been conscious of this.

In keeping with traditional aristocratic values, Solon wanted to excel among all, but in a completely new and personal way. By thrusting away the idea of tyranny, he claimed, 'he had further surpassed all others'. That was the sort of glory he hoped to achieve. There had been no shortage of people who had opposed this form of rule, but often enough such critics were among those who aspired to become tyrants themselves. In Solon, we encounter a principled rejection of tyranny as fundamentally antithetical to *eunomia*. Tyranny is but an unjust evil that can bring no lasting blessings. Solon obviously thought as a citizen, as one among many, and he is the first person we know of to do so.

In addition to his efforts to combat indebtedness and forced servitude, Solon also enacted a whole series of laws, 'valid for both high and low, fashioning straight justice for everyone'. The corpus of his legislation, which was too extensive to fit on the walls of any building and thus was written on wooden boards attached to four revolving rectangular wagon axles (*axones*), was for centuries the basis of Attic law. Solon probably more or less took up and perhaps reformulated existing legal ideas and earlier laws, for example, against the establishment of one-man rule. But he also seems to have taken new situations into account and sought answers to new problems. Examples are his *stasis* law, his precise regulations concerning Attic citizenship, his interventions in the subdivision of citizenry, and perhaps also his reform of the division of census classes, which were crucial for the distribution of burdens and access to offices.

Many of Solon's laws dealt with economic problems. For example, he is said to have decreed an export ban on all food products except olives. He required parents with insufficient property to ensure that their children learned a trade; if they failed to do so the children were not obliged to provide for their parents in old age. For some people, he restricted access to citizenship while facilitating it for craftsmen willing to settle in the city. They should increase Athens's wealth and teach their skills to others. In addition, he set limits on the amount spent on luxurious funerals and is said to have changed the system of weights and measures.

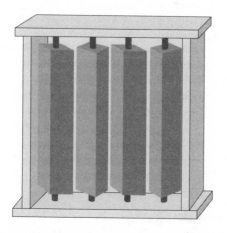

Figure 15. Solon's *axones*. Solon's laws were carved into rectangular whitened wooden boards, with the letters presumably painted. To protect the wood against the elements, they were displayed in a roofed space. Because of the amount of text, the boards had to be mounted on revolving wagon axles (this is the original meaning of *axōn*). Here is one attempt to illustrate how they may have looked.

Especially interesting is his introduction of popular prosecutions. Not possessing a state, Greeks had no public prosecutors either. If a murder occurred, it was up to the victim's relatives or the leading members of the victim's subdivision to bring the case to court. The same applied to other crimes. There had been earlier attempts to extend the circle of persons entitled to act as prosecutors. Solon took up these efforts and seems to have increased the scope for bringing charges in this way. The right to prosecute was to be open to everyone who wanted to use it, and not just in instances of murder but many other sorts of cases. What was impossible for the community as such was to become the province of individuals who felt responsible for justice being done. (All too often, though, as it later turned out, people abused this freedom to get back at enemies or persons they disliked, or simply to swamp them with frivolous allegations and legal challenges, but Solon could hardly have foreseen that.)

Because they lacked sufficient historical sources at the time when they developed a stronger interest in their history, the Greeks tended to attribute in retrospect all kinds of institutions and laws to the few personalities they knew to have been lawgivers. So we do not know whether Solon actually decreed everything that was later attributed to him. In particular, doubts remain about various reforms of Athens's political and legal order. Some historical 'facts' were invented retrospectively. It is very questionable, for example, whether Solon set up a second council that, in contrast to the aristocratic council on the Aeropagus, was to be elected every year. And even if this new council is authentic, it could hardly have played a major role since it lacked the support of an active citizenry.

It would be an exaggeration to treat Solon as the founder of a new constitution. The conditions necessary for such an effort were utterly lacking. However many decrees he made in individual cases, he could not resolve what would soon emerge as the crucial problem. In accordance with his maxim of giving everyone his due, he was content to see 'the people' regain their property and freedom. He emphasized that he neither increased nor took away their honour, that is, their political rights. The people were to be neither too free nor too tightly leashed; in this way, they would best follow their leaders. Those leaders, however, though certainly within the limits Solon set, were supposed to continue to come from among the aristocrats—the very class many of whose members he himself had earlier accused of greed and blamed for all the misfortune they had brought upon the city. He seems to have thought that with the restoration of *eunomia*, they would not be able to do any further harm. And he probably saw no other option for the city's leadership. In this respect his insight was apparently limited.

As fundamental as Solon's contribution to the solution of social and economic issues was, the main political problem remained: constantly renewed struggles for power and domination, or *stasis*. Furthermore, portions of the citizen body had recently been radicalized. Suddenly, much seemed not only conceivable, but possible, and new paths were opening up. On the other hand, the aristocracy and their followers had hardly changed at all. The leaders of society seem to have continued to be primarily concerned with their power, splendid lifestyle, and glory.

To alleviate those ills, a force would have been needed that was able to form an alternative to traditional ways. But in the absence of a monarchy such a force had to grow out of the citizenry. Even if Solon had hit upon the idea, the size of Attica made it much harder to mobilize the citizenry as a whole than was the case anywhere else in Greece, except in situations of widespread popular uproar.

At the end of his term, Solon presented his catalogue of laws to the popular assembly, which was asked to swear an oath not to change anything for ten years. He then went abroad for extended travel.

Some time after his return, Solon had to watch Peisistratus establish a tyranny. In this period he composed the poems in which he criticized his fellow citizens for being as clever as foxes individually but possessing an empty head collectively. Again he connected his observation of a political process unfolding according to necessity with the assertion that it could be prevented: great men should never be allowed to rise too high. Moreover, since Solon too had suffered the experience of those whose insight is superior to that of his contemporaries, he did not neglect to mention that they would soon see how crazy he was. Once tyranny had been established, he placed his weapons in front of his house. Their presence, lonely and deserted, was a shameful reminder that the citizens had to defend themselves—he himself was too old for that. But did anyone register this admonition or take it seriously?

Solon's poems may have bolstered the Athenians' sense of responsibility and also their confidence in the assumption that there was a just order, intended by the gods, and that such an order could be realized.

His reforms were left to stand, protected by deep fears that the demons he banished might revive. But there were many points of dissatisfaction that were simply waiting to be invoked again.

In the short term, the struggle between two aristocratic factions dominated the political stage. One was based in the central plains of Attica, the other along the coast. They were called, respectively, the *pediakoi* and the *paraloi*, and each group was led by the head of a powerful family. If these men were interested in establishing a tyranny, they mutually prevented one another from succeeding. But they also cooperated. In 566–565, for example, the great Panathenaic festival of Athena was instituted. The first temple devoted to this goddess was constructed on the Acropolis.

The end of that decade saw the rise of the man who at the time towered above everyone else in Athens with his decisiveness, daring (or should one say boldness), lack of scruples, and willingness to risk everything on a single card. He was unconventional and burning with ambition. He came from Brauron on Attica's eastern coast. Peisistratus drew his followers, on the one hand, from the area around Marathon: these were likely families who had not much to say in Athens proper. He is also reported to have won the support of the farmers from Attica's mountainous interior. They formed a third faction called the *diakrioi* or *hyperakrioi* (hill people) who competed with the other two. While these were mostly composed of aristocrats, Peisistratus mobilized those who had thus far been disadvantaged. Thanks to his outstanding performance in the wars with Megara, he enjoyed general respect in the community at large that was enhanced by the glamour of his appearance, his generosity, and his amiability.

When he first tried to take control of Athens, he faced only a few minor hurdles. The popular assembly, which was probably dominated by his supporters, did not need much evidence to be convinced that he had been subject to an assassination attempt, and granted him the bodyguard he asked for. He used it to seize the Acropolis. The political situation was sufficiently volatile to permit such coups, provided the usurper was bold and imaginative enough. But Peisistratus' success was short-lived; the two rival factions banded together to put an end to his shenanigans. Nonetheless, a bitter struggle soon erupted between them, and when the Paralians came under pressure, their leader tried to rescue himself through an alliance with the usurper he had previously helped depose. This leader was Megacles of the Alcmeonid family, the husband of Agariste, whose hand he had won in the famous bridal contest in Sicyon. His grandfather of the same name had once had the followers of Cylon murdered. He negotiated with Peisistratus. The result was that Peisistratus would once again become tyrant, while Megacles would somehow share in the power. The alliance was to be sealed through the marriage of Peisistratus and Megacles' daughter.

The way in which the banished (or perhaps self-exiled) leader staged his return to Athens was bizarre indeed. As Herodotus relates, a young woman—'nearly six feet tall and well formed'—was costumed as Athena; runners preceded the chariot on which she rode into the city to proclaim that the goddess herself was leading her favourite, Peisistratus, to her fortress. The Athenians seemed to accept this, even without laughter—with gods, one never knew what they were up to. The citizens let the 'goddess' pass in respectful silence and prayer, and before they knew it, the tyrant was reinstalled. But again his reign was short. His alliance with the Alcmeonids broke down, according to Herodotus, because Peisistratus refused to consummate the arranged marriage. His reason may have been the curse haunting the family since the murder of Cylon. In addition, Megacles may have noticed that his power-sharing agreement with the ambitious tyrant was hardly implemented equitably and he was probably subjected to severe pressure by his own factional allies.

Peisitratus fled once more but did not give up, although it must have been clear to him that he would not be able to take over such a large city again with a simple surprise coup. For ten years, he stayed away while keeping his eye on Athens. During that time, he did what must have seemed obvious to a grand and ambitious lord. He gathered wealth and power. Adopting a method that was to become frequent and successful among Greek aristocrats, he established a foothold on the northern Aegean coast. He seems to have founded a settlement there and exploited the region's gold and silver mines, presumably in concert with the ruling Thracian princes, who felt flattered by his attention and received a cut of the profits. He also established sources of income and connections in other areas. Thessalians, Thebans, and men from Argos are especially mentioned as allies, as is Lygdamis, a lord blessed with wealth and followers, whom Peisistratus would help to establish a tyranny in his home *polis* of Naxos.

Finally, Peisistratus went to Eretria, which was favourably disposed towards him. There he assembled his forces and made the passage to Attica, which was, as so often, preoccupied with internal matters. His armies camped out at Marathon on friendly territory, and followers from throughout Attica streamed in. Only when the army began to march on Athens did the city send troops of its own to confront the aggressors; but that army does not seem to have taken its mission very seriously. In any case, Peisistratus was able to attack and rout it.

His third period of rule, established in 546–545 BC, elicited a positive reaction for being *politikōs*, that is, entirely in the interest of the *polis*. Thucydides, for example, praises the reason and essential fairness of the tyrant and his sons, and later on his rule became known as a golden age of Cronus. For the general population, life was relatively free of worries. That, however, was hardly true for the aristocrats who were Peisistratus' rivals, who had been defeated, were banished, or forced to surrender their sons as hostages. Otherwise, the rosy picture of Peisistratus' third reign may well be fairly accurate. The tyrant ruled cleverly. The fact that tyrannies had already failed in most places taught him that there were limits to what one could achieve with violence and exploitation. Peisistratus' rule was secured with bodyguards and mercenaries, and he reportedly disarmed the citizens. He himself had no intention of enlisting Athenians to wage war, even if wars occasionally proved necessary, at least under his sons. We do not know whether, in time, at least parts of the citizenry acquired weapons again.

Like other tyrants, Peisistratus basically left the political order unchanged and merely saw to it that offices were occupied by men of his choice. He levied taxes, encouraged farmers to work, and improved their conditions by ensuring that they were protected from arbitrary verdicts in aristocratic jurisdiction. He also built grandiose temples and constructed aqueducts and fountain-houses. His sons improved Attica's road system. Economically, the reigns of Peisistratus and his successor and son, Hippias, who took over after his death in 528 BC, were highly beneficial to both the city and the countryside. Solon's reforms had laid the groundwork, but it was under the tyranny that Athens's economy seems to have truly blossomed. This is also attested by the many magnificent dedications offered by craftsmen on the Acropolis. Without knowing it, the tyrants thus created the preconditions for the future participation of broader segments of the citizen body in politics.

Among the gods, the tyrants particularly worshipped Athena and Dionysus, whose cult Peisistratus relocated from Eleutherai on the Attic border to the southern slope of the Acropolis in the city proper. Around 535 BC, to honour Dionysus, Peisistratus sponsored the first competition of tragic poets. The winner was Thespis of Icaria. His innovation, in contrast to earlier pure choral songs, was to have an actor confront the chorus, thus making a plot possible. From around the same time, the Panathenaic festival, which was probably enhanced by the tyrants, featured performances of the Homeric epics.

Peisistratus' sons, in particular the second oldest, Hipparchus, maintained good relations with interpreters of oracles and with poets. Among his favourites were Simonides and Anacreon, who had lived at the court of Polycrates of Samos and whom Hipparchus brought to Athens on a trireme (a warship) after that tyrant's fall.

If we look solely at the practical sides of their tyranny, Peisistratus' and Hippias' regimes were intelligent, focusing on internal peace and stability, legal security, prosperity, and worship of the gods. In the competition between aristocrats that transcended individual *poleis*, they could boast their wealth, which they apparently enjoyed rather modestly, their power, and the magnificence of their buildings. From a historical perspective, their significant contribution to calming and consolidating this large city was important. But that was as far as they could go. The rulers could not merge with the *polis*, because the *polis* was the citizenry. There was ultimately no way to legitimize personal rule.

Peisistratus once famously declared that the Athenians should take care of their domestic affairs, while public matters were the task of the tyrant. In the long term, that view had little future. On the other hand, what did broad segments of the populace have to gain by replacing the tolerable, indeed useful rule of the tyrants with a return to aristocratic power struggles? True, in the meantime in other cities, broader classes of citizens had achieved a more active and regular role in politics, but it was unclear whether that was even possible in a community of Athens's size. The Greeks understood concepts like participation and presence literally. Hence those who opposed the tyrants were mostly the aristocrats, and the tyrants presumably needed to protect their regime primarily from them.

Many of them lived in exile. One of them, Miltiades, from a very noble family, had established his rule at the Hellespont over the Thracian Chersonese, with Peisistratus' support. In time, the tyrant seems to have allowed several of his rivals to return to Athens. Megacles' son Cleisthenes was even permitted to occupy the highest Athenian office of *archōn*. Yet soon thereafter he again went into exile.

In 514 BC, fourteen years after his father's death, Hippias' regime became more oppressive after his brother Hipparchus was murdered by Harmodius and his lover Aristogeiton. The assassination attempt was actually aimed at Hippias himself as well and intended to end the tyranny. The attack was supposed to happen in public during the procession at the Great Panathenaea; the conspirators hoped that it would inspire broad support. But the two assassins, believing that they had been betrayed, spared Hippias and hastily attacked his brother, whom they considered their actual source of offence. Hipparchus had tried to seduce Harmodius and, when rejected, had insulted his sister. As was so often the case with tyrants, their arbitrariness was especially visible in matters of love. Both assassins and several others were killed.

That prompted the exiled aristocrats, under the leadership of members of the Alcmeonid family, to try to liberate Athens by force. When this attempt failed, they occupied Leipsydrion, a small village on the south-west slope of Mount Parnassus. But expected support failed to materialize, so this action, too, had to be cancelled. The general mood in Athens may well have been turning against the ruler, but it was not easily converted into action—to say nothing of action that required courage.

At that point, Cleisthenes decided to take matter into his own hands. Following Peisistratus' own example from several decades earlier, he deemed that only an army could rectify the situation. He went about raising such a force in very circumspect fashion, drawing upon a previously acquired advantage. Years earlier, the Temple of Apollo at Delphi had burnt down and was scheduled to be rebuilt, for which money was raised, and a contractor was needed who would be willing to supervise the construction. Cleisthenes won the assignment. He supposedly used his own wealth to build a more spectacular temple than originally planned. As a result, and perhaps because of some additional contributions in pure gold, Cleisthenes had won the favour of the oracle. He arranged for the priestess, the Pythia, repeatedly to advise the Spartans to liberate Athens. And although they were bound by a relationship of guest friendship to the house of the Peisistratids, they eventually obeyed. They may have been motivated by piety, although the Athenian tyrants' relationship to Sparta's rival Argos may also have been a factor.

However, the Spartans also initially underestimated how internally secure and externally well supported the Peisistratids' power truly was. The force the Spartans sent to Athens was relatively small, and it collapsed under counter-attacks by Thessalian cavalry, which Hippias had enlisted. Even the far larger army that the Spartan King Cleomenes then led to Attica was only successful by an accident of chance. Hippias had retreated with his relatives to the fortified Acropolis. The Spartans were not experienced in siege warfare. But when they happened to capture the tyrant's children, who were being sent abroad for their protection, Hippias capitulated upon the promise of safe conduct.

Figure 16. Harmodius and Aristogeiton. Copies of sculptures made by Critius and Nesiotes. Their exact placement vis-à-vis one another is disputed. This monument was erected in 477–476 BC in the agora in Athens as a replacement for one by Antenor, which had been looted by the Persians.

Athens was liberated in 510 BC, and we have no way of knowing how the Athenians reacted to this watershed event. In later years, they preferred to repress memories of the Spartan army's intervention and revered Harmodius and Aristogeiton as their liberators. They honoured them with a monument in the agora; its sculptor, Antenor, was one of the most highly regarded of his day. It was the first time that meritorious personalities were memorialized in this way. Earlier, sculptures had served only as cult images, dedications in sanctuaries, and decorations of tombs. The pair of heroes were also celebrated in songs. Thucydides was later to remark dryly that the fear of tyranny which regularly flared up among his fellow citizens in times of crisis could be traced back to the fact that they had not been able to liberate themselves.

But if Cleisthenes had assumed that the leading role in Athens was now going to be his, he was mistaken. A struggle developed between him and Isagoras, one of the most prominent aristocrats to have remained in the city during the tyranny. Both were probably supported by the customary retinues of allies and followers, and there was not necessarily widespread sympathy for the newly returned exile, as powerful as his family once had been. When Isagoras gained the upper hand, Herodotus reports, Cleisthenes tried to win over 'the people', for whom he had previously cared little, by making an astonishingly bold suggestion. The citizenry, he proposed, should be fundamentally reorganized, with the aim of tying them more closely to political activities and giving them regular opportunities to participate substantially in decision-making.

We know of no precedent for this, although there surely must have been some in other places. What Cleisthenes did was entirely different from the many attempts of usurpers who made promises to the people, but when they succeeded merely provided them with some economic advantages while they seized power for themselves. Cleisthenes was not going to use the people as a springboard. He wanted to attain political influence by putting them in an entirely different political position, although presumably he expected to reap gratitude and authority from this. His plan apparently corresponded well with the interests of those in the middle. Economic conditions had been consolidated, and in many *poleis* members of the broader classes were already participating more and more in politics. Those who were still miserably poor no longer offered a reliable political base.

Remarkably, Cleisthenes had used his time in exile not to stew in resentment but to look around in the world at large. He was highly intelligent and had made himself sufficiently acquainted with smart minds and political thinkers to know whom he could ask for advice when he needed it. Still, apparently he would initially have been content, given the circumstances in which he found himself upon returning to Athens, just to win the power struggle with Isagoras. It is an open question whether he already had a long-term plan for comprehensive reforms. The idea could have been in the air, but even if this were the case, it does not follow that he really wanted to engage in it. After all, it was anything but easy to restructure such a large citizenry over relatively large distances so that its members could be politically present in Athens.

Perhaps his advisers urged him. Perhaps Attic citizens confronted him with their expectations. Or perhaps he just suddenly decided to take the risk. In any case, Cleisthenes made his plan known in outline, and it must have attracted major support. The sources are silent about this, but the popular assembly must have approved the plan and authorized him to carry it out.

Thus began what is known as Cleisthenes' 'tribal reform'. This colourless, bureaucratic-sounding term should not obscure the fact that this was an act of the greatest significance, nothing less than a fundamental restructuring, a lasting activation, and a complete reconstitution of the Attic citizen body. In a sense, Cleisthenes transformed the majority of Athenians from community members with limited political rights into citizens in the full Greek sense of the word: men who saw politics as an important and central focus of their lives and who were united in common interests that aimed not just at participation, but at status within the public sphere and the community. This was the form of social and political rise that was typical of this society and meaningful for the broader classes involved. In these common interests too lay the possibility of forming horizontal solidarity on a large scale. Under the conditions prevailing in Greece at the time, men could not afford to be *bourgeois* if they wanted to be *citoyens*, or to use politics to pursue domestic or economic interests, which would have collided with other such interests and inevitably led again to the predominance of vertical forms of solidarity.

In so far as such a change took place in what was by far the largest *polis*, it concerned not just the Athenians. The balance of power began to shift everywhere in Greece. It is hardly an exaggeration to credit this reform with world-historical importance.

The reform began with a new division of the citizen body. The lowest unit consisted of 139 'demes', small towns, villages, and in some cases the sum of a few hamlets or quarters of Athens and its environs, including the coast where its ports were located.

These demes were organized into ten 'tribes' (*phylai*), which henceforth formed the main subdivisions of the citizen body. The basis was a division

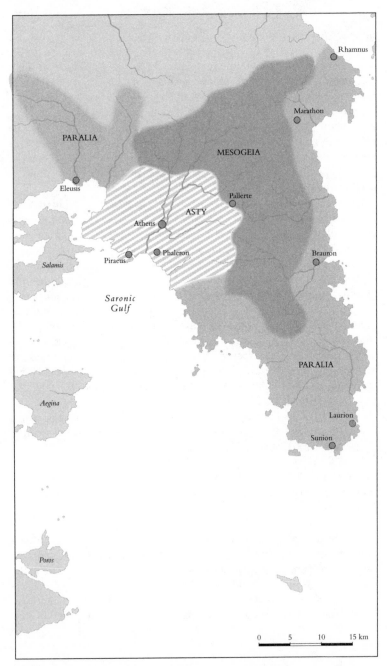

Map 4. The three regions of Attica in Cleisthenes' time.

of Attica into three distinct regions: Athens proper (*asty*, including the plain surrounding it, and the ports), the interior (*mesogeia*), and the coastal area (*paralia*). In each of these three regions, the demes were combined into ten 'trittyes' (thirds). Three trittyes, one from each region, made up a *phylē*. According to historical tradition, this was done by lot. This could have led to dramatic inequalities between the tribes, though, and perhaps the lot was used only in certain cases, for instance, to decide between trittyes roughly similar in size. Interestingly, the trittyes in any given tribe usually did not border with one another. Most significantly, no one *phylē* was more than a tenth of the entire citizen body, and all contained citizens from each of the three regions. In this way, the new organization was much better able than the old one to connect and integrate different parts of the citizenry. The intended result, borne by the 'middle ones', was a new communal spirit both in the whole *polis* and within its individual parts.

Communal life in the demes henceforth proceeded entirely according to the principles of grass-roots democracy. In small associations, where people knew one another personally, less prominent individuals could also speak up and help take care of common tasks. At issue were not just local affairs, but also the keeping of the lists of those eligible for the hoplite army. Solidarity was encouraged by the common practice of cult rituals.

The tribes, which consisted of somewhere between two and four thousand citizens, were responsible for distributing tasks and rights. Yet they were also intended to foster a communal spirit. No one, neither individual nor deme, was supposed to feel lost in the whole; everyone was to have his place at every level. One aim was probably also to encourage a sense of common pride in these new units. Members of each tribe served in the same regiment in the phalanx, and at the festival of the Great Dionysia choruses composed of members of the tribes were to compete against one another as well. Every one of these artificially created subdivisions was assigned a patron hero who gave his name to the tribe and was revered in common cult. Cleisthenes had sent a list of a hundred names to Delphi, from which the oracle selected ten. The fiction of some kind of common descent encouraged solidarity within these subdivisions.

Above all, though, the members of tribes were to work together in a newly established council. The Council of the 500, the heart of this new order, comprised fifty men per tribe. The councillors were most probably chosen proportionally from the demes—perhaps by lot from the beginning, or initially still by vote—and they served for one year. Presumably, Cleisthenes had already made sure that the councillors rotated year by year. And it was probably his idea that the fifty councillors from each tribe—representing an arbitrary cross-section of the citizen body—should be present in Athens for one-tenth of the year. This could have been one of the crucial conditions of the new order's success.

Out of a total of some 35,000, there was one councillor for every seventy citizens. If only two of them alternated in office, the ratio declined to 35 to 1; if four, it was less than 20 to 1. The councillors thus remained closely tied into the circles from which they came and to which they continually returned.

By cooperating in this way with their fellow councillors from diverse parts of Attica, broad segments of the middle classes (who alone had the time and means to serve), gained an advantage that had previously only been available to the aristocracy. They came to know each other well. And since neighbours often belonged to different tribes, the network of acquaintances quickly expanded.

While the whole of the citizenry could never be present in Athens, a relatively large number did through the rotation of councillors. In establishing a circulation between the individual parts of the territory and the common centre and back again, the system succeeded in creating a partial form of the unmediated political presence that was desirable for the citizenry. Keeping the councillors tied to the demes, moreover, had the effect of making them less susceptible to the influences, prevailing winds, and currents of urban politics, except in situations where the political fronts had been radicalized. And if one considers the fact that many people enjoyed leaving the narrow confines of their village or region, another benefit was to break through the relative isolation of many parts of Attica. Distances shrank the more frequently community representatives travelled.

The task of the Council of 500 was the discussion and preparation (*probouleuma*) of decisions to be made by the popular assembly, and such preliminary consultation was no doubt a *sine qua non* for the effectiveness of such resolutions. The council was an important instrument as well for preventing smaller groups of aristocrats, together with their allies and supporters, from passing resolutions in their own particular interest. The council here had the function of a filter. We do not know whether members of the Aeropagus Council were allowed to serve in this council as well. Relations between officials, Aeropagus, and the Council of 500 still had to develop a stable pattern.

Cleisthenes retained previous divisions of the citizenry into four *phylai* and various subcategories. The *phratries*, for example, were still responsible for decisions about accepting and registering newborn babies in the citizen lists. But the traditional dependence of members of these old tribes on the aristocrats who played a dominant role in them must have been lessened, the more the citizenry as a whole strengthened its position within the community. One thus did not need to eradicate the old structures. It was enough to truncate their political dimension.

As leaders of the ten tribal regiments, ten *stratēgēgoi* (generals) were elected. That office was to become the most important in Athens. An oath of office was introduced for the councillors, who swore 'not to dissolve the *dēmos*'. Originally that can only have referred to the organizational form, the citizenry that Cleisthenes had constituted and made capable of political action, and that was represented by the Council of 500. But the term *dēmos* would soon come to designate the entire order. It was thus the first term for what would eventually be understood as democracy. As early as 500, perhaps, the Athenians constructed a new meeting place for popular assemblies, called the Pnyx, above the city's agora.

Cleisthenes was thus able to achieve something that had eluded Solon: to stabilize the community, to bring about internal peace and law and order, and to end the struggles for power. *Eunomia* was achieved through *isonomia*. Even if political offices in Athens remained in aristocratic hands for decades, the whole situation had changed thanks to the increased presence of those in the middle.

Perhaps there was no other Greek community that so depended on founding itself upon the broader classes—assuming that Athenian aristocrats were particularly difficult to keep under control. The greater the distances in Attica and the effort needed to bridge them, the greater the energy with which this community now seems to have been filled— and the greater its self-confidence.

In so far as these citizens could only be the *polis* by leaving their specific domestic interests as farmers, traders, and craftsmen at home, they had to find it important to elevate their role as citizens above everything else. They had to develop an identity as citizens and a sense of brotherhood between themselves. Participating in politics had to become an end in itself and not merely a means to achieving other, purely individual and private goals.

That a large part of the Attic citizenry (in the country but probably also in the city) understood what Cleisthenes wanted to achieve and was prepared to support him is suggested by the fact that his rival Isagoras panicked and called upon the Spartan King Cleomenes, his guest friend, to assist him. Cleomenes was ready and willing. Was it just because he wanted to help out a friend? Or did he sense the opportunity to achieve something great, which would have fitted in well with his general ambition? Or might he perhaps have feared that the introduction of *isonomia* in Athens would catch on and disrupt the system of aristocratic relationships on which Sparta so heavily depended? Was he afraid that the citizenry in Athens, once it had achieved integration and unity, might flex its political and military might far beyond its own borders? In any case, Cleomenes marched on Athens with a small army. He probably assumed it would be sufficient to send one group of aristocrats into exile—as had so often been the case in Greece before and as the competing heads of factions probably had intended to do in order to prevail with Solon's help. Moreover, the tyrant, whose power the Spartans had underestimated not long before, was not there any more.

Cleisthenes was able to flee, and hundreds of his followers were banished from the city. Isagoras dissolved 'the council', most probably the old aristocratic council on the Aeropagus, and began forming a new one with three hundred members. But then the improbable happened. The council resisted Isagoras' plans, and masses of citizens from all over Attica marched on the city to support the council. Cleomenes was forced to withdraw to the Acropolis, where he capitulated with his troops and Isagoras after two days of siege, on condition of safe withdrawal.

A number of Isagoras' supporters, and not just those from Athens, were executed. Cleisthenes returned and carried out his reforms. But the Athenians remained nervous. Fearing a new attack by the Spartans, they sent emissaries to the Persian satrap in the Lydian city of Sardes to seek an alliance (which, however, is not mentioned later on in the historical sources).

In fact, Cleomenes did not give up so easily. He now raised a large army on the Peloponnese in an attempt to install Isagoras as tyrant. Athens's neighbours, the Boeotians to the west and the Chalcidians on Euboea, simultaneously invaded Attica. The forces involved were thought to be sufficient to ensure Athens's future obedience. But the Spartan army hardly advanced beyond the Attic borders. In Eleusis, a quarrel flared up between Cleomenes and Demaratus, Sparta's second king. That most likely encouraged the Corinthians to refuse to continue the invasion. They had no interest in contributing to the establishment of a new tyranny. The army turned back home. The Athenians exploited the opportunity to score major victories against Sparta's allies, first the Boeotians, then the Chalcidians. In Chalcis, they stripped the aristocracy of major portions of their land and divided it up among reportedly four thousand of their own citizens. Ransom for Boeotian captives also earned Athens a princely sum, at least part of which may then have been distributed among Athenian hoplites or citizens in general.

Herodotus saw these victories as evidence for the excellence of an order characterized by *isēgoria* (equality of speech—a synonym for *isonomia*). As soon as the citizens fought for themselves and not for a tyrant, their hearts were in the fight. Having been liberated from tyranny, the Athenians became, in Herodotus' view, far and away the leading people in Greece. For the first time, the *polis* was fully able to make use of its potential power.

A few years later, when the Thebans banded together with the Aeginetans against the Athenians, they, too, had no success, even though the Aeginetan fleet was able to cause much damage along the Attic coast. The alliance might well be taken as a sign of how few were willing to accept Athens in its new form.

The Spartans finally began to consider whether to reinstall Hippias as a tyrant so that Athens, once again held in check by a sole ruler, would yield to their authority. But such plans also failed because of the resistance of Sparta's allies. If the historical tradition is accurate, the decisive point for many *poleis*, especially Corinth, was the issue of political constitution. Just as they themselves did not want a tyranny, they felt that Athens should not be subject to one either. In their view Sparta, which had helped overthrow a number of tyrants, must not reverse its usual policy. By contrast, Cleomenes' main motive was to maintain Sparta's leading role in Greece. In terms of foreign policy, the constitutional argument aimed at the coexistence of equal powers. Sparta, by contrast, was worried about the potential rival and considered the contrast with Athens and the dangers inherent in the new situation only too obvious and real. But the old order could no longer be restored.

Was it just a matter of time before the Attic citizenry was reorganized—so that Cleisthenes only did something that would have happened sooner or later anyway? Or were Cleisthenes' achievements beyond the scope of men less able and daring? And would Cleisthenes ever have attempted such massive reforms, had he not been defeated by Isagoras in the first place? Was it perhaps only Sparta's attack on the reformers that motivated the Athenians, who until then had merely welcomed the changes, to put all their energy behind supporting them? After all, often one of the conditions for the ultimate success of something new is resistance by the defenders of the status quo, who sense the threat to their position but fall short in their efforts because they fail fully to comprehend the power and potential of the new ideas. Yet it is precisely the counter-attack of the old guard that alters the playing field to such an extent that they themselves now are obvious in being wrong. As a consequence, the new forces pass their first crucial test and begin to gain ever more power and momentum.

In any case, Athens henceforth was no longer just an overarching structure in which actions and changes took place but it was, in the full sense of the *polis* concept, its citizens—no longer just a domain for aristocratic power struggles, but the cause of the citizens. The more difficult and strenuous it was in the largest Greek *polis* to maintain the citizens' presence, the more energy they mustered and the more intense life and politics in the *polis* must have become. The Athenians must have been inspired by the experience of just how much they could achieve, both militarily and in dealing with the outside world, but especially by making the foundations of their political order and the organization of their community the objects of their political thought and action.

24

The Aegean World around 500 BC: Greeks and Persians II

Two hundred and fifty years had passed since the Greeks had sent out their first colonizing expeditions and begun to intensify their contacts with the Orient to such an extent that they were able to expose themselves to the entire richness of those venerable ancient cultures. At the same time, the parallel existence of a large number of small *poleis* had persisted, as had the particular forms of life that were so closely connected with them. In their struggle against everything that made their lives difficult, the Greeks had absorbed what they could and extended their feelers in all directions. They had secured their place in the world and found a strength and a stance that allowed them to weather all storms.

As a result, they had been able to ride out all the turbulences that had been caused by the (at times) explosive increases in freedom and ambitions. What had split apart had eventually been tied together again. Autocracy occurred, often opening up a path out of misery, impending civil strife, and other crisis symptoms of a culture that was beginning to differentiate itself, but it could not be maintained for long.

Hence the ideals of independence, freedom, and the cultivation of an all-round personality retained their power. Important habits were preserved: understanding the community primarily from the perspective of the public sphere, direct political participation, and the internal and external exclusiveness of the communities of property owners. The high valuation of the agonistic impulse, so well suited to the world of *poleis*, was by now deeply rooted, and the same was true of the importance of aesthetics. A specific type of people had emerged and proved itself. The Greeks had learned to live for the most part on their own and by their own devices, constantly asserting themselves; they had also learned to balance a variety of interests and needs within and among themselves—not least with the help of poetry. They had developed customs that allowed even war to support the diversity of the *polis* world. A great number of insights had been revealed. In their search for the golden mean, in their enquiries into the laws that governed the *polis*, nature, and the cosmos, and in their political thought, the Greeks had introduced new norms and commitments.

Finally, an alternative to aristocratic regimes had developed. What was general and common to the *polis* began to find strong advocates. Possibilities for instituting deep reforms, and especially for activating broad segments of the citizenry, had dramatically expanded the radius and potential which shaped politics. Isonomic systems had arisen especially in relatively turbulent poleis. The aristocrats' political and military freedom of action had been curtailed. Things were more or less under control.

On the other hand, in Sicily, under very particular circumstances, power was concentrating in new forms. Tyrants began to implement unusual policies of conquering cities and resettling their citizens. Conflicts with Carthage were on the horizon. Around 500 BC, however, the Greeks could hardly be concerned with such issues, just as they could hardly be aware of the question of how long the conditions that had allowed the formation of the *polis* world would continue to exist in the Aegean.

We can assume that by then the Greeks had grown accustomed to the fact that the Persians had ruled the western coast of Asia Minor since 547 BC, for so far the Persians had just been one power among others participating in the political games of the other Greeks. Here and there, the Persians established dominance over an island, and Greek aristocrats enlisted them in their affairs often enough, for example, to provide assistance in an individual's effort to establish a tyranny in his home city. Quite similarly, the Athenians had attempted to win over the Persian satrap to protect them in their conflict with Sparta. Hippias too had hoped he could tap the satrap's power to regain his tyranny in Athens. Later, Thessalian aristocrats would ally themselves with the Persians, preferring to become vassals of the Great King to allowing broader classes of citizens to dominate their communities. Persian assistance, of course, always came at a price. Those seeking aid were forced to submit to the Persian king and to pay tribute. But many people seem to have thought that was a price worth paying, while others simply had no choice.

There was no major contrast between Greeks and Persians. Whether someone was for or against the latter was hardly relevant. The Persians were simply there and could be enlisted occasionally in the tug-of-war between factions in and among Greek *poleis*. True, Persian rule over the *poleis* in Asia Minor may well have been perceived by some as oppressive.

Although the Persians basically left the Greeks alone, the satraps, of course, had their whims, preferences, and idiosyncrasies. And the tyrannies upon which Persian control was based were not exactly popular. But presumably this was one of the facts of life that had to be accepted, at least as long as no other options were available.

How long could such a situation last? The question must be asked from both sides. Would the Persian drive towards conquest not have to reach the Greek mainland at some point? And could Greek isonomic systems—those political orders in which broader segments of the citizenry were very much involved politically, thus restricting the free play of the aristocrats—tolerate potential and lasting interference from the giant empire in the East? Even if problems usually arose only in isolated cases, was there not enough potential for conflict to cause small struggles to explode into large ones? Was it not just a matter of time before the Persians began throwing their weight around in the Aegean? And there was another factor that had the potential of influencing the situation.

It was due to chance (and chance alone, since the contributing factors have nothing else in common) that two communities on the Greek mainland stood out by far from all the others by virtue of their size. One was Athens, of which this had been essentially true since the Mycenaean era, and the other was Sparta, which, for a variety of reasons, had conquered not only Laconia but also Messenia.

This latter *polis*, which had the strongest army in all of Greece but also had to defend itself against potential uprisings by the helots, had by the mid-sixth century concluded close and mutually binding alliances with most of the communities on the Peloponnese. The result was what we call the Peloponnesian League. This was not, however, a formal, political association (neither a federal state nor a confederation), but rather a collection of Spartan allies, who were politically independent, but closely connected with the hegemonic power. Sparta sometimes invited league members for joint consultations, at which decisions over war and peace could be made. De facto, there were therefore ad hoc assemblies that met as the need arose and might create the impression of a political league. Sparta ensured that it could rely on the most influential circles within the other communities, the aristocracy, no matter what position their influence was based on. As a result, in the sixth century, by virtue of its own military might and the strength of its allies, Sparta had achieved the generally recognized status of Hellas' leading power and most vigorous champion (*prostatēs*).

As long as this power had no rivals, it served to stabilize the *polis* world. But as soon as the large and newly reorganized citizenry of Athens came into play, the result was dualism. Whereas Sparta was defensive, Athens had to become offensive—for the simple reason that Sparta consistently tried to keep the power of Athens in check. Thus, the large area in which, overall, most Greek *poleis* had simply coexisted with each other became a dynamic political field in which almost everything (or at least many things) had to be oriented towards these two centres. Pressure must have arisen for other Greeks to take sides, whether in a friendly or hostile way, if they did not live far out on the periphery or were not willing to accept the risks associated with neutrality. Within this field, considerations of sheer power began to take precedence over the traditional principles of agonistic interaction. The self-sufficiency and self-centredness of the *polis* world, with its many zero-sum games, could no longer continue. And internal tensions were all too easily directed outward.

Circumstances in the Aegean thus began to come to a head during this period, initially because of the Greeks themselves. But in the long term, the fundamental changes wrought by the Persian Empire upon the Orient and the rest of the known world had far-reaching consequences for practically everything else.

Whether western Asia Minor was ruled by the Lydian kings or the Persians made a huge difference. The Lydians had been powerful enough to subjugate the Greek cities along the coast one after another, although had those cities followed Thales' advice and joined together, they might perhaps have been able to repel the attacks. At any rate, the Lydians were neither in a position nor did it occur to them to reach out across the Aegean Sea to confront the Greeks on the other side (apart perhaps from some of the islands). And if they had, the Greeks would probably have been able to exploit connections with other Oriental empires located to the Lydians' rear. The Greeks might thus have been drawn into the power struggles in this larger world, and it may be interesting to speculate about the consequences.

The Persians, on the other hand, had no rival empire at their backs. They ruled over the entire space once occupied by eastern empires and far beyond. In case of a major conflict, either they would subjugate the mainland Greeks or, if the Greeks successfully defended themselves, a deep divide would open up between the two peoples and worlds. Hence the formation of a single global empire in the East opened up the possibility of a deep split between East and West, Asia and Europe.

By 500 BC, however, things had not gone that far. Whatever Greek intellectuals might have thought concerning the future, whatever the plans of the Persian kings, their courts, or the satraps living in the former Lydian capital Sardes, for the time being the Aegean remained on the margins of Persian interests. Greece may have seemed like the centre of the world when viewed from a Hellenocentric perspective. But we should not forget that it took some ninety-three days to get from there to the Persian capital Susa.

The royal residences from which the Persian Empire was ruled were located on the eastern edge of Mesopotamia (Susa), in the bordering mountain regions (the ancient capital of the Medes', Ecbatana), or many hundreds of kilometres to the south-east in the Persian core area (Pasargadae and Persepolis). That was the centre of the empire. Ionia was as far away from that centre as the Persian territories in the Indus Valley.

Furthermore, the Persians did not pay much attention to Asia Minor because it was relatively firmly in their grasp. There had not been any insurrections, as there had been in Mesopotamia and Egypt or in the east and the north. Nor were there any problems with peoples living beyond the borders.

It had been a good fifty years since Prince—and later King—Cyrus II from the house of the Achaemenids united more closely or perhaps for the first time various parts of the tribes of the Persians. Previously they had primarily raised livestock in the mountains to the north of the Persian Gulf. Then they had grown into a military and political power that first conquered neighbouring Elam with its capital Susa and then vanquished the Medes, a related people who lived in the Zagros mountain region. That gave the Persians a foothold in Mesopotamia since the Medes had taken control of the old Assyrian Empire in the late seventh century BC.

All this happened in a short space of time. We do not know whether Cyrus originally strove for anything more than predominance in his immediate region. There is evidence, in any case, that he did not attack but was attacked by the Median king. Whatever the case may have been, Cyrus disrupted a relatively stable balance of power between the Median, New Babylonian, Egyptian, and Lydian Empires. At least one of the rulers concerned, the Lydian King Croesus, refused to accept this change, possibly because he hoped to gain control over at least some of the remnants of the Median Empire. If he allied himself in advance with the other powers against the interloper, they initially held back. Croesus seems to have started his campaign against Cyrus alone. Before departing, he had asked the oracle at Delphi about his prospects and received the famous answer: When you cross the (border river) Halys, you will destroy a great empire. That would have been quite a clever prognosis, since even major wars sometimes end without a winner.

Again we do not know whether Cyrus was motivated by a desire for further expansion when he took up arms, or whether he was merely responding to the Lydian challenge. In any case, the Lydians made a mistake when they assumed, after the initial, indecisive battle in the late summer of 547 BC, that the war would only be continued in the following year. Croesus now summoned his allies, the Egyptians, the Babylonians, and the Spartans. But Cyrus ignored the seasons. He marched upon Sardes and took the city after a brief siege.

Barely a decade later, he conquered the third of the Oriental empires, the New Babylonian (539). At some point, before or soon after, he also staged campaigns to the north and the east. They led him into Central Asia, a region that had thus far been beyond the interests of rulers in Mesopotamia. In many locations through which Cyrus marched, he established relationships of dependency. By the time he died, in 530 BC, during a campaign south of the Aral Sea, his empire encompassed a territory far larger than the sum of the other empires that had thus far dominated the Oriental political landscape. Egypt alone maintained its independence.

Egypt then fell to Cyrus' son, Cambyses, who ruled from 533 to 522 BC. He extended his campaign to Libya, but was forced to abandon a march upon Carthage. The quarrels about the succession that commenced with Cambyses' death ended with Darius I, a relative of Cyrus, ascending to the throne. Within a year, he succeeded in putting down a series of rebellions.

Darius, too, added further territory to the empire, extending it eastward to the River Indus and taking additional parts of Libya. In 513, he crossed the Bosporus. His goal, though, was not to attack the Greeks, but to integrate Scythian territories north of the Black Sea into the empire. People remembered that a century earlier tribes from that region had laid waste and partially ruled some of the Near East. Darius was probably motivated by the desire to secure the borders along the Caucasus. Despite some initial successes, the campaign ultimately failed, but it was continued in the subjugation of territories in the northern Aegean, Thrace, and Macedonia.

Step by step, the Persian Empire was growing. However the first of the Persian kings may have come to take this path, he served as a model for all his successors. By the late sixth century, the Persians had run out of evenly matched adversaries, and there were no obvious limits upon how far their empire could expand. When Darius ordered the geographer Scylax of Caryanda to explore the sea routes between the Persian Gulf and Egypt and sent others on similar missions to Greece and Sicily, map-making was probably not the only thing on his mind. The interval between the conquests of Cyrus (up to 530), Cambyses (525), and Darius (513 and earlier) were never long. In addition, there were other things to be done, especially securing and organizing the conquered territories. That was one of Darius' primary achievements.

The Persian Empire, which Alfred Heuss has called 'a historical curiosity *par excellence*', was only in a limited sense the empire of the Persians and their close allies, the Medians. Above all, it was the empire of the Persian kings, or 'Great Kings', as they called themselves. They were the ones who received tribute. They proudly had long lists inscribed of the lands and peoples over which they ruled, and they took credit for great deeds such as campaigns, conquests, and the suppression of rebellions. They assumed the roles of the kings of Babylon or the pharaohs. They represented the whole and held it together, which was necessary, since the individual parts of the empire had little in common with one another.

Nor was it in the interest of the Great Kings to advance the forming of their empire. The inscription on Darius' tomb reads: 'I ruled over them, they paid me tribute, and what I told them, they did.' The kings thus ensured order and, if necessary, justice, and carried out improvements here and there. Otherwise, everything could basically stay as it was. Not even the imperial army was unified. The various troops that were enlisted alongside the standing army of Persians were as colourful and diverse as the empire itself. Some of the kings, princes, and tribal chiefs who had been subjugated were allowed to continue to exercise power; others were replaced. Persian authority was simply laid on top of existing power structures.

The subjects were allowed to retain their religion, lifestyle, and their political order and laws; those of the Egyptians were recorded upon Darius' orders. The Persian kings served their own god Ahuramazda, the principle deity of Zoroastrianism, whom they credited with all their triumphs. But they also portrayed themselves as servants, even the chosen ones, of Marduk in Babylon or Amun-Re in Egypt. They allowed the Jews, who had been exiled to Babylon, to return to their homeland, and they contributed towards rebuilding their temple. Thus they would almost certainly have been tolerant towards the Greeks too, whose god Apollo enjoyed their special respect. The sheer size of the empire left

Figure 17. The Persian King Darius, with a bow in his left hand and his right hand raised in prayer, marches over the rebel Gaumata. In front of him are nine rebel leaders, dressed in their native costumes. The last one is a Scythian. A rope around their necks binds them together, and their hands are tied behind their backs. The relief is carved into the Bisutun mountain on the route between the Persian capital Ecbatana and Babylon and is dated 521–520 BC.

them with no other option. Whatever their natural inclinations or desires, the Persian Great Kings had to allow the various countries and peoples they ruled to live as they chose. The only condition was obedience and loyalty to the king. There was no pardon for rebellion.

The ruling classes among the Persians and Medians bore the primary responsibility for keeping the empire together, and they provided the bulk of its mighty army. For that, more than a few of them were rewarded with land. The Persian king needed loyal allies in a great variety of regions. The children of the ruling classes were educated communally at royal courts, where they learned to ride, shoot with the bow, and tell the truth. Loyalty was considered an especially important virtue. We do not know whether it was possible for others to rise into these classes.

Persian administration was divided between the central government in the capital cities and the twenty satraps, who served as something like viceroys of the large districts (satrapies) into which the empire was divided. They were primarily responsible for maintaining public order, supervising local powers, collecting taxes, and commanding the local military or at least raising troops whenever needed. Nonetheless, the Persian kings tried to keep as much control as possible in their own hands. To do that, they called upon the services of a large administrative apparatus and a number of agents, who were known as the eyes (and ears) of the king. Their job was probably not just to watch over the satraps, but generally to form their own impressions of what was going on in the empire. The kings placed great emphasis on being able to learn about the complaints of their subjects and to remedy their problems, in some cases by doling out money.

Internal connections were of great importance in this great empire. Roads were constructed and improved. The long King's Road from Sardes to Susa was well known among the Greeks, and it was certainly not the only road of this sort. Postal stations allowed riders to change horses quickly, and Persian couriers enjoyed the reputation of being faster than cranes. These roads, of course, also increased the mobility of the Persian army. Darius, as is well attested, achieved a long-standing aim of the Egyptian kings by building a canal between the Nile and the Red Sea. We do not know precisely why he did so. Even if he intended to increase trade the project also promised eternal fame, much like the massive construction projects the kings ordered in their royal residences.

All in all, the constellation that had emerged around the Aegean by 500 BC was highly unusual. Orient and Occident, if one can use those global terms, encountered one another in truly novel fashion. No longer were interactions solely commercial in nature or cultural impulses moving from east to west. The encounters were now political and military. The regional power vacuum, in which the Greeks had existed for so long, was being filled. The Greek world of *poleis* was colliding with the new Persian Empire that would become, in Heuss's term, an 'epilogue' to the two-and-a-half millennia of ancient Oriental rule.

For almost half a century, this Oriental empire took scant interest in the Greeks on the other side of the Aegean. And that fifty-year period was precisely the time Athens needed to reorganize itself so that the Greeks on the mainland found themselves for the first time in a position to counter a potential Persian attack with a defence that was not completely without chances. Without *isonomia*, Athens would probably not have been prepared for this effort.

But that was hardly the entire story. The Greeks owed their eventual victory both to a series of improbable triumphs and to several temporal coincidences. When the Persian offensive came, it was crucial not only that Athens was already so strong, but that Sparta still possessed the power and authority to assemble a whole coalition under its leadership. This would likely not have been possible had Greek dualism taken a destructive course. The death of Darius the Great in 486 BC further delayed the start of the Persian campaign so that Athens had time to finish constructing its fleet. If there is a deeper conclusion to be drawn here, it is that the Persians underestimated the Greeks. If Darius had attacked them instead of the Scythians in 513, everything would surely have turned out differently.

If the Persians had defeated the Greeks, they certainly would not have choked off all the developments that had taken place in Greece in the preceding five hundred years. While they ruled over Ephesus, Heraclitus was still able to philosophize there, just as Anaximander and Hecataeus were free to pursue their philosophy and science in Miletus. The same is true for many others. On the other hand, Xenophanes and Pythagoras, together with the men of Phocaea and Teos, probably knew well why they left their home cities. The freedom that was such as an essential part of Greek life and society had to be able to flourish both within the *polis* and outside it, without the tyrants, whom the Persians tended to install to maintain their authority, and without restraints on the right to wage war.

Most significantly, a Persian victory might have prevented the development of what the Greeks saw themselves challenged to achieve in light of Athens's exceptional role in the fifth century, that is, the Greek classical culture. Conversely, it is hard to imagine this classical culture emerging without the Greek victory, made possible by the Persian attack, specifically without the smooth and meteoric rise of Athens in the wake of that victory, and without the host of new challenges it would not have faced otherwise. Just as earlier Greeks had not been able simply to develop further what they had borrowed from the Orient, so, too, they could not just persist in their established ways after their victory over the Persians. The classical culture was certainly built upon what had been achieved before it and should not be considered a completely new start. But it is hard to see how it would even have been possible without the massive challenges Greek society faced because of its confrontation with the Persian Empire.

When facing such unusual connections and coincidences, the historian may be tempted to speculate about the deeper meaning of history. But where would that lead?

25

Outlook

In conclusion it is perhaps interesting to cast a glance at what came next—the history of the fifth century.

There are not many centuries—if indeed there are any at all—in which so many improbable things happened. Rarely has so much depended on so few men. It was the century of Athens, at least as far as the Aegean was concerned. But it was precisely there that entirely novel possibilities for human culture were opened up and exploited—with enormous consequences.

The century began with an act of stupidity on the part of Athens, which compounded a previous one. In 500, the Ionian cities of Asia Minor decided to break away from the Persian Empire. They asked Athens and Sparta for help, and Athens felt compelled to send twenty ships and an army contingent. The military importance of these forces was almost negligible, but their mere presence made the Persians want to punish Athens for its intervention, once they had put down the ill-considered insurrection. That was the beginning of the Persian wars against the Greek mainland.

Did the Greeks have any idea of whom they were tangling with? The gigantic size of the Persian Empire was obvious—its contours were plainly visible on the maps that Anaximander and Hecataeus had drawn. The Greeks also knew that a journey of ninety-three days was required to get from Ephesus to the Persian capital of Susa. The Spartans had rejected the Ionian pleas for help as soon as they realized this. We do not know whether the Ionian ambassadors sought to downplay the dimensions involved when they made similar entreaties in Athens, or whether the Athenians even thought to ask appropriate questions. Herodotus merely remarks that 30,000 Athenians were easier to deceive than one Spartan king. Moreover the much-travelled, anything but naïve, and well-respected scholar Hecataeus of Miletus had recited for the Ionians the list of the many peoples over whom the Persians held sway. In the consultations preceding the uprising, he left no doubt about the military capacities of the Persian king.

The Greeks therefore could have known how inferior they were to the Persians in terms of military might. But what one should or indeed does know often enough appears not nearly in the same vivid colours as what one wishes for. Optimism often obscures dim prospects, and as Thucydides writes, people who crave something tend to abandon themselves to hope, 'uncircumspect' though it may be. The leaders of the uprising were also probably going at full steam before it dawned on them precisely what they were doing. 'When men go to war', says Thucydides, 'they begin by taking action, which they ought to do last. Only after they have suffered, do they engage in reasoned thinking.' The Austrian dramatist Arthur Schnitzler stated the matter even more drastically, writing that men only engage in serious thinking once they have tried everything else.

In this case, it is also possible that the Greeks simply could not fully comprehend what they knew about the Persians. Such knowledge just did not fit in with the realm of possibilities in which the Greeks were used to operate and which they had learned to take into account. They had never fought against the Persians and were accustomed to wars that were decided by a single battle. They probably just measured bravery against bravery, armaments against armaments, and felt themselves to be superior. That was certainly true for the leader of the rebellion, Aristogoras of Miletus. His attitude was arrogant but not untypical. The distances, dimensions, and time frames in which people thought and acted in the Persian Empire and in Greece were completely different. For Greeks, everything was continually present, whereas the Persians first had to organize and assemble much of what they needed. The relaxed routine made necessary by the size of the Persian Empire may have seemed a weakness to the Greeks. The rhythm of life in the *poleis* was different from that of the Great Empire. Even if the Ionians had lived under Persian domination for half a century, they could, but might not, have had a clear understanding of whom they were dealing with.

Yet, improbable as it may sound, perhaps the Greek cause was not entirely hopeless. To succeed, though, they needed to transcend their own limitations. In clear knowledge of their enemy's superiority, they would have had to rely fully on their own potential strengths and the advantages offered them by their entirely different situation and characteristics. After his suggestion to avoid the uprising was ignored, Hecataeus did not slip into hopeless resignation. Instead he declared that if the Ionians absolutely wanted to pursue their plan, they should at least go about it using reason and sparing no effort. He recommended melting down the valuable dedications in the sanctuary of Apollo at Didyma near

Miletus in order to build a large fleet in addition to the considerable number of warships they already possessed. In Hecataeus' view, the Ionians had to do everything they could to dominate the seas. The Persians laying siege to their cities would soon have to give up unless they controlled access from the sea. By ruling the waves, the Ionians could turn the coastal cities into islands, threaten the long coastline of the Persian Empire, and convince others to defect from the Persians. Water was the element on which the underdogs could bring pressure to bear even on the mighty ones.

It is very questionable whether the Persians would have been prepared to yield cities they had already subjugated. In any case, the Ionians found Hecataeus' second suggestion unacceptable too, and their rebellion was put down in 493. But the ideas that were developed at the time may have continued to exert an influence.

Ten years later, having failed to avenge themselves upon Athens at the Battle of Marathon in 490, the Persians prepared a massive military campaign against the entire Greek mainland. Athens meanwhile was building the large fleet that would enable it, in Aeschylus' words, to vanquish 'all of Asia'. The powerful Persian land army had problems manoeuvring in the narrow confines of the Greek terrain. Even so, the Greeks would hardly have emerged victorious, if they had not succeeded in gaining superiority at sea. The challenge was to defeat the large Persian fleet that was supporting the land army. Athens had prepared itself to do just that.

And Athens achieved success, one of the most astonishing, difficult-to-comprehend military successes in world history. Themistocles, a brilliant strategist and politician, was able to analyse the situation with the utmost precision and go beyond normal ways of thinking, transcending what seemed obvious to the eye, drawing the proper conclusions, and convincing the popular assembly that his plan was right. The entire city was turned on its head, and the Athenians placed all their bets on one card. They did not stay in their homeland, but abandoned the city to fight the Persians at sea. To top it all, they succeeded in drawing their enemy into an unfavourable position, the straits of Salamis, where their fleet could be destroyed. Outmanned and underpowered, the Greeks directed the course of the war so that they could emerge victorious.

True, the Athenians did not fight alone, but without them, victory would have been impossible. In total, some thirty communities took up arms against the Persians, but most of them were rather insignificant. Following on the heels of victory at Salamis, the Greeks, led mostly by the

Spartans, in 479 BC also prevailed on land at Plataea. By that time, it was clear that the Persians could not conquer Greece.

Nothing was ever the same thereafter. Greeks on the other side of the Aegean demanded liberation. Victory in the West raised the possibility of success where rebellion in the East had failed. Motivated by the unexpected triumphs, a large number of Greek *poleis* united in a naval alliance under Athens's leadership. The Persians were pushed back, but their claims to rule in Asia Minor persisted. The Greeks had to stay armed for all eventualities.

The Aegean had gone from being a region of scant political interest to one of extreme tension, and political considerations began to encroach upon personal and commercial contacts. Where many more or less independent communities had coexisted, more concerned with honour and status than power, and focused more on providing a framework and communal structures that enabled their citizens to live together than on pursuing active foreign policies, a coherent political field now emerged. In a meteoric rise, Athens, a minor regional power, became a major international power, upon which Greece's prospects for defending itself against Persia rested. The city's radius of activity and interest extended far beyond Greece to the Persian Empire, stretching along its periphery from Egypt to Cyprus and the Black Sea. In the west, it would later encompass Sicily, while to the north Athens began exerting influence to secure the supply of raw materials, chiefly wood for the fleet, in Macedonia and Thrace. Athenian fleets were constantly roaming the seas. There were costly wars. A newly empowered *polis* flexed its muscles, filling a vacuum in world politics.

With the Persian Empire mostly posing little concrete danger, many *poleis* were eventually tempted to leave the naval alliance, but Athens forced them to maintain the partnership. The Persians, it was argued, could return at any time. But Athens primarily wanted to retain its leading role. Gradually, its allies became subjects, the alliance a sphere of domination, and Athens a 'tyrant city'. That, however, also meant that Sparta and its allies became Athens's opponents and rivals. A Greek dualism began to crystallize and eventually resulted in a twenty-seven-year-long, extremely bitter war (431–404) that affected the entire Greek world, brought suffering to huge numbers of people, and drew the Persians once again into Greek history.

Thanks to its atypically large size, fifth-century Athens became both an irritating foreign body in the *polis* world and an extreme example of how possibilities open to the Greeks could be realized. In Athens, it was not living one's life, measuring oneself against others, and pursuing enjoyment that were uppermost. The focus was on intense engagement for the community, political activity, creativity, and war. Thucydides gives voice to some contemporaries' criticism: 'Their view of a holiday is to do what needs doing; they prefer hardship and activity to peace and quiet.'

Unlike Sparta, which gradually built up its alliances and only concentrated on preserving the status quo, Athens acquired its huge circle of allies in one fell swoop. Having become dominant in the Aegean, after overcoming initial hesitation, Athens had to arrange many things in new ways and suddenly began to go down entirely new paths. A gulf opened up between tradition and necessity, and in its planning and actions Athens constantly had to override custom and expectations. In the eyes of its contemporaries, Athenians were the 'eternal innovators'. That reputation was deserved. Athens had no other choice, either externally or internally.

For the first time, and precisely in the most important Greek *polis*, a democracy arose. In the popular assembly, which was now ruling with virtually unlimited power, day-labourers (the *thētes*), who served as oarsmen in the Athenian navy, and craftsmen (both members of the lowest class of citizens, without substantial landed property), played a significant role. The Athenian *polis* departed from its age-old tradition and restricted horizons as a community of property owners. It became much more than the sum total of all citizens because it set itself tasks and accepted challenges that called upon all citizens to enter intensively into its service. The citizens were willing to rise above themselves and establish rule and political domination—something only the tyrant of Samos, Polycrates, had been able to do previously.

'They are keen in planning', the same critic in Thucydides remarks, 'and quick to implement what they have decided... They are accustomed to tackle challenges beyond their strength and seek out risk in the face of reason, while remaining confident in dangerous situations... When they vanquish enemies, they advance as far as possible, and when they are defeated, they only retreat as much as they have to.' No one among the Greeks had ever before experienced anything like this.

That made Athens exciting, but also hated and misunderstood. It also hindered rivals from taking it seriously while there was still time. Blinded by the force of self-evident tradition, many contemporaries could hardly imagine that something so unfamiliar and new could last. But Athens did last—for decades—and became all the more fascinating. Many Greeks found it terrifying in its power and ruthlessness. But it also attracted huge interest and exerted an almost uncanny appeal, not only because of what it did and achieved but also because of what one could study about and learn from it. Thousands of people poured into Athens from the rest of Greece, Egypt, and other parts of the world to work there as artisans or traders. Others signed on as oarsmen for the Athenian fleet. A large number of slaves were imported. In the markets of the Piraeus, customers could get anything they desired. It was said that if one walked along the stands, one would not know what season it was. In addition, ambassadors arrived from everywhere as well as artists, intellectuals, and philosophers. Athens became a destination for prominent people.

The fifth century saw Athens's rise and fall. In its glorious hubris, its greatness, and descent into blinkered arrogance, it has much in common with tragedy. This was also the century that produced almost the entire body of what we have grown accustomed to associating with Greek classicism: the works of the three great tragedians and the comedian Aristophanes, of the sculptors Phidias, Polyclitus, and Myron, and the architects behind such landmarks as the buildings on the Acropolis. The writing of history was invented, based on the ability to reconstruct historical events and processes empirically, and among the first historians are two of the great masters of the discipline, Herodotus and Thucydides. The Sophists introduced a previously unknown form of intellectual discourse. Socrates posed his famous questions. Moreover, even if Socrates' disciple Plato, who was born in Athens in 427, wrote his works in the fourth century, his philosophy resonated with the experience of his home city's tragic downfall and transgressions as well as the enquiries and eventual fate of his teacher.

The conditions that enabled all this must be sought first of all in the experiences made in and by this community that so suddenly found itself thrust onto the centre stage of world politics. Its situation was the most extraordinary one can imagine. Athens's series of successes was dizzying; the city continually achieved what had previously hardly been even thinkable: victory over Persia's world empire, radical democracy, domination in the Aegean—a chain of ruptures, one following hot upon the heels of another. The Athenians were unprepared for this and could hardly perceive or absorb the rapid process of change. They focused all the more on what had to be done and what they were experiencing.

A historical process like this can rob a society of its senses and awaken the need to shut itself off from change and its possible consequences. But in fifth-century Athens and beyond, citizens confronted all this with stupendous interest and great openness. Nothing was off-limits; on the contrary, much potential was freed up. In tragedy especially, we can see how, for example, the often unusually difficult and unprecedented decisions that the Athenian popular assembly had to take provoked thought and debate. The questions that arose did not end with political resolutions, but continued to affect those who had made them. They had to find some way of harmonizing their choices with received wisdom. They had to work, if you will, on the mental infrastructure of the community.

The issue of whether the Greeks were really safe from further Persian attack was not just a political and military question; it also depended on the will of the gods. Did the gods want the Aegean to be a boundary, as Aeschylus believed? Did the Persian king, again as Aeschylus suggested, really suffer defeat because he had failed to respect this boundary? Furthermore, the Greeks believed in the envy of the gods, which would strike down anyone who became too powerful. Was this the fate that now threatened Athens after all its unlikely successes? Or did it depend on whether one had justly acquired such power and how one used it? But what was ultimately just and unjust?

In a citizen body where planning and reason reached so far and were so prominent, the question had to arise whether the gods still played any role at all. Did everything ultimately depend only on humans? Were people really autonomous? Or were they simply deluding themselves? Could the gods not visit them with *atē*, delusion, which would make disadvantage look like advantage? How much progress could one make with enlightened thought, and how much with arbitrary legislation? Did not the unwritten 'laws' or norms that were sanctioned by age-old traditions demand a respect of their own?

Indeed, how far did human potential reach? What was human destiny? Did humans really deserve the benefits of utterly unfamiliar, unhoped-for developments? What was man, anyway, as great and yet all-too-weak (and soon shabby as well) as he came to perceive himself, especially whenever more depended on him? What could man know about himself?

These were general questions of the kind that people keep asking themselves, completely independent of politics, and those question multiplied with time. At stake was people's understanding of themselves and how they were to find their way as well as a just order in the world. But here a whole citizenry was asking them, and it did so with greater urgency the more such questions were connected with multiple needs for action, with the citizenry's very existence. They were not just private matters or subjects of casual conversation that touched upon topics only to move on equally quickly. On the contrary, the great questions of the time formed the public discourse of the entire city—and quite intensely as well.

Before and especially after the realization of radical democracy, Athens was not dominated by small circles of people who ruled. It was the entire citizenry that carried the community and decided everything. The citizenry, with its hopes and perhaps arrogance, as well as its worries and fears, was not just heavily involved in all events, it was also accustomed to taking responsibility for the community. In some sense, at least, it was used to being held accountable for what happened. And it wanted to know where it stood and expected this demand to be fulfilled. These citizens had been schooled for decades in political thought. They placed great value upon others being able to express themselves comprehensibly before them, as in the theatre.

It must also have made a difference that the members of this society tended to see events from various perspectives, depending on the many roles they had to play in deliberating, making decisions, acting, suffering, and continually observing.

Moreover, the dimensions of all that required public consensus-building, accountability, and self-assertion were drawn especially wide in art, which potentially offered objective distance. That had always been the case, and it was even truer now. Beyond dealing with daily necessities, the citizens needed not only the rationality of political thought, but also the ideas, images, and stories offered by the arts to help them interpret, understand, and visualize the unusual and unsuspected. And because all needed such help, for themselves and in concert with one another, working on these arts was a public task.

In Thucydides, we read that the Athenians risked their bodies for the community as if they were not their own. They needed their minds, however, as 'that which was most their own', in order to do the city any good. Thucydides was primarily thinking about politics. But could life in the *polis*, under the circumstances prevailing at the time, be reduced to just politics? Significantly, large parts of the citizenry attended the performances of tragedies.

These audiences were probably unique in world history. The orator Gorgias, for one, praised the Athenians for being smart and fond of language. And when else have democratic committees been responsible, in such minute detail, for such a grandiose construction project as the Acropolis, which both preserved traditional standards and stretched them to their absolute extreme? Popular and high culture converged here.

Such statements may sound unbelievable. But obviously what was produced at the time was incredible too. It would have been a miracle if the conditions allowing for such excellence had not been exceptional as well.

Athens was full of questions. Perhaps it had almost become addicted to questioning. It went through highs and lows. Grandiose, rationally based plans and triumphs alternated with uncertainties. But for a long time, the Athenians must have been driven by enormous confidence in their own success—articulated in a magnificent consciousness of ability that helped them clear many hurdles. They moved with great bravura about the space that had opened up. And they did so under the conditions of competition, not just among the tragedians, before an ever more demanding public.

The search and striving for the right measures that were fuelled by this culture for the sake of freedom must have determined the forms of the plastic arts. Artists too gained great freedom with the alternatives that opened up in the political realm. But everything remained connected to a human dimension, to an image of humanity that was essentially an ideal to be distilled out of what seemed to be the basis of all phenomena.

In short, within a few decades, albeit after 500 years of history, a single city and its citizens became the centre of unparalleled human experiences. They were manifested 'classically' in the widest variety of areas and forms. The more things came apart, the more one had to force them back together. Tonio Hölscher has called classical Greek culture uncanny, and that word seems to reflect something of the threatening and fearsome nature of the worries classicism sought to vanquish.

Athenian citizens were *homines politici*, and they were so to an extraordinary extent. This played a decisive role in what they experienced. But precisely as such, they were also paradigms of what is generally human. After all, the Athenian citizens were not a bourgeoisie, not a class with its own particular sphere of life, a high regard for work, its own achievements, and perhaps some wealth. They had no special bourgeois ways, tried and tested for centuries, and there was no discrete circle of intelligentsia. Nor were they a society unto themselves, separate from the state, whose members were primarily private individuals and whose interests were mostly directed towards economic and social affairs, and the rarified realm of their own private sphere. They knew nothing of the mediations and abstractions with which modern personalities define themselves in relation to the whole. Nor did they experience the division of society into distinct sectors, the specialization that creates so many particular spheres of achievement and prestige.

As a consequence, their experiences were not those of isolation, moodiness, internal division, and disorientation, or proving oneself in many specialized areas. The Athenians did not go through the psychological abysses that continually and repeatedly must affect specific individuals. Nor did they know any of the similar dispositions which modern literature and art have unlocked. The Greeks had no inkling of a world in which, to paraphrase the sociologist Niklas Luhmann, it was hardly any more possible to imagine human beings in anthropomorphic terms.

On the contrary, as Jacob Burckhardt put it, the Greeks wanted to be 'a whole unto themselves'. Their experiences concerned social interaction and coexistence with others as equals, quarrel, compromise, struggle, and continual existential threat, not just for the individual, but for the entire community. They worked through the questions that arose for them both individually and communally with often shocking openness and rigour, and they found answers that prove to be relevant time and again even today, influencing not least the very heart of philosophy and science. Their questions are still our questions, no matter how many others have been added throughout the centuries. Thus it is only logical that these free citizens in the horizon of antiquity and far beyond—were, by virtue of being *homines politici*, also *homines maxime homines*. It is worth asking whether experiences of this sort and intensity were unique in history and could only have been made so productively under the most extraordinary circumstances.

Epilogue

The major part of this book has been devoted to the question of how the Greeks came about, how this unusual and exotic people developed into what they were—or to put that question another way: how they developed a culture that was so different from all the other magnificent high cultures that emerged before and beside them in world history. Political rule was usually the driving force that propelled, unified, and shaped everything that was part of a high culture: political organization and mentality, ideas, myths, modes of thought, technical capabilities, religion, poetry, art, and science. With the Greeks, the motor was freedom, specifically, a broad circle of free men in many cities, who saw themselves challenged to secure and expand their free way of life against all encroachments. The result of their efforts reflected that difference.

One cannot trace the development of cultures back to genes or innate abilities. What the Greeks were, they became in the course of their history, with and as a direct result of their culture, which they developed in the process and needed as a means of giving themselves support in their further development. The historian's task is to find out how this happened, to explain it, and, if possible, to make it comprehensible.

Yet such questions about the Greeks should not just be posed for their own sake, but also with an eye towards the history of Europe. Legitimate arguments exist about whether the Greeks represent Europe's prehistory or the first chapter of its history. This issue is the topic of the first part of this book.

The two parts of this book are the first of seven in total that are intended to form the first volume, on the ancient world, of a series of volumes on the history of Europe. For various reasons I have chosen to publish these two parts in advance. One deserves mention here. If I am not mistaken, discussions are intensifying in our time about the development and particularity of Europe, and specifically about Europe's relationship to the Orient. They open up more general questions about the origins of cultures, their openness to others, the conditions of, and time needed, for their formation and further development, as well as the difficulties and time needed to gain access to and participate in them.

We sometimes notice that we need to think about all this. On the other hand, it is not easily obvious to see why we should. To far too great an extent, we today live under the illusion that the achievements of all cultures are readily available, as in a supermarket, and can be consumed by anyone in whatever mixture he chooses—and not just by individuals but by whole societies. It may be, however, that this situation tempts us to misunderstand and ignore much that is important about all earlier history. In any case, history as a discipline is called to contribute to this discussion what it can in whatever field and in whatever way, even if it is merely a matter of drawing attention to what has been neglected and thus expanding the realm of possible topics for debate. History though can no longer function as a *magistra vitae*, and it does well to remember that fact.

The other parts of the book on the ancient world unfortunately remain work in progress. They should have been completed years ago.

The often troubling difficulties I encountered in working on this book (which also explain the delays in the publication), were caused in part by an unexpected need to conduct much additional research—even though I had concerned myself for decades with many of the issues involved. This was true for the analysis and interpretation of sources and in particular for the synthesis, the effort to understand and present how everything fitted together. This may also have been the result of the particular questions I posed and how I understood them. And there is a special difficulty: an author who tries to define what is special about a given culture needs to distinguish it from others, in theory from all others, which involves making a host of comparisons. Today, this is very difficult, if not impossible. Some relief was offered by the fact that it is possible to reach a reasonable understanding at least of the main subject of comparison, the ancient Near East. Nonetheless, some of my assertions may seem overly bold. I thought it better to make such statements than to remain vague, and I have tried to indicate where I am speculating. Moreover, the limited sources we possess for countless historical phenomena often do not allow for precise and certain statements. Precisely marked imprecision is the closest one can get to meeting the demand for precision.

Another special and truly testing difficulty was given by the genre of history in which I am trying to operate. On the one hand, the material has to be presented so as to be comprehensible and interesting to a broad readership without leaving out or unduly simplifying anything essential. Others will have to judge whether I have succeeded in this regard.

If readers do not notice the effort spent in producing this book—count-less pages had to be written before those that made it into the printed volume could stand—then the trials were worth it.

On the other hand, I had to try to find a form that would make the larger context of what happened and developed among the early Greeks understandable and concrete. Alfred Heuss very accurately character-ized the problem that arises in the process. 'As in a picture,' he wrote, 'the various individual parts have to be placed in a relationship with one another. That is an independent undertaking since the parts themselves and the limited information they provide are insufficient to complete this task. Historical synthesis is thus a special, constructive achievement.' For further thoughts on this issue, see my essays 'Programm einer Geschichtsschreibung', in Jürgen Trabant (ed.), *Sprache der Geschichte* (Munich 2005), 149ff.; and 'Alfred Heuss als Geschichtsschreiber', in H.-J. Gehrke (ed.), *Alfred Heuss—Ansichten seines Lebenswerkes* (Stuttgart, 1998), 115–40.

For much of early Greek history, the historical sequence of events can only be sketchily reconstructed, and whole sets of topics can only be given their due in special sections. Topics like the Greeks' relationship to the Orient, the two hundred years of Greek colonization, the early epics, the *polis* within its pan-Hellenic context, lyric poetry, political thought, philosophy, and many others had to be given chapters of their own. Only late in the story, with the decisive stages of the history of Athens in the sixth century, could I pursue a more narrative type of historical writing. Hence diachronic sections comprising the entire time period intersect with thematically focused chapters. This is the only way to do justice to the multifaceted character of the Greeks. Rome is entirely different: all is focused there on politics, the military, constitu-tion, and law; there it is possible to narrate events and developments with a few digressions summarizing issues like constitution, law, and (closely connected) religion.

The Greeks' extremely daring, if not positively adventurous develop-ment of a culture for the sake of freedom by necessity evolved much more broadly and in a rich spectrum of dimensions. Accordingly, I had to include many issues that hardly existed or were negligible in ancient Rome. It is symptomatic of the early years of ancient Greece, in contrast to Rome, that we know little about its political history. At the same time, again in contrast to Rome, we possess a whole series of sources from this period that are of extraordinary quality but of a literary and later philosophical nature. They include the epics of Homer and Hesiod, lyric poetry, fragments of works dealing with political thought, philosophy, and science—not to mention inscriptions and other archaeological evidence.

Obviously, this fact must reflect a basic element of Greek culture. Such sources are not just the results of a special Greek artistic talent, but products of specific ways and needs of living and surviving. In short, the Greeks felt the need to preserve and develop what they most valued, which can be summed up in two words: independence and freedom. This required a special amount and special ways of understanding the world and communicating about it, including the ability to balance interests in small communities free of political domination, asserting oneself, finding moderation, bearing, skill in expressing oneself in thought and words—to name just a few qualities. All this explains why the Greeks could become and remain so free, what they needed in order to achieve that, and what ultimately allowed a world consisting of tiny *poleis* to vanquish the massive Persian Empire. The key was to combine freedom with social order and later military might, which, of course, brought a set of new risks along with it.

Writing for a broad audience is both an opportunity and a problem. My work was made more difficult by the need to avoid specialist terminology, jargon, and the habits of thought that underlie them, to emancipate myself from the various discourses of academia with their no longer completely conscious assumptions. Nor was it always easy to suppress lengthy justifications for presenting my subject matter as I did and to suggest, rather than to fully explore my own arguments. My ambition was to make an alien and faraway world accessible to today's readers without concealing its basic foreignness, my desire to make it imaginable and comprehensible in everyday language. This was alluring and opened up interesting perspectives. But it also took a long time before I had even halfway finished.

Glossary of Greek terms

(Please note ou is pronounced as u: *kouros* = *kuros*)

agón   competition

agorá   public square for public events and markets

ápeiron   that which is limitless

arché   beginning, rule

árchōn (*pl.* **árchontes**)   leader, magistrate

areté   manly excellence, virtue

aristeía   effort to excel beyond all others

áristos (*pl.* **áristoi**)   the best

atimía   loss of civic honour and citizenship rights

autárkeia   self-sufficiency

basileús (*pl.* **basileís**)   leader, lord, king

cháris   grace

démos   people

díkē   justice

dysnomía   bad order

eirénē   peace

éphoros (**ephor**)   overseer, Spartan magistrate

éthnos (*pl.* **éthnē**)   tribe

eunomía   good order

gymnásion (**gymnasium**)   place for athletic exercises

hetaíra, hetaera   courtesan

isomoiría   'equal shares', redistribution of property

isonomía   'order of equality', equality before the law, political equality

katartistér (*pl.* **katartistéres**)   'straightener', specialist in bringing things into order, straightening things out

koiné   common feature, area sharing common features

koúros (*pl.* **koúroi**), **kórē** (*pl.* **korai**)   statue of young man or woman

krátos   power

lógos   word, story, principle, reason

nekrópolis (**necropolis**)   burial site, cemetery

nómos (*pl.* **nómoi**)   custom, law, convention

orchéstra   circular space for dances and performances

palaístra (**palaestra**)   wrestling ring

phrátra (**phrátry,** *pl.* **phrátries**)   brotherhood, civic subdivision

phýlē (*pl.* **phýlai**)   tribe, civic subdivision

pólis (*pl.* **poleis**)   city-state, citizen-state

stásis (*pl.* **stáseis**)   civil strife, civil war

xénos (*pl.* **xénoi**), **xenía**   guest friend, guest friendship

Sources and Further Reading

To add detailed documentation in footnotes would have contradicted the purpose and character of the present book. If I had wanted to cite adequately all the sources as well as all the arguments and considerations upon which my work is based (as well as justifying omissions), the size of this book would easily have doubled. I have mentioned important arguments for my reconstruction where this seemed appropriate. The process by which I reached my understanding of conditions, developments, and events, and the justification of this understanding, is mostly comprised in my narrative.

The selective bibliography I had included in the German edition served two purposes. It highlighted works that were especially important to me and from which I had quoted. And it included a small number of works that could help readers gain an overview of the sources and scholarship. In the present English edition some of the German titles have been replaced by English ones.

Moreover, for the present edition Kurt Raaflaub has integrated into this bibliography a longer list of works in English (and occasionally another language) for further reading. It is intended to assist those readers who wish to gain fuller access to recent research on the issues discussed in this book. I am very grateful to him not only for providing these references but also for revising the entire text of the English translation. His suggestions have been extremely useful in both respects.

Evidence

Sources for Greek history between 1000 and 500 BC are sparse. Only four works survive in their entirety: the two Homeric epics, *Iliad* and *Odyssey*, and Hesiod's *Theogony* and, with special value for our present purposes, *Works and Days*. Richmond Lattimore's translations (*Iliad*, paperback, Chicago, 1961; *Odyssey*, paperback, New York, 1975) follow the Greek text closely. More modern, somewhat freer, more easily readable translations are by Donald Fagles (with introductions by Bernard Knox, New York, 1990, 1996, respectively) and Stephen Lombardo (with introductions by Sheila Murnaghan, Indianapolis, 1997, 2000). Hesiod's works are most easily accessible in the annotated translations by Apostolos Athanassakis (2nd edn, Baltimore, 2004) and M. L. West (Oxford, 1988).

Most of what has survived of lyric and elegiac poetry is fragmentary; fortunately it includes a sizeable amount of the poetry of the great Athenian reformer Solon. The Greek text of iambic and elegiac poetry is collected in anthologies edited by M. L. West, *Iambi et Elegi Graeci Ante Alexandrum Cantati* (I, Oxford, 1971; II, 2nd edn, 1992), and Bruno Gentili and Carlo Prato, *Poetae Elegiaci* (2 vols, Leipzig, 1985–8). The Loeb Classical Library (Cambridge, Mass.) contains bilingual Greek/English editions: *Greek Elegiac Poetry*, ed. Douglas E. Gerber

(1999); *Greek Lyric*, ed. David A. Campbell (5 vols, 1982–93). Among several translations of both elegiac and lyric poetry, that of M. L. West (*Greek Lyric Poetry*, Oxford, 1994) is easily accessible; a broad selection with interpretation is in Hermann Fränkel, *Early Greek Poetry and Philosophy*, trans. Moses Hadas and James Willis (New York and Oxford, 1973).

The fragments of the early philosophers are collected by Hermann Diels and Walther Kranz, *Die Fragmente der Vorsokratiker* (3 vols, 10th and 11th edn, Zurich and Berlin, 1961, 1964), trans. Kathleen Freeman, *Ancilla to the Pre-Socratic Philosophers* (paperback, Cambridge, Mass., 1983) and (with interpretation) by G. S. Kirk, J. E. Raven, and Malcolm Schofield (2nd edn, Cambridge, 2007); selections (with interpretation) are also in Fränkel (above).

One can glean further information from the histories of Herodotus and Thucydides, written in the late fifth and very early fourth centuries, respectively (both are available in multiple translations; Rex Warner's Penguin trans. has been used here). The school of Aristotle (second half of the fourth century) produced a well-preserved survey of the history and working of the Athenian constitution: *Athēnaiōn politeia* (*The Constitution of the Athenians*); see P. J. Rhodes, *A Commentary on the Aristotelian Athenaion politeia* (Oxford, 1981) and Rhodes's translation, *Aristotle: The Athenian Constitution* (Harmondsworth, 1984). In addition, we have scattered references in later authors, which are cited (together with relevant archaeological finds) in the scholarship listed below.

Surveys

Among surveys on early Greek history, *The Cambridge Ancient History* (*CAH*), vols III.1, III.3, and IV (2nd edn, Cambridge, 1982, 1988) and Salvatore Settis (ed.), *I Greci. Storia Cultura Arte Società*, II.1: *Formazione* (Turin, 1996) offer the most comprehensive treatment of many relevant aspects. See also Oswyn Murray, *Early Greece* (2nd edn, Cambridge, Mass., 1993); Paul Cartledge (ed.), *The Cambridge Illustrated History of Ancient Greece* (Cambridge, 1998); Robin Osborne, *Greece in the Making, 1200–479 BC* (2nd edn, London, 2009). Jacob Burckhardt, *Griechische Kulturgeschichte* (new scholarly edn, Munich, in progress); *The Greeks and Greek Civilization* (trans. Sheila Stern, ed. and intro. Oswyn Murray, New York, 1998) still proves inestimably rich and in many ways the most relevant treatment of the subject.

On the Greek Bronze Age Civilization and its destruction: John Chadwick, *The Mycenaean World* (Cambridge, 1976); Oliver Dickinson, *The Aegean Bronze Age* (Cambridge, 1994); Cynthia W. Shelmerdine (ed.), *The Cambridge Companion to the Aegean Bronze Age* (Cambridge, 2008). On the 'Dark Age': Anthony Snodgrass, *The Dark Age of Greece* (2nd edn, Edinburgh, 2000); Oliver Dickinson, *The Aegean from Bronze Age to Iron Age* (London, 2006). On the Archaic Age: Alfred Heuss, 'Hellas. Die archaische Zeit', in Golo Mann and Alfred Heuss (eds), *Propyläen*

Weltgeschichte, III (Berlin, 1962), 69–213; 'Die archaische Zeit Griechenlands als geschichtliche Epoche', in Heuss, *Gesammelte Schriften*, I (Stuttgart, 1995), 2–38; Anthony Snodgrass, *Archaic Greece: The Age of Experiment* (Berkeley, 1980); Nick Fisher and Hans van Wees (eds), *Archaic Greece: New Approaches and New Evidence* (London, 1998); Jonathan Hall, *A History of the Archaic Greek World* (Malden, Mass., 2007); H. A. Shapiro (ed.), *The Cambridge Companion to Archaic Greece* (Cambridge, 2007); Kurt A. Raaflaub and Hans van Wees (eds), *A Companion to Archaic Greece* (Malden, Mass., 2009).

Much material is collected in Elke Stein-Hölkeskamp, *Adelskultur und Polisgesellschaft* (Stuttgart, 1989). On literature, Albin Lesky, *A History of Greek Literature*, trans. James Willis and Cornelis de Heer (New York, 1966); Fränkel, *Early Greek Poetry and Philosophy* (cited above); see also Kurt Raaflaub, 'Intellectual Achievements [of Archaic Greece]', in Raaflaub and van Wees, *Companion* (above), 564–84. On the concept of freedom: Raaflaub, *The Discovery of Freedom in Ancient Greece* (first English edn, rev. and updated from the German, Chicago, 2004).

In many cases, the reader will find easy access to an issue or item through the brief surveys (with references to sources and bibliog.) in the recent *Brill's New Pauly: Encyclopedia of the Ancient World* (multiple vols, Leiden, 2002–).

Part I

A number of studies have examined the origins of the particular characteristics of Europe. To Max Weber, it was important with regard to the development of capitalism. Recent works that have revived the discussion include Werner Dahlheim, 'Verwehte Spuren. Die antiken Wurzeln des modernen Europa', in *Deutsche Akademie für Sprache und Dichtung. Jahrbuch 1997*, 111ff.; E. L. Jones, *The European Miracle: Environments, Economies, and Geopolitics in the History of Europe and Asia* (3rd edn, Cambridge, 2003); Michael Mitterauer, *Why Europe? The Medieval Origins of its Special Path*, trans. Gerald Chapple (Chicago, 2010).

Chapter 4

On Anaximander, see Kirk, Raven, and Schofield, *Presocratic Philosophers* (cited among sources), 100–42; the fragment discussed here is A6 in Diels and Kranz, *Fragmente* (cited above among sources). On Hecataeus of Miletus, see Lionel Pearson, *Early Ionian Historians* (Oxford, 1939), ch. 2; Stephanie West, 'Herodotus' Portrait of Hecataeus', *Journal of Hellenic Studies* 111 (1991), 144–60. The most important passage is Herodotus 4.36ff. On maps: J. B. Harley and David Woodward, *The History of Cartography*, I (Chicago, 1987); O. A. W. Dilke, *Greek and Roman Maps* (paperback, Baltimore, 1998).

Chapter 5

Aeschylus' *Persians* is included in *Aeschylus, Prometheus Bound, The Suppliants, Seven Against Thebes, The Persians*, trans. Philip Vellacott (Harmondsworth, 1961); Edith Hall offers a bilingual edition with commentary (Warminster, 1996).

Chapter 6

On the Greek concept of Europe and the division between Asia and Europe: Martin Ninck, *Die Entdeckung Europas durch die Griechen* (Basel, 1945); James Romm, 'Continents, Climates, and Cultures: Greek Theories of Global Structure', in Kurt Raaflaub and Richard Talbert (eds), *Geography and Ethnography: Perceptions of the World in Pre-Modern Societies* (Malden, Mass., 2010), 215–35. The quotation by Ernst Jünger is from *Der gordische Knoten* (Frankfurt am Main, 1953). On the contrast between Greeks and barbarians: Olivier Reverdin (ed.), *Grecs et barbares* (Vandoeuvres, 1962); Pericles Georges, *Barbarian Asia and the Greek Experience* (Baltimore, 1994). Hippocrates' treatise, *Airs, Waters, Places*, ed. Jacques Jouanna, *Hippocrate*, II: *Airs, Eaux, Lieux* (Paris, 1996), is translated in G. E. R. Lloyd (ed.), *Hippocratic Writings* (Harmondsworth, 1978); on Hippocrates, see Jouanna, *Hippocrates*, trans. M. B. DeBevoise (Baltimore, 1999).

Chapter 7

Rémi Brague, *Eccentric Culture: A Theory of Western Civilization*, trans. Samuel Lester (South Bend, Ind., 2002).

Part II

Chapter 8

References on the end of the Greek Bronze Age civilization and on the Dark Ages are listed above among surveys. On early Mesopotamian history, see esp. Hans Nissen, *The Early History of the Ancient Near East, 9000–2000 B.C.* (Chicago, 1988); see also e.g. J. N. Postgate, *Early Mesopotamia: Society and Economy at the Dawn of History* (London, 1992); Amélie Kuhrt, *The Ancient Near East, c.3000–330 B.C.* (2 vols, London, 1995); Marc Van de Mieroop, *A History of the Ancient Near East, ca. 3000–323 BC* (Malden, Mass., 2004).

Chapter 9

On the eighth century and the archaic period, see above under surveys. On public spaces: Tonio Hölscher, *Öffentliche Räume in frühen griechischen Städten* (Heidelberg, 1998). On colonization, see below under Chapter 11. On early Greek law: Kurt Latte, 'Der Rechtsgedanke im archaischen Griechentum' and 'Beiträge zum griechischen Strafrecht', in Latte, *Kleine Schriften zu Religion, Recht,*

Literatur und Sprache der Griechen und Römer (Munich, 1968), 233–51, 252–93; Louis Gernet, *The Anthropology of Ancient Greece*, trans. John Hamilton and Blaise Nagy (Baltimore, 1981) esp. pt. III; Michael Gagarin, *Early Greek Law* (Berkeley, 1986); *Writing Greek Law* (Cambridge, 2008); Vincent Farenga, *Citizen and Self in Ancient Greece: Individuals Performing Justice and the Law* (Cambridge, 2006). On Homer, see under Chapter 12.

Chapter 10

Walter Burkert, *The Orientalizing Revolution: Near Eastern Influence on Greek Culture in the Early Archaic Age*, trans. Margaret E. Pinder and Walter Burkert (Cambridge, Mass., 1992); Burkert, *Babylon, Memphis, Persepolis: Eastern Contexts of Greek Culture* (Cambridge, Mass., 2004); M. L. West, *The East Face of Helicon: West Asiatic Elements in Greek Poetry and Myth* (Oxford, 1997); Johannes Renger, 'Griechenland und der Orient—der Orient und Griechenland. Oder zur Frage von ex oriente lux', in Monika Bernett, Wilfried Nippel, and Aloys Winterling (eds), *Christian Meier zur Diskussion* (Stuttgart, 2008), 1–32; Kurt Raaflaub, 'Early Greek Political Thought in its Mediterranean Context', in Ryan Balot (ed.), *A Companion to Greek and Roman Political Thought* (Malden, Mass., 2009), 37–56; 'Zeus and Prometheus: Greek Adaptations of Near Eastern Myths', forthcoming in Kenneth Sacks (ed.), *Appropriation and Exchange in the Ancient World: A Periplus of the Mediterranean*.

Chapter 11

On colonization, see the relevant chapters by A. J. Graham and J. M. Cook in *CAH* III.3 (1982), and, more recently, by Carla Antonaccio and Irad Malkin, respectively, in the *Companions* on archaic Greece listed above among surveys. On the role of Delphi: Irad Malkin, *Religion and Colonization in Ancient Greece* (Leiden, 1987).

Chapter 12

On Homer, see Joachim Latacz, *Homer: His Art and His World*, trans. James Holoka (Ann Arbor, 1996); Latacz (ed.), *Zweihundert Jahre Homer-Forschung. Rückblick und Ausblick* (Stuttgart, 1991); Ian Morris and Barry Powell (eds), *A New Companion to Homer* (Leiden, 1997); Robert Fowler (ed.), *The Cambridge Companion to Homer* (Cambridge, 2004). Especially important for my interpretation: Fränkel, *Early Greek Poetry and Philosophy* (above under Sources); Karl Reinhardt, 'Tradition und Geist im homerischen Epos', in Reinhardt, *Tradition und Geist. Gesammelte Essays zur Dichtung* (Göttingen, 1960), 5–15; *Die Ilias und ihr Dichter* (Göttingen, 1961); Bruno Snell, *The Discovery of the Mind: The Greek Origins of European Thought*, trans. T. G. Rosenmeyer (Cambridge, Mass., 1953); Snell, *Poetry and Society: The Role of Poetry in Ancient Greece* (Bloomington, Ind., 1961). I also quoted from Kurt Latte's review of Fränkel's work, in Latte, *Kleine Schriften* (above under Chapter 9), 713–

26; Jean-Pierre Vernant, 'A "Beautiful Death" and the Disfigured Corpse in Homeric Epic', in Vernant, *Mortals and Immortals: Collected Essays*, ed. Froma I. Zeitlin (Princeton, 1991), 50–74; Richard Harder, *Eigenart der Griechen: Einführung in die griechische Kultur* (Freiburg i. Br., 1962). On 'epic society', Hans van Wees, *Status Warriors: War, Violence, and Society in Homer and History* (Amsterdam, 1992); Kurt Raaflaub, 'Homer und die Geschichte des 8. Jhs v. Chr.', in Latacz, *Zweihundert Jahre* (above), 205–56; 'Homeric Society', in Morris and Powell, *A New Companion to Homer* (above), 624–48; 'A Historian's Headache: How to Read "Homeric Society"?' in Fisher and van Wees, *Archaic Greece* (cited under Surveys), 169–93. On the epic of Gilgamesh, see now Andrew George, *The Babylonian Gilgamesh Epic: Introduction, Critical Edition and Cuneiform Texts* (Oxford, 2003), and George's translation, *The Epic of Gilgamesh: The Babylonian Epic Poem and Other Texts in Akkadian and Sumerian* (Harmondsworth, 1999). On Hesiod see the introductions to M. L. West, *Theogony* (Oxford, 1966); *Works and Days* (Oxford, 1978); Robert Lamberton, *Hesiod* (New Haven, 1988); Friedrich Solmsen, *Hesiod and Aeschylus* (new edn, Ithaca, NY, 1995); Jenny Strauss Clay, *Hesiod's Cosmos* (Cambridge, 2003); Franco Montanari, Antonios Rengakos, and Christos Tsagalis (eds), *Brill's Companion to Hesiod* (Leiden, 2009). On early political reflection in Homer and Hesiod: Kurt Raaflaub, 'Poets, Lawgivers, and the Beginnings of Greek Political Reflection', in Christopher Rowe and Malcolm Schofield (eds), *The Cambridge History of Greek and Roman Political Thought* (Cambridge, 2000), 23–59; Dean Hammer, *The Iliad as Politics: The Performance of Political Thought* (Norman, Okla., 2002).

Chapter 13

Walter Burkert, *Homo necans: The Anthropology of Ancient Greek Sacrificial Ritual and Myth*, trans. Peter Bing (Berkeley, 1983);   Burkert, *Greek Religion*, trans. John Raffan (Cambridge, 1985); Burkert, 'The Formation of Greek Religion at the Close of the Dark Ages', *Studi italiani di filologia classica*, NS 10 (1992), 533–51; Louise Bruit Zaidman and Pauline Schmitt Pantel, *Religion in the Ancient Greek City*, trans. Paul Cartledge (Cambridge, 1992); Paul Veyne, 'Culte, piété et morale dans le paganisme gréco-romain', in Veyne, *L'Empire gréco-romain* (Paris, 2005), 419–543; Richard Harder, *Eigenart* (see under Chapter 12); Michael Flower, *The Seer in Ancient Greece* (Berkeley, 2008).

Chapter 14

See the works on archaic Greece listed among surveys. In addition, E. R. Dodds, *The Greeks and the Irrational* (Berkeley, 1966); C. G. Starr, *The Economic and Social Growth of Early Greece, 800–500 B.C.* (New York, 1977); *Individual and Community: The Rise of the Polis, 800–500 B.C.* (New York, 1986); A. W. H. Adkins, *Merit and Responsibility: A Study in Greek Values* (Oxford, 1960); *Moral Values and Political Behavior in Ancient Greece* (New York, 1972); Walter Donlan, *The Aristocratic Ideal and Selected*

Papers (Wauconda, Wash., 1999). On the dedications on the Acropolis: A. E. Raubitschek, *Dedications from the Athenian Acropolis: A Catalogue of the Inscriptions of the Sixth and Fifth Century* (Cambridge, Mass., 1949). On the emergence of the agora as a public square: Roland Martin, *Recherches sur l'agora grecque* (Paris, 1951); Hölscher, 'Öffentliche Räume' (see under Chapter 9); John M. Camp, *The Athenian Agora* (London, 1986). On early coinage: Colin M. Kraay and Max Hirmer, *Greek Coins* (New York, 1966); Christopher Howgego, *Ancient History from Coins* (London, 1995).

Chapter 15

Hans Schaefer, 'Das Problem der griechischen Nationalität', in Schaefer, *Probleme der Alten Geschichte* (Göttingen, 1963), 269–306. On the 'agonistic impulse', see Ingomar Weiler, 'Wider und für das agonale Prinzip—eine griechische Eigenart? Wissenschaftliche Aspekte und Grundsatzüberlegungen', *Nikephoros* 19 (2006), 81ff.; John Dayton, *'The Athletes of War': An Evaluation of the Agonistic Elements in Greek Warfare* (Toronto, 2006). On *xenia*: Gabriel Herman, *Ritualised Friendship and the Greek City* (Cambridge, 1987). On the emergence of the pan-Hellenic sanctuaries and games: Catherine Morgan, *Athletes and Oracles: The Transformation of Olympia and Delphi in the Eighth Century B.C.* (Cambridge, 1990); Morgan, 'The Origins of Panhellenism', in Nanno Marinatos and Robin Hägg (eds), *Greek Sanctuaries: New Approaches* (London, 1993), 18–44; M. I. Finley and H. W. Pleket, *The Olympic Games: The First Thousand Years* (New York, 1976).

Chapter 16

On Sparta and related issues, see M. I. Finley, 'Sparta and Spartan Society', in Finley, *Economy and Society in Ancient Greeece* (New York, 1982), 24–40; Nigel Kennell, *The Gymnasium of Virtue: Education and Culture in Ancient Sparta* (Chapel Hill, NC, 1995); J. F. Lazenby, *The Spartan Army* (Warminster, 1985); Graham Shipley, 'Other Lakedaimonians: The Dependent Perioikic *Poleis* of Laconia and Messenia', in M. H. Hansen (ed.), *The Polis as an Urban Centre and as a Political Community* (Copenhagen, 1997), 189–281; Paul Cartledge, *Spartan Reflections* (Berkeley, 2001); *Sparta and Lakonia: A Regional History* (2nd edn, London, 2002); S. B. Pomeroy, *Spartan Women* (Oxford, 2002); Nino Luraghi and Susan Alcock (eds), *Helots and Their Masters in Laconia and Messenia: Histories, Ideologies, Structures* (Washington, DC, 2003); Jean Ducat, *Spartan Education* (London, 2006); K.-W. Welwei, *Sparta* (2nd edn, Stuttgart, 2007); Nino Luraghi, *The Ancient Messenians: Constructions of Ethnicity and Memory* (Cambridge, 2008). On the world of *poleis* beyond Sparta and Athens: L. H. Jeffery, *Archaic Greece: The City-States c. 700–500 B.C.* (London, 1976); Hans-Joachim Gehrke, *Jenseits von Athen und Sparta. Das dritte Griechenland und seine Staatenwelt* (Munich, 1986); R. A. Tomlinson, *Argos and the Argolid* (Ithaca, NY, 1972); J. B. Salmon, *Wealthy Corinth* (Oxford, 1984); Thomas Figueira and Gregory Nagy (eds), *Theognis and Megara: Poetry and the Polis*

(Baltimore, 1985); Graham Shipley, *A History of Samos, 800–188* BC (Oxford, 1987); V. B. Gorman, *Miletus, the Ornament of Ionia* (Ann Arbor, 2001); M. I. Finley, *Ancient Sicily* (Totowa, NJ, 1979); Astrid Möller, *Naukratis: Trade in Archaic Greece* (Oxford, 2000).

Chapter 17

On archaic Greek warfare and hoplite fighting, see Jean-Pierre Vernant (ed.), *Problèmes de la guerre en Grèce ancienne* (The Hague, 1968); V. D. Hanson (ed.), *Hoplites: The Classical Greek Battle Experience* (London, 1991); Hanson, *The Other Greeks: The Family Farm and the Agrarian Roots of Western Civilization* (New York, 1995); Hanson, *The Western Way of War: Infantry Battle in Classical Greece* (2nd edn, Berkeley, 2000); John Rich and Graham Shipley (eds), *War and Society in Ancient Greece* (London, 1993); Paul Cartledge, 'The Birth of the Hoplite: Sparta's Contribution to Early Greek Military Organization', in Cartledge, *Spartan Reflections* (above under Chapter 16), 153–66; Hans van Wees, *Greek Warfare: Myths and Realities* (London, 2004); Adam Schwartz, *Reinstating the Hoplite: Arms, Armour and Phalanx Fighting in Archaic and Classical Greece* (Stuttgart, 2009). On the agonistic element: Jan Huizinga, *Homo ludens: A Study of the Play-Element in Culture*, trans. R. F. C. Hull (London, 1949); W. R. Connor, 'Early Greek Land Warfare as Symbolic Expression', *Past & Present* 119 (1988), 3–28; Dayton, *Athletes of War* (above under Chapter 15). On the origins of the phalanx and Homeric warfare: van Wees, 'Homeric Warfare', in Morris and Powell, *A New Companion to Homer* (above under Chapter 12), 668–93; van Wees, 'The Development of the Hoplite Phalanx: Iconography and Reality in the 7th Century', in van Wees (ed.), *War and Violence in Ancient Greece* (London, 2000), 125–66; Kurt Raaflaub, 'Archaic and Classical Greece', in Raaflaub and Nathan Rosenstein (eds), *War and Society in the Ancient and Medieval Worlds* (Washington, DC, 1999), 129–61; Raaflaub, 'Homeric Warriors and Battles: Trying to Resolve Old Problems', *Classical World* 101 (2008), 469–83. On the Beginnings of Naval Warfare: H. T. Wallinga, *Ships and Sea-Power before the Great Persian War: The Ancestry of the Ancient Trireme* (Leiden, 1993).

Chapter 18

On the origins of citizenship, P. Brook Manville, *The Origins of Citizenship in Ancient Athens* (Princeton, 1990); Uwe Walter, *An der Polis teilhaben. Bürgerstaat und Zugehörigkeit im archaischen Griechenland* (Stuttgart, 1993). On 'private and public' in the Greek *polis*, see relevant chapters in Oswyn Murray and Simon Price (eds), *The Greek City from Homer to Alexander* (Oxford, 1990). On public spaces and squares, Martin, *Recherches sur l'agora grecque*, and Hölscher, 'Öffentliche Räume' (above under Chapter 14). The importance of charm (*charis*) is explored in Meier, *Politik und Anmut* (Stuttgart, 2000). Revenge: Hans-Joachim Gehrke, 'Die Griechen und die Rache. Ein Versuch in historischer Psychologie', *Saeculum* 38 (1987), 121–49;

see also Jon E. Lendon, 'Homeric Vengeance and the Outbreak of Greek Wars', in van Wees (ed.), *War and Violence* (above under Chapter 17), 1–30. On the archaic aristocracy, Donlan, *The Aristocratic Ideal* (above under Chapter 14); Gregory Nagy, 'Aristocrazia: caratteri e stili di vita', in Settis, *I Greci* (cited among Surveys), II.1: 577–98. On civic subdivisions and institutions: Victor Ehrenberg, *The Greek State* (2nd edn, London, 1969); Nicholas F. Jones, *Public Organization in Ancient Greece: A Documentary Study* (Philadelphia, 1987); S. D. Lambert, *The Phratries of Attica* (Ann Arbor, 1993). Assemblies and councils: Kurt Raaflaub, 'Politics and Interstate Relations in the World of Early Greek *Poleis:* Homer and Beyond', *Antichthon* 31 (1997), 1–27; Françoise Ruzé, *Délibération et pouvoir dans la cité grecque de Nestor à Socrate* (Paris, 1997). On laws, see the collections by Reinhard Koerner, *Inschriftliche Gesetzestexte der frühen griechischen Polis*, ed. Klaus Hallof (Cologne, 1993); Henri van Effenterre and Françoise Ruzé (eds), *Nomima. Recueil d'inscriptions politiques et juridiques de l'archaïsme grec*, 2 vols (Rome, 1994–5); see also the works cited under Chapter 9; Kurt Latte, *Heiliges Recht* (Tübingen, 1920), Karl-Joachim Hölkeskamp, *Schiedsrichter, Gesetzgeber und Gesetzgebung im archaischen Griechenland* (Stuttgart, 1999); relevant chapters in Lin Foxhall and D. E. Lewis (eds), *Greek Law in its Political Setting* (Oxford, 1996); Hans-Joachim Gehrke, 'States', in Raaflaub and van Wees, *Companion* (cited under Surveys), 395–410. On the concepts involved, see Ostwald, *Nomos* (below under Chapter 21). On the enforcement of traditional norms in rural communities: Winfried Schmitz, *Nachbarschaft und Dorfgemeinschaft im archaischen und klassischen Griechenland* (Berlin, 2004).

Chapter 19

On the 'archaic crisis', Stein-Hölkeskamp, *Adelskultur und Polisgesellschaft* (cited under Surveys). On *stasis*, Andrew Lintott, *Violence, Civil Strife and Revolution in the Classical City, 750–330 BC* (Baltimore, 1982); Meier, 'Revolution', in Otto Brunner, Werner Conze, and Reinhart Koselleck (eds), *Geschichtliche Grundbegriffe*, V (Stuttgart, 1984), 665–6; H.-J. Gehrke, *Stasis* (Munich, 1985). Revenge: Gehrke, 'Die Griechen und die Rache', and Lendon, 'Homeric Vengeance' (above under Chapter 18). The most complete treatment of tyranny is in Helmut Berve, *Die Tyrannis bei den Griechen*, 2 vols (Munich, 1967); see also e.g. H. W. Pleket, 'The Archaic Tyrannis', *Talanta* 1 (1969), 19–61; Sian Lewis, *Greek Tyranny* (Exeter, 2009), and the chapters by Victor Parker and Elke Stein-Hölkeskamp, respectively, in the *Companions* to archaic Greece listed under Surveys. On mediators and 'straighteners', see Michele Faraguna, 'La figura dell'aisymnetes tra realtà storica e teoria politica', in Robert W. Wallace and Michael Gagarin (eds), *Symposion 2001: Papers on Greek and Hellenistic Legal History* (Vienna, 2005), 321–38; Robert W. Wallace, 'Charismatic Leaders', in Raaflaub and van Wees, *Companion* (cited under Surveys), 411–26. On those 'in the middle', see under Chapter 22 below.

Chapter 20

On lyric poetry in general, see the works of Lesky (above, under Surveys) and
Fränkel (above, under Evidence); also Albrecht Dihle, *A History of Greek Literature*,
trans. Clare Krojzl (London, 1994), and, on art in general, Jeffrey M. Hurwit, *The
Art and Culture of Early Greece, 1100–480 B.C.* (Ithaca, NY, 1985); Robin Osborne,
Archaic and Classical Greek Art (Oxford, 1998). On the symposium: Oswyn Murray
(ed.), *Sympotica: A Symposium on the Symposion* (expanded paperback edn, Oxford,
1994); William J. Slater (ed.), *Dining in a Classical Context* (Ann Arbor, 1991); on its
oriental background: J.-M. Dentzer, *Le motif du banquet couché dans le Proche-Orient et
le monde grec du VIIème au IVème siècle avant J.-C.* (Paris, 1982); Walter Burkert,
'Oriental Symposia: Contrasts and Parallels', in Slater, *Dining in a Classical Context*
(above), 7–24. On individual poets: Anne P. Burnett, *Three Archaic Poets: Archilochus,
Alcaeus, Sappho* (Cambridge, Mass., 1983); Anthony J. Podlecki, *The Early Greek
Poets and Their Times* (Vancouver, 1984). On the *kouroi*, see Hurwit, *The Art and
Culture of Early Greece* (above), 186–202; Osborne, *Archaic and Classical Greek Art*
(above), 75–85.

Chapter 21

On the beginnings of Greek political thought, see Meier, *The Greek Discovery of
Politics*, trans. David McLintock (Cambridge, Mass., 1990); Raaflaub, 'Poets,
Lawgivers' (above, under Chapter 12); Raaflaub (ed.), *Anfänges des politischen
Denkens in der Antike. Die nahöstlichen Kulturen und die Griechen* (Munich, 1993).
I quote Arnold Gehlen, *Urmensch und Spätkultur* (Frankfurt am Main, 1964). On
Solon: Wolfgang Schadewaldt, *Anfänge* (below, under Chapter 22), 113–21;
Werner Jaeger, 'Solon's Eunomia', in Jaeger, *Five Essays* (Montreal, 1966), 75–
100. On the 'Seven Sages', Bruno Snell, *Leben und Meinungen der Sieben Weisen*
(Munich, 1971); Richard Martin, 'The Seven Sages as Performers of Wisdom', in
Carol Dougherty and Leslie Kurke (eds), *Cultural Poetics in Archaic Greece: Cult,
Performance, Politics* (Cambridge, 2003), 108–28; see also Faraguna, 'La figura
dell'aisymnetes', and Wallace, 'Charismatic Leaders' (above, under Chapter
19). On those in the middle: Peter Spahn, *Mittelschicht und Polisbildung* (Frankfurt
am Main, 1977); Ian Morris, *Archaeology as Cultural History* (Malden, Mass., 2000),
esp. pt. 3. On the emergence of *isonomia*, Martin Ostwald, *Nomos and the Beginnings
of Athenian Democracy* (Oxford, 1969), 96–173; Meier, *The Greek Discovery* (above),
29–52; Gregory Vlastos, 'Isonomia', in Vlastos, *Studies in Greek Philosophy*,
I (Princeton, 1995), 89–111; Meier, 'Zum Aufkommen des Demokratie-Begriffs',
in Tassilo Schmitt, Winfried Schmitz, and Aloys Winterling (eds), *Gegenwärtige
Antike—Antike Gegenwart* (Munich, 2005), 49–83, esp. 56–61.

Chapter 22

On the beginnings of Greek philosophy and science, see the works cited above (under Evidence and Surveys), esp. Fränkel, *Early Greek Poetry and Philosophy*, and Kirk, Raven, and Schofield (*Presocratic Philosophers*); see also, Jean-Pierre Vernant, *The Origins of Greek Thought* (Ithaca, NY, 1982); W. K. C. Guthrie, *A History of Greek Philosophy*, I: *The Earlier Presocratics and the Pythagoreans* (Cambridge, 1962); Uvo Hölscher, *Anfängliches Fragen. Studien zur frühen griechischen Philosophie* (Göttingen, 1968); M. L. West, *Early Greek Philosophy and the Orient* (Oxford, 1971); Wolfgang Schadewaldt, *Die Anfänge der Philosophie bei den Griechen. Die Vorsokratiker und ihre Voraussetzungen* (Frankfurt am Main, 1978); Jonathan Barnes, *The Presocratic Philosophers* (paperback, London, 1982); A. A. Long (ed.), *The Cambridge Companion to Early Greek Philosophy* (Cambridge, 1999). Specifically, on cosmology, Keimpe Algra, 'The Beginnings of Cosmology', in Long, *Companion* (above), 45–65; on Anaximander, C. H. Kahn, *Anaximander and the Origins of Greek Cosmology* (New York, 1960); on Xenophanes, James Lesher, *Xenophanes of Colophon* (Toronto, 1992); on Heraclitus, Kahn, *The Art and Thought of Heraclitus* (Cambridge, 1979); on Parmenides: Karl Reinhardt, *Parmenides und die Geschichte der griechischen Philosophie* (2nd edn, Frankfurt am Main, 1959); Hans-Georg Gadamer, *Philosophisches Lesebuch*, I (Frankfurt am Main, 1965); David Gallop, *Parmenides of Elea, Fragments: A Text and Translation with an Introduction* (Toronto, 1984); on Pythagoras: Christoph Riedweg, *Pythagoras: His Life, Teaching, and Influence*, trans. Steven Rendall (Ithaca, NY, 2005). On the beginnings of science: Otto Neugebauer, *The Exact Sciences in Antiquity* (2nd edn, Providence, RI, 1957); André Pichot, *La Naissance de la science* (Paris, 1991); B. L. van der Waerden, *Science Awakening*, trans. Arnold Dresden (4th edn, Dordrecht, 1988); Meier, 'Griechische Anfänge von Wissenschaft', in *Nova Acta Leopoldina*, NS 93, no. 345 (2006), 259–74.

Chapter 23

On the history of Athens in the late seventh and sixth centuries, see relevant chapters in *CAH* III.3 (1982), and IV (1988); Karl-Wilhelm Welwei, *Athen: Vom neolithischen Siedlungsplatz zur archaischen Grosspolis* (Darmstadt, 1992); Christian Meier, *Athens: A Portrait of the City in its Golden Age* (1999), chs. 2–4; Kurt Raaflaub, Josiah Ober, and Robert Wallace, *Origins of Democracy in Ancient Greece* (Berkeley, 2007). In addition, on Draco: Ronald Stroud, *Draco's Law on Homicide* (Berkeley, 1968); Michael Gagarin, *Drakon and Early Athenian Homicide Law* (New Haven, 1981). For Solon's poetry, on which the present reconstruction is primarily based, see the references to elegiac poetry above in the section on evidence. Solon's laws are collected in Eberhard Ruschenbusch, ΣΟΛΩΝΟΣ ΝΟΜΟΙ. *Die Fragmente des solonischen Gesetzeswerkes mit einer Text- und Überlieferungsgeschichte* (Wiesbaden, 1966); Ruschenbusch, *Solon: Das Gesetzeswerk—Fragmente*, ed. Klaus Bringmann (Stuttgart, 2010) now provides a German trans. and commentary. For the section on Solon in Aristotle's *Constitution of the Athenians*, see above under evidence;

Plutarch's *Life of Solon* is translated in *Plutarch, The Rise and Fall of Athens*, trans. Ian Scott-Kilvert (Harmondsworth, 1960). On Solon, see further Werner Jaeger, 'Solon's Eunomia' (above, under Chapter 21); Ronald Stroud, *The Axones and Kyrbeis of Drakon and Solon* (Berkeley, 1979); Stein-Hölkeskamp, *Adelskultur* (above, under Surveys); Kurt Raaflaub, 'Solone, la nuova Atene e l'emergere della politica', in Settis, I: *Greci*, II.1 (above, under Surveys), 1035–81; Josine Blok and André Lardinois (eds), *Solon of Athens: New Historical and Philological Approaches* (Leiden, 2006). On *eunomia*, see Ostwald, *Nomos* (above, under Chapter 21), 62–95. On Cleisthenes' reforms: Martin Ostwald, in *CAH* IV (1988), 303–46; Meier, 'Cleisthenes and the Institutionalizing of the Civic Presence in Athens', in Meier, *Greek Discovery* (above, under Chapter 21), 53–81; Greg Anderson, *The Athenian Experiment: Building an Imagined Political Community in Ancient Attica, 508–490 B.C.* (Ann Arbor, 2003); see also John S. Traill, *The Political Organization of Attica* (Princeton, 1975); David Whitehead, *The Demes of Attica, 508/7–ca. 250 B.C.: A Political and Social Study* (Princeton, 1986). On *isonomia*, see above, under Chapter 21. On the evolution of the concept of citizenship, Manville, *The Origins of Citizenship*, and Walter, *An der Polis teilharben* (above, under Chapter 18); on that of equality, Kurt Raaflaub, 'Equalities and Inequalities in Athenian Democracy', in Josiah Ober and Charles Hedrick (eds), *Dēmokratia: A Conversation on Democracies, Ancient and Modern* (Princeton, 1996), 139–74. On the 'Harmodios Song' and the statues of the tyrannicides: Victor Ehrenberg, 'Das Harmodioslied', in Ehrenberg, *Polis und Imperium* (Zurich, 1965), 253–64; David Castriota, 'Democracy and Art in Late-Sixth- and Fifth-Century B.C. Athens', in Ian Morris and Kurt Raaflaub (eds), *Democracy 2500? Questions and Challenges* (Dubuque, IA, 1998), 197–216.

Chapter 24

On the Persian Empire, the conquest of the eastern Greeks by the Persians, and the Greek–Persian wars of the early fifth century, see *CAH* IV (1988); Pierre Briant, *From Cyrus to Alexander: A History of the Persian Empire*, trans. Peter Daniels (Winona Lake, Ark., 2002). On the impact of the Persian Wars: Margaret C. Miller, *Athens and Persia in the Fifth Century BC: A Study in Cultural Receptivity* (Cambridge, 1997); P. J. Rhodes, 'The Impact of the Persian Wars on Classical Greece', in Emma Bridges, Edith Hall, and P. J. Rhodes (eds), *Cultural Responses to the Persian Wars: Antiquity to the Third Millennium* (Oxford, 2007), 31–45; see also Deborah Boedeker and Kurt Raaflaub (eds), *Democracy, Empire, and the Arts in the Fifth Century* (Cambridge, Mass., 1998). On Sicilian tyranny: David Asheri, in *CAH* IV (1988), 739–80, V (1992), 147–70.

Picture Acknowledgements

Photo credit: Erich Lessing/Art Resource, NY
Figure 1, Figure 2

Photo credit: Bildarchiv Preussischer Kulturbesitz/Art Resource, NY
Figure 4, Figure 12, Figure 14

Used with permission, AKG Images
Figure 5, Figure 9, Figure 16

Photo credit: Vanni/Art Resource
Figure 7

Used with permission, Bridgeman Art Library International
Figure 8

Photo Credit: Foto Marburg/Art Resource, NY
Figure 10

Photo Credit: Scala/Art Resource, NY
Figure 11

Photo Credit: Christa Koppermann
Figure 13

Used with permission of Peter Palm, Berlin, Germany
Figure 15

Wikimedia.org (public domain)
Figure 17

The publisher and the author apologize for any errors or omissions in the above list. If contacted they will be pleased to rectify these at the earliest opportunity.

Index